THE BAREFOOT ARISTOCRATS

Jacket illustration
Early emblem of the Amalgamated Society of
Operative Cotton Spinners produced by the firm of
Gow Butterfield in the 1880s.

Frontispiece
Emblem of the Bolton Province designed by Charles
E. Turner.

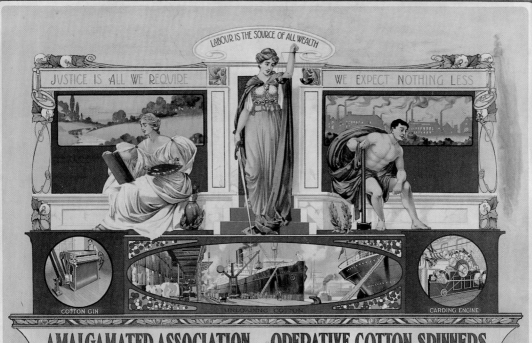

LABOUR IS THE SOURCE OF ALL WEALTH

JUSTICE IS ALL WE REQUIRE

WE EXPECT NOTHING LESS

COTTON GIN

UNLOADING COTTON

CARDING ENGINE

AMALGAMATED ASSOCIATION of OPERATIVE COTTON SPINNERS

THIS IS TO CERTIFY THAT
Mr WILLIAM MONKS
was admitted a Member of the
Bolton Province Branch of this Association
on the 6th day of May . 1882

General Secretary

UNION IS STRENGTH

Branch Secretary

ARKWRIGHT

CROMPTON

ACCIDENT

MODERN SPINNING MILL

OUT OF WORK

OLD HAND MULE

TWINING MULE

SPINNING MULE

CHAS E. TURNER

THE BAREFOOT ARISTOCRATS

A HISTORY OF
THE AMALGAMATED ASSOCIATION
OF OPERATIVE COTTON SPINNERS

edited by
Alan Fowler and Terry Wyke

with contributions from

Andrew Bullen	John McHugh
Alan Fowler	Brian Ripley
John Mason	Terry Wyke

Littleborough
GEORGE KELSALL
1987

THE BAREFOOT ARISTOCRATS
1987

ISBN 0 946571 09 0 hardback
ISBN 0 946571 10 4 paperback

Published by
GEORGE KELSALL
The Bookshop
22 Church Street, Littleborough
Lancashire OL15 9AA
Tel. 0706 70244

Printed and Bound by
SMITH SETTLE
Ilkley Road, Otley
West Yorkshire

Contents

Abbreviations

A.A.O.C.S.	Amalgamated Association of Operative Cotton Spinners
C.S.A.	Cotton Spinners' Association
C.S.M.A.	Cotton Spinners' and Manufacturers' Association
C.W.A.	Cotton Workers' Association
F.A.R.A.	Factory Acts Reform Association
F.M.C.S.A.	Federation of Master Cotton Spinners' Associations
G.F.T.U.	General Federation of Trade Unions
G.G.U.	Grand General Union of Cotton Spinners
I.L.P.	Independent Labour Party
L.R.C.	Labour Representation Committee
N.A.P.L.	National Association for the Protection of Labour
N.A.U.T.P.L.	National Association of United Trades for the Protection of Labour
U.C.S.A.	United Cotton Spinners' Association
U.T.F.W.A.	United Textile Factory Workers' Association

Illustrations

We are extremely grateful to Oldham Local Interest Centre, Manchester Central Library, Andrew Bullen, Audrey Linkman and Joseph Richardson for supplying us with photographs. Edmund and Ruth Frow of the Working Class Movement Library kindly provided us with the emblems which appear in this book.

Note

In order to save space contributors were asked to reduce footnote references and with the exception of long quotations, references have been gathered together at the end of paragraphs.

Appendices

Foreword

The Trustees of the Amalgamated Association of Operative Cotton Spinners invited, in 1984, the Department of Economics and Economic History at the Manchester Polytechnic to write a history of the Amalgamation in order to commemorate the work of the union and its officers. During the years when the union was nearing its end there had been a long-felt need amongst the officials for a commemorative history. With the exception of H. A. Turner's work in the early 1960s the cotton unions had not received the attention they deserved from historians. The hope was that in writing such a history the knowledge of the Amalgamation's wide-ranging activities would be made available to a wider public.

The history has been funded from the original pension fund of the Amalgamation. In 1906 it was decided to establish a 'Mawdsley Memorial Pension Fund' for the purpose of perpetuating the memory of James Mawdsley who had served as General Secretary for 24 years from 1878 until his death during 1902. £2,000 was allocated for the purpose of paying five shillings per week, from the interest on the capital, to the five eldest surviving union members.

Further sums were later allocated and the number of pensioners increased, following the deaths of other stalwarts:

£2,000 in June 1914 to the memory of Thomas Ashton, Chairman from June 1878 to March 1913;

£2,000 in September 1917 in memory of William Marsland, General Secretary from 1904 to March 1917;

£2,000 in September 1926 in memory of Edward Judson, Chairman from 1913 until August 1926;

£2,000 in March 1951 to commemorate the memory of Henry Boothman, General Secretary from 1917 to November 1943;

a further sum of £1,000 was added in December 1953 in memory of Albert Knowles, Chairman from September 1940 until his death in July 1953.

Early in 1975, faced with the inevitability that the Amalgamation would cease to exist in the foreseeable future, coupled with the problems created by the diminishing contact with former members and the problem of administration in the future, it was decided that the payment of pensions should cease and that the purpose for which the fund was created and built up, ie to perpetuate the memory of former officials, would be best served in some other tangible and lasting manner. Accordingly a decision was made to finance the publication of a history of the Amalgamation with the balance left in the fund.

It was considered that in this way not only the memory of the six named former officials would be preserved, but also all the officers of the Amalgamation since its re-organisation in 1870. Equally, so will the memory of a large number of members of the Executive Council, both officials and members working at the trade. Some of these later served on the Executive Council for up to and in excess of forty years. To mention only a few whose names were synonymous with the organisation, in alphabetical order and with apologies to an even larger number not named we had, Messrs. Arnfield, Boyson, Banks, Billington, Bullough, Furness, Gregson, Mercer, Mellor and Rimmer.

Of equal importance, there is evidence of the existence of organisations of mule spinners for 180 years. Throughout that time these early organisations and the Amalgamations of mule spinners were active in the promotion of legislation to improve the working and living conditions of their members and the working classes generally. Nothing would have been achieved without the initiative, drive, perseverance and loyalty, often at considerable personal sacrifice, of the hard working Shop Committees, Shopmen and Chairmen, Locals and Committees of the many Provinces and Districts throughout the county.

To their memory and to all former mule spinners this book is dedicated.

J. RICHARDSON

Preface

This study provides the first detailed account of the origins, development and decline of the Amalgamated Association of Operative Cotton Spinners, one of the leading trade unions in the English cotton industry. It has been written at the request of the Trustees of the Spinners' Amalgamation and with their generous financial support. We would like to thank the Trustees, William Nally, Joseph Richardson and Clifford Wynn for their encouragement and advice during the preparation of this book. The project for a history of the Spinners' Amalgamation was begun originally some years ago by Professor Roger Dyson but due to personal reasons he was unable to complete it. We wish to thank him for making available to us the results of his own research, including a manuscript draft relating to the earlier part of the Spinners' Amalgamation's history, and for his helpful comments during the writing of this book. When the project passed to Manchester Polytechnic we were conscious of the Trustees' desire that the history be completed quickly and it was decided that this could be best achieved by bringing together a small team of historians, each working on a specific time-period or aspect of the union's history. Although working within an agreed agenda of themes, contributors were free to offer their own interpretations on the various aspects of the Amalgamation's activities covered in their particular time-periods. The project was based in the Department of Economics and Economic History and we would particularly like to thank George Zis for his constant encouragement throughout the researching and writing of the book. Andrew Bullen was appointed as Research Fellow for the project and apart from contributing his own chapters, his encyclopaedic knowledge of the cotton industry and research skills were of immense value to the other contributors. Dr D. A. Farnie was kind enough to read the complete manuscript and offered many constructive suggestions. We are equally indebted to Arthur McIvor who read the manuscript in full. Our thanks also go to Steve Jones, Neville Kirk, Dr Robert Murray and Mike Rayner who read parts of the manuscript and for the interest they showed in the work. We are grateful to Edmund and Ruth Frow for the loan of their union emblems which are reproduced in the book.

Many libraries and Record Offices have been used during the project and we would especially like to thank Dr P. McNiven and Dr J. Laidlaw of the John Rylands University Library Manchester for their help in making available the uncatalogued collection of records relating to the Spinners'

Amalgamation. Our thanks also go to their colleagues at Deansgate for the prompt and courteous way in which they made material available to the authors. We are also much obliged to Julian Hunt and the staff of the Oldham Local Interest Centre, John Cole of Rochdale Local Studies Library and the staff of the Lancashire Record Office who have all helped to make the work of researching this history a pleasure.

In preparing the book for publication we are indebted to our typist, Wyn Morris, who worked miracles in deciphering an untidy manuscript. Our publisher George Kelsall has also been very helpful in transforming, with a speed not always associated with the book trade, the manuscript into its final form.

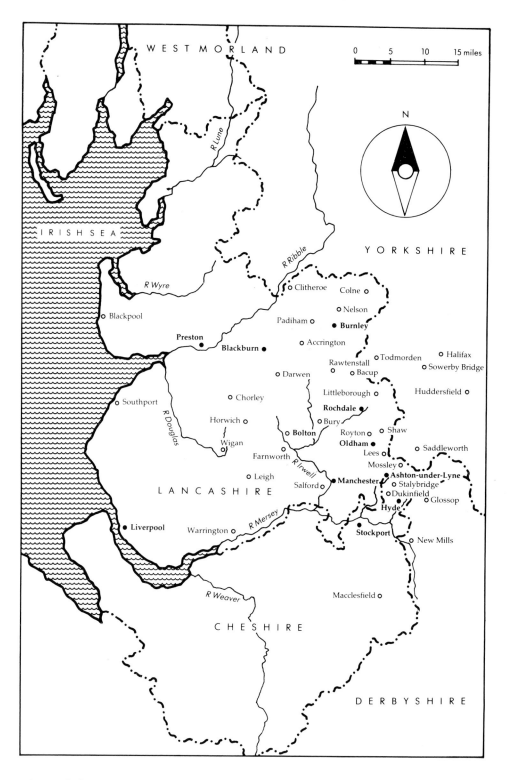

WESTMORLAND

N

YORKSHIRE

I R I S H S E A

R Lune

R Ribble

R Wyre

○ Clitheroe   Colne ○
                                        ○ Nelson
○ Blackpool   Padiham ○   ● Burnley

Preston ●   ○ Accrington

Blackburn ●   Rawtenstall   ○ Todmorden   ○ Halifax
                                                  ○   ○ Bacup   ○ Sowerby Bridge
            ○ Darwen
                          Littleborough ○   Huddersfield ○
○ Southport   ○ Chorley   **Rochdale** ●
                                        ○ Bury
            Horwich ○   ○ Shaw
R Douglas   Wigan ○   **Bolton** ●   Royton ○
                                    Oldham ●   ○ Saddleworth
                      Farnworth ○   Lees ○
                                    Mossley ○
L A N C A S H I R E   ○ Leigh   Salford ○ ● Manchester   **Ashton-under-Lyne** ●
                                                    ○ Stalybridge
                                                    ○ Dukinfield   ○ Glossop
● **Liverpool**   Warrington ○   R Mersey   **Hyde** ●
                                        Stockport ●   ○ New Mills

R Weaver   Macclesfield ○

C H E S H I R E

D E R B Y S H I R E

THE COTTON TOWNS OF NORTH-WEST ENGLAND

CHAPTER ONE

Cotton Spinning in the Industrial Revolution

Samuel Crompton's spinning mule was one of the inventions that revolutionised the English cotton industry in the eighteenth century and transformed it by the nineteenth century into the nation's principal exporter and one of its leading employers of labour. The country's textile trade had until then been dominated by the production of woollen cloth with linen and silk far behind. Consumer choice had been widened in the seventeenth century as the British East India Company began to import fine all-cotton cloths from its trading bases on the Indian sub-continent. As this new trade expanded the woollen industry sought to protect its interests and in the early eighteenth century obtained government legislation which restricted the sale of Indian cottons in England. But consumers had been captivated by the new material, particularly the printed designs, and English manufacturers quickly moved to imitate the banned commodities. Lancashire fustians, cloths manufactured from linen warps and cotton wefts in a variety of types and some easily printed upon, helped fill the gap and also found a ready market overseas. Small quantities of cotton had been worked in Lancashire since the turn of the sixteenth and seventeenth centuries and the region's entrepreneurs now developed extensive manufacturing networks. Raw materials were put out to families working in their own homes; women, aided by children in the preparatory processes, spun whilst men worked the looms.[1]

The expansion of the Lancashire industry encouraged the development of new techniques. By the 1760s weavers were adapting their looms to the use of the flying shuttle, a Lancashire invention originally intended to speed up the production of woollen cloth but subsequently deployed in the weaving of fustians. Women preparing cotton and linen yarn on the spinning wheel and the flax wheel were increasingly unable to supply the weavers with the quantity demanded. In 1770 James Hargreaves patented the spinning jenny, a multi-spindle machine which imitated, albeit duplicating many times, the drawing, twisting and winding actions of the spinning wheel, but the yarn produced had its limitations, not being strong enough for use as warps on the hand-loom. The production of such a warp was made possible by Richard Arkwright's water frame, a machine constructed on different principles from the jenny; it used pairs of rollers operating at different speeds to draw out the cotton, and employed a spindle similar to that of the flax wheel to give the requisite twist. Thus manufacturers were in a position to produce English all-cotton cloth. Whilst Hargreaves's jenny was soon being employed in

1

workshops it was extensively used in the cottage and thus facilitated extension of the domestic system; in contrast Arkwright's frame was designed for use in the water-powered mills of the type operated by the silk industry and thus marked the first stage of spinning's transition from cottage to factory.[2]

The cotton industry had first taken root in north-west England but the growth that came in the wake of the spinning wheel's replacement by Hargreaves's spinning jenny and Arkwright's water frame led to dispersion into the east Midlands where cotton yarn was extensively used in hosiery manufacture and, as the search for water power intensified, into the further Pennines and northwards into Scotland. Yet Lancashire became the centre for the manufacture of the all-cotton cloths that were to become the trade's staple product; its weavers who had worked the linen and cotton yarn into fustian now worked on warps from the Arkwright water frame and weft from the jenny. The demand for more and better yarn led the industry's organisers and workers to construct larger machines and seek out modifications. Samuel Crompton was working a jenny of eight spindles a year before Hargreaves took out his patent and, doubtless like many other Lancashire weavers familiar with the new machine, he tried to improve upon it. By 1779 after some years of effort he had perfected a 48 spindle machine that produced a good quality yarn suitable for either warp or weft. His 'mule', so called because it combined the drawing action of the jenny and the roller principles of the Arkwright frame, had its own novel feature, never patented, whereby the spindles that spun and collected the yarn were set on a wheeled, moveable carriage — thus giving to the spinning mule its most characteristic feature. At first Crompton only spun sufficient warp and weft for his own use but, discovering that he could spin yarn of 40s, 60s, and even 80s count, he gave up weaving and concentrated on working the new machine. In cotton spinning the fineness of the yarn is represented by a number known as a count which is determined by the number of hanks, each 840 yards in length, obtainable from 1 lb of yarn. In 1780, 80s count was considered to be extraordinarily fine but it was later possible to distinguish between coarse (less than 50s), medium (50s-90s), fine (80s-150s), and superfine (150s-300s); confusingly some contemporaries distinguished between coarse spinning (50s and below) and fine spinning (all those above). Unable to afford the cost of the patent application Crompton revealed the secrets of his invention for a paltry sum. In the following years others were to improve and modify the mule and adapt it for use in the factory. By 1811 the mule dominated the British cotton spinning industry: in England there were 4.2 million spindles compared with 310,516 water frame and 155,880 jenny spindles. These figures, collected by Crompton in an effort to persuade government to reward him for his invention, are believed to underestimate the proportion of water frame spindles. The Arkwright machinery's successor, the throstle, continued to be widely used for the spinning of lower counts.[3]

The expansion of the cotton trade from the late eighteenth century was breathtaking and has left an indelible mark upon historical interpretations of the period; for E. J. Hobsbawm 'Whoever says Industrial Revolution says cotton'. Yet the inadequacies of data make precise analysis of the industry's development difficult.

Consumption of cotton increased from 5.1 million lbs in 1781 to an annual average of 82 million lbs in 1808-12 and 936.8 million in 1856-60. The number of spindles increased from 4.7 million in 1811 to 30.3 million by 1861; even these figures under-estimate the industry's growth for production per spindle also increased, almost trebling in the years 1811-61 (Appendix VIII). The numbers employed by the industry as a whole increased to 446,000 on the eve of the Cotton Famine in 1861. Reliance on imported raw materials was matched by a growing dependence on exports for the disposal of the industry's output. Whilst domestic markets remained the richest and most profitable outlet, continued growth was dependent upon the exploitation of overseas markets. In 1820, Europe, the USA and Latin America took 90 per cent of exported piece goods but thirty years later only 54 per cent; India, in the eighteenth century the supplier of fine cottons for English customers, had by 1850 become the greatest single overseas market for the produce of the industry. But reliance on overseas raw materials and markets brought risks; to the volatility of the home market, much affected until the 1840s by the vagaries of the harvest, was added the potential for disruption of raw material supply and the inherent instability of overseas trade. The experience of sharp cyclical swings that had characterised cotton's emergence during the French and Napoleonic wars was to be repeated throughout the nineteenth century and constituted the backdrop to the conduct of the trade's industrial relations.[4]

The spinning mule was manually operated during the 1780s, spinners either working for themselves or taking raw material from the putter-out. Many small businesses responded to the opportunities and Ashton, Bolton, Stockport and Manchester became mule spinning centres. Spinning had traditionally been women's work but the high pay, technical finesse, and the need to train and supervise assistants set the mantle of craft upon mule spinning and led to the appropriation of the trade by adult men. The high rewards, especially for working the finer counts, attracted recruits from other trades. Unlike the worker at the Arkwright water frame whose task was to supervise and piece the yarn passing through the continuously spinning machinery, the mule spinner was required to manoeuvre his machine through a series of stages. He applied power to the mule by rotating the handle of a large flywheel set to the right of the frame. At the first stage, the draw, this moved the carriage out and powered the rollers and spindles, thus stretching and spinning the roving between the former set on the fixed back of the mule and the latter attached to the carriage. When the carriage was fully out he continued to rotate the flywheel until he had given enough twist to the yarn. The spinner's next task was to wind the newly spun yarn to form a cop upon the spindle. He first gave the flywheel a reverse turn which unwound the yarn down from the tip of the spindles to the position where he was to form the cop. He then rotated the flywheel which returned the carriage and at the same time powered the spindles which thus wound the yarn; meantime, in a crucial process, he operated with his left hand a wire faller running the length of the carriage which guided the yarn onto the spindles to form a cop of the required shape. With the carriage returned to the back of the mule, he raised the faller clear of the yarn and gave the flywheel a further turn, thus to bring the final length of yarn to the spindle tip from where he could repeat the cycle. Experience and improvements brought extensions in the size of the mule and by 1785 carriages of 100 spindles seem to have become standard. Assistants, no doubt principally family members, were soon employed to help with the routine tasks of 'piecing' the broken ends, 'doffing' the full cops from the spindles, cleaning away the dust from the carriage, and placing fresh bobbins of roving on the creel, the frame at the back of the mule. Thus the adult hand-mule spinner came to concentrate on the powering, manipulating and maintenance of the machine.[5]

By the late 1780s numbers of mules were probably being brought together in workshops or mills; there the owner could make use of the water or steam-powered carding machinery that processed the raw cotton into rovings and better organise the work of the mule spinner. The realisation that the mule was more productive than Arkwright's frame, the high prices fetched by mule yarn and the high wages and alleged independence of the mule spinner, encouraged efforts to automate the mule's various processes so that expensive and perhaps obstreperous male craftsmen could be replaced with teenage operatives as in mills using the Arkwright machinery. William Kelly at New Lanark, Scotland, in 1790 was the first to successfully automate part of the mule's cycle by amending its operation so that the drawing out of the carriage and the turning of the rollers and spindles at the drawing out and spinning stage could be powered from belts attached to the mill gearing. But, instead of replacing men with women, mill proprietors increased the size of the mule to the physical limits of the male spinner and by the early years of the nineteenth century carriages of 300 spindles were being operated. Kelly's improvement had a further advantage. It was realised that the spinner, freed from the need to operate the flywheel handle in the drawing-out stage, could operate more than one mule. By the 1790s the classic mule room plan had evolved whereby mules were placed opposite each other with the headstocks right of centre, one drawing-out as the other was put up, thus enabling the spinner to move from flywheel to flywheel for the still manually powered winding and putting up stages. The size and expense of these mules and the preparatory carding and roving machinery, their powering and housing, and the falling price of yarn consequent on increased output, meant that mule spinning was only economic within the mill. Whilst hand-loom weaving remained in the cottage and the workshop, the domestic system of spinning withered and mule spinners became factory operatives.[6]

The day-long operation of a pair of mules put the spinner at the limits of his strength and little further increase in size occurred in the first two decades of the nineteenth century. However, in an environment conducive to technical change — the years after Waterloo saw the development of powerloom weaving — the wish to maximise the mill's output, and, from the 1820s, a growing desire to circumvent the well-organised, highly paid spinners with more docile women and children, led cotton masters to seek out further improvements in the mule. These took two forms; the development of the self-actor, a mule which automatically progressed through the stages of the spinning process, and the improvement and increasing scale of the common mule. Kelly had patented a fully automatic mule in 1792 but the subsequent failure to adopt it suggests that it was less than satisfactory. Others also took out patents but it was not until the 1820s that a successful self-actor was patented. In 1825 a group of master spinners, anxious to break the grip of adult mule spinners, approached Richard Roberts of the engineers Sharp, Roberts & Co., and commissioned him to construct a self-actor mule; some five years later he had all but perfected his device. The putting up of the carriages was easily powered but the keys to success were the quadrant winding mechanism which controlled the spindle speed during winding, and a counter-faller which dispensed with the need for manual operation of the faller in the crucial cop-forming process. Although the theory of Roberts's machine was not to be surpassed it was to be some fifty years before the self-actor became fully automatic. For many years the quadrant had to be manually adjusted by means of a nut, failure to do this causing nicks, snarls or sawneys, whilst to obtain a perfect cop a further nut, known as the nosing motion, had to be adjusted as the spindles filled up with cotton. The conversion of spinning rooms from the hand-mule to the self-actor system was made easier and cheaper by the discovery that the existing frame and carriage could be utilised with a new self-actor headstock. However the harsh and sometimes imprecise action of the early self-actors made them unsuitable for the finer yarns. Though being introduced from the early 1830s the self-actor was not universal for the coarser counts until the 1860s and even then it should not be automatically assumed that hand-mule spinners were being displaced for many employers had previously preferred to use the throstle (the successor to the Arkwright's water frame) for the spinning of coarser counts. Indeed the little studied throstle continued to spin a significant proportion — in some mills up to one-quarter — of the lower count yarns. Only from the late 1850s did the self-actor begin to mount an effective challenge to the medium counts and it did not supersede hand-mules for counts up to 90s until the 1880s, and for the very finest counts hand-mules were in use until towards the end of the century.[7]

For much of the nineteenth century medium and higher count yarns continued to be spun on the common mule. Its survival was due to a number of factors — the technical deficiencies of the self-actor, especially for finer spinning, the higher fuel costs and greater piecing requirement of the new machine, and above all the technical improvements to the common mule that enabled larger numbers of spindles to be operated at greater speeds. In 1825, as part of the search for a self-actor, a putting up motion was developed which gave power assistance during the rotation of the flywheel for the movement of the carriage in the putting-up stage. A lengthening of frames ensued. Manchester fine spinners introduced 400-500 spindle mules in the late 1820s and some worked 600 or more in the 1830s. The greater production of these innovating long-wheel masters threatened the commercial viability of the small-wheel (shorter carriage) masters and set in train a general lengthening of mules. This was taken up by the coarser spinner who also engaged in the 'coupling or double decking of mules, by which one man is able to work twice the number of spindles'. This meant putting two mules side by side and running them both from one headstock. Further technical improvements made the hand-mule

more precise, faster, and smoother in operation. Harold Catling has concluded that
the mule constructed in the Bolton area for the spinning of higher counts 'may well
qualify as the most complex and most highly refined manually controlled tool
which has yet been, or will ever be, mass produced'. The application of power to the
different processes had by 1880 made even the common mule virtually a self-actor.
Only in the last decades of the century were self-actors introduced for spinning the
finest counts. The improvement upon Crompton's original machine had thus
travelled two paths: the gradual and sustained improvement of the common mule
to the stage where it too was almost automated, and the extension of Roberts's self-
actor to embrace ever higher counts.[8]

The first cotton spinning factories were operated on the Arkwright system and
many were located on water-powered sites outside north-west England, principally
in Derbyshire and Nottinghamshire, Scotland and North Wales, but when
Crompton conducted his survey in 1811 the cotton spinning industry was shown to
have grown most rapidly in south-east Lancashire and the adjoining district of
north-east Cheshire (Appendix II). Behind this movement lay the attraction of
Manchester, increasingly the trade's centre, the development of the manufacturing
and finishing sector of the industry in the region, and the application of steam
power to the mills and the evident advantages of location on the Lancashire coalfield.
This concentration was further encouraged in the next two decades as master
cotton spinners constructed weaving sheds adjacent to their mills and introduced
the new powerlooms. The Stockport-Manchester area was the first to experience
the rise of these combined enterprises which rapidly grew to dominate the industry.
By 1850 in Lancashire there were 436 combined spinning and weaving mills, 517
spinning mills and 196 specialising in weaving only. The mixed firms, larger in size
than the industry's average were at their peak in the 1850s. From then the industry
became increasingly specialised between single process spinning and weaving
firms; moreover a regional specialisation became evident with spinning becoming
concentrated around Ashton, Bolton, Manchester, Oldham, Rochdale and
Stockport, and weaving around Accrington, Blackburn, Burnley, Chorley, Colne,
Darwen, and Todmorden. Some districts had both spinning and weaving. The
concentration and specialisation of the industry within the North West was highlighted by the industry's decline in other regions — the Scottish industry had
passed its peak by mid-century and was badly affected by Lancashire competition
and the problems of the early 1860s.[9]

The increasing sophistication of the equipment developed from Crompton's first
mule enabled differing types of cotton to be spun in an increasing range of counts.
District and firms developed their own specialities. By the 1790s Manchester was
already emerging as the centre of the fine spinning industry though numerous other
Manchester firms were engaged in the production of coarse and medium counts.
Stockport originally specialised in the finer counts but was soon engaged in spinning
coarse and medium. Nor did the cotton towns develop at an even rate. Stockport
grew rapidly during the late eighteenth and early nineteenth centuries but growth
slowed from the 1830s; Oldham was one of the earliest cotton towns but only from

the 1850s did it commence its rise to world importance as a spinning centre; Preston, in the early nineteenth century, home to Horrockses, the country's largest cotton spinning firm, enjoyed its greatest influence from 1820-50, but declined relatively after 1854. Whilst no area was to achieve the significant presence in both fine and coarse counts that was Manchester's until the 1840s, the pattern of specialisation gave certain districts a predominance in particular counts. Though Manchester retained its hold in superfine spinning, the medium and fine trade was to pass to Bolton and its adjacent districts. Preston became a centre for the spinning of higher coarse and low medium counts. In contrast the districts to the east and south-east of Manchester generally concentrated on the coarser counts. Scattered amongst the larger towns lay smaller factory communities, frequently dominated by single firms and each displaying its own speciality. At Turton, near Bolton, was the fine spinning enterprise of the Ashworths, at Compstall, near Stockport, the integrated spinning to printing enterprise of the Andrews family, and at Styal, one of the Greg's spinning and weaving mills. These water-powered mills were amongst the industry's largest but whilst some survived into the twentieth century, most gave way before the combined effect of more efficient steam power and the dislocation of the Cotton Famine.[10]

Cotton towns were different, not just in their timing and pace of development but in the nature of social relationships within them, the parochialism of town life and the culture of the factory. Some historians have described factory communities in the first half of the nineteenth century as being sharply split on class grounds, others have emphasized the lack of class feeling, and sectionalism and division amongst the workforce; it would seem that the latter may have become more typical from mid-century. Manchester became a cosmopolitan centre with its elite living outside the town and the majority probably knowing or caring little about working-class conditions. In contrast the divisions between employers and working classes may have been less apparent in the medium and smaller towns. Whilst it is clear that many proprietors in the factory villages and towns exhibited a paternalistic attitude towards their workers — Hugh Mason of Ashton-under-Lyne being one such example — expecting in return social acquiescence, it is not yet possible to generalise about the overall experience of the cotton districts. In the absence of detailed local studies historians are divided, some suggesting that the transition of weaving to the mills and the arrival of a complete factory system enabled paternalistic mill communities to develop within towns, others asserting that the paternalistic and deferential relationships were skin deep, with the society still being prone, especially at times of economic distress or industrial dispute, to fierce social conflict. But as the population growth of cotton towns slowed, parochialism and differences between towns may have been heightened. The extent to which cotton towns constituted a society with a shared experience should not be over-stated. Whilst employers came together at meetings for business or civic purposes, for working people contact was inhibited by the difficulties and expense of transport, the lack of free time, and the social and sometimes legal prohibition or discouragement of inter-town working-class organisation. Social variation and distance thus compounded the economic and industrial distinctiveness of the separate cotton towns.[11]

Though mill work was the principal activity of the cotton town, differences in size and equipment make the typical mill as elusive as the typical industrial town. The organisation of the cotton industry in its early years can be described as a pyramid with a small number of large firms at the apex giving way to a large number of small units at the bottom. The surveys of cotton factories from the 1790s to the 1840s indicate a spread from units employing more than 1,000 workers to others that must have been little more than workshops. Smaller firms were the numerically preponderant — in 1841 more than two-thirds of Lancashire firms employed less than 100 hands whilst just six of 80 fine spinning firms, four of 500 coarse spinning firms, and 73 of 321 combined spinning and weaving enterprises employed more than 500 hands. The combined mills aside, the greater proportion of large mills were to be found amongst the fine spinners. The writings of contemporaries, particularly Andrew Ure, who drew on the large Travis Brook mill built for Ralph Orrell at Heaton Norris, Stockport, suggest that the larger mill was becoming more typical. Yet whilst it is probably correct that competition was making the climate more difficult for the smaller firm, recent work suggests that due to technological constraints and the problem of managing what were generally family enterprises, the medium-sized firm was better suited to the conditions of the cotton industry. There was little more than a gradual increase in the size of cotton mills from 1811 to 1870. The majority of the industry's labour force served its time in mills employing fewer than 500 hands, in single process spinning firms fewer than 250 hands.[12]

The structure of mill labour forces varied according to the processes, spinning or spinning and weaving, being conducted, and the technology employed, be it the less important Arkwright method or the Crompton common mule and Roberts self-actor systems. Their age and sex structure changed during the nineteenth century as successively more effective legislation led to a reduction in the proportion of younger children employed and an increase in the number of women and youths. Management and day-to-day control was invariably in the hands of the owner, members of his family, or, in some of the largest firms, a managing partner. Harold Catling has described the conduct of a mill in the industry's later years. The operation of the mill came to lie with the engineer who was responsible for the powering of machinery, the carder who received the raw cotton and supervised its preparation for the spinner, and the spinning room overlooker. The spinning room overlooker supervised his room and was responsible for the spinners under him; in single process spinning firms he would send completed work to the warehouseman, in combined firms he would despatch it to the loomsheds. Although the workforce was recruited from the same community, workers at the different processes, and particularly the spinners, developed a tradition of independence from their fellows that spilt over into their social lives and was particularly evident in the separate development of their trade unions and the conduct of industrial disputes. The number of spinners employed in mills varied with the unit's size, from perhaps no more than half-a-dozen in the smallest mills to one hundred or more in the largest. Of those employed in the cotton spinning industry during the mid-nineteenth century perhaps no more than 10 per cent would have been operative spinners —

the remainder, a small number of adult males, women, juveniles and children were either their assistants or engaged in other processes. The mule spinning room was predominantly staffed by males.[13]

Within the early mill the spinners aspired to the craftsman status they had acquired in the first years of mule spinning. This air of independence was substantially fostered by mill proprietors who were content to pay the spinner for the yarn produced whilst leaving him to maintain and operate the machine, and recruit, train and pay his assistants. In some of the early workshops and mills a small number of spinners seem to have hired machinery and power and operated their own small businesses; this system may have influenced the early nineteenth century deductions from the spinners' wages of charges for candles or gas lighting — a practice which persisted in amended form at Bolton until 1859. However the vast majority of, and eventually all, mule spinners were wage employees and as such subject to the common and statutory laws that bound them to their employers. Even so the system of sub-contracting was to continue, little altered, until the demise of mule spinning in the twentieth century. The number and age of the spinners' assistants varied with the size and type of machine and custom, but at pairs of hand-mules worked on the Kelly system, one spinner usually employed a big piecer, and two or more small piecers, children aged ten to thirteen years old being preferred, and a scavenger to clean the machinery. The big piecer was, albeit not in the traditional craft sense, an apprentice; deputed to temporarily supervise the mules when the spinner was otherwise engaged, he could, at least until the 1830s, look forward to work his own mules at the age of eighteen. With the advent of the self-actor the spinner was himself free to piece and could thus dispense with one of the small piecers. The spinners' enjoyment of an earnings differential over that of other workers was in part made possible by the low fixed weekly wage which he paid to his assistants; himself motivated to maximise output, the unscrupulous spinner could, without the need to pay more, pass much of the burden on to his assistants. On the other hand, if the assistants were his relatives, their employment would boost family income. Within the area bounded by the two mules, the mule-gate, the piecework motivated spinner exerted an effective authority, benevolent or otherwise over his assistants. The big piecers were kept in check by the expectation of their own promotion to the rank of spinner. They had much in common with the mule spinners but they were also the trade's Achilles' heel, a pool of workers who knew the spinners' work and from whom employers might draw strike breakers, cheaper labour, or, in preference to mule spinners, the operatives to work the self-actors. Thus security evaded the mule spinners. Never free of the fear of technological redundancy, they too were driven by overlookers and employers seeking to maximise production.[14]

The extent to which mule spinners can justly be described as craftsmen remains open to question. Gareth Stedman Jones has written of the hand-mule spinners that:

> from the start the cotton spinners described their occupation as a 'trade', were strongly organised, successfully imposed a wage level comparable to that of

the artizan, and achieved limitation of entry into the trade and a degree of control over hours of work — in other words a form of craft control comparable to that within (pre-factory) manufacture.[15]

The spinners' aspirations were not in doubt but the available data on nineteenth-century wages suggests that the net income of mule spinners whilst favourable in comparison to those of other factory workers varied according to location, type and count of spinning. The generality of hand-mule spinners may have enjoyed higher than average wages down to the 1820s, but from then until the second half of the 1860s, only the minority producing counts in excess of 100s-120s received net wages comparable with those of other higher grade skilled workers and artizans. Though the spinner might recruit and train his own assistants, this was a practice far removed from the apprenticeship system by which the traditional crafts had controlled entry into the trade; the piecer system, whatever appearance of spinner control it might suggest, led to the creation of a pool of potential spinners far in excess of the number required by employers. Whilst employers may have allowed spinners to decide which piecers should be promoted, such control should not be taken for granted; in the small mill towns, in non-union shops, or at times of stress within the industry, employers may well have exerted their authority. The ready supply of labour meant that for all their craft aspirations, wages, and this is clear from their short term volatility, were principally determined by market forces. The evident qualifications to this are the high wage differentials that accrued to the fine spinners and the particular wage structures obtained by the Glasgow spinners; here shop and district craft organisation played their part but even so, the fine spinners' wages must be partly explicable by employer willingness to pay more for the greater skill that high count working required. In a competitive environment it was incumbent upon employers to exploit their investment to the full. Until the introduction of effective factory legislation in the 1830s and 1840s the spinner had no control over hours of work — indeed some of the early mills worked day and night and even when this practice ceased in the early 1800s fifteen hour days were not uncommon. Conditions within the mills — temperature, noise, lack of ventilation, sanitation, humidity — were regarded as unpleasant whilst exacting discipline and rigorous routine constituted best practice. Whilst the first mule spinners could work the machines at their own pace, automation of some processes and the power-aiding of others meant that their successors had to cope with more frequent draws of the carriage and higher spindle speeds. Apart from their role as sub-contractors, their monopolisation of particular spinning operations, and the high wages to which a minority might aspire, the greater number of mule spinners had little claim to the title of artizan.[16]

The introduction of the self-actor was intended to remove them from their place of work altogether; its patentees and manufacturers claimed that it would enable 'The saving of a spinner's wages to each pair of mules, piecers only being required, one overlooker being sufficient to manage six or eight pairs of mules or upwards.' E. C. Tufnell, a Factory Commissioner asserted that the 'introduction of the invention will give a death blow to the Spinners' Union, the members of which will have to thank themselves alone, for the creation of this destined agent of their extinction . . . in a few years the very name of working spinner, as well as the follies and oppression of their combination, will only be found in history.' Stedman Jones has suggested that the threatened effect of the self-actor 'was to transform the operative from a specialised worker into a machine minder and to allow the replacement of the male artizan by female or juvenile labour'; a threat aimed not only at wages but at the mule spinners' "real" control over production (and) all means of control over recruitment, hours and conditions of work until then enforced by the spinners.' Yet this may be an incorrect interpretation. It has already been argued that mule spinners had no control over conditions and hours within the mills and that control of entry should not be overstated. The hand-mule spinners' principal control lay, like that of all modern factory proletariats, in their ability to disrupt the flow of production within the mill. This was enhanced by the subcontract system that gave them the means to bring out their big piecers — the only people who, in the short run, could replace them. It was this power, deployed in support of wage claims rather than non-existent craft controls that the self-actor machine was intended to destroy. Given that employers did not generally choose to abandon the subcontract system when self-actors were introduced and that the mule spinners displaced or redeployed in the first decades of the new machine's use would have been working the lowest counts, its impact upon spinning rooms should not be overstated. There mule spinners had already been subject to the discipline of master, mill and machine. Moreover the part-automation and power-aiding of the common mule had already anticipated the effects of the self-actor, the main result of which was to increase the unskilled element in, and intensity of, spinning work.[17]

The further automation of the spinning process that the self-acting mule introduced meant that the new machine's operators were engaged in a technically different job than their predecessors. To distinguish between operatives on the old and new machines, contemporaries referred to the self-actor men as 'minders'. Though isolated cases exist of employers seeking to operate their self-actors with women and teenagers, adult men were preferred; nevertheless there is some indication that in the 1840s minders were being appointed at the age of eighteen whilst hand-mule spinners, though once appointed at that age, were not being given a pair of wheels until their mid-twenties. The new machines were probably staffed by replaced or unemployed mule spinners or big piecers. Except where appointment meant on the spot demotion the work was doubtless preferable to unemployment whilst for older teenage piecers appointment to a self-actor meant a considerable increase in earnings. The differential between coarse hand-mule spinners' and self-actor minders' earnings would have narrowed with the collapse of the former in the 1830s whilst for older minders the continuance of subcontracting meant that they would be able to supplement family earnings by the employment of relatives.[18]

The number and distribution of hand-mule spinners and self-actor minders is difficult to assess. Setbacks of trade apart, they increased to perhaps 7,000-8,000 in

1811, 10,000 in 1817, and 15,000 in 1834; the expansion of the mid-1830s further increased their ranks but it would seem that their number rose only slightly, if at all, in the 1840s, probably stabilising at about 20,000, before rising again in the 1850s. These are crude estimates and should be regarded as no more than a rough suggestion. Calculation of the number to be found spinning the different counts is even more hazardous, partly because of the definition of what constituted the different qualities of yarn was changing until the early nineteenth century, but principally because the nineteenth century commentators and recent historians have failed to use a common standard. The available data suggests that less than 10 per cent of spinners would have been employed in the working of superfine counts, a little less than 15 per cent in fine and medium, and something more than 75 per cent in the coarser counts. Whilst the higher count spinners were immune from the influence of the self-actor until after 1860, the coarser-count hand-mule spinners were faced with its spread from the 1830s. The new self-actor minders formed perhaps no more than 3 per cent of the total in 1834, increased to perhaps one-third by the mid-1840s, and to something more than 60 per cent during the 1850s. The 1860s on, saw their conquest of the remaining counts. Because of the uneven growth of the cotton spinning districts, and the specialisation and concentration of particular areas upon the different counts, the different types of mule spinners and minders were unevenly distributed across the cotton spinning region. Mule spinners, in large numbers, remained prominent, particularly in the Manchester, Ashton and Bolton areas, until the eventual surrender of higher-count spinning to the self-actor. In contrast the self-actor minders though being present in many cotton towns from the 1830s, made steady advances in the coarser spinning districts of south-east Lancashire and north-east Cheshire and the coarse spinning districts around Blackburn and Rossendale. The number of spinners and self-actor minders in the different cotton communities would evidently have changed with the fortunes of the separate districts.[19]

The mule spinners and self-actor minders had a unique standing within the industry but there was much difference of skill and status within their ranks. The potential range of experience between spinners in fine, medium and coarse spinning districts, large and small towns and rural factory communities, the giant, medium and smaller mills, has already been suggested. The difference between the hand-mule spinners, particularly the fine and medium, and their eventual successors the self-actor minders was real and more than could be concealed by similar manning practices. Amongst all mule spinners the nature of work varied according to the length of carriage and number of spindles, the count and type of yarn being spun, the type and construction of the mule, and the room conditions for spinning. Though the differences would have been more apparent between districts and, in the more complex communities, between mills producing different counts, the possibility of a variety of mule spinning systems within single mills should not be discounted. Thus shifts in markets, raw material problems or technological change would be experienced differently in the separate cotton districts. And whilst the information on nineteenth century wage rates suggests that spinners shared a common experience be it improvements, slump or stability the variations between districts and the type of spinner and spinning is the more striking. Though cotton spinners and minders were sometimes easily united in common cause, the potential for divisions within their trade was to be a source of weakness that was to take a century to overcome.[20]

CHAPTER TWO

Mule Spinner Societies and the Early Federations

The mule spinners' small numbers and, with the shift of production into the factory, their concentration, provided a natural basis for association and organisation. The strategic position which they occupied within the cotton industry thrust them to the fore in disputes with employers, at least until the emergence of weavers' militancy in the 1840s, and even then spinners alone — the cardroom hands were late to organise — maintained an ability to stop the entire mill. The Webbs, in their *History of Trade Unionism*, used the spinners' history to illustrate the progression of nineteenth century trade unionism through three stages — the struggle for existence (1799-1825), the revolutionary period (1829-42), the new spirit and the new model (1843-60). The thesis that the mid-century marked a turning point in the spinners' history — from a revolutionary to a sectional role — still runs strong in the literature and has recently been given additional weight by the claim that these years saw a stabilisation of industrial relations following widespread conflicts associated with the technological changes from the late 1820s to the early 1840s. Though the spinners' history can be divided into periods which exhibit specific features and illustrate the engagement of spinners and particularly their leaders in broader working-class movements, it is the continuity of purpose, the pursuit of spinners' industrial interests and the search for the organisational means to achieve that end, that provide the central theme. This chapter is concerned with the history of the hand-mule spinners down to 1837; chapter three concentrates on their and the self-actor minders' experience in the mid-century decades that were concluded by the Cotton Famine.[1]

The first spinners' societies were formed in the 1780s and 1790s when the industry's workers were still spread amongst cottages, workshops and the new factories. They may have been established by spinners who came from crafts that already possessed rudimentary trade unions for regulating apprenticeship, trade practices and wages or, in the case of weaving, friendly societies to which members would contribute their pence in exchange for benefits in time of need. Spinners may also have been influenced by the calico printers who operated a strong Lancashire society from the 1780s. A society of jenny spinners, which may have been open to mule spinners, was established at Stockport in 1785 and societies especially for mule spinners at Stockport and Manchester in 1792. These early societies clearly had amongst their purposes the regulation of wages and the conduct of disputes with employers or middlemen; but caution was essential, for in the wake of the

French Revolution and the outbreak of war in 1793, government opposition to working men's organisations hardened, culminating in the legislation of 1799 and 1800 which made combinations of both workers and employers illegal. However, association for mutual benefit purposes was possible and from 1793 societies sprang up to take advantage of legislation which gave protection to registered friendly society funds; by 1800-1 Lancashire had 820 societies, some of which were operated by mule spinners. Registration had its dangers: at Stockport, in an evident attempt to control their operatives, employers supported a new mule spinners' society in March 1795; Manchester mule spinners now claimed their society existed 'only to Relieve our Fellow Labourers in Distress'; the Oldham mule spinners' rules provided for the expulsion of members who 'combined together to raise their wages contrary to the law'. Such provisions may have been cosmetic in intent for spinners were not to be deterred from the pursuit of industrial issues; strikes occurred at Manchester in 1795 which concluded in a unique agreement to link wages to the price of yarn, whilst in 1799 a spinners' representative was on the Lancashire trades committee that unsuccessfully demanded repeal of the first Combination Act. The penalty for transgressing the country's laws could be severe: in 1798 Charles Radcliffe, a Stockport spinner, and possibly one of many who became engaged in organised political opposition to the government, was sentenced to seven years' transportation for administering the revolutionary United Englishmen's oath to another spinner.[2]

The establishment and survival of spinners' societies in these critical years was due to a number of circumstances: the indifference of employers, except when under threat; the protection of friendly society legislation; the support they gave to members; the resolution and courage of individual mule spinners; and, primarily, their spontaneity. The earliest organisation, consisting of domestic or workshop based mule spinners, was probably the village or town society but, with the movement of workers into the factories, the shop clubs of spinners employed in a particular mill would have been increasingly significant. Working together and living in close proximity, spinners were tied by bonds that employers might find hard to penetrate; they spoke of their shop mates and, either together or through shop committees, sought to establish a hold, a closed shop, in the mill. The shared experience and a consciousness of interests different from those of employers would have encouraged a mutuality that family links and the subcontracting system would have readily diffused to new recruits. Alongside shop clubs developed town or district societies. These latter, consisting of all members in the area, were governed by committees composed of 'head shopmen' from the shop clubs, either elected or serving in rote. Perhaps because of the fear of legal action and the need for efficiency, committees could be reduced in size; the prolonged Manchester strike of 1818 was organised by a committee of twelve, whilst that at Bolton in 1823 was led by one of seven. In some societies committee and officers regularly changed in order to share a burden exacerbated by the long working day. Members blacklisted for their trade union activities were sometimes established and supported as small tradesmen or beerhouse keepers and might serve as officers. The strength of district societies, as of shop clubs, lay in their simplicity; raided by the authorities or abandoned by members at the termination of a disastrous dispute they could be reformed easily by a handful of activists or shop delegates, and more elaborate regional or trade-wide organisations could be erected upon them.[3]

Combination for defence of trade interests was at the heart of spinner organisation. To that end district society rules sought to standardise procedures and establish a firm discipline over shop clubs. The Oldham rules of 1797 declared that 'in every shop . . . there shall be one person appointed . . . who shall regulate any particular business, control the Committee (if found necessary) and collect for the members in the shop where they work.' And the Manchester and Oldham rule book provisions for the public conduct of their members, whilst possibly an effort to moderate the societies' image, would also have served to bind members more closely. Both Manchester and Oldham rules provided for the control of entry into the trade. The subcontracting system may have made such regulations largely irrelevant, but the attitude of societies and clubs would have created a climate hostile to incomers from other trades. The extent to which districts and shops went beyond their rule books to dictate to employers which spinner or piecer should be set to spare mules is generally without record; however, entry by outsiders was still taking place as late as the depressed years at the end of the French wars. Individual spinner acceptance of what the society regarded as the appropriate rate was crucial to the maintenance of standards and the 1785 Stockport instruction to members 'not to work under the usual prices' doubtless found echoes elsewhere. Similarly, the 1792 Manchester requirement upon members not to work in a shop where a strike had taken place constituted the means by which spinners might influence their employers. During industrial disputes, at the behest of their shop mates, or on the instruction of the district committee, a delegation from the shop might approach the master; however a wish to protect activists frequently led to the use of representatives drawn from other shops or districts. The prosperity of the 1790s may have encouraged spinners to make demands not imitated by those of later generations; in 1797 spinners employed by M'Connel & Kennedy informed their employer that they would not have any more wefting, apparently their preference was for the more highly paid warp spinning.[4]

Benefit provision was an aspect of their activities that spinner societies were willing to publicise, if not detail. Accounts for the early period have not survived but rule books and public statements indicate the pattern of income and expenditure. The high pay of the early mule spinners and the size of their societies made a comprehensive range of benefits possible. Funeral benefits and 'out of work' pay to those unable to work or looking for employment were widely disbursed; whilst the former was given in a lump sum, more regular benefits probably varied according to the society's ability to pay. Some societies asked new members to pay an entry fee; whilst this may have been to ensure that members paid in before becoming a burden, it may also have served to restrict the entry of migrant spinners. Though efforts were to be made to introduce allowances for members 'tramping' in search of work, there was opposition to this form of mobility; as late as 1829 the Glasgow society opposed such a scheme for fear it might undercut pay in the higher wage districts. Aside from regular benefits the societies' funds would be called upon to provide 'out of work' pay to striking members and their piecers. Whilst district societies were usually able to finance, sometimes generously, 'partial' or shop strikes, 'general' district strikes were difficult. The striking members would be supported in a number of ways: by levies on their fellows — at Manchester in 1829 coarse spinners paid about 15 per cent of their net earnings to support striking fine spinners; by payments, to the fury of the authorities, from sympathetically managed friendly societies; by credit from sympathetic or intimidated shopkeepers; and, again demonstrating the scope of spinner organisation, funds raised by delegates despatched to other trades or towns. The extent to which all spinner societies adopted a comprehensive benefits policy should be qualified. The chief evidence comes from the wealthier societies; it is possible that societies in the lower paid or isolated country districts and others whose existence was intermittent were unable to support such activities and were primarily industrial in purpose. Whilst most societies continued to provide death benefits, there is evidence that from the 1830s, with extensive unemployment, falling wages amongst coarse spinners, and the provision of many benefits by specialist friendly societies, there was a wide-scale abandonment of comprehensive benefits provision.[5]

The nature of mule spinner unions in the early nineteenth century is concealed by the absence of records but references to strikes, though misleading in that they direct attention away from the more commonplace activities, give some indication of their character and distribution. Strikes to raise wages broke out at Manchester, Stockport and Stalybridge from 1801 to 1803; of these only the 1802 Manchester dispute seems to have been successful. The most extensive dispute seems to have been at Manchester in 1803 when the employers raised a fund of £20,000 to break the spinners. The pattern of future disputes involving the mule spinners can already be discerned: their readiness to strike in periods of expansion; their ability to sustain long disputes; their general disdain of the Combination Acts; and the willingness of masters to combine to break them. The Manchester spinners' payments to and from Yorkshire woollen workers at this time is a pointer to later inter-trade co-operation whilst the replacement of striking Salford spinners by women in 1807 served to raise a fear of male redundancy that was to persist through the century. Inadequate documentation makes it futile to enquire whether spinners' societies were continuously active during these years; at Glasgow a trade union tradition was beginning, at Manchester unions evidently continued to operate, whilst some societies, such as Stockport, were probably broken by employers. But cotton spinner trade unionism evidently survived, for in 1810 the spinning district raised their organisation to new heights.[6]

In that year spinners demonstrated the ability to build upon their shop clubs and district societies. As trade improved spinners from the principal towns were 'organised under the denomination of a General Union, and conducted by what was termed a General Congress'. This, the spinners' first federation, originated in Manchester and that town dominated the congress of forty to fifty delegates, one for each Manchester shop and each country district. Like subsequent spinner federations the General Union was concerned solely with wages issues; friendly society benefits were the responsibility of district societies, whilst craft control considerations were outside its ambit. The strategy and tactics initiated by this body were to be repeated many times at both regional and district level. To maintain or advance wages in the high paying districts, of which Manchester was the principal, the low wage country districts first had to be advanced. To this end the General Congress invented the rolling strike — supported by working districts, the low paid districts were successively to strike until their wages were advanced. In May 1810 Preston and Stalybridge spinners turned out and were subsequently financed by working districts. The employers, their hand strengthened by a sudden contraction of trade, established their own association and set out to break the strike; their means was to be a lockout of working spinners which would deprive those on strike of support. Work ceased in Manchester and most of the principal cotton towns. Estimates of the number of spinners turned out range from 3,000 to 8,000. A count of likely mule spinner numbers in the places affected would suggest 5,000 as a probable figure. Up to 30,000 other factory operatives were reported to have been involved. The dispute became a trial of strength; the Spinners' leader, Joseph Shipley, 'was as "a general in the army", the commander of thousands of willing agents, who performed his bidding with the utmost promptitude', but the strike was doomed:

> When the contribution of those in work failed, such of the men as had laid by money in the days of their prosperity, resorted to it for support, and then the hard-earned savings of perhaps years of industry, were consumed in this hopeless warfare. Furniture, clothes, every article of comfort or convenience that their cottages contained, was then disposed of, and these unhappy victims of their own folly underwent a series of privations, which would appear incredible to those who do not know the force of pride, and the enduring pertinacity, with which the English working classes will not infrequently remain, what they call 'true to each other'.[7]

The strike began to break in the autumn and the spinners returned on the employers' terms, reputedly at wages half the previous level.[8]

The following six years reveal a diversity of experience. Though the Federation was abandoned some of the spinners' district societies, and maybe some of the local employers' associations, survived. Their activities were dominated by the volatility that characterised the economic history of the cotton trade during the final years of the Napoleonic wars. Spinners' and employers' behaviour varied with trade conditions. In 1811, as the slump of trade intensified, Manchester mills struck against further wage reductions; by the year's end short time had made such acts futile. And trade union activity may have been put aside with the government repression that followed the weaver-inspired Luddite outbreaks of early 1812 in which some spinners may have been involved. But as trade improved spinners again advanced: in 1813 Manchester fine spinners successfully turned out for higher wages, whilst in 1814 the Preston society was reorganised. Employers also may have been learning to anticipate and fend off demands; in 1814 the Bolton masters published a 'town list', that 'our prices might be generally known, as being higher than in other towns in the neighbourhood'. Lists at their simplest were tables indicating the difference piece rates payable for spinning specific quantities of the various counts, and carried the implication that employers would pay the standard rate and might be seen as a concession to or recognition of trade unions. Yet industrial harmony was to be elusive. As trade slumped in 1814 Oldham spinners conducted a two-month strike against wage cuts. At Stockport, after strikes against wage reductions at one or two mills, spinners and masters negotiated short time at the same rates. Short-time working was to be preferred to wage cuts by operatives in adverse periods and insofar as it enabled a liquidation of stocks it also had appeal to employers; nevertheless, as at Stockport, it usually delayed rather than put off wage reductions. The sharp downturn that came with the ending of the Napoleonic war continued through to 1816 and again the response of district societies to further wage reductions varied; at Preston spinners turned out and paraded around the town before returning defeated whilst at Stockport and Manchester, mule spinners accepted reductions on the promise that employers would restore them when markets again permitted.[9]

The readiness of some mule spinners to enter into agreements with employers may have been encouraged by the experience of those cotton spinners who had formed Manchester's first short-time committee in 1814. In 1815-16 the campaign for a limited working week for children attracted the support of some of the industry's best known names, Sir Robert Peel and Robert Owen to the fore, and some Manchester manufacturers and merchants, particularly Nathaniel Gould, gave it their help. Despite this support the interests of master and operative spinner were to differ, for behind the public campaign for children, whose presence as piecers and assistants was essential to the operation of the mule, emerged a clear intent by the operatives to limit the hours of adult labour. A six day working week of from seventy to eighty hours had become common; in 1816 Thackeray's Manchester mill worked fourteen hours a day 'no time being allowed for meals'. Working conditions were generally poor and, apart from the humanitarian urge to improve the lot of child labour, became a powerful argument in the spinners' own claims to justify their relatively high wages. The spinners pointed to their long hours of work in hot and humid conditions. Though critics could assert that spinners were the often willing drivers of children, their commitment to shorter hours was genuine; whilst they were to experience sharp changes of fortune the spinners, particularly the Manchester fine, were never to abandon the short-time committee. Peel introduced a Bill into the House of Commons in 1815 that would have limited the hours of work of persons under eighteen to 10½ hours per day; but numerous political campaigns and empty Factory Acts were to pass before that object was satisfactorily attained.[10]

As prosperity returned to the cotton spinning industry in 1817-18 the integrity of employer promises to restore wage cuts was put to the test. Wage advances and reductions of hours were the twin demands of a prolonged strike at Manchester. Bolton, Stockport, Wigan and Glasgow spinners were to be engaged in lesser disputes. Though there is some evidence of mutual support and co-ordination, there is little indication of the prior organisation that made the 1810 General Congress so formidable; moreover the principal conflict was to occur at the industry's high wage centre. In the autumn of 1817 the Manchester spinners asked their employers to fulfil their promise to restore wage cuts. 'Some declared they could not give it; others they would not; but the great part, that they would, if others did, but they should not like to be first.' The spinners may have later made piecemeal advances with individual employers but they did not force the issue until June 1818 after bricksetters, joiners, carpenters and dyers had successfully struck for higher wages; then some 2,200 Manchester spinners gave notice to their employers and turned out on the same day, bringing out nearly 20,000 other operatives who depended on them. Mill delegates elected a committee of twelve to finance and conduct the strike. Initially the strike was peaceful. The spinners congregated or placed pickets outside the few working mills, and, drawn up in ranks by shop, paraded the town twice daily. For the first few weeks the strikers received strike pay and, to discourage any urge to break the strike, piecers also received an allowance. At the beginning of August the magistrates encouraged the employers to re-open their mills, yet the strike continued solid. By August 12th some employers had conceded two-thirds of the advance, their mills were back at work, and a spinners' victory seemed possible. But many employers were evidently determined to starve the spinners back and on August 24th they again opened their mills. The sight of working spinners, the introduction of knobsticks, and the growing shortage of funds compounded by the disappearance of the committee's treasurer with the strike fund had their effect — the peaceful and disciplined dispute gave way to riot and the calling out of the military. Pickets and committee members were arrested and, following scenes of violence, a spinner was killed and others wounded when shots were fired at a 'mob' storming a working mill. The spinners quickly formed a fresh committee but by early September, without funds and impotent in the face of military force, the strikers drifted back to work; James Norris reported to the Home Office that 'many of the large mills [were] completely filled, and the rest filling as fast as can reasonably be expected'.

The Manchester dispute was the cotton spinning industry's most serious since 1810 and was a measure of employer and trade union strength. Both sides looked to outside support. Seeking to influence public opinion, the mule spinners distributed a broadsheet by way of justifying their claims for an advance. To help finance the strike they re-activated the delegate system that had probably been dormant since 1810, sending delegates across the country in search of funds. Whilst little was raised the contacts with other towns and with spinners in Scotland and Ireland probably inspired the unrealised proposal for a 'general rising or turn out' of spinners throughout the United Kingdom. And spinners and other trades together established at Manchester the 'Union of all Trades called the PHILANTHROPIC SOCIETY'; though short-lived, it brought together groups of craftsmen and workers across the country. Both schemes anticipated future occasions when spinners would seek to broaden the scope of their activities but they could not conceal the failure to match will with resources. The spinners' discipline had held until late August but the sustaining of the industry's largest single society through a long town strike was evidently beyond them. Nor were the employers without weakness, for the differences that had marked their responses to the spinners' initial request for advances were to persist throughout the stoppage; the majority may have been content to starve the spinners back, but the advances given by some employers and the evident panic of others in the face of the violence may well have led to a crumbling of their position. That they continued to refuse the advances was probably due to the action of the magistrates, stiffened by Tory government resolve to break the spinners; after previously complaining about the inadequacies of the Combination Acts and the laws dealing with picketing, the magistrates clearly took the initiative. Alerted by reports from its Manchester spies, suspicious that the strikers might be influenced by anti-government agitators, and hostile to any form of organisation amongst the lower orders, the Home Office was determined that the strike must be broken.

If the years from 1814-16 marked a period of possible recognition and agreement between masters and men, it was clearly terminated by the 1818 strike. The bitter-ness of the dispute sharply polarised relations between employers and mule spinners whilst the intervention of the Home Office effectively turned the spinners into legal outcasts. As the spinners returned to the mills employers and authorities gave full vent to their vindictiveness: Norris, the Manchester magistrate, informed the Home Office that 'the worst people amongst the turnouts . . . will never be received again into any mill'; up to 100 or more were blacklisted, and eleven years later Daniel Brough, 'the captain of the pickets', was eking a living as a rag and bone man; others were forced to sign 'a written declaration that they will not in future be concerned in any combination'. The arrested committee members and pickets were sent for trial to the Lancaster assizes; the former were released after pleading guilty but three of the latter, including the eighteen-year-old John Doherty, later to rank amongst the century's greatest trade union organisers, received two years' imprison-ment. At the end of September, employers decided to reduce the hours of labour from Monday to Saturday to twelve, exclusive of mealtimes. Long hours were later described as 'the main origin of the late turn-out'. The Home Office was concerned that such a reduction would be seen as a concession to the strikers; more likely employers were seeking to anticipate Peel's campaign for legislation to limit hours. Warned of the employers' pending concession the Home Office was anxious that defeat should not be softened.[11]

The determination of the authorities to use the law to suppress trade union activity was also exhibited in other cotton towns. At Stockport jenny spinners and powerloom weavers embarked on strikes for wage advances; while the former were successful the latter were defeated by employers supported by the military and yeomanry under the direction of John Lloyd, the vigorous clerk to the magistrates and a Home Office agent. Though Stockport mule spinners were organised they seem to have been weak in comparison to their Manchester fellows; Lloyd's zeal in suppressing their activities was to be held up by the Home Office as an example of how to handle trade unions. Lloyd demonstrated how the law could be used to isolate the activists and threaten the existence of their societies. At the Heaton Norris mill of William Smith, William Temple, an ex-soldier who had served with Sir John Moore on his retreat from Corunna, along with some colleagues, gave notice to quit his employment and seek higher wages elsewhere in the town:

> The result was, I left his service on Saturday; and he said I must not consider myself as his servant again. . . On Monday the 18th, he sent my name with twenty more, round to the masters not to employ me and the rest . . . one of my shopmates had got on employ at Mr Ruths . . . Between three and four in the afternoon he sent for him and told him, he had got his name on a list from Mr Smith, and he must quit his employ; he instantly turned him away after working three quarters of a day. I went to Mr Jesse Howard . . . and he said, I have got your name upon a list from Mr Smith, and must not employ you.[12]

Temple called a town meeting and went to each factory in the Stockport district asking the men to send representatives; he then collected money for the strikers in Stockport. He also visited an attorney on whose advice he commenced a legal action against Smith for depriving him of work elsewhere. Lloyd's wrath fell upon him — along with fourteen others he was charged under the Combination Acts for the action at Smith's which was finally heard on appeal at the Lancaster assizes. For calling a town meeting and collecting money in Stockport he and five others were charged with conspiracy which was to be heard at Chester. Lloyd thus ensured that Temple, the only one accused at both centres, was held in prison for six months until supporters were able to raise his £400 bail. Though granted a discharge at Lancaster he and two shopmates were sentenced at Chester to three months' imprisonment; John Barnett, another spinner, was sentenced to twelve months for helping Temple call the meeting, whilst another named Bolton was imprisoned for three months for meeting a person in the street and saying, 'I wish you would come forward for those men, otherwise they will drop through'. On release Temple was deprived of work for a further twelve months. Lloyd's action broke the strike and seized papers subsequently revealed that the spinners' shop had been supporting striking Wigan spinners and raising funds to support Temple and his mates. Nor was Temple broken, for six years later the old soldier was sent to London to give evidence to the 1824 parliamentary committee that led to the repeal of the Combination Acts.[13]

  Though the spinners were not to the forefront of the political campaigns for the extension of the vote in the Napoleonic and post-war period, the behaviour of the authorities during strikes may have encouraged many to participate. At the beginning of the Manchester strike Norris commented, 'I do not by any means think that the system of turning out in the different trades is connected with this idea [reform] or that the sentiment itself has taken root in the minds of the mass of the population, yet I am disposed to think that this idea gained ground'. The arrest of the committee, increasing agitation amongst the weavers, and violence, placed Manchester 'almost in a state of military law' and created a climate for radicals to exploit. On 1 September 1818 some 500 striking Manchester spinners marched to a public meeting at Stockport where speakers demanding parliamentary reform advocated violence, threatened to assassinate government ministers, and mooted the establishment of a National Convention. Yet spinners' leaders continued to make use of the parliamentary process. Factory workers at Manchester and Bolton had petitioned the House of Commons for a 10½ hour factory day early in 1818. And after a House of Lords committee had been packed in the summer of that year by witnesses supportive of the masters' case, spinners at Manchester, Bolton and Stockport sent witnesses of their own to a second committee sitting in the following year. Their efforts may have enabled the passage of the first general factory act which prohibited the employment of children under the age of nine and limited the working week for those under the age of 16 to 72 hours; however, it did nothing to ameliorate the condition of male operatives and was widely ignored by employers. When the Manchester and Bolton witnesses returned home:

> . . . they were flung out of employment and so persecuted by the masters throughout the country; that they had no employment for weeks and months after; and some of them were obliged to leave the country for America, in consequence of giving evidence.[14]

The efforts of employers, magistrates and government to break the spinners made 1818 and 1819 the most critical years in their history.[15]

The resurgence of the spinners was marked by a rumoured meeting at Stalybridge in October 1820 and fresh talk of a turn-out. As trade improved in the following years local societies were again mobilised. Lesser disputes occurred at Blackburn, Preston and Stockport. Major disputes broke out at Bolton in 1822-3 and at Glasgow between 1823 and 1825. The Bolton dispute began as a mill by mill rolling strike to advance wages but after early successes which brought wage advances the spinners were halted by Mr Jones of Tyldesley who took in knobsticks, prosecuted his workers for assault not combination, and broke the strike. The Bolton masters then counter-attacked. Their trade had been increasingly built upon the production of medium to fine yarns for the district's muslin weavers and some mills had introduced the longer mules that high count spinning made possible. They revised their 1814 wage list to take account of the increase in mule size: for every dozen spindles over 324 — and amongst the fine spinners carriages of up to 420 were now being used — a discount was made on the piece rate paid; previously the general rule had been to pay a standard rate according to the amount and count of yarn turned off. The threat to the more highly paid fine spinners was clear and 500 stopped work, bringing out ten times that number of ancillary workers. The concern which spinners attached to discounting is evidenced in the support Bolton received; operating in contravention of the Combination Acts, spinners at most of the major centres, including Manchester, contributed to the turnouts. The support was probably solicited by delegates and there is no evidence that a federation such as that of 1810 was in existence. After the arrest of their committee the Bolton spinners negotiated an arrangement with their employers which conceded half the proposed discount; though not a total defeat the principle had been conceded, and it was to encourage masters to develop longer mules and had as its sequel the disputes of 1829-31.[16]

The Glasgow spinners, though in touch with Lancashire, had established their own trade union tradition; formed in the early nineteenth century their members were engaged in strikes in 1811, 1817, recurrently through the 1820s, and again in 1837. Unlike Lancashire and Cheshire, where wages were the principal issue, spinners at Glasgow turned their attention to conditions of work and the establishment and maintenance of the closed shop as a base from which to handle employers and keep their wages high. Their opponents were led by Henry Houldsworth, cotton spinner and magistrate and, through his Manchester interests, a ruthless antagonist in the disputes there in 1818. Houldsworth and Dunlop, a second Glasgow employer, and three Glasgow mule spinners, gave evidence on the 1823 dispute to the 1824 *Select Committee on Artisans and Machinery* and it is impossible to determine who was lying. Houldsworth and Dunlop alleged violence and intimidation and an effort by spinners to usurp the employer's control over his factory; the spinners complained of insanitary conditions, dismissal of workers for protesting against payment in truck, fraud and fines, and in effect demanded a closed shop and the right to have dismissed spinners and overseers with whom they disagreed. Defeated after a Glasgow-wide lockout concerted by Houldsworth, they failed a second time in 1825 after about 650 had been engaged in a dispute that originated in a demand for the dismissal of a manager. In such actions the Glasgow men were making demands which went beyond those normally considered proper in England; though the Manchester committee originally sent support to Glasgow, it was over-ruled by a general meeting of the town's spinners which denounced all pretensions to interfere with 'the rights of employers' and offered to mediate between the two parties. The Stalybridge strikers made control of entry an issue in the 1810 dispute, and Bolton strikers in 1830 demanded the ending of the apprenticeship system whereby employers promoted piecers to man mules at a reduced rate, but there is little evidence of English spinners generally engaging in closed shop disputes comparable to those of the Glasgow men.[17]

Cotton spinner trade unionism in the early 1820s was conducted in an environment free of the popular radicalism and protest which had attracted the fear and hostility of the authorities and the support of many mule spinners in 1818-19. Yet, following the efforts of John Lloyd and his colleagues in 1818, the laws, and particularly the Combination Acts, seem to have been increasingly used against trade unionists. Though the proliferation and continuation of society activity indicates that the law was unable to stem the spinners, it undoubtedly aided the breaking of strikes and the disruption of some local organisations. To imprisoned trade unionists the Combination laws were indistinguishable from the other laws, statute and common, which were one-sidedly applied against them; to many employers and magistrates they were clumsy and unworkable. To those influenced by political economy the labourer's wage was determined by the supply of and demand for labour, and the Combination laws, by preventing discussion between the two sides, exacerbated rather than prevented conflicts. However, the question of repealing the Combination Acts was raised in the House of Commons in 1822 and subsequently taken up outside parliament; the adroit handling of this campaign by Francis Place, which included the channelling of petitions from Manchester and Stockport spinners, encouraged witnesses to appear before the Parliamentary committee and helped bring about the Acts' repeal in 1824. Henceforth workers would be free 'to enter any combination to obtain an advance or to fix the rate of wages, or to lessen or alter the hours or duration of the time of working, or to decrease the quantity of work, or to induce another to depart from his service . . . ' The Acts' repeal brought a mixed response from spinners. It encouraged those who believed that change could be achieved through Parliament and that conciliation and agreements with employers was possible. In the winter and spring of 1824-5 factory workers campaigned and petitioned for a fresh factory act; employers were approached for their support and whilst the majority threw their weight against major reform, 32 of Manchester's leading masters declared their backing for a 66-hour week. An Act of 1825 finally reduced the hours for children from 72 to 69 as against the original demand for 63½ hours. Out of such co-operation emerged the view that agreement with 'honourable' masters was possible, but that they were wary of being undercut by the illegal hours and low wages of the 'dishonourable' and particularly the country masters. However, for other trade unionists the 1824 repeal was an opportunity; mill strikes at Manchester and Stockport and the re-opening of the Glasgow dispute were the prelude to more extensive activity amongst the country's cotton spinners.[18]

The legislation of 1824, whilst leaving untouched many of the laws that could be used against those engaged in industrial action, did allow workers openly to organise, proselytise and strike. It was now possible for activists more easily to promote trade federations and pre-planning of the kind that seems to have made the General Union of 1810 so formidable. The Manchester society had been re-established by 1822 and from the summer of 1824 it was at the centre of a fresh effort to construct a general spinners' union; in December 1824 two of its delegates visited the striking Glasgow spinners to 'establish a union of operative cotton spinners over all the three kingdoms'. Although the union received support from Glasgow the main impact of the organisation was felt in Lancashire and north-east Cheshire. The federation's promoters claimed some 4,000 members in December 1824 and anticipated that their numbers would shortly increase to 16,000. Co-ordinated by a Manchester based committee, associated societies re-adopted the 1810 General Union's policy of attempting to bring up the outlying towns to the Manchester wage rates. But the ability to direct districts was evidently far less than in 1810; instead of harnessing resources and commencing rolling strikes a rash of disputes erupted, at Preston, Oldham, Ashton, and most bitterly at Hyde, which brought more out on strike than there were employed to support them. The actions were not to be successful. Knobsticks, picket violence, the drift back of the weak, loss of confidence, dismissals and blacklisting became the pattern.[19]

This wave of trade union activity was not without consequence. Government gave way, not unwillingly, before the pleas of employers, and permitted a fresh Parliamentary inquiry into trade unions which led in 1825 to legislation that, whilst recognising the right to combine, so hedged it with fresh offences as to render most forms of trade union activity illegal. Employers at Manchester and Stockport had petitioned against repeal of the Combination Acts in 1824 and others now adopted a more aggressive attitude towards trade unions. Cotton masters were encouraged to sink their differences and form or re-establish associations which rapidly displayed a ruthlessness and vindictiveness sufficient to break their opponents. At Hyde the paternalistic employer Thomas Ashton, who had been dismissive of workmen's combinations in evidence to the 1824 committee, now became a vigorous exponent of employer authority and was, with other employers, sufficiently concerned about the spinners' strength as to commission Sharp, Roberts & Co., the Manchester engineers, to construct a self-actor mule, thus to dispense with skilled male spinners. And as trade collapsed in 1826 employers seized the initiative in wage bargaining. At Stockport and Bolton workers accepted reductions on the promise of a return to the old rate when trade permitted whilst at Ashton and Oldham spinners struck only to return defeated on the employers' terms. Perhaps S. J. Chapman was correct in asserting that masters 'learnt . . . that by precipitating disputes in times of bad trade they might insure being unhampered when trade improved', for in 1827 and 1828, as consumption of raw cotton reached record levels, employers outside Manchester seem to have been little troubled by industrial disputes.[20]

For many societies the years following the defeats of 1826-7 were probably ones of consolidation. The society that had most evidently grown in strength in the 1820s was that at Manchester. By 1824 it had recovered from the defeat of 1818 and its spinners, though avoiding direct participation in the strikes of the mid-1820s, had determined policy and helped organise and finance other districts in dispute. Manchester's mills dominated the fine spinning industry and were the largest single force in coarse spinning. Workers in the two sectors faced distinct problems; the fine would have been aware of the dangers that the introduction of longer mules and discounting on the lines of the Bolton list posed to their standards, while the coarse would have been conscious of the lower rates being paid in the country towns. Despite the difference of interests, one that could have been exacerbated by the gulf in the earnings, the two classes of mule spinners stood together. By 1828 Manchester's mills were all but a closed shop; membership fees were high but members received a range of benefits, and most importantly, were given substantial support if called upon to strike. Behind this strength lay skilful leadership; the society's leaders, some of whom had suffered imprisonment or proscription for trade union activity, contained men adept at union organisation, and experienced in inter-trade collaboration, parliamentary and political campaigning and propaganda. In the mid-1820s the society seems to have oscillated between policies of conciliation and confrontation; the election of John Doherty as Manchester's secretary in 1828 has been seen as marking the beginnings of a more militant phase. At the end of that year the Manchester union commenced action to bring up the lower paying firms; whilst two conceded rather than be turned out, a third resisted and a mill strike commenced.[21]

Perhaps the Manchester men drew confidence from their society's strength for they made no attempt at this stage to re-establish the federal organisation of 1824-5. Instead it was to be the employers who seized the initiative. At Manchester a Masters' Association was formed and in January 1829 resolved to reduce the wages of the working spinners who were supporting the strike by 5 per cent until the turnout was ended. The society ordered the men to return to work; behind their action lay the probable realisation that their resources were going to be needed elsewhere. A major dispute had also broken out at Stockport in January 1829 where, in a move which threatened wage rates throughout the cotton districts, employers demanded a 10 per cent reduction of all factory workers. Before the end of the month some 10,000 operatives were on strike and Manchester initially, then other districts, rallied to their support. In a pattern that was to be repeated through the century the separate groups of factory operatives, although no doubt co-ordinating, each organised and financed their own members. In March Thomas Ashton chaired a meeting of employers from Manchester, Hyde, Stockport and the neighbouring communities; alarmed at the support being given to Stockport strikers they formed their own association for the 'suppression of combinations'. At Manchester the Fine Spinning Masters seized their opportunity and presented a wage list to the spinners — drawn up by Henry Houldsworth — which superseded the existing individual mill lists, reduced wage rates, and, in imitation of the Bolton list of 1823, introduced discounting on the larger mules. No doubt the masters wished to take advantage of the larger 400-500 spindle mules then being built; but the timing of their demands would seem to have been designed to stretch and break the Manchester spinners already deeply committed to the Stockport dispute. Though the Manchester spinners' leaders saw the danger and sought to persuade their members to compromise and not to strike, they were out-voted by the rank and file; in April, the fine spinners possibly believing that the self-interest of individual employers and the support of the still working coarse spinners would see them through, withdrew their labour.

The spinners were now striking on two fronts. At Stockport the employers made use of a dual strategy: firstly, to starve the strikers back, to which end Hyde workers contributing to their Stockport colleagues were either dismissed or forced to sign the document; and secondly to undermine their confidence by initiating the strike-breaking cycle of knobsticks. The previously peaceful strike gave way to public disorder. The vitriol-throwing and violence which greeted the knobsticks was the prelude to scenes of riot only quietened by volleys of gunfire from troops, whilst the spinners' committee, falsely implicated in the violence, was arrested. One worker was sentenced to be hanged and three others to transportation. In September, after nine months of struggle, the last of the defeated Stockport strikers returned. In October the six month Manchester dispute ended. The Manchester employers had bound themselves to abide by their Association with £500 bonds whilst the strikers, with Stockport taking much of the out-of-town funding, sustained themselves with an average strike pay of 2s. 2¼d. a week, funded primarily by a levy of 3s. 0d. on the coarse spinning members of the Manchester society. The employers never lost the initiative, first sitting the strike out and publicising their own case — which emphasised the very high wages of the fine spinners — then in late July announcing the opening of their mills and subsequently rejecting all suggestions of compromise. Though the government became sufficiently concerned about the dispute as to discuss it in Cabinet, the discipline and peaceful nature of the strike was maintained; the union's strategy was to present its own case through the press and public addresses, and to seek arbitration. The strike's turning point came on 2 September when the Manchester coarse master spinners joined the fine masters to break the strike, threatening their workers with wage reductions unless they signed an agreement that they would not aid the strikers. The coarse spinners, rejecting this demand, came out on strike, thus depriving the fine spinners of financial support. When the committee organised a mass meeting to determine whether members were prepared to accept the employers' terms, on a show of hands there was a majority against; it was then agreed to hold a secret ballot. The result was declared to be a majority of seven in favour of acceptance, and the spinners returned. Nine years later it was revealed that the ballot result had been a majority of three for rejection, but that the committee, afraid of the crumbling of the strike, the possibility of violence and a break-up of the union, had changed the figures.[22]

Unlike previous major defeats which had been followed by a collapse or lull of trade union activity, those of 1829 were the prelude to major organisational innovations. The spinners' leaders were motivated by the bleak prospects that now faced them: discounting was an evident encouragement to the development of longer mules for use throughout the trade, and carried with it the double threat of further wage reductions and redundancies, whilst the defeat at Stockport was a blow to the policy of maintaining high wages at Manchester by raising or holding those in surrounding districts. As the strike was ending the Manchester leadership took steps to build on the delegate system that had solicited and brought help from working spinners and other trades. On 20 September 1829, spinners' delegates from Lancashire and Cheshire resolved to form a 'Grand General Union of Cotton Spinners throughout the United Kingdom' (G.G.U.). The promoters obtained support from spinners in Scotland and Ireland and in December a conference of seventeen delegates representing 12,000 to 13,000 delegates from the United Kingdom's principal cotton towns was held at Ramsey in the Isle of Man. Riddled by parochialism — Bolton 'would not allow Manchester to govern them' — the delegates rejected proposals for a single national committee, and established three national committees subject only to an annual meeting. Yet this was 'a real federation' whose purpose was to equalise wages within and between districts; the delegates confirmed John Doherty as secretary and reached agreement on a number of central objectives including the restriction of entry, the rejection of tramping, the exclusion but separate organisation of women, finance, a fresh application to Parliament for an amended Factory Act, and the need if not the means to co-ordinate and exercise control over district strikes. In the last week of the Manchester dispute Doherty also convened the first of a series of meetings that was to lead in 1830 to the formation of the National Association for the Protection of Labour (N.A.P.L.), a general combination of trades formed, from the spinners' view, for the purpose of increasing the resources available to workers from member trades in dispute with their employers.[23]

The new organisations soon had an opportunity to prove their worth as employers sought to build on their victories of 1829. Strikes to prevent wage cutting occurred at Hyde early in 1830 when workers were apparently supported by some masters. At Bolton in March the fine spinning masters attempted to re-establish their competitive position by introducing the Manchester list, and although Bolton spinners were willing to compromise, they were drawn into bitter and violent strikes by firms demanding 25 per cent reductions to the full list. Though Bolton was supported by the N.A.P.L., the G.G.U. was not to be seen; doubtless events confirmed Bolton's suspicion of the federal body for Doherty was later blamed for the strike's failure. A second conference of the G.G.U. was held at the Isle of Man in June 1830 though it came to late to aid the Bolton spinners. As a major dispute set to unfold at Ashton, the G.G.U. was to display its skills. Following a threat by the Ashton masters to reduce rates to those prevailing in the notoriously low-wage Stalybridge area, it convened a meeting attended by 4,000 spinners from south-east Lancashire and north-east Cheshire, obtained their support, and then requested employers to withhold their reductions and give the G.G.U. a chance to raise wages in Stalybridge. The masters agreed and after two mills had been turned out Stalybridge rates were brought up to a compromise level. The G.G.U.'s success, the campaigning of the N.A.P.L. and the concurrent July Revolution in France enthused a previously poorly organised area; the Ashton spinners' society grew rapidly in the course of the year and commenced successful rolling strikes for wage increases against Ashton masters. But in November 1830 the combined masters of Ashton, Dukinfield, Stalybridge and Mossley again presented their July demands and, for the first time in the coarse spinning districts, insisted upon discounting. At a meeting 20,000 strong on Ashton Moss, complete with bands, tricolours, guns and hatchets, the Ashton spinners and their supporters rejected calls for compromise and struck for the old rates. The third general meeting of the G.G.U. held in Manchester in December 1830 decided to finance them and, in contravention of its Ramsey policy of husbanding resources and not striking for advances, called a general strike of all spinners working below the Ashton rate. Despite hopes raised by the G.G.U. and the N.A.P.L. the general strike call was largely ignored and funds for the Ashton strike were not forthcoming. The Ashton strike became violent — Thomas Ashton Jnr., of the Hyde mill owning family, was murdered, allegedly at the instigation of the local union, and assassination attempts made against other masters — and the spinners, rejecting compromise, became more obstinate; but after the mills were opened on February 3rd the strike rapidly collapsed and ended amidst blacklisting and extensive victimisation. The G.G.U. collapsed and the spinners, increasingly lukewarm, withdrew their support from the N.A.P.L. In the following months employers at Hyde and Oldham forced the gap first opened at Bolton in 1823 and introduced discounting and further wage reductions.[24]

The cluster of strikes from 1829 to 1831 directly involved fine and coarse spinners in most of the north-western cotton towns. Whilst these were primarily wage disputes, involving either discounting or district and mill rates, their resolution, particularly in fine spinning, stimulated the more widespread introduction of the longer, more productive mules that had encouraged Manchester employers to implement a Bolton-style list of 1829. However, at Manchester, some employers, lacking either the wish or the means, did not introduce the new machinery, and in the winter of 1830-1 the still well organised spinners' society, after some unsuccessful efforts to reverse the 1829 wage cuts and prevent the employment of women on smaller mules, attempted to exploit divisions between the masters to reverse the tide of discounting. In the winter of 1830-1 they received support from the small-wheel masters in attempts to influence the long-wheel masters to amend their rates; when these overtures failed a meeting of some masters and men agreed a list which increased rates on the largest wheels but reduced those on the small and medium wheels. But the long-wheel masters who had not attended now further cut their rates in line, and when spinners turned out at two mills to enforce the proposed list, speedily replaced them from the ranks of the unemployed. Thus an attempt at negotiation had brought an even further cut in rates. To stay in business the small-wheel masters turned to the coupling of mules to form longer pairs and turned off the surplus spinners. Battered by strike failure, wage reductions and unemployment, the Manchester spinners abandoned their society. The 1829-31 disputes have been described as structural and a result of the tensions generated by the destabilising influence of long mules on the family economy and employment prospects of the spinner. But this may be a lop-sided perspective. The small 1830-1 dispute at Manchester apart, the strikes were about wage cutting, discounting at Manchester and, most clearly at Stockport, simple wage reductions. Unemployment was sequel rather than cause.[25]

Defeat in the wage campaign did not end the spinners' struggles. Those still active returned to their second aim, legislation to limit factory hours. In November 1828 Doherty had initiated the Society for the Protection of Children Employed in Cotton Factories, to enforce the 1819 and 1825 Acts. Just as the wages equalisation policy was aimed at low paying masters, so this campaign was directed at those masters who, through excessive working, sought lower costs and thus threatened working and wage standards throughout the industry. An Act of 1829 made prosecutions under the existing legislation easier but though some were initiated — particularly at Wigan — the society's activities were superseded by the industrial campaign. However in April 1830 the society set in train a campaign for a new 60½ hour factory bill — 10½ hours Monday to Friday and 8 on Saturday; the Manchester Short-Time Committee was reformed and, dominated by former or working spinners, conducted proceedings in co-operation with the Yorkshire leaders. Through this movement the spinners hoped to attain their industrial objectives: short time would effectively reduce output and therefore excessive competition, and help maintain prices and wages in the trade; moreover further expansion would have to be met from fresh capacity and thus create jobs for unemployed spinners. The movement had wide appeal; to some master spinners anxious to prevent the undercutting of the unscrupulous, to humanitarians wishing to advance the conditions of factory children, and to Tory opponents of the emerging millocracy. From the start spinners solicited help wherever it could be found. Legislation was passed in 1831, but this provided for a 66 hour week and excluded the woollen industry. Enraged, the Yorkshire and Lancashire co-ordinating committees launched a fresh movement, and short time committees — organisationally distinct from the trade union societies but drawing much of their leadership and support from them — were established in most cotton towns in support of Sadler's parliamentary campaign for a ten hour day and a fresh inquiry. But the efforts of employers and a newly returned Whig Government were to defeat them. After a Royal Commission inquiry, boycotted by the spinners, an Act was passed in 1833 which, whilst it established a factory inspectorate and provided for enforcement, actually threatened an increase in spinners' hours, by limiting child labour to eight hours but enabling its use in relays. The thorough nature of the Act, and a willingness, even amongst some reformers, to observe its operation, were to effectively prevent further amendments in the 1830s. Doherty and other members of the short-time movement threw their efforts into the Robert Owen inspired National Regeneration Society which sought to restrict factory working by non-parliamentary means; however attempts to obtain a shorter day by industrial action and through agreements with employers were of limited local significance. Further ten hour campaigns, in 1836 and 1837, and 1840-1, though gaining increased parliamentary support, failed to break the resistance of employers and government.[26]

The employer victories of 1829-31 and the adverse economic climate ensured that the early 1830s were generally free of trade disputes. The activity of spinners in the factory campaign, paralleled by the participation, particularly of many of their leaders, in the 1830-2 movement for parliamentary reform, was not matched by a readiness for confrontation on the industrial front. The exception was at Oldham; the district was apparently unaffected by the short time then being worked in other towns, and in late 1833 its spinners, who had formed a Central Union Club, commenced strikes against wage reductions, the coupling of mules and, in a local continuation of the short-time movement, for a reduction of hours. In April 1834 the police raided the public house where the committee was meeting and arrested two of its members and charged them with oath taking; coming weeks after the Tolpuddle Martyrs had been sentenced to seven years' transportation, the arrests were seen as part of a government-employer onslaught upon trade unionism. For ten days Oldham experienced a general strike, mass meetings, the shooting of a spinner, and the standing by of troops and special constables. Disputes in cotton towns could rapidly polarise into conflicts between authorities and the masses, as at Manchester in 1818, Stockport in 1829, and Ashton in 1830-1. However the nature of the Oldham events is still in dispute — variously interpreted as 'fundamentally trade unionist', 'a powerful confirmation of local class solidarity' and 'mass action' with 'more than a touch of revolution in the air'. Irrespective of the nature of the Oldham dispute it was not to be imitated elsewhere and can hardly be described as typical. Moreover, by the end of the month, a short period by spinner standards, even the original demands had been abandoned and the workers requested employers to take them back.[27]

The Oldham dispute may have had sympathisers in other cotton towns but, if so desirous, the spinners' societies would still have been too weak to act. Many of the fine spinners who remained in work, though paid lower rates, were operating longer mules at higher speeds, probably maintained their wages and were perhaps less interested in trade union activities. For coarse spinners the consequences of the 1829-31 disputes had been more severe. Until then their wages, in many cases supplemented by child earnings, would have maintained a level comparable with that of the majority of skilled non-factory workers, but, following the defeats, they seem to have followed a downward trend, arguably discernible from the 1826 slump, which took them further apart from the elite fine spinners. With the evident failure of their societies and perhaps the prospect of paying heavy fees to maintain out-of-work pay to the growing numbers of unemployed, many remained outside the societies. In 1834 the revived Manchester Society had only 700 members out of three times as many spinners, Preston in 1836 had 250 to 300 out of 660 spinners. Doherty returned as Manchester's secretary in 1834 and attempted to rebuild the society; to increase member participation he replaced the system of mills, lodges and lodge committees by the Quinquarticular System with each five members electing a tithing man, five of whom elected a constable, five of whom elected a warden, the wardens forming the committee and the whole subject to quarterly meetings and jurors to handle complaints. To prevent excessive costs, regular payments to the unemployed were replaced by lump sums whilst sick pay schemes were abandoned — both noticeable reversals of the earlier high benefit policy. This may have been a consequence of the emergence of well-established specialist benefit organisations; at Stockport in 1840 some 300 spinners, perhaps half the town's total, were members of the local Oddfellows' Friendly Society and presumably had less interest in their trade society. Though Manchester's leaders managed a partial revival of their society's influence they could not completely reverse the tide and in June 1838, only 1,060 spinners were on roll, some mills had no members, and unemployed spinners were not counted. Manchester's failure to re-establish its full strength after the disasters of 1829-31 marked the end of the virtual hegemony that it had exerted over neighbouring towns in the preceding decades.[28]

Yet the upswing of trade in 1834-6 was to herald a revival of trade union activity, a fresh campaign to advance wages, and a further attempt at federal organisation. In 1835 Bolton spinners, doubtless seeking to recover the cuts made following their 1830 defeat, successfully struck for higher wages. Though pressures built up in the following year few societies followed Bolton's lead. Despite their society's weakness, Manchester leaders still ranked amongst the trade's strategists and in October 1836 they met to consider 'the propriety of organising upon a firm basis a union of the trade throughout the country, for protecting the prices of labour'. Shortly afterwards 22 delegates from Lancashire and Cheshire cotton towns met, indicatively, at Bolton and decided on a combined movement and to 'use every legal means in their power to raise wages to the Bolton standard'. Perhaps the Manchester leaders were seeking to imitate Bolton's success. Though that town would have contained fewer spinners than Ashton and Oldham, and a fine-spinning trade perhaps only a third that of Manchester's, it had a history of activity from 1795 and a record of repeated industrial actions. As the discount compromise of 1823 and the attitude of its delegates at Ramsey in 1829 illustrate, it was ready to take an independent view of the trade. Given the weakness of Manchester and the coarse spinning centres, Bolton's anchor role was perhaps inevitable. However, the 1836 Federation seems to have been more typical of the 1824-5 than the 1829-31 predecessor. It was probably no more than a formalisation of inter-district delegate meetings and the rash of subsequent wage demands or disputes has been seen as evidence of 'no strong central authority to control the constituent societies'. The Bolton society had unsuccessfully encouraged Preston spinners to commence a wages campaign after its own success in 1835. However, the new federation, at least according to employers, seems to have played a major part in initiating and sustaining the Preston dispute of 1836-7. After recruiting most of the town's spinners, the Preston society was reformed in October 1836 and simultaneous demands made to the masters for the Bolton list. Preston employers had an anti-union reputation and they now reformed their association; gaining support from Manchester employers and determined to resist, they responded by offering 10 per cent on condition that spinners renounced their union. On these terms being refused, employers locked out all their factory workers. Spinners and their piecers, who had already struck, were supported from union funds and by other trade delegates for three months. Other factory operatives thrown out of work by the dispute and without strike pay were to experience extreme poverty. Employers refused all offers of mediation and after the mills had been opened, the funds exhausted or dried up, and combined with a downturn of trade, the spinners returned on the employers' terms — a declaration not to become members of any union, and, surprisingly, the full 10 per cent; some 200 of the most active, a third of the total, were replaced by new hands. The Federation seems to have been abandoned. As trade worsened the spinners in other districts fought their separate disputes, but now against wage reductions; at Oldham, the spinners' society suffered another major defeat early in 1837. In April 1837 the Preston employers reclaimed their 10 per cent.[28]

The employers' victories of early 1837 were to be rendered comprehensive by the breaking of the most powerful spinners' society — that at Glasgow. Though participating in the 1824-5 and 1829-31 federations, the Glasgow society had maintained its exclusive stance. The bitter disputes of the 1820s had resulted in a truce of sorts, whereby masters paid a standard rate irrespective of mule size — the agreement that the Manchester operatives sought — but apparently on the understanding that the society would bring up undercutting employers. In a period which saw downward pressure on piece rates, Glasgow's policy, backed by heavy expenditure and therefore high subscriptions, was to keep wages up by striking, by regulating the supply of labour through the closed shop, and by the promotion of emigration schemes. The society also supported the short time movement. The truce with employers was apparently maintained and, during the booming trade of 1836, wages were raised. But the masters then informed the men that the advances would be withdrawn unless wages at Duntocher, a country mill, were also raised; the spinners subsequently fought an unsuccessful strike which cost the union £3,000. The employers may have colluded, for in 1837, with the union's funds exhausted, the Glasgow masters, separately and then together, demanded wage reductions and, as at Manchester in 1829, discounting. After thirteen weeks, marked towards the end by the inevitable violence including murder, vitriol-throwing and incendiarism, the spinners were defeated and returned on the employers' terms; subsequently the union's committee were arrested and charged with the organisation of the violence and the appointment of a secret committee to assassinate masters. Employers and authorities blackguarded the spinners, and historians have tended to follow them; but the English spinners and trade unionists were more inclined to see the prosecution as another example of government and employers attacking trade unionists. Although the more serious charges were not proven, the members of the committee were sentenced to be transported. The Glasgow union did recover from the strike, but was weakened due to victimisation, unemployment following the shift to long mules, the employment of women on the smaller mules, and the introduction of self-actor mules.[30]

The employers' victories of 1829-37 were a real check on mule spinner trade unionism. Though the spread of district societies, the general prolongation of trade disputes, the federations and the efforts to stimulate a broader trade union movement suggest considerable achievement, the nature and scope of the spinners' organisations needs to be heavily qualified. The mule spinner advances were based upon a spontaneous trade unionism deeply rooted in the mill shops but it was limited; whilst some societies seem to have drawn strength from their role as friendly societies and may, at the times of their greatest influence, have aspired to traditional-type craft control, the trade unionism of the expanding coarse spinning districts seems to have been increasingly linked to short term wage issues which thus gave it an extra volatility. The district societies' lack of continuity is a further qualification of their impact: Manchester had periods of influence, before 1810, 1818, 1824-31 and possibly 1835-6, but in between it was a broken or defeated body; though Bolton could claim continuity since 1795, the experience of many north-western societies, admittedly with considerable variation, tended to be ephemeral. None of the Lancashire and Cheshire societies approached the influence that Glasgow seems to have commanded over its immediate area, particularly from 1827 to 1837. The most influential societies seem to have been the largest and those with a significant number of fine spinners. Though there was always the danger that the fine–coarse spinner wage differential would become a source of division, the experience of the early period, and particularly at Manchester in 1829, suggests the instinct of the two groups was for unity. Apart from their willingness to remain true to each other, be it through friendly society support, or more dramatically, during industrial disputes, and their capacity to reform and fight again, the spinners' principal achievement lay in their reaching out to their fellows in other towns. It was this, given shape in the trade federations, that constituted their principal contribution to early nineteenth century trade unionism; in bringing down an even more powerful employer response, it was also the cause of crushing defeats. The spinners' participation in and stimulation of broader trade union movements seems impressive, yet should be qualified. The initial motive was to obtain extra support for spinners' campaigns, with any broader trade union advances coming after; moreover the overtures that led to the formation of the N.A.P.L. in 1829-30 contrast with the exclusivity of the 1829 G.G.U. and the failure of the spinners to extend their organisation to embrace operatives in all branches of factory work.

What did spinner trade unionism achieve for its members? Local variations apart, it might be asserted that the advance of technology was not impaired, and conditions and hours of work were only slightly influenced. For those in societies operating as friendly societies, the benefits would have served as a cushion against the uncertainties of the new industrial age. But what of wages? Whilst their volatility, moderated by employer willingness to pay, would suggest that market forces and the supply of appropriately skilled labour were the principal determinants, the effectiveness of trade unions in the short term may have been of some significance The Bolton list, aspects of Manchester trade unionism in 1828, the concessions by Ashton masters in 1830, and the Glasgow spinner-employer relations, suggest that societies may at times, albeit with employer consent, have gained some form of district consolidation; certainly the successful disputes seem to have been those designed to bring mills or sub-districts up to a district level. Similarly the sustained disputes reflected the spinners' belief in their ability to influence short-term wage rates. And Doherty pointed out in 1837 that the existence of unions may have led employers to delay, if only for a short time, wage reductions. The major disputes of 1802-3, 1810, 1818, 1824-5, 1829-31 and 1836-7 have been seen, 1829-31 apart, as efforts to raise wages, and three of these followed periods in which wages had been beaten down; the failure to affect their course suggests that mule spinner influence upon wages was limited. The high, albeit fluctuating, wages of the war years, the post-war slump, the early 1820s advances and the subsequent downward trend were largely outside their control. From 1824-5 employers were determined not merely to defeat the spinners' unions, but to break them: at Manchester, Ashton and Preston, many hundreds of 'the most active, bold, intelligent and influential, without whom they were nothing' paid the penalty of proscription and victimisation. The scale of employer victories suggests the limited effectiveness of mule spinner trade unionism, and the commitment of members during disputes indicates the extent and depth of shop and district consciousness.[31]

CHAPTER THREE

Spinners and Minders

The breaking of the strongest district societies at Manchester and Glasgow, the smashing of the mid 1830s strikes, and the collapse of efforts at federation, left the mule spinners powerless to halt the introduction of longer mules and the unemployment, discounting and cutting of piece rates that followed. A new threat had also emerged; the concluding phases of the Preston and Glasgow strikes had each been marked by single firms seeking a solution through the employment of self-actors. From the 1830s the spinners had to watch the spread of the new system and come to terms with the new class of workers, the self-actor minders, who operated them. Though the two groups were sometimes to combine they were no longer the single trade union influence in the factories that mule spinners had been down to the 1830s; the shift of weaving from cottage to mill brought in a much larger separately organised occupational group that by the nature and scale of its activities was to relatively diminish the importance of spinners and minders in cotton's industrial relations. The significance of cotton spinners in the country's trade union movement was also to diminish; the construction of the railways, the expansion of coal, iron and engineering industries meant that trade union developments were increasingly to take place outside the cotton industry. But the tradition established by the mule spinner did not fade. The mid-century period bounded by the crises of 1837-42 and 1861-5 continued to provide a volatile environment for the conduct of industrial relations and the issues that concerned the mule spinners — wages, hours and technology — did not disappear with the defeats of the 1830s.[1]

Of concern to mule spinners in the 1830s was the threat that technical change posed to their status. Yet the immediate impact of the self-actor machine has not been charted. At the outset of the Stockport dispute in 1829 a visiting Manchester delegate dismissed the new machine as of no consequence. Though the self-actor was soon in operation across the cotton districts, albeit in small numbers, there seems to have been no resistance to its introduction. And when introduced as a strike breaking weapon at Preston and Glasgow, societies were in no position to halt its operation. Moreover the self-actor's slow conquest of the higher counts meant that fine spinners, the group most able to resist, were unaffected until the 1860s and 1870s. Nevertheless many hand-mule spinners seem to have regarded the self-actor with contempt; at Glasgow in 1837 mule spinners at one mill lost all prospects of employment after refusing to man the new machines at the strike's end. Even so it may be that mule spinner societies were immediately open to the male minders; the Webbs suggest that the Bolton society was reformed in 1837 and open to both groups. The operation of the two systems in the same mill and the possible drawing of some of the early minders from the ranks of the unemployed spinners or the surplus of piecers would certainly have encouraged such a move. However the earnings and skill differences between spinners and minders were to persist until the former's demise. Wages of fine, medium and coarse spinners already exhibited significant variations and the new self-actor minders, at the lower end, received wages little more than those of urban labourers. In the 1830s fine spinners earning up to 45 shillings per week earned perhaps 50 per cent more than the medium, 100 per cent more than coarse and a further 5 shillings per week more than minders whose earnings were around 16-18 shillings per week when a full week was worked (Appendix V). Such differentials may not have barred minders from mule spinners' societies; the abandonment of more extensive benefit provision by many societies meant a lowering of subscriptions and the fees reportedly paid by a Bolton spinner in 1833 — 3d to his society and 1d to the Short Time Committee — were not beyond the self-actor operator. It is likely that the question of mule spinner opposition to minder membership did not arise in the 1830s; their small numbers, perhaps little more than 3 per cent of the total, may simply have swelled the ranks of mule spinners who had abandoned their trade unions.[2]

The weakness of spinner trade unionism was to be revealed in the years of economic uncertainty from 1837-42. The decline of spinners' wages, especially of the lower medium and coarse as against the fine, arguably evident from the slump of 1826, accelerated in the late 1830s, plumbing a low in 1842 when short time gave way to unemployment. For the spinner these problems were compounded by the continuing coupling and lengthening of mules. Federal organisations were absent whilst at Manchester, certainly, there were shops without any union members. Disputes were few and 'from mid 1838 to late 1839, there were no large strikes in the mills and very few strikes of any kind' whilst 'from 1840 to 1842 the round of reductions were received with sullen acquiesence and a few small scale, inevitably short, unsuccessful strikes.' Nevertheless, spinners' leaders and many of their members were to become engaged in other working-class organisations. The 1836-7 disputes had re-activated the tradition of inter-trade support and led to meetings of spinners and trade delegates to raise funds. The Manchester spinners, working through the town's trades council which had been established in 1837 to consider political questions of interest to trade unionists, participated in the extensive 1837-8 campaign for the Glasgow spinners and in 1838 gave evidence to the *Select Committee on Workmen's Combination*. The Glasgow prosecutions and the parliamentary inquiry were seen as the prelude to a major governmental and employer onslaught upon trade unionists and, coming on top of the failed Ten Hours campaigns, were major factors behind the spinners' renewed support for parliamentary reform. Spinners had taken part in working-class political movements since the 1790s and were therefore amongst the promoters and financiers of the 1838-9 campaign for parliamentary reform enshrined in the People's Charter. Many of those spinners who provided leadership or support for Chartism in the cotton towns would probably have agreed with John Doherty that universal suffrage 'means nothing more than a power given to every man to protect his own labour from being devalued by others' and seen it, alongside normal trade union activity and parliamentary lobbying, as a further means to their ends. Bolton spinners who supported the Charter eventually articulated their demands in terms that included the ten hours day, employer observation of list prices, abandonment of the apprenticeship system, unnecessary deductions from earnings, and abolition of gas charges. However after the first Chartist upsurge of 1839 direct organisational links between spinners and Chartists were few; interchange of personnel was enough and spinners were no doubt anxious to protect their societies from association with Chartism's more illegal activities. Even so support for the Charter did not prevent the spinners from engaging in parliamentary lobbying for factory reform and in the summer of 1841 they accompanied Lord Ashley on his tour of Lancashire.[3]

The extent of the spinners' support for Chartism was to be revealed in the Plug Plot riots that spread through the textile towns in the summer of 1842. The strikes in the cotton industry stemmed from a wages dispute. In the spring of 1842, after two years in which successive wage reductions had been accepted with little struggle, cotton workers and spinners at a number of Lancashire towns, Bolton, Blackburn and Preston struck, albeit unsuccessfully, against further wage cuts. In July four Ashton and Stalybridge firms threatened their weavers with wage reductions and started a dispute that was to spread through the cotton districts. Local Chartist leaders seized their opportunity and after a meeting at Mottram Moor which pledged to stay out for the Charter, marchers visited other cotton towns to stop working mills. At Manchester in mid-August meetings and conferences of trade delegates passed resolutions endorsing the strike for the Charter. That end was not to be attained but whilst some towns returned to normality as soon as the marchers passed, others settled into strikes of which a minority persisted after the general collapse at the end of the month. Although spinners' delegates from Manchester, Bolton and Heywood and unspecified groups of factory operatives from Ashton, Hyde, Stalybridge, Mossley and Lees attended the Trades Conferences, the spinners' attachment to the 'plot' must be qualified. At Manchester, though spinners and carders met together and struck, other spinners were amongst the special constables enrolled to repulse the Ashton 'mob'; at Oldham mills returned to normal the day after the marchers left although workers subsequently came out again in demand of 1840s wages and the ten hours day; at Preston, where the town's mills were virtually stopped by riot, visiting Blackburn and Chorley spinners were subsequently unable to persuade spinners to join striking weavers. In contrast Stockport mills were at work until brought out by a visiting Ashton 'mob', but spinners persisted with a strike demand for the wages of 1840 until late September. Doubtless the participants' objectives varied from the radical to a simple demand for higher wages; whilst the former had always claimed some spinners amongst its supporters the behaviour of many spinners during the summer months points to a committed concern with the latter. It is tempting to view in the spinners' diverse response a split between the well paid minority of fine and medium spinners and the greater number of more lowly paid coarse and self-actor spinners, but evidence of such is not yet available. It is the geographical rather than the horizontal division of the trade that is revealed by the dispute of 1842; whatever their support for Chartism at the different towns, either in association with other factory groups or alone, spinners pursued their separate ends.[4]

Limited though the spinners' engagement in Chartism and the 1842 Plug Plot may have been, it is possible that the forum of the trades' committee and the apparently uncoordinated continuation of the post-plot disputes at Bolton and Stockport, together with contacts through the short-time movement, may have again turned the spinners' minds to mutual aid and inter-district co-operation. According to notes in the Webb collection a new federation 'The Association of Operative Cotton Spinners in the United Kingdom' was formed in the autumn of 1842. Whilst it is possible that delegate contacts took place, the Webbs' dating of the federation's establishment is tendentious — in their *History of Trade Unionism* they suggest about 1843. The first evidence of spinner re-organisation was at Oldham where during or shortly after a dispute concerning the manning of self-actors, in the winter of 1842-3, the Oldham Operative Cotton Spinners' Provincial Association consisting of centres in a radius of about five miles around Oldham was formed. Initial references to the federal organisation come from the minute books of the 'Associated Cotton Spinners, Self-Actor Minders, and other Factory Operatives' of Bolton and refer to general meetings of delegates from September 1844. The first newspaper account is of a meeting of delegates from Manchester, Ashton-under-Lyne, Oldham, Astley, Stockport, Heywood, Bury, Blackburn, Preston, Chowbent, Wigan, Hindley, Farrington, Cuerden Green, Lees, Waterhead Mill, Chorley, Horwich, Ashton-in-Makerfield and Hyde, held at Bolton on Sunday 10 November 1844. The first exact reference to the title used by the Webbs is in January 1845 whilst into the August of that year minutes and circulars continued to be addressed to 'The Operative Cotton Spinners of Lancashire, Cheshire, Yorkshire and Derbyshire'. It would seem that the Association was a loose federation of delegates of the kind that had operated from Bolton in 1836. Moreover members of that earlier body were amongst the participants; William Arrowsmith who addressed the delegates in 1836 was still Manchester's secretary, and an active member in the new body. Behind Bolton's choice as location for the new Association may have lain a continuing distrust or weakness of the trade's centre, Manchester, already revealed in 1829 and 1836. By 1845 the Association was holding fortnightly delegate meetings, rotating them through the different cotton towns, had a central committee, chairman and secretary, the whole being financed by levies raised according to need from the constituent societies. Bolton provided the officers and central committee meetings were held in that town.[5]

The purpose of the Association was to combine and advance the interests of all spinners. Contrary to the evidence of later divisions between mule spinners and minders, the Association was evidently intended to embrace both. The titles of local societies — the Stockport Spinners and Self-Actor Minders and the Manchester Operative Cotton Spinners and Self-Actor Minders — suggest that the central body may have played a guiding role in a reconstruction of local societies after the 1842 dispute. The Association first came to prominence in the autumn of 1844 as its members made demands for wage advances. The pace was set at Stockport where the local society, failing to obtain an average based on fifteen spinning centres, persisted with 'demands for a rise of 10 per cent on the hand mules and 20 per cent on the self-actors'. At Manchester spinners asked 'less than was taken from us in times of depression' from the employers and 'carefully abstained from the use of language which was in any way calculated to disturb the good feelings which exist between us'. The masters at Wigan, Ashton and Manchester, speaking as a body, sought to anticipate or split the spinners by proffering their own advances, generally of 5 per cent, whilst Daniel Dronsfield of Werneth Mill, Oldham 'agreed to give advances to the spinners' but 'declined to increase the wages of self-actor minders'. Though Ashton spinners seemed to have accepted the terms, strikes broke out at Oldham, Manchester, Wigan and Stockport; whilst the three former seem to have won further advances, employers at Stockport held the line, permanently rid themselves of some strikers, and forced the remainder back to work. The Association supported spinners at Manchester, Wigan and Stockport but it would have been impossible to sustain a prolonged dispute at all three; evidently without a rolling strike strategy, the Association's role seems to have been to encourage rather than to lead. This first round of extensive disputes revealed fundamental problems at the local level. Behind the brave rhetoric of the Stockport committee lay shop weaknesses — barely two weeks into the strike twelve mills were fully at work, six partially and only nine all out. Dronsfield eventually paid twice his original advance to both spinners and self-actor minders yet he may have been correct in probing the divisions between them; by the spring of 1845 spinners at Ashton, Manchester and Warrington had split into separate mule spinner and self-actor minder societies. It is tempting to see in this a sharpening realisation amongst the more highly paid fine spinners, that at the local level their interests would be best served by a separate organisation.[6]

The 1844 wages campaign probably increased inter-district co-operation to its highest level since 1836-7 and encouraged further societies to join the Association. Founded in a more buoyant period, with employers anxious to take advantage of trade, the Association had time to consolidate and develop. A delegate meeting at the beginning of 1845 requested members to consider the following 'Objects and Rules of the Associated Operative Cotton Spinners, Twiners, and Self Acting Minders of the United Kingdom':

1.   That the object of this Association shall be the permanently bettering of the condition of its members, by locating our surplus members on the land.
2.   A more equitable adjustment or distribution of labour, by means of shortening the hours of labour.
3.   And the prevention of all unnecessary turn-outs.

The Association's geographical limits were to be Lancashire, Cheshire, Yorkshire and Derbyshire. Whilst the first objective was to be given separate consideration by

Oldham and Bolton, it was clearly beyond the means of smaller societies and never adopted by the Association. The second objective had been a central plank of spinner campaigns since 1814 and was to be pursued through the Lancashire Central Short-Time Committee. The final objective had taxed the promoters of the Grand General Union of Cotton Spinners (G.G.U.) and the principles adopted by the Association in 1845 were not a great advance on those arrived at in Ramsey in 1829. The eventually agreed purpose of the Association, clearly outlined at the head of each circular, was 'to afford assistance when any district is turned out for an advance or against a reduction in prices and for the redressing of any grievances between employers and employed; but that no turnout be allowed, under any circumstances, until every legal means have been tried to adjust the same honestly and fairly to both parties'. In January 1846 the Association agreed to make Bolton's Thomas Brindle its permanent secretary at a salary of £1 per week. However there do seem to have been points of tension within the organisation. Though day-to-day business was generally delegated to the Central Committee, the delegate meetings (possibly reflecting local jealousies) were concerned to restrict its powers; the Association rules were amended to limit its ability to sanction strikes and to engage in political activity. Failure to delegate authority to its executive may have been a fundamental flaw inhibiting the Association's development.[7]

By 1845 the Association had become the most successful in the spinners' history. Despite division at the district level, it remained open to hand mule spinners and self-actor minders and the divided Manchester, Ashton and Warrington groups separately re-affiliated. In the seventeen months to May 1846, 49 societies were represented at meetings, some two dozen regularly, and the Ashton, Bolton, Bury, Manchester, Oldham and Preston societies almost always. As the period progressed delegates from Blackburn, Dukinfield and Mossley became regular attenders whilst the peripheral cotton communities of West Yorkshire were also drawn in; noticeably weak was Stalybridge, the storm centre during the 1842 plug riots. The Association sought to encourage the weaker societies — in March 1845 it appointed a delegate to organise the Stalybridge area and in December urged the stronger societies to send delegates to Hyde 'to assist in organising that district and the surrounding areas'. Whilst delegate meetings continued to move around the districts, proceedings were increasingly being held at Manchester and though this may have reflected the town's location, its still large fine and coarse spinners' societies and the revival of the short-time campaign probably pushed it to the fore. The Webbs were later informed that the Manchester Fine Spinners were the backbone of the Association and William Arrowsmith and William Fair, ex-spinner and now proprietor of the Woodman's Hut Tavern, successively their secretaries, were amongst its leading figures. The enlargement of the Association and the shift to Manchester cost Bolton its pre-eminence; though Thomas Brindle continued as secretary, on matters of control, policy and expenditure Bolton was increasingly at odds with the central body.[8]

The opportunities open to a spinners' federation less ambitious and more disciplined than those of the 1820s and 1830s were to become apparent in the wages campaign of 1845, itself made possible by the continuing buoyancy of the cotton trade. Districts were instructed to request advances and employers, evidently anxious to take benefit of the times, agreed. In July the Association delegated a representative to attend the tea-party called to tender thanks to the Bolton employers 'for their great kindness in advancing their operatives before those of every other district'; advances were subsequently made throughout the region. Whilst the Association was ready to encourage districts to pursue wage advances it differed from earlier federations in that instead of implementing policies designed to equalise wage rates throughout the cotton districts, it concentrated on the consolidation of district rates and the raising of low paying firms within them. Existing studies of the cotton industry have generally followed S. J. Chapman in maintaining that lists were uncommon amongst the spinners until after the Blackburn list in 1853; however this is a narrow interpretation for the 1845 and 1846 minutes clearly refer to 'lists' and 'district prices' at Preston, Mossley, Bury and Stockport. Indeed Bolton Masters had operated a list since 1814 and Manchester since 1829. These were different from the later jointly negotiated lists and inevitably at employer discretion; nevertheless they provided a basis for employers and unions to negotiate. Employers paying the list were advantaged in that, short of a general stoppage, strikes would be aimed at their undercutting rivals whilst the Association was provided with a framework within which it could conduct its district consolidation policy and 'legitimately' depute delegates or Association officers to visit and lay the case or conduct strikes against employers paying below the list. At Manchester in 1845-6 fine hand-mule spinners received 50s. 0d. to 60s. 0d. per week — as much as at any time until the 1870s — medium hand mule spinners 23s. 6d. to 32s. 7d. and self-actor minders 16s. 2d. to 20s. 2d.; at other centres the increase on the 1837-42 wages was comparable though given Manchester's monopolisation of the superfine spinning trade, differentials were not as great. In August 1845 the Central Committee congratulated 'fellow workers' that 'a better system has been adopted to gain our object'. However, success brought the Association up against a hard core of obdurate employers; it also encouraged the smaller and weaker societies, more likely to demand than to contribute resources, to enter the Association. Between August 1845 and May 1846 the Association became involved in numerous separate disputes. In November it was drawn into a dispute at Wood's Mill at Wigan where, for four months, the Association supported spinners and piecers in a small but expensive strike that was to end in failure; eight societies contributed 60 per cent of the funds and probably became increasingly concerned at the extent to which their resources were being drawn upon. The minutes of the Association for May 1846 record the delegates in dispute with, or demanding advances from, firms at Ashton-under-Lyne, Mossley, Stalybridge, Dukinfield, Lees and Warrington and offering to support Glasgow spinners in a proposed general strike.[9]

The activity of the spinners on wages was paralleled by the part they played in the factory movement. A succession of campaigns from 1844 onwards culminated in the passage of a Ten Hours Act in 1847. Despite the frenzied activities of agitators such as the Rev J. R. Stephens and Richard Oastler, the popular campaigns in

Lancashire were largely orchestrated and supported by factory operatives through their short-time committees; in the cotton districts these were co-ordinated by the Lancashire Central Short-Time Committee, the leaders of which were in touch with London and the parliamentary advocates, particularly Lord Ashley. The deep involvement of the spinners with the short time committees has been long recognised; however it would seem that in the mid-1840s the Lancashire Central Short-Time Committee was a junior body of the Spinners' Association. This is indicated in the Association's records: in January 1845 delegates were asked 'to consider renewing the struggle for a Ten Hour Bill in the next session of Parliament', in February they agreed that Doherty's famous *Letter to the Factory Operatives . . . on . . . the Ten Hours' Bill* be paid for by the Committee and distributed throughout the Districts, in March they resolved that 'the Lancashire Central Short-Time Committee be instructed to draw up forms of petitions . . .'. Districts were levied for the Central Short-Time Committee funds and from October 1844 to October 1845 the spinners provided 70 per cent of the finance. The Central Short-Time Committee meetings were held at William Fair's public house and the district short-time committees, particularly in the smaller communities, were probably open or reconstituted gatherings of the spinners' societies. Indeed it is tempting to see in the March 1844 Lancashire Central Short-Time Committee's petition demanding the Home Secretary's dismissal, the first list of the affiliated societies of the Association.[10]

The spinners' success in mobilising both trade union and short-time movements in 1844-6 seems to have led to the Lancashire Central Committee's separate reconstitution. At a conference of Lancashire delegates in April 1846 a new Lancashire Committee of seven was established. Nevertheless it included Harry Green, the previous secretary, and Thomas Mawdsley, a future secretary of the Spinners' Association and meetings continued to be held at William Fair's. There seems to be little reason to doubt Philip Grant's assertion that 'from the days of Thomas Foster and John Doherty to the present time 'the operative fine spinners of Manchester were the mainstay of the short-time committee in Manchester'; it would seem that, not least through Fair, their influence continued to be significant. It was this body that conducted the successful Lancashire campaign in 1846-7. However in the absence from Parliament of the spinners' advocate, Lord Ashley, the Westminster campaign was led by the radical Todmorden millowner, John Fielden, who was prepared to take more account of Oastler and the Yorkshire campaigners. The Ten Hours Bill was successfully passed through Parliament and it became law in two stages; for women and young persons, eleven hours were to be worked from July 1847 and ten hours from May 1848.[11]

The successful wages and factory campaigns of the 1840s are a mark of the Association's considerable achievements. That it has been generally underestimated is possibly due to its having been overshadowed by the northern Chartist campaigns of 1842 and 1847-8. Ironically the Association's moderation and pragmatism are amongst the principal question marks to be set against the assertion that the spinners of the early 1840s were of a revolutionary hue. In the wake of the 1842 Plug Plot societies sought to exclude political discussions from their meetings. But inevitably the Ten Hours campaigns and ordinary trade union interests made this object difficult. The Association maintained the spinners' tradition of supporting other trades in dispute and in 1845 played a part in the early activities of the National Association of United Trades for the Protection of Industry (N.A.U.T.P.I.), a fresh effort to construct a general trade union forum. Delegates were clearly divided as to membership but after meetings which agreed to support the N.A.U.T.P.I. the Association leaned to the Bolton view that seemingly rejected all organised engagements outside the trade. In 1845-6 the Spinners' Association launched and financed a campaign in the cotton towns to promote the repeal of the Corn Laws, an old radical platform but one that had fallen into disrepute on becoming the orthodoxy of employers. The Association's annual report for 1845 adopted employer policy stating that 'if the ports of the country were opened . . . provisions would be reasonable in price, trade would continue to flourish and things again wear a cheerful aspect'. Despite the ban on political activity, Chartist views surfaced in the Association. The proposal to settle unemployed labourers on the land, though rejected as an Association objective in 1845, was a central feature of later O'Connorite Chartism. Whilst it can be perceived, along with short time and emigration, as a further, albeit prohibitively expensive, means by which spinners sought to redress the balance of the labour market it clearly drew on working-class political economy. Moreover many of the societies that joined the Association in 1845 were from districts active in the 1842 disturbances.[12]

By the late summer of 1846 the mid-1840s expansion of the cotton trade was coming to a halt. In August 1846 Bolton spinners, probably fearing wage reductions, memorialised their employers 'to work shorter time in order to prevent the accumulation of stock at home and foreign speculation in cotton'. Twelve months later short-time and unemployment was evidence of a slump almost as severe as that of 1842. And it was to Chartist-type solutions that some of the Association looked. At Oldham and Mossley the local societies eventually obtained land on which they established unemployed spinners; at Bolton the society considered the land scheme and some members subscribed to the National Land Plan. Fearful of reductions the Association determined upon a more imaginative policy; a special delegate conference held at Manchester in August 1847 suggested to employers that the industry's problems could be solved by 'entirely suspending operations in cotton mills for a few weeks' thus to eliminate the surplus of stocks. Whilst the *Manchester Guardian* recorded the scheme observing that 'few of our readers will have forgotten the beneficial effect produced upon the trade by the general turn-out in August 1842', the employers' response was to be of a different order. In September 1847 masters at Mossley announced a 10 per cent reduction of wages.[13]

The Spinners' Association were now caught in circumstances similar to those that had wrecked the G.G.U. in 1830-1. The Mossley spinners agreed to resist the reduction and amidst fears that it would be extended throughout the cotton districts, delegates from other spinning centres flocked to a public meeting held at Charlestown 'to see what could be done'. The local and veteran Chartist leader, Richard Pilling, was elected to the chair from where he suggested a general stoppage of the cotton industry. Whilst the meeting could do little more than agree 'to assist to its uppermost the spinners of Mossley', Pilling's demand was taken up by Manchester's William Arrowsmith and the Association's secretary, Thomas Brindle. Whatever Pilling's motives, and he may have envisaged a re-run of 1842, Arrowsmith and Brindle were in effect seeking to implement the policy outlined at the August meeting of the Association. By early October their motive was clear for despite a 5 per cent levy on earnings the extent of the short-time and unemployment was such that the 500 striking Mossley spinners could not be supported; only through a cessation of work that would sharply reduce the industry's stocks could spinners hope to maintain wage rates. But the rank and file did not respond to the call for a general stoppage. Yet this was the policy endorsed by October delegate meetings of the Association, the only dissenters being Bolton, Lees and Tyldesley; Oldham sat on the fence. At this point the Association was overtaken by events when Ashton employers reduced wages to the levels applying before August 1844; there too spinners struck. At a delegate meeting on 20 October the Association variously renewed its call for a general stoppage, instructed Districts to request of employers that they 'allow men their former list prices' and agreed on a deputation to the government. By late November the Mossley and Ashton strikes were broken and the men had returned on the employers' terms. Elsewhere resistance was absent; at Preston, Stockport and Bolton (where spinners first sought to negotiate with employers but eventually agreed to strike only to rescind their decision a week later) reductions were accepted in anticipation or on the promise of a restoration when trade permitted.[14]

The trade collapse of 1846-7 was a severe blow to the Association and heralded its decline. Though delegate meetings continued to be well attended into the autumn of 1847, societies at Blackburn and Preston were unable to attend 'being so long out of employment'; many other societies had their books called in for inspection by the Association. But the slump took its toll. Recession and reductions brought a collapse of living standards. By 1849 earnings of Manchester fine spinners had fallen to 36s. — 40s. and of medium and coarse hand mule spinners to 21s. per week; in contrast self-actor minder earnings had started to recover and certainly had not fallen at a rate comparable with those of their more highly paid fellows. Manchester Fine Spinners, perhaps unwilling to finance the Association any further, left in 1848 whilst many of the smaller societies unable or unwilling to pay melted away; Stalybridge self-actor minders were expelled for non-payment of the levy and Hyde and Newton Moor societies collapsed. Bolton, perhaps disenchanted by the 1847 debacle, withdrew until it could find 'more confidence in the parties constituting the Central Committee' and for the next two years it was to oscillate between isolation and participation. Lacking the support of some major societies it would have been difficult for the remaining societies adequately to support the employment of a General Secretary and there is no evidence of Thomas Brindle being in post after 1848. However Mawdsley's Lancashire Central Short-Time Committee, represented at 1847 Association meetings by two delegates, now played an increasingly influential role in the Association.[15]

As trade began to recover in 1849 the spinners' organisations were faced with a new challenge. At Bolton and Stockport spinners unsuccessfully petitioned their employers for restoration of the 1847 reductions; at the former, spinners also decided to rejoin the Association. However the nature of the problem facing spinners changed when employers, once more working full time, effectively sabotaged the Ten Hours Act by working relays of children, thus avoiding the framers' intention to restrict the length of the working day. Though some Stalybridge operatives walked out of the mills in the spring it was the Spinners' Association and the Lancashire Central Short-Time Committee that took the initiative. At Preston 'the spinners, acting on the advice of their federation, decided in March to defer their wages demand until the legality of the relay system had been determined'. In the late summer the two issues were to become increasingly entangled. After a meeting at the Woodman's Hut in August which agreed on the principle of a general turn-out to enforce the ten hours day, the Association delegate meetings encouraged districts to promote the Lancashire Central Short-Time Committee's policy; and early in the next month, probably inspired by advances given to Blackburn operatives, 624 of 838 Bolton spinners struck for 10 per cent and the ten hours day. However there was little appetite for strikes amongst factory workers; the Bolton dispute quickly crumbled whilst at Manchester factory operatives were urged to accept the logic of the market. The Short-Time Committee, faced by a lack of district support, was forced to rescind its call for a general turn out. The Mawdsley group had lost ground to Oastler and the Fieldenites in 1846-7 and with the latter now demanding 'Ten Hours and No Surrender' they now compounded their error by association with the Ashley manoeuvres that effectively resulted in a 10½ hour compromise Bill. The abortive general strike call and the ideological divisions over the Ten Hours Act broke the influence of the Lancashire Central Short-Time Committee — although it continued to meet in the early 1850s and was later refounded — and, along with the failure of the 1847 and 1849 wages campaigns wrecked the Association. In the autumn of 1849 that body still had 3,000 members and, with Preston, Clitheroe, Bolton, Oldham and Mossley in membership, could claim to be a regional federation. Shortly afterwards Oldham withdrew and it was a disintegrating Association that co-ordinated support for the striking Heywood society in June 1850. In August 1850 the Bolton society, now led by a new secretary, David Holt, after failing in an attempt to re-establish its own pre-eminence, withdrew 'until such time as Manchester, Oldham and other large districts manifest a disposition to form a general union'.[16]

The disintegration of the Spinners' Association, coming after seven years of continuous activity and at a time of more solidly based union organisation amongst other industries, has never been adequately explained. Constitutional flaws, disenchantment in the face of impotence and defeat, possible differences over Chartism and the Ten Hours campaign — Bolton's departure came in the same month that saw the final break between the Fieldenite and Mawdsleyite short-time movements — may all have played their part. However these difficulties may have been a reflection of deeper structural problems. The wages campaign of the 1840s did little to abolish the pay differentials that, compounded by the regional specialization of the spinning trade, effectively made fine, medium and coarse spinners, and self-actor minders distinct trades and interests. Moreover from the mid-1840s until the demise of hand-mule spinning in the 1890s, mule spinners and self-actor minders allowed the inexorable advance of new technology to drive a wedge between them. The most serious divisions were those at Manchester and Ashton; without unity at the trade's largest centres the prospects for a permanent and effective trade-wide association were bleak. Behind these divisions the Webbs saw James Mawdsley's argument that 'in the old days the hand-mule spinners used to greatly despise and look down on the self-actor minders'. But economic sense rather than disdain is a more likely explanation, for the divisions seem to have been most acute in those communities where fine and coarse or medium and coarse trades were carried on; here the hand-mule spinners would have constituted a genuine labour aristocracy, highly skilled and well paid, with earnings enabling them to maintain a full range of benefit payments. In a joint society the low wages that were until the 1860s the lot of the self-actor minders would have made such benefits difficult. Nevertheless the majority of societies remained open to both mule spinners and self-actor minders and even the existence of separate spinner and minder societies in the same town did not preclude both from affiliating to the Association. It is possible that such joint organisation and co-operation was the principal means by which the low paid minders acquired the trade union tradition and values of the elite mule spinners. Yet in the mid-century, the gulf of skill and remuneration between spinners and minders was a further element inhibiting co-operation.[17]

Such divisions over policy and status are not unusual in trade union organisations. They can hardly have been much greater amongst the spinners than the engineers who at this time were establishing a new model of national organisation involving a strong central executive, a common rule book for local societies, and a high benefit and trade protection policy. Perhaps the chief explanation for the collapse of the Spinners' Association is to be found in the presence of alternative organisational forms that effectively limited the need for a trade-wide organisation. From the 1840s District societies were combining together to form provincial groupings. The Oldham Provincial Association established in 1843 was maintained after the Oldham District's withdrawal from the Association and was to remain apart from the Association until 1870. A similar provincial association was operating in the Ashton area from the 1850s and may have been the reason why that town's societies also resisted wider trade links. However the greatest threat to unity was posed by Bolton, the principal instigator of the 1840s Association. After its withdrawal from that body in 1850 the District society established a provincial association which in 1853 it extended to 'all those districts governed by the Bolton list'. Thus an industry-wide federation for the mutual support of other districts engaged in possibly dubious disputes may have appeared to be of less relevance. Whilst organisation for wage disputes had been the principal reason for the establishment of trade wide federations and the founding of district societies in the low paid coarse spinning districts, the well organised and fine mule spinners had traditionally looked to their trade clubs as much for friendly society benefits; in keeping with the experience in the late 1840s and 1850s of other high paid crafts they extended their range of benefits. Set apart from their irregularly organised and lower paid fellows in other districts, the spinner elite was increasingly prone to separatism. The Manchester Fine Spinners' abandonment of the Association in 1848 would suggest that this previously outward looking society had become more insular. H. A. Turner has suggested that prior organisation of the skilled workers in the cotton industry may have impeded the organisation of the lesser skilled; it is possible that in the existence of provincial associations and the more exclusive mule spinner district societies, a similar process, to the detriment of a more general organisation of all spinners, was at work.[18]

The history of the spinners from the Association's abandonment at the end of the 1840s to the great Preston strike and lockout of 1853 has left little record. There is a possibility that an Association rump connected with the Lancashire Central Short-Time Committee continued to meet. Certainly that latter organisation was still conducting business in the early 1850s and its secretary, Thomas Mawdsley, was to become secretary of the revived Spinners' Association in 1853. William Fair, secretary from 1844 to 1876 of the Manchester Fine Spinners, was later described as treasurer 'since about 1849' of the Spinners' Amalgamation. Traditionally spinners had supported their leaders in small businesses. Mawdsley was described as a provisions dealer in 1851 whilst Fair operated the spinners' principal meeting place, the Woodman's Hut Tavern in Manchester. This can be viewed as the interim step in the progress of the full time official. Whilst depriving the spinners of the professional bureaucrats who were to knit the later organisation together they did compensate by providing flexibility in response to changing conditions. Around Mawdsley and Fair may have gathered societies such as Mossley which later claimed early membership of the Association, Preston, and the Manchester, Dukinfield, Blackburn and Darwen groups that had rallied to Mawdsley's short-time committee in the disputes of 1850. Certainly, when the district societies again turned to trade federation and factory reform it was from the Mawdsley-Fair group that they accepted leadership.[19]

In the absence of a central body, provincial and district organisations became the centres for the formation of spinner policy. The 1840s had been characterised by a moderate policy towards wages, and as trade picked up in the early 1850s this approach was again tried. In north-east Lancashire at Blackburn where the Association had had much influence, employers and operatives sat down together in 1852-3 to jointly agree a new type of list, the standard list, which set a price for the standard job and calculated variations according to the quality of the product, manufacturing conditions, and machinery. Negotiated by both spinners and weavers it placed pressure on employers to observe the standard rate and on the union to bring up the lower payers and discipline their more aggressive members. In accepting that 'in future any disputes should be brought before the joint committee' it was the harbinger of a new attitute to industrial relations. Whilst joint negotiation had long been sought by the spinners, action in defence of justifiable demands was never ruled out; though spinner societies were not engaged in general disputes with their employers in the early 1850s, the Bolton society supported the A.S.E. in its 1852 dispute. In contrast the lower paying districts around Hyde that had provided the mass protest in the 1830s and 1840s saw the retreat of trade unionism.[20]

The recovery of the economy and the cotton trade from the slump of 1847-50 was a spur to a further wave of spinner trade unionism which had as its purpose the recovery of the 1847 reductions. It was anticipated by wage demands and organisation amongst many groups of workers outside textiles. In January 1853 the Bolton Provincial Association asked their employers for an advance of 10 per cent, 'in consequence of the continued prosperity of trade.' The local employers' association agreed to offer 5 per cent. Their compromise was identical to that of 1844 and suggests that employers, at least those in the fine spinning trade, were prepared to play the wages game in periods of buoyant trading. An air of reality similarly pervaded the union for the Bolton spinners agreed to accept the 5 per cent, considering that given the 'disorganised state of the spinners generally, it would be imprudent to offer any resistance to the masters' proposal'. It was not until March 1853 that a general wages campaign commenced. Employer reaction varied — at Blackburn spinners but not weavers were offered advances, whilst at Preston a re-formed employers' association prepared to blacklist spinner activists. From March the weavers stole the limelight and their leaders' tactic was to employ mass meetings and parades to rouse and mobilise the unorganised behind demands for wage advances which were then presented as ultimata to employers. In June, to better co-ordinate their campaign, spinners and weavers separately held delegate meetings at which resolutions demanding nothing short of 'an unconditional advance of ten per cent' were passed. Clearly of a different order from the responsible negotiating practices of the Bolton spinners earlier in the year, the campaign brought an inevitable reaction from employers who whilst initially prepared to advance the smaller number of spinners, were unwilling to advance or even negotiate with weavers. After Stockport's employers had crumbled and conceded 10 per cent in face of a two month strike, Preston employers locked out their entire workforce 'until those now on strike are prepared to resume their work, and a better understanding is established between the employer and the employed.' With the financial support of a trade-wide association, they starved or cajoled their weavers and spinners back after a thirty-eight week dispute. The operatives were finally broken by a disastrous renewal of the Stockport strike and a general downturn of trade which led to a collapse of support from other workers consequent on the withdrawal of advances they had obtained.[21]

The spinners' campaign was initially organised by loose, trade-wide delegate meetings of which the first was held at Bolton in June but the initial Stockport success and the enthusiasm generated at the commencement of the Preston dispute led to further developments. Abandoned societies were reconstituted, co-ordination between districts was improved and the spinners' Association was refounded. Its title, The Equitable and Friendly Association of Hand Mule Spinners, Self-Actor

Minders, Twiners and Rovers of Lancashire, Cheshire, Yorkshire and Derbyshire suggests a continuity with the previous federation. The Bolton committee — no doubt anxious to preserve its early advances by raising the lower districts — and its Provincial Association joined the body though the initiative probably came from the remnants of the defunct Association and the rump of the Lancashire Central Short-Time Committee associated with Thomas Mawdsley and William Fair who were respectively confirmed as secretary and treasurer of the revived body. A meeting held at Ashton-under-Lyne in January 1854 brought together delegates from most of the societies active in the earlier Association — although noticeably absent were representatives from Oldham. The Preston society's willingness during the strike to follow faithfully the instructions of the delegate meetings may be partly due to the earlier connection with Fair and Mawdsley: it had been an important member of the Association in the 1840s and moreover most of the Preston spinners' leaders in 1853 were former short-time agitators. The delegate meetings exerted considerable influence over the local societies during the strike — in August 1853 they agreed the terms that Preston men should demand; but their command was not total — in April 1854 Stockport spinners were eventually to ignore conference advice not to strike. Throughout the dispute Preston spinners and their piecers were supported by funds and levies from the working districts — at Bolton the names of non-payers were printed and circulated through the mill — and towards the strike's end the Association probably became the 'inexhaustible box' from which spinners threatened an indefinite strike. Though employer power, the gradual breaking of the weavers, and their own slow crumbling in face of need and knobsticks sent some back, the mass of spinners held out for two weeks longer than the weavers and only returned on the recommendation of a delegate meeting held in Manchester.[22]

As the lengthiest dispute involving spinners and weavers since Stockport in 1829, the Preston strike has attracted considerable attention. Generally viewed as 'little more than a wages dispute' it has recently been depicted as an example of employer unwillingness 'to recognise trade unions' and as evidence of a revival of 'general class conflict'. Inevitably the dispute polarised the textile communities as employers, factory operatives, and other workers each rallied to the support of their own. Preston employers justified the lockout that started the strike by objecting to their workers being directed by 'a designing and irresponsible body . . . having no connexion with the town' and subsequently refused to recognise the spinners' and weavers' committees. However many employers had previously negotiated and accepted terms with deputations from their own spinners who were clearly pursuing a common trade policy; and towards the end of the strike the employers secretly informed a publicly nominated Mediation Committee that 'the only matter now in dispute . . . is the amount of wages' and abandoned the demand for renunciation of the union. But whilst employers were prepared to live with or recognise local spinners' trade unions they were not willing to be stampeded into paying higher wages or to be dictated to by trade-wide worker combinations. The realisation probably lay behind the 1840s Spinners' Association's policy of consolidating district rates; indeed it was the spinners' delegates led by Bolton advocates of this policy and activists from the earlier Association who first broke rank in March 1854 urging their Preston colleagues to surrender the 10 per cent in exchange for a district or county average. Though the spinners' language waxed on 'the social war . . . being waged by capitalists' there was no intent to turn the dispute into a broader class conflict: in November 1853 the spinners' secretary, Thomas Mawdsley, in words that echoed Doherty's on the formation of the G.G.U., informed *Manchester Guardian* readers that spinners had no intention 'to interfere with their employers, either with regard to the management of their concerns, or as to whom they shall or shall not employ', and expressed a desire for binding arbitration; and when the Chartist Socialist, Ernest Jones, visited Preston, spinners were probably amongst those on the operatives' committee who 'objected to him taking a part in the proceedings, being resolved to keep the wages question apart from all others'. Though the Stockport and Preston campaigns of mid-summer 1853 perhaps indicate that a group committed to rolling strikes and wages equalisation was making the running at the spinners' meetings, the Bolton settlement of January 1853 and the volte-face of March 1854 suggests that the more moderate tone of the 1840s was also asserting itself.[23]

The Preston strike did much to re-establish the authority of the millowners that had been called into question by the victory of the Ten Hours Movement and the abject surrender of the Stockport masters in the summer of 1853. Whilst some employers would have agreed with Henry Ashworth's description of the Preston strike as a struggle of 'property against communism' and shared his detestation of trade unionism, the protracted and intense dispute may have led others to search for different relationships with their workforces. Some, particularly the larger, attempted to adapt to the town the paternalistic control over workers that was evident in rural factory communities. The mid-1850s saw employers investing in social and recreational facilities and spending money on treats and outings, thus to stress the mutuality that bound master and hands and cut across the ties that led workers into trade unions. Whilst there is evidence that such prudential investment may have had results, the extent to which trade union activity was inhibited should not be over-estimated. Employer attitudes to trade unions had traditionally been ambivalent and diverse, embracing a wish to see them eliminated by law, ignoring their presence as powerless, encouraging their friendly society activities, or making use of them either against competitors or as a means of controlling the more militant elements. The experiences of the mid-1840s and of the Blackburn list negotiations in 1852-3 clearly demonstrate that employer–trade union relations were possible at least during buoyant periods. The 1850s brought a spread, particularly among weavers, but extending to spinners, of the jointly negotiated district list of the Blackburn type. Not all of the employers were of this mentality but some seem to have been considering and evolving a relationship with trade unions which was more than the opportunism that characterised their joint discussions during times of stress and went beyond the individual employer and worker representative negotiations of the 1840s.[24]

For spinner trade unionism the mid-1850s represented a further period of consolidation. The delegate conferences had served their purpose and the Manchester-based Association, though not abandoned, stepped into the background. Its rule book has not survived except in the amended 1860 format. Objectives were little different from those of the 1840s, emphasising the importance of wage considerations and continuing interest in the Factory Acts, albeit now in their enforcement. The autonomy of Provincial and District societies was clearly recognised and the executive was controlled and appointed by regular delegate meetings. Again in keeping with the objectives of the more moderate attitudes of the 1840s Association, the rule book sought to control, through its potential to levy districts, the ability of societies to call town strikes. Some of the spinners' societies, particularly the fine, would have been at the local level, amongst the strongest trade clubs in the country and their lack of interest in or renewed failure to organise on a trade-wide basis again contrasts markedly with the Amalgamated Society of Engineers, which, after their disastrous 1852 lockout, went from strength to strength. More strikingly the spinners' failure contrasts with the efforts of the more lowly paid cotton power loom weavers to build up an inter-district organisation; though still maintaining the independence of the local societies they developed a professional bureaucracy to cater for the administrative complexities of the Blackburn list. Though the spinners had emerged from the Preston strike better organised than they had entered it, the subsequent tendency was to proceed along the previous seemingly sectionalist path. The Oldham and Ashton Provinces continued to conduct their business in isolation whilst Bolton and its affiliates left the Association in 1857. Ashton and Manchester Fine Spinners seem to have left the Association after the Preston dispute (though William Fair continued as the Association's treasurer). However the middle ranking societies, Preston, Rochdale, Hyde and Mossley and perhaps some of the smaller societies seem to have maintained their membership. By the 1850s these societies, principally in the lower medium or coarse spinning areas, would have been dominated by self-actor minders. Thus through the mid-1850s the Association would have continued as a forum for both spinners and minders with the balance of participation probably decisively shifting to the latter. However the trend of spinner trade unions was towards the Provincial and District societies; and business and disputes seem to have been conducted without consideration of broader trade interests.[25]

The 1850s also seem to have brought about a further consolidation of the manning system that appears to have underwritten the spinners' strength as trade unionists. The years of economic expansion in the mid-1840s and 1850s witnessed the further deployment of the self-actor. Despite an effort to work with a multiple machine system at Manchester in the early 1830s and again at Oldham in the early 1840s, the minder-piecer system was not generally challenged. However after the 1837 dispute Glasgow employers seem to have introduced a manning system similar to that envisaged by the machine's promoters — women under the supervision of an overlooker working a number of mules. A small number of mule spinning firms had employed women, some of whom were active trade unionists, but by the time of

Doherty's G.G.U., male hostility to their existence and union membership had become explicit. However the introduction of the self-actor may have encouraged a number of Lancashire firms, particularly away from the principal centres, to make use of women. It may be that further research will indicate a more complex array of manning patterns than the later dominance of a minder to a pair of mules suggests. At Ashton in 1849 seven of the fourteen minders at Cheetham's Mill were dismissed and the remainder instructed to work two pairs of mules instead of one; and some mills were reputedly working three pairs to a minder. At Manchester in the winter of 1855-6, a major wages dispute between employers and self-actor minders and their piecers, came to turn in part on a conflict over manning levels. Apparently some firms engaged minders on a single mule basis. Yet, despite their evident strength, employers did not move to introduce women or a multiple machine system; rather they looked to standardisation with the regularly manned self-actors in Stockport and Oldham mills. At Bolton in 1857 in different circumstances the hand mule spinners' society put its resources into a single mill dispute where an employer was operating the apprentice system which the spinners regarded as a threat to practices throughout the town. This 'abominable system' entailed a promoted piecer operating a pair of mules at a lower wage rate than a full spinner. The same practice was brought to an end at Chorley in 1857. In February 1859 the Bolton committee passed 'a vote of thanks to [the] masters for giving up the Apprentice System'. At Bolton the mule spinners demonstrated the ability of union strength to influence manning levels that was to be a prime characteristic of self-actor minders in the late nineteenth century; however for the 1850s as for the 1830s, it is clear that the self-actor manning system reflected not union strength but an employer perception that traditional control and practice was also in their best interests.[26]

With technology no longer posing a threat to machine manning, legislative control of the factory day and increased employment opportunities due to the expansion of trade, spinners were free to concentrate on wage issues. The leaders who directed spinner trade unionism in the high Victorian period had experienced the successful Ten Hours Movement, the 1840s wages campaigns and the Preston strike; and whilst prepared to fight they were also aware of the need for compromise. But the extent to which the seemingly conciliatory moves on the part of employers were reciprocated by spinners is difficult to assess. Negotiated lists on the Blackburn model held out a genuine opportunity for trade unionists; whilst tending to confirm the status quo, and subject to sharp amendment, particularly during downturns of trade, they also enabled workers to justifiably strike against firms paying below the rate. The memorial of Preston spinners to their employers in 1856 stating that 'our interest is closely allied with yours' and that it would be both 'suicidal and dishonest in us to ask for any concession not warranted by the state of trade' might be dismissed as special pleading in support of a wages claim but it does indicate an appreciation of the determining role of market forces. The revised Association constitution of 1860, drawing on practice in the 1850s and recognising that 'it is the scarcity or redundancy of labour in the market which regulates the rate of wages', a view which had long underwritten the spinners' earlier commitment to a shorter day, emigration and land schemes, also displayed an awareness of the vital importance of trading conditions. Rule XVI stipulated:

> That the real state of trade may at all times be known, it shall be the imperative duty of each and every district or local committee, as also the General Secretary, to purchase such publications, periodicals or newspapers, as shall be found to convey the soundest and most reliable information on that subject; and they shall come to be entered weekly, the current prices of cotton, with a memorandum of the state of the market, with a view of enabling the Association to determine the time to ask for an advance of wages, or to resist reductions; every fact of special importance to the trade to be communicated by the local secretaries to the General Secretary, to enable him to decide on the proper time to call a meeting.[27]

It would seem that the 1850s were witnessing the emergence of a market rather than conflict orientated approach to wages. This tendency may have been encouraged by the upward trend of wages from the mid-1850s. Though the Preston and Stockport disputes prevented a general advance, wages, bearing in mind regional and local divergences, recovered from the low of the late 1840s. It would also appear that the mass of still low paid self-actor minders may have been experiencing the beginning of the higher wage trend that eventually was to gain for them an aristocratic position within the industry. Admittedly the wages were underwritten by the greater intensity of work that higher spindle speeds made possible but for all groups there was the knowledge that earnings were based upon a statutorily limited 10½ hours day.[28]

The weakness of the spinners' central Association and the inherent localism of District and Provincial organisations meant that they were ill-placed to take advantage of the 'unprecedented prosperity' at the end of the 1850s. A general wages movement affecting all classes of workers spread across the cotton districts. The initiative was seized by weavers whose first Amalgamation attempted to push up pay in north-east Lancashire but, as in the 1840s and early 1850s, employers were unwilling to accede to general wage advances by this the most numerous factory class. In contrast employers strove to seize the initiative from spinners, being prepared to concede advances to this less numerous but more strategic group. In September 1859 the Ashton minders asked for a 10 per cent advance and declared strikes to be 'the scourge of civilization'. However in the following March they rejected a 5 per cent advance and threatened a strike within ten days unless employers agreed to 'the standard list of the Associated Minders of Lancashire'; subsequently a new list was introduced in the town and then extended to Dukinfield, Stalybridge and Mossley. At Preston in 1859 self-actor minders asking for an advance received their first town list. In August 1859 Bolton spinners applied for a 7.5 per cent increase and the masters responded by abolishing the traditional gas and bobbin charges; in March 1860 they obtained a 5 per cent advance. Oldham was without a town list until 1872, wages apparently being agreed on a mill basis, but the fact that the district seems to have been free from disputes was probably due to employers having to pay a reasonable rate in order to attract and keep the spinners that the town's expanding industry required. Thus in the principal spinning areas, employers granting advances and the principle of the town or district list generally anticipated spinners' demands. The improvement, particularly when set against the high rates of the mid-1840s, should not be exaggerated; in 1860 fine hand-mule spinners were earning 38s. 0d. per week, the medium-fine Bolton spinners 35s. 6d. per week, Oldham spinners (most of whom would have been minders) 27s. 10d. per week, and Manchester coarse self-actor minders as little as 18s. 0d. Employers were not everywhere ready to grant concessions; at Clitheroe the Association was called upon to support its members in a dispute with the secretary of the local employers' Association. However the central body's militancy should not be over-emphasised; Preston, Hyde and Mossley were amongst its principal supporters and they clearly acquiesced in the employer-led policy.[29]

This movement on the wages front may also have stimulated a fresh interest in wider associations. The moribund Lancashire Central Short-Time Committee was revived in 1858 as the central operative body to campaign for an extension of the Factory Acts to bleaching works. The campaign lasted three years, was largely financed by spinners, and Mawdsley, Grant and Thomas Banks were its delegates. Thus as in the 1840s this body served to link spinning communities. The wages movement also encouraged the refoundation of a number of district organisations and renewed interest in the Association amongst societies anxious to consolidate their own advances by working in an organisation which held out the possibility of bringing up rogue firms and low-paying districts. It is not clear what the 'standard list of the associated minders of Lancashire' aspired to by the Ashton minders was (perhaps the Blackburn List) but it suggests that the Association's influence was again extending. It would seem that some 4000 spinners and minders were in membership at this time. Apart from its influence in north-east Cheshire, parts of south-east Lancashire and the Preston area, the 1859 Clitheroe dispute suggests that it was also entrenched in the north-eastern cotton districts around Blackburn. Yet the rapidly growing Oldham district still stood aside from the Association and may have been attempting to establish a rival body. However the Mawdsley-Fair Association was unique in that it still aspired to be an organisation for both spinners and minders. The Bolton society, led by David Holt, re-affiliated and the rules were again revised. Whatever may have been the officers' views — Mawdsley and Fair continued in office and Hyde's William Leigh was chairman — the central executive was abandoned and the autonomy of provincial organisations recognised. Bolton certainly would have been anxious to avoid disputes and the constitution specified that districts in dispute with employers must first request arbitration and, even if this was refused, only the central body, through its delegate meetings, could sanction a district strike and a levy; as in the 1840s this also meant that delegates could over-rule the 'wisdom' of officers and engage in dubious actions. Given the Association's policy in the 1840s and the 1850s, reinforced as it was by the 1847

Ashton and 1853-4 Preston and Stockport defeats, it would seem that the Association was envisaged as a supporter and consolidator of district activity rather than as a vehicle for general action.[30]

As in earlier mid-century periods of prosperity, moderation seems to have been a predominant characteristic amongst spinners in the second half of the 1850s and may have facilitated a reaching out to employers; as sustained expansion gave way to over-production in the face of saturated markets, spinners' strength and conciliatory attitudes were to be questioned. Employers across the cotton districts began to make wage reductions for all workers early in 1861 but the spinners' response was to be locally rather than centrally directed. At Blackburn employers refused weaver demands for short time rather than wage cuts and locked out 16,000; whether spinners became involved is not known. Ashton spinners accepted a 5 per cent reduction on the grounds that it was necessitated by the state of trade and disassociated themselves from striking weavers; but by March and April they too had become engaged in a dispute which stretched through most of the north-east Cheshire cotton towns. At Bolton the spinners' leaders urged members to accept the 5 per cent reduction but the rank and file were otherwise inclined and struck, remained out for 12 weeks, and only returned when the funds of their society, probably the spinners' wealthiest, were almost entirely depleted. The resignation of their secretary, David Holt, was accepted following his assertion that strikes were subversive to the rights of labour, gave rise to 'unnecessary class hatred' and left the spinners 'helpless at our masters' feet'. Yet he was subsequently reinstated in his post. The small number of Bolton self-actor minders continued on strike for a further three weeks; they then returned to work but after a dispute with the mule spinners concerning the respective rights of self-actor minder piecers or unemployed mule spinners to work additional self-actors they left to form their own Bolton society under the secretaryship of Eli Fielding. The Bolton society had spent a considerable sum sustaining the strikes but they received little support from the Association, though encouraged by it to embark on the dispute; left to fight alone the Bolton mule spinners again withdrew from the central Association. Though some of their provincial associates stood with them, they were in fact beginning thirteen years of isolation from the rest of the trade which was founded on a policy of increasing collaboration with employers. The dangers of localism and lack of interest in wider association that had under-written the industrial relations advances of the 1850s became evident as spinners found themselves involved in disputes in different parts of the cotton districts. Despite the framework of local and provincial bodies, the central Association and the experience of their leaders, the spinners were adrift.[31]

In the summer of 1861 spinners and minders fell into a number of distinct groups: the mass of self-actor minders, many of whom through their districts were associated with the Mawdsley-Fair organisation; the coarse spinners and minders of the Oldham province; the separately organised mule spinners at Manchester and Ashton; the mule spinners of the Bolton Province; and the unorganised. By 1862 the market problems were being compounded by the American Civil War and the blockade of the southern cotton exporting ports. The fine spinning centres like Bolton, with a greater stake in the home market and able to extend the use of Egyptian cotton, were least affected; the districts such as Blackburn, Oldham, parts of Ashton and north-east Cheshire producing the lower count yarns and cloth for export and most dependent on American cotton, the worst. Though businessmen sought to adapt — as at Oldham where the self-actor was modified to take Surat cotton — no area was unaffected. By December 1862 half of Hyde's operatives were working short time, the other half not at all; even at Bolton little over half continued in full time work. Spinners who had withstood the rigours of strike, short time and trade depression were flung out of work and sustained either by Poor Relief given in exchange for 'oakum picking and the stoneyard' or charity. The stoic endurance of the operatives emphasised by some commentators was not everywhere true; at Ashton, Stalybridge and Preston rioting broke out, only ended in the latter by three companies of infantry bearing fixed bayonets and after a plea from the secretary of the spinners' union. In such circumstances spinners' unions were rendered all but useless; strikes would have had no meaning whilst benefit funds were called on to meet a demand greater than ever intended. At local level little union business was conducted and advertisements were placed in the Bolton press asking for old newspapers and periodicals for distribution to out-of-work members. Some societies ceased to operate whilst others existed in name only. Mossley suspended its activities and its membership, continuous since 1845, of the Association.[32]

Weakened as it must have been, that body continued to operate; moreover it firmly established itself as the only effective voice for cotton spinners. In August 1862 Mawdsley and the leaders of the Hyde, Stockport and Preston district societies formed a deputation that visited government ministers, M.P.s and distributors of relief; their purpose was to press for 'some discrimination . . . as to the sort of work given to spinners who objected to being classed with paupers'. In 1863 the Association was strengthened by the affiliation of the Bolton self-actor minders' society. However in 1864 only 13 districts are known to have been affiliated; even so these were from across the north-west and included the not insignificant Preston, Blackburn and Hyde societies. Moreover all would have been dominated by self-actor minders. By the time of its September meeting the Association had adopted a policy of despair; though unable to organise a central plan it called on each district to carry out:

> More extensively than ever its own system of emigration, experience having proved that it is only by emigration that the position of the working classes can be improved. It is, moreover, equally certain that any individual member of the Association who neglects to promote to the utmost of his power the emigration movement at this important crisis, neglects a duty which he owes to himself, whilst inflicting a serious injury upon his fellow workmen.[33]

The Association did not lose sight of its industrial role; members were urged to support Chorley spinners, all of whom had been thrown out of work by a cardroom dispute and requested: 'Constantly bear in mind, so that when trade shall have once more assumed its normal character, they may be prepared to vindicate an

equitable price for spinning on coupled mules and compensation of extra turns.'
Mawdsley and his colleagues were safely conducting the central body through the
greatest crisis in the industry's history.

   The spinners' history between the hand-mule spinner defeats of the 1830s and the
weakness and collapse of the spinner and minder unions during the early 1860s was
complex. Sandwiched between the dramatic confrontations that highlighted the
mule spinner era and the moderation and closed shop discipline of the later Victorian
self-actor minders' Amalgamation, the middle decades of the century have been
seen as a period of little advance. Yet despite the vulnerability of spinners in the face
of economic uncertainty and the threat that technological change posed to their
occupational status, this was a period of progress for cotton spinner trade unionism.
Though some societies were still prone to collapse in adverse periods, the continuity
of the leading district societies was either maintained or established. The trade-wide
Association established in 1842, though reflecting the trade induced surges and collapse of support that characterised the early nineteenth century efforts at federation,
achieved a size and continuity (the possible abandonment of 1850-3 apart) surpassing
that of its more widely written about predecessors. Thomas Mawdsley and his associates lacked the charisma and the self-advertisement that enabled Doherty to tower
over his contemporaries. The decline of the Manchester industry also meant that
they lacked the platform that had enabled the early Manchester society to impose its
policy on other districts. But whilst they generally steered clear of the set piece battles
that engaged the earlier generation, their achievements may have been the more
substantial. Their contribution to the popular campaign that supported the parliamentary advocates of the Ten Hour Bill was fundamental; besides giving the spinners
a real, albeit vicarious, control over the length of the working day, it protected the
groups most susceptible to millowner exploitation and, according to spinner leaders,
did something to redress the balance of the labour market in their favour. Through
the Association and many of the district societies, spinners promoted, with varying
degrees of success, the district wages consolidated policy that was to be the hallmark
of the later nineteenth century organisation; the 1850s in particular saw widespread
moves towards genuine negotiations with employers and the promotion by the spinners of the principle of arbitration. The 1847 calls for a general stoppage apart, it
would seem that spinner trade unionism in the years after the 1842 Plug Plot was
based on a more realistic appraisal of operative strength. However the volatility and
trend of wages during the mid-century (the mid-1840s gains that followed the 1837-42
slump were largely lost at the 1847 slump and only slowly clawed back in the 1850s)
indicate the continued dominance of market forces. The success of the little known
group that maintained the Association in the face of employer hostility and district
indifference was even more important; they provided the forum for the more highly
paid fine spinners and the increasing number of lowly paid self-actor minders to
meet and were thus the means by which the craft aspirations and moderation of the
mule spinner aristocracy was passed on to self-actor minders with little claim to any
of these attributes. Yet in the Spinners' Association and the provincial and district
societies the potential for a future spinner advance was evident.

CHAPTER FOUR

The Founding of the Amalgamation

Between the Cotton Famine and the mid-1880s the Spinners' union faced a number of new challenges as the industry underwent major changes to its structure, ownership and trading environment. Production continued to expand, increasing consumption of raw cotton by 50 per cent and yarn exports from 175 to 275 million lbs during these years, but at a reduced level of profitability. Apart from a brief respite in the early 1870s, the state of trade was either suffering intermittent dislocation or full-blown crisis resulting from overproduction and collapsing prices. From 1873 to 1880, the value of those increased exports of yarn fell by 30 per cent, bringing losses not offset by the growing sales to home producers of cloth. Despite this, expansion continued, and the total United Kingdom cotton labour force, made up of two-thirds women, rose by 50,000 to 500,000. The number of cotton spindles rose from 34 million to 44 million between 1867 and 1885, Lancashire in the latter year boasting 41 million as its share. More importantly, the growth of Limited Liability Companies at Oldham accelerated the move away from Manchester and North Lancashire, where the Spinners' recent power base had lain. The new spinning mills were bigger, over the period almost doubling the average number of spindles of 18,000 that each contained in 1870 and employing 50 per cent more labour per mill. Specialisation intensified, leading to the further demise of the combined spinning and weaving firms, leaving only a third of capacity in their hands by 1885. Productivity rose by 30 per cent and as competition increased some old as well as new firms attempted to run overtime, introduce inferior raw materials and quicken the speed of machinery. Average mule size rose by 20 per cent from around 800 spindles in 1870, and with the increased efficiency of the self-actor mule, the further decline of the remaining hand-mule spinners was assured.[1]

For the first time also came a new threat, a possible rival to replace the self-actor mule itself. The throstle frame, an improved Arkwright water frame, had continued to be used in Britain to produce stronger yarns on a small, but not insignificant scale operated by female labour. Shortage of mule spinners in the U.S.A., however, had led to the throstle's development into the ring frame, particularly effective for lower counts and again employing female labour. Little interest in the new technology had been shown by the Lancashire cotton masters prior to the late 1870s, but as further improvements were made from the early 1880s the introduction of ring spinning in a very limited way began. The belief in the self-actor mule's superiority meant initially that any threat to jobs was minimal, although rings were used effectively in the process of doubling, the twisting of two or more threads together, to produce a stronger, more even yarn. All this was taking place as the employers were organising themselves in their own associations and whilst not to the same county-wide extent as the Spinners, increasing co-operation between towns and districts was evident.[2]

As yet the Spinners' Association was not in a position to meet the challenge presented by the coming of industrial change. The 4,000 members out of a possible 20,000 spinners represented only one half of those organised with two of the main Districts, Oldham and Bolton, outside its ranks. Headquarters was an office at 55 Store Street, Ancoats, Manchester, a building too small to use for Delegate Meetings, which had to convene in nearby public houses. Subscriptions of a farthing per week, compared with District Association rates averaging sixpence and even separate shop club dues of a penny a week or more, reflected to some extent the relatively low importance given to the Association. As a collection of District Associations, some with hundreds of members while others had less than twenty enrolled, there was little in the way of organisational uniformity. Local subscriptions, benefits, levels of unionisation, wages and to a lesser extent work practices, differed widely. Two or three Districts had offices and full-time secretaries, but most maintained their organisation with lay officials and a box kept in a public house, in some cases owned by ex-spinners who acted as the treasurer. Oldham, the largest organisation outside the Association, with nearly 2,000 members, was said to have kept their records in the Chairman's hat, and most were lost when a gust of wind blew the hat over a fence! The shop remained the bastion against possible encroachment on working practices, but here also meetings were used to dissipate the funds on drink. Employer acquiescence in the absence of major technological changes, more than the Spinners' own strength, appeared to be sustaining standards. A stronger central Association, better organisation and uniformity between District Associations were needed in the coming period. The late 1870s saw many of the lesser skilled unions in other industries disappear in trying to defend wages and associations of craft workers becoming cautious, conservative and increasingly unwilling to take industrial action. If the Spinners were not to follow the same path, but defend wages and oppose changes in work practices, central finances had to be reorganised and divisions reconciled. Given fiercely protected District independence, such a programme of reorganisation would entail many setbacks and considerable time before a real commitment was manifest, more pressing were the immediate problems of the post-Cotton Famine years.[3]

The recovery of trade following the Cotton Famine was for a number of years neither smooth nor complete, the dislocation during the war period being carried over into peacetime. Between 1864 and 1866 the industry suffered three waves of bankruptcies which provided an uncertain stage for the re-emergence of the Spinners' unions. Not all sections of the industry had suffered or were about to suffer the same degree of crisis and, in consequence, not all District Associations were faced with the same problems. Some had gone out of existence altogether, others losing active members through schemes for emigration fostered by unions.

All, however, had seen some diminution of membership and the need for reorgani-sation was paramount before effective action could take place. Particularly important was on whose terms, masters' or men's, the restoration of pre-famine practices and procedures would be achieved. The unwritten informal agreements that regulated the relationship between union and employer had been allowed to lapse and both sides determined that any new found consensus should reflect cherished concessions from previous struggles. Understandably, therefore, the first two years after the Cotton Famine saw a spate of small disputes focusing on the restoration of the 1861 and wartime wage reductions, and around which local associations re-emerged. Oldham was one of the first to reorganise in 1864, their local industry making some success of spinning Surat. Bolton Fine Spinners' Association, in a district the least affected by the Cotton Famine due to its use of Egyptian cotton, revised their rules in 1865. The Central Association also, despite the absence of these two associations, revived with the re-affiliation of Stockport (1864), Warrington (1865) and Burnley (1866). Likewise new wage lists were adopted, and, more importantly, the restoration of employers' associations to negotiate and implement them.[4]

Having less need for a formal structure, constitution and organisation than the operatives, the masters easily responded to the upsurge in union activity by recon-stituting their associations. Whilst Bolton Masters were formed in 1861, most of the permanent employers' associations date their formation from 1866 and afterwards. In that year a general wage movement covering all trades swept Lancashire and as in 1853 and 1860, when similar movements occurred, cotton workers in each town began their agitation. During March, Blackburn Spinners won the 5 per cent taken off in 1861. In April, Preston Spinners gained 7.5 per cent and a new standard list, while others struck for 10 per cent or comparability with surrounding districts. In the north of the county the employers of Preston, Blackburn and Burnley responded by forming the North-East Lancashire Cotton Spinners' and Manufacturers' Association (C.S.M.A.) and in the south new district associations of employers were formed in Stockport, Hyde, Bury and Oldham. Unfortunately the good trade of 1866 was short-lived, and before the year was out trade had turned and a series of reductions began to be imposed and short-time implemented. By the end of 1867 Ashton Spinners had suffered their third reduction of 5 per cent, strikes having taken place in Bolton, and, with the Central Association's support, Stockport. This latter dispute at Stockport lasted some sixteen weeks and resulted in a local wage list which left the Spinners worse off than before. The local association paid out £3,235 during the strike and £494 in victim pay. The Central Association's share of these amounts, £2,969 and £289 respectively, may have helped quicken the leaders' search for a plan of reorganisation and a more financially secure constitutional form. Certainly there was some doubt of the union continuing as it was, and in one opinion, expressed years later, 'The General Association was on the point of being broken up several times and never seemed to have gained a solid footing until the commencement of 1868'.[5]

The new rules of 1868 began the process of restoring to the Central Association the powers and functions lost in the 1850s and early 1860s. The Executive was expanded from three officers, to include five others elected from Quarterly Delegate Meetings, payment for attendance at such meetings being revived. Benefits which had been restricted to strike, and in certain cases victim pay for those dismissed for union action, were extended to include accident benefit. Under the title of The Equitable and Friendly Association of Operative Cotton Spinners and Self-Actor Minders of Lancashire and Adjoining Counties, the tramping system whereby members were encouraged to travel to other towns looking for work with vouchers cashable at the visited District Association, was recognised. On the other hand to prevent criticism of financial imprudence, the old rules concerning extra levies for strikes were altered so as to limit the power of the delegates to impose fresh calls without the support of those Districts forced to pay. In regard to the rest of the rules few changes were made. The contributions to the Association continued at ¼d. per week, the central authority remained the Delegate Meeting and strikers still would not receive financial support until the employer had rejected binding arbitration. With an eye on the *Royal Commission on Trade Unions and Employers Association Organisations and Rules*, then sitting, Thomas Mawdsley took the opportunity in his preamble to vouchsafe the Spinners' law-abiding character by declaring, 'this Association sanctions no proceedings opposed to the laws of the country, whether economic, social or moral'.[6]

Under the new rules the Central Association prospered, District affiliations rising to 36 during the first year and membership increasing to 8,000, double the 1866 figure. Of the major District Associations only the Bolton Hand-Mule Spinners and Oldham remained outside the Association. However, before the new rules could prove their worth, trade took a turn for the worse. Margins, the difference between the buying and selling price of raw cotton and spun yarn, dropped in 1869 to the lowest since the height of the Cotton Famine, and a savage round of wage cutting followed. Blackburn had 5 per cent taken off in March, whilst Preston a month later faced cuts of between 10 and 15 per cent. After a bitter struggle lasting several months and costing £8,000 the Spinners' resistance collapsed and masters in other Districts, waiting on the results of this conflict, imposed varying levels of wage reductions of their own. The Central Association's failure was obvious to member Districts as well as Oldham and Bolton outside its ranks. One reaction was to disaffiliate, and Rochdale did so, complaining of intolerably high levies in aid of the striking Districts just when local funds were at their lowest. Some small Districts went out of existence, but others met the challenge by formulating policies for the reorganisation of the Central Association with a special emphasis on the establishment of a reserve fund.[7]

The concern to create a new and more secure organisation was expressed in the circular issued in November 1869. Perhaps exaggerating the extent of some of the divisions among the local associations, the circular called for a conference of all Districts irrespective of previous affiliations with a view to reorganisation. Signed by William Leigh (Chairman), and Thomas Mawdsley (Secretary), the circular stated:

Fellow Workmen,

The unsatisfactory state of the cotton trade during the last eight years and the sacrifices we have had to make in defending our position are facts well known to all of you.

Though our effort to defend the fruits of our toil have not been wholly useless, it may be affirmed that had we, as we might have at a cheap and easy rate, accumulated funds both central and local, the most powerful capitalists would hesitate before attempting any encroachment.

The power of union must be obvious to all, yet we as a body of workmen are more split up into sections, more divided in our actions and counsels, than were our predecessors in the same trade twenty-five years ago. Not only are the districts too frequently isolated from each other and different organisations of the same branch of operatives to be found in the same district, but separate organisations are recognised by men working in the same mill. With a view to remedying this state of things the Committee are desirous of conferring with representatives from all districts for the purpose of considering such measures as may be judged necessary.[8]

The conference in January 1870 adopted a new set of rules under the title of 'The Amalgamated Association of Operative Cotton Spinners, Self-Actor Minders, Twiners, and Rovers of Lancashire and Adjoining Counties'. Thomas Mawdsley's plan had been to, firstly, discuss the question of whether it was desirable and practicable to form one grand Federated Association of every organised body of cotton spinners in Lancashire, Yorkshire, Derbyshire and Cheshire, and then to decide if general and local objects, rules, contributions and benefits ought to be identical. In practice the results of the conference were more modest. The inclusion of the term Amalgamated in the title, whilst the first use of the word by the Spinners, signified no major change in the constitution. The new body remained as the old, a federation of fairly autonomous District Associations, with their own rules, subscriptions and benefits in addition to those provided by the Amalgamation. Similarly the naming of rovers and twiners in the title signalled no extension of the Union's occupational boundaries. Rovers, those operatives who prepared the product of the cardroom for finer spinning by giving it extra twist, were already in membership, as were twiners and doublers. Twining, mostly located around Oldham, was a method of doubling, twisting two or more threads together, carried out on mules instead of special frames and may have been included in the title to recognise its importance in Oldham where operatives using the technology were later to form a separate branch. Both occupations, roving and twining, were however faced with technical improvements that threatened employment opportunities and perhaps their inclusion in the title as separate groups was meant to boost morale. The constitution of this revitalized body expanded the executive from five to seven and doubled subscriptions from ¼d. to a ½d. per week, but more importantly it created a reserve fund of 1d. per week to be kept partially at local level with the aim of building up a fund to withstand a major strike without having to impose levies on the membership.

This latter provision, while not establishing a sufficient reserve on which any future success eventually depended, was the reason why at least one District, Rochdale, which had refused to attend the conference, rejoined the Amalgamation in December. Rules for arbitration were extended to include the option of a Board of Conciliation, and the Delegate Meeting was now to be known as a Representative Meeting, but essentially the rest of the rules remained the same.[9]

The significance of the 1870 changes therefore was not so much due to the constitution adopted, but rather in the addition of Oldham to its ranks. That the Amalgamation was courting both Bolton and Oldham was obvious, not least in holding the conference in Bolton where the Secretary of the local Hand Spinners, David Holt, had been the Amalgamation's strongest critic. Oldham, on the other hand, had already begun to realise the need to belong to the larger organisation. Having failed to convince their employers in 1869 to forgo a wage reduction of 10 per cent and instead work short-time, they had allowed the dispute to go to arbitration where the difference had been split. The 5 per cent reduction was bitterly resented in the town, strikes occurring, particularly at firms outside the Masters' Association, before the cut was accepted. This Provincial Association covering Oldham, Chadderton, Hollinwood, Lees, Middleton, Royton, Shaw and Waterhead, had 2,226 members in 1868 and had only recently revised its own rules following the election of Thomas Ashton as its Secretary in that year. Unfortunately, the ending of Oldham's twenty years isolation was not matched by Bolton. It was not until 1874, after thirteen years outside the main body, that the Bolton Hand Spinners submerged their interests within the larger Association, a year later Holt retired. The accession of Oldham with its nine branches, however, was enough to give the enlarged Amalgamation a new financial stability and authority not seen since the 1840s.[10]

Between 1870 and 1873 the patchy recovery of the industry following the Cotton Famine came to an end, these were years of prosperity and growth. The Franco-Prussian War had stimulated demand from the maturing economies of Europe and the USA and unions in all British industries were given an impetus to organise. Unskilled farm labourers, railwaymen, dockers and seamen, as well as skilled workers, formed new associations, winning advances. Home demand for cotton products was therefore buoyant, ushering in a period of full employment and speculative mill building. This was the period of the Oldham Limiteds, when company after company was floated with the encouragement of the machine-makers, who were eventually to equip the mills. Limited companies had been seen before, but not on this grand scale. In the eighteen months prior to March 1873, fourteen new mills had commenced running and a similar number were under construction. These bigger factories containing larger, technically improved mules, the Oldham Limiteds brought a new level of competition to the industry, a new system of ownership and the creation of a managerial class. For J. B. Tattersall, a member of the Spinners' Executive and for a time its Auditor, this meant the opportunity for personal advancement as a director of a number of companies. For the spinners continuing to work in the mill it meant both increased job opportunities and the increased work load of minding larger mules at faster speeds. For the small private master, especially those who rented 'room and power' in buildings owned by the class of rentier mill landlords, it meant the driving of their own workforce to compete with the Limiteds' efficiency and economies of scale. Sooner or later major adjustments would have to be made to accommodate the growth of the Limiteds, but while the boom lasted many of the consequences of the speculation were hidden.[11]

For a period therefore the Spinners' Amalgamation was in a favourable situation to pursue an improvement in their members' position. With the demand for labour being not only high but fairly consistent for a period of three years, the opportunities for advances and equalising wages between districts existed. The idea of a Universal List whereby all operatives producing similar counts would be paid the same, not just a standard for each town, was however on the decline. Comparisons between towns were still made the basis of wage claims, but only by the badly paid districts such as Hyde, Stockport and Burnley. Thomas Ashton spelt out the policy in high paying Oldham during the 1873 wages campaign there. In his view, what other districts were paying was no business of Oldham's, 20 shillings in one town was worth 22 shillings in another. The interpretation of the objective of a 'fair reward for their labour', contained in the Amalgamation's rules, had come to mean simply that each district was to get the best they could. This is not to suggest that the Amalgamation had abandoned all concern for the inequality between districts, but rather the concern was expressed in a different form. At the same time in 1873 the Amalgamation extended and codified the piecemeal rule changes that had taken place since the last major revision in 1870. Allowances were given for spinners who lost their jobs and were forced to return to piecing, and emigration benefit was made available for victims and those on strike. Accident payments were extended and the reserve fund was brought further under central control. The 1872 rule change recorded by the Webbs debarring women from membership, however, was not included in the new codification. Perhaps it was thought the restriction was sufficiently incorporated in local Association practice not to be needed in the Amalgamation's own body of rules. Local Associations also extended their range of benefits and besides the 'topping up' of Amalgamation allowances and the universal funeral grant, some paid out-of-work, breakdown, emigration, sick, leaving trade and even superannuation benefit.[12]

Taking advantage of the prosperous trade and their new organisation, the Spinners' Amalgamation initiated an attempt to raise wages. Thomas Banks, the veteran Preston leader, in a circular to his members explained the policy, suggesting that the town was to be once again the 'centre of struggle'. The thirty-seven Districts of the Amalgamation, he told them, had decided to wrest back from the employers the losses of 1869, beginning at those firms which had made the greatest reductions. Launched officially in May 1870, the campaign was fairly successful in gaining a 5 per cent advance, but not without a war of attrition in many of the smaller Districts. Indeed some of the larger towns had already embarked on a second wage claim before others had won the first. When therefore a further general campaign to raise wages in 1873 met with greater resistance, the movement was allowed to drop.

Instead the Amalgamation's policy increasingly switched to giving power to spinners at individual mills to take action on their own behalf to improve wages, involving at times the rejection of existing procedures and the idea of standard wage lists. In north-east Lancashire, where such a policy was already underway, this led to the moribund C.S.M.A. being reformed when it became evident 'that the local Masters' Association would be unable to cope with the solid array of the combined spinners' associations, or to resist demands ruinous in tendency to the prosperity of the cotton trade'. Faced with such determined opposition on wages, the Amalgamation turned its attention to improving working conditions, the abolition of overtime, the banning of joining, claims for increased cleaning time, and, most importantly, the reduction of hours.[13]

Just when the campaign to reduce hours began is not certain. Hugh Mason, the Ashton employer, claimed to have initiated the campaign in 1870 by granting a twelve o'clock finish on Saturday instead of the usual 2.00 p.m., but there is evidence of a movement already in existence prior to this, not least the 1867 campaign for the eight hour day. Mason's action, however, did play a part in spurring the various operatives' associations into further action, more especially in the immediate vicinity of Ashton, where the noon finish became general. Perhaps as important was the active campaign in other industries, notably engineering. Whatever the impetus the hours reduction drive, known originally as the Saturday Half-Day Holiday Movement, the eventual outcome was the regeneration of the old Factory Acts Reform Association (F.A.R.A.) in 1872. Indeed, it may be argued that this new movement was nothing more than the revamping of the old factory movement of the 1840s. Certainly a level of continuity is demonstrated by the same account book being used for this movement as that of the 1850s campaign. Amongst the leaders in 1870 were William Fair and Phillip Grant, who were active in the earlier campaign, whilst Thomas Mawdsley, who had been a member of the 1847 Short-Time Central Committee, was now the F.A.R.A.'s General Secretary. As in the 1840s, the new movement was 'Spinners' Union led', contributing leadership, organisation, the bulk of funds, and over half the affiliating organisations.[14]

In policy too there were echoes of the earlier Ten Hours Movement and while there was a suggestion that this time the fight would not be carried on 'behind the women's petticoats', part of the claim was made 'on the grounds of education, recreation, morality and health, more especially for women and children'. Public sympathy was more easily evoked for female and child labour and the leaders used this argument knowing that any restrictions on those operatives' hours would mean employers conceding similar arrangements for adult males. The Act of 1847 had eventually led to all operatives working from 6.00a.m. to 6.00p.m. with 1½ hours for meals Monday to Friday, and 7½ hours on Saturday with breakfast from 8.30 to 9.00a.m. What new arguments there were, besides references to hours reductions in other trades, essentially centred on the worsening of conditions since the 1847 Act was passed. Machines were larger and faster, needing more work — an estimated 40 per cent additional effort on behalf of the operative was claimed. In order to return to the benefits intended in the 1847 Act, hours needed to be reduced again.[15]

The movement for shorter hours however did not begin with the petitioning of Parliament for a new Factory Act, but rather with an attempt by the Spinners' Amalgamation to gain a reduction of the working week by collective bargaining. After some initial successes, concessions by individual employers came to a halt in December 1870, when the Oldham Spinners approached their masters. Already Spinners in Ashton, and surrounding towns, had won the reduction in hours, but there was a threat that if other towns did not follow, the two o'clock finish would be reverted to. Some Oldham firms conceded the operatives' claim, but the local employers' association was determined to resist, writing to other associations to establish a united front against the operatives. Employers' groups in north and south Lancashire responded and during February 1871 a number of meetings pledging resistance were held in Manchester. Meanwhile, Oldham employers pursued a stalling campaign, using the time to recruit more firms into their Association. Agitation on the operatives' side also increased, conferences and public meetings being held, occasionally gaining the concession from individual firms. Both sides began to prepare for an eventual conflict with the operatives organising the largest demonstration for a single trade Oldham had seen.[16]

The date agreed on to insist on the noon finish was 8 April, and the Masters resolved to lockout the town if the operatives took unilateral action. It was at this point that the lack of unity among the employers began to show, demonstrating the poor coverage of employers' associations even at Oldham. Firms not affiliated to the Employers' Association met privately in Manchester and then sent a deputation to the Oldham Masters' Association to inform them of their decision to offer the compromise of one o'clock. Faced with this breakaway the Employers' Association agreed the compromise as a common policy, although adhering to the original decision to lockout if the operatives left at twelve o'clock. After again meeting with representatives of the other towns, notices were posted, signed by over 105 firms, offering the compromise and threatening to withdraw the offer if it was not accepted. The operatives' leaders, however, had no authority to make concessions and with some regret they turned down the offer. On 1 May 1871 the mills of Oldham closed.[17]

The lockout ended the scenes that had attended the campaign prior to May, when the doors had been locked to prevent the operatives leaving the mills before the time the masters insisted upon. In the previous three weeks both women and men had been forced to climb the walls and scale outbuildings in order to gain their freedom. Now, with 128 Oldham employers signing a pact to close their works, 200 mills shut their doors and some 20,000 operatives were on the streets. Had the lockout continued, the cost to the Spinners' Amalgamation at a dispute pay of 6 shillings would have been £6,000 per week; unable to afford this, the leaders sued for peace on the third day. The negotiations were led by Thomas Mawdsley accompanied by other executive members of the F.A.R.A., who came prepared to offer a range of compromises, all of which the employers refused. Their counter-offer of arbitration and in the meantime a finish at one o'clock was agreed by the parties, and the lockout ended with both sides relieved at its conclusion.[18]

The immediate consequences of the lockout were detrimental to both masters and men. On return to work employers found some of their operatives had been enticed away by firms that had kept working, whilst the Oldham Spinners' saw its membership fall from 2,500 to 2,100. The only immediate beneficiaries were the six East End families brought up to Oldham by the masters, intent on bringing into the town the unemployed of London. Outside the district, on the other hand, the compromise pending arbitration became the new demand and Manchester gained the hour as did the operatives at Bolton firms within a few weeks. Bolton as a whole then joined in the movement adding to the list of reasons for the one o'clock finish the opportunity they would have to take advantage of the new railway excursions then being introduced. Meanwhile the arbitration arrangements proceeded, the employers failing to get some financial guarantee in the form of a deposit that the award would be accepted. Similarly, no agreement could be reached on a single arbitrator in the event of deadlock and, eventually, when the two persons appointed failed to agree, the arbitration scheme collapsed.[19]

It was at this point, following a mass meeting of delegates at Manchester in January 1872, that the campaign to reduce hours by collective bargaining was replaced by a Factory Act movement. Members of Parliament were approached and, as before, the hours restriction was to be on women and children. However, instead of aiming for a 58-hours week, the new demand was for 54 hours. Already, it was pointed out, there was a shortage of raw cotton and, at the same time, a glut in the product market. A panic was forecast, bringing ruin to the operatives as well as the masters; the reduction of hours would benefit both. A week later the leaders met with 'Friends' at Todmorden, where the movement was designated the Factory Acts Reform Association and an organisation along the lines of those of the 1840s was set up, secretaries were appointed — Mawdsley from Lancashire and William McWeeny, another veteran from Yorkshire. Eschewing strikes, as in other trades, the F.A.R.A. issued appeals for employers' support in carrying a Bill through Parliament, claiming a desire not to disturb the friendly feeling between masters and men. Given the recent history, especially the victimisation of a Shaw spinner for his part in the agitation, this was perhaps a little misleading, but clearly the appeal was for a wider public support. For similar reasons of public as well as Parliamentary sympathy, the T.U.C. was not utilised to press their case, but old relationships with sympathisers at Westminster were rekindled. Eventually Anthony Mundella, the Liberal M.P. for Sheffield, brought forward the proposals in Parliament, while in Lancashire a series of mass meetings was arranged and the signing of petitions began in earnest. Almost immediately the employers for their part began a counter-campaign to defeat the operatives' proposals. A survey of individual firms by the F.A.R.A. in February 1872 indicated 56 employers in favour of the hours reduction and 156 against, but this did not reflect the true level of opposition. Following the first reading of the Bill in late April, the Manchester Chamber of Commerce began to organise opposition by writing to M.P.s discouraging their support for the Bill without a Royal Commission and along with the reformed National Association of Factory Occupiers they succeeded in delaying progress at the Bill's second reading.[20]

The Liberal Government's position on the Bill was ambiguous, and despite sympathetic noises, instead of coming out directly in favour, it initiated an inquiry under the Home Secretary, H. A. Bruce, to discover the detrimental effects of factory work on women and children. For this inquiry the F.A.R.A. organised the giving of evidence as well as collecting information from medical practitioners in the manufacturing districts. By this time each town had its own local organisation, often initiated by the Spinners' Amalgamation and meeting in their rooms. Such bodies were able to persuade local Mayors to call town meetings and pass resolutions in favour of the Bill, so when the inquiry took place it was in an atmosphere of considerable agitation favourable to the operatives' cause. The report issued in May 1873 of the *Select Committee into Sanitary Conditions of Textiles in the United Kingdom* despite the fears of operative leaders, was in favour of some change in the law, paying particular attention to the obnoxious substances introduced for sizing during the Cotton Famine which had become more prevalent, and which allowed the use of inferior materials. The Report, however, did have reservations, particularly about the attitude of the women themselves:

> We have reason to believe that the workpeople are by no means unanimous on the other side of the question and that among the women especially there is a considerable amount of apathy, and possibly in some cases of positive opposition to the proposed change.[21]

Indeed it was true that some female organisations were against the Nine Hours Bill; the Liberal M.P., Henry Fawcett, acting in their interest had expressed opposition to the measure in the House. The F.A.R.A., however, could point out that of the 200,000 who signed the petitions, some 60 per cent were women. It was obvious from this point that some legislation in favour of the hours reduction was likely and the employers responded in July 1873 with a compromise. In exchange for their support they were prepared to offer 57 hours, if the operatives would abandon any further changes for a specific number of years. When this was refused the masters had the Bill talked out the next day. Not until after the 1874 election, in which the Spinners took an active part in questioning candidates, and with some behind the scenes manoeuvring, did the new Tory Government put forward its own compromise Bill of 56½ hours. Not wishing to see further delay, the majority of operatives accepted the offer and the Factories (Health of Women etc.) Bill became law. The campaign closed with the Spinners taking a greater interest in the T.U.C. than ever before and a pledge by the unions to raise wages as soon as possible so as to make up the income lost by the reduction in hours.[22].

The reduction in hours was almost universally welcomed by the operatives, but one question remained: when were the 56½ hours actually to be worked? Ignoring part of Mundella's justification for the Act, that children would be spared the necessity of leaving their beds at an early hour, the Spinners insisted that the old starting time of six o'clock remain. Against some employer opposition this was implemented, the Spinners arguing it was better to start work before the beer houses which then opened at six o'clock. Not all the problems of the Act's implementation were however so easily solved. The legislation had raised starting ages to ten years for half-timers and fourteen for full-timers, and had not provided for any compensatory increase in wages to take account of the fewer hours. Both questions had immediate implications for piecers, exacerbating existing problems and highlighting the old tensions in their relationship with the spinners.[23]

It is possible to overstate the nature of the subordinate position of piecers to spinners, especially at this time. Historians searching for examples of exploitation of one group by another privileged one can easily caricature the spinner-piecer relationship. Just because the spinner acted as a sub-contractor by employing in his team a big and little piecer, however, did not mean the assistants were necessarily in any way downtrodden. It is true, with the exception of Manchester where some piecers received piece rates, that all types of spinners were paid by results, while their assistants received a standing wage and therefore it was the spinner who gained the rewards for increased production. On the other hand the relationship was paternal, although perhaps in the 1870s only a minority of the piecers were actually members of a spinner's family. Individual spinners no doubt misused their supervisory role, but isolated incidents should not be taken as the norm. Maximising production depended upon team work, not mutual antagonism. Spinners in most areas had the responsibility of recruiting their own assistants, and if they did not have their full complement of piecers, the employer had the right and the sanction of the union to dismiss them and fill the positions with someone who had. Obtaining, training and keeping satisfactory piecers was therefore high on the spinners' priorities, especially after a strike when it was not always possible to re-employ the old assistants. At this time too, the problem of the big piecer growing old in his job, attempting to bring up a family on low wages while waiting for a vacancy as a spinner in his own mill was not yet evident. Representative information on the average age at which piecers became spinners is difficult to obtain and there were, undoubtedly, differences between districts. North-east Lancashire for instance, with its slower growth would not have seen the promotion of the piecer to spinner that was evident in the faster growing Oldham district. Figures for the ages at which spinners were admitted into the Bolton union may therefore provide a rough guide to the average, not least because of its high union density which excluded most of the late entrants one might normally find. Here in 1873 and 1874 members were admitted at an average age of around twenty-four, in the latter year, when the fine trade was already suffering a recession, nine individuals joined at eighteen years old and a further sixteen at nineteen. With wages up to and over £1 per week for a big piecer depending on the size of mules, wages at this point were far more than most apprentices might receive.[24]

The seniority system whereby the oldest piecer filled any vacancy, while widespread, was not universal. Indeed the spinners insisted where they could that jobs went to the unemployed adult men from elsewhere and members on the books were encouraged to go piecing until a spinners' job became available. Any idea that the spinners kept their piecers 'in place' by operating the seniority system at this time is therefore questionable. That the spinners were training twice as many youngsters as there were adult jobs at any one moment is true; but this was not the problem it later became. The turnover of spinners leaving the industry was quite high, special rules existing for setting up beer houses and other businesses. Failing eyesight caused many to leave in their fifties. Moreover, not all little piecers went on to be big piecers, ending their careers as half-timers, especially in Manchester where many more than the average two piecers was exceeded and where alternative employment and apprenticeships were available. Given the Amalgamation's prohibition on women becoming members, the employment of female piecers in many districts also kept down the numbers available to become spinners.[25]

By far the most important factor in keeping down the over supply of trained spinners, however, was the growth of the industry itself, and in the early 1870s that was creating its own problem of a piecer shortage, particularly at Oldham. There Thomas Ashton complained that mere boys were being employed as spinners and only an inferior type of piecer was left, making additional work for the spinner. In neighbouring Rochdale, the shortage was so great that 2s. 6d. was offered to any piecer willing to leave a non-unionist spinner to work for members. By 1872, Hollinwood, in the Oldham Province, experienced growing numbers of spinners being stopped, unable to get little piecers. In order to increase the supply wages were advanced and strikes occurred as spinners attempted to pass on the rises to the employer. Throughout 1873-4 the pressure increased, especially in places such as Oldham where the wage list was not a gross wage out of which the piecers' remuneration was deducted. Here, where the spinners had no incentive to keep assistants' wages down, the masters claimed the price of piecing was increasing unnecessarily, and they prepared to make a stand. Their solution was to foster the idea of a list of piecing prices to be incorporated into a new spinners' Gross List; rejecting the idea of a separate piecers' list which they thought would entail the creation of another operatives' organisation with whom they would have to negotiate. Confidentially, Thomas Ashton told the employers that the idea of a piecers' list could not work as supply and demand in each location was different and for a while the question was left in abeyance. With new mills opening and the demand for labour high, employers were unwilling to start a dispute, the Masters' secretary complaining that he did not like giving in, 'letting them have all they ask for — something must be decided upon or they will be on top of us'. What brought the matter to a head, however, was the introduction of the hours legislation. Understandably Oldham Province was not happy at the raising of starting ages from nine to ten years. Thomas Ashton complained not only of the poor parents who were denied the extra income of now idle hands, but the even greater shortage of piecers that would result. Notwithstanding this problem, it was decided to reduce the piecers' wages by an amount appropriate to the reduction in hours. The year 1875 therefore opened with the piecers striking of their own volition against the cuts and another round of wage rises at individual mills to pay the piecers the old rate.[26]

Before 1870 Oldham did not have a wage list of its own, but following the arbit-rated wage cut of 1869, the Masters' Association suggested negotiations should commence with the union to form one based on the average of the town. The Spinners' leaders, however, doubted that one could be made that covered all the variations in mules and materials produced and eventually it was decided that instead of a standard list of prices there should be a standard list of earnings. Whereas other districts paid wages according to a piece price list, Oldham's spinners were to receive whatever price it took to earn a specified amount. Each side submitted their own list of earnings, but negotiations broke down without agreement, the Masters attempting to impose their version. Not until 1872 was there a mutually agreed list, which despite the intentions of the employers gave some 80 per cent of the spinners an advance. With the further introduction of 'indicators', a mule attachment which allowed payment by length rather than weight, for a time disputes over wages in the town abated, helped by the introduction of new procedural agreements which began with the 1870 wage settlement. The employers had proposed, and it was accepted, that twenty-eight days notice be given by either side for any changes in wages and that all mills were to start and finish on the same day in cases of general disputes. With the agreed list of 1872 these rules were extended to allow Thomas Ashton to go along with the employers' secretary to establish the facts of a dispute inside the mill, and only when the two committees had failed to agree on a settlement was there to be any action. By 1875, however, the system was coming under pressure, necessitating numerous meetings, partly because of the piecers' agitation, partly because minders were demanding compensatory wage rises for the hours reduction, but most importantly due to the demands being made for extra payment for increased speed. Faster machinery was principally worked by the Limiteds who unofficially rewarded their operatives with payments of 2 shillings to 4 shillings above the list, but with no fixed payments the opportunities for disputes were widened. Other towns which paid a standard wage list had no need for a speed clause, although some did, because the extra production would be reflected in the wage packet. At Oldham, on the earnings list, the employer officially received all the benefit from increased output. When therefore the 1872 list came to an end in February 1875, both sides were determined to effect fundamental changes, the operatives demanding a speed clause and the masters a gross list that incorporated piecers' wages.[27]

Negotiations on a new list had begun some months before the old one expired, but broke down as neither side would accept the demands of the other. Both masters and men allowed the town to be operated without an agreed list in the hope that eventually the other side would capitulate to end the uncertainty. For a short time, settlements were reached on the old list, pending the introduction of a new one, but the operatives became reluctant to continue the practices regarding it as an unnecessary delay. 'We are at the end of the string,' wrote the Employers' Secretary, in June 1876, 'and everybody seems to be afraid to take action. A struggle is imminent and wants marshalling.' A few days later the employers declared their intention of implementing their own list unilaterally, and in July 130 of the 200 mills in the District closed, throwing, according to some estimates, 18,000 operatives onto the streets. The strike or lockout, depending on whose perspective one adopts, was by no means complete, two mills reopening within days and several Limited Companies continuing to run on the old list. Irrespective of the incompleteness, however, the dispute was beyond what local union resources or factory workers could afford, some operatives attempted to sell their Limited shares when loan capital was called in. Spinners also tried to get the local Co-operative Society to withdraw its investments in local companies as an extra lever in the dispute. The Oldham 1876 dispute was the first general strike undertaken by the Amalgamation since its reorganisation in 1870. It was the Amalgamation which took over the leadership of the dispute and it was the General Secretary who, in August, asked to re-open negotiations for an honourable settlement. Themselves in difficulties, the employers withdrew their list providing the operatives accepted the principle of gross lists, and a new list incorporating piecers' wages was eventually agreed. Despite the inclusion of piecers' wages into the agreement, the six weeks dispute was hailed as a victory, the new list including for the first time a 'speed clause', an allowance for the extra mule speed which gave the operatives half of the increased production. Together with other changes this meant that on average there was a 6.5 per cent gain for the spinners. For the Amalgamation, too, there was some room for congratulations, notwithstanding their eagerness to have the dispute ended. Unlike all previous town general strikes no extra levy was imposed upon the membership, increasing the Amalgamation's status, affiliations and members.[28]

CHAPTER FIVE

A Modern Spinners Union

In April 1874, Thomas Mawdsley, the General Secretary of the Spinners' Amalgamation, retired through illness after twenty-seven years' service. Two months later William Heginbotham was appointed to take up the vacant post at £150 per annum. Heginbotham was a local official from the Hyde district but now he was being asked to manage a county-wide Amalgamation in a difficult period of the industry's history. Prices had begun to fall in 1864 and continued to do so until 1898, with only the temporary respite of 1869-72. Within this longer period, three particular groups of years were noted for the severity of their depression, 1877-9, 1884-5 and 1891-3. Exacerbating the long-term decline in prices were the four cotton corners of 1879, 1881, 1888 and 1889, when financiers bought up raw materials in the hope of creating a false scarcity. What caused this long deterioration in trade and its attendant crises was debated extensively at the time. At first, some argued that it was the necessary adjustment to the creation of over-capacity in the boom of 1870-3. Later, over-production, under-consumption, foreign competition, tariffs (particularly those of India) and the adulteration of the product were advanced as contributory explanations of the industry's problems. In the latter third of the period, fluctuations in the price of silver became a fashionable scapegoat, Amalgamation leaders advocating a fixed exchange rate as with gold. D. A. Farnie, in the best modern analysis of the late Victorian cotton industry, has concluded that essentially there was a relative decline in demand and an over-expansion in supply. At the time, however, surrounded by closures, short-time and wage reductions, cool appraisals were the exception and both masters and men reacted in frustration and despair in trying to protect their livelihoods.[1]

Apart from mutual co-operation to reduce tariffs, the employers and the unions did not agree as to the responses required to meet the industry's problems. Essentially the operatives wanted to curtail output by working short-time, while the masters for the most part wanted to cheapen production by any means possible. Usually reducing production costs was synonymous with reducing wages, but the employers resorted to new as well as the traditional responses. In Bolton and elsewhere there was the continued substitution of self-actor mules to replace the old hand mules, undermining Bolton's older union and wiping out those in other districts. In Oldham's case, particularly in the Limited Companies, the response was to increase both the size and more especially the speed of the mules. Machinery wore out more rapidly causing excessive breakdowns and in consequence the spinners were not only forced to work faster, but to spend extra time mending broken thread. Despite the additional work 'speed up' entailed — which over-stocked the market even more — such action was not resisted by the spinners as long as they were paid for the extra production. Similarly, despite the Amalgamation's active and reasonably successful campaign to eradicate overtime, the rank and file often connived with their employers to maximise their income in contravention of the Factory Act. Given the unemployment and occasional bouts of short-time working when only partial wages were earned, it was understandable that workers wanted to earn as much as possible when market conditions permitted. In the north-east of the county, on the other hand, for those combined firms running both spindles and looms, the response to declining markets was to close down their spinning capacity and buy in yarn from Oldham. Specialist spinning companies did not have that option and instead they reacted by introducing inferior materials, resulting in a mushrooming of bad spinning disputes.[2]

In resisting such attacks upon the terms and conditions of their members, the Spinners' leaders were not unsympathetic to the plight of the employers. They recognised that the industry was in trouble and that wages could not be paid unless profits were made. In that attitude they had accepted that what was good for the industry was good for them. Excess profits and over-expansion of capacity might be a bone of contention, but they took pride in the legitimate growth of their trade and wished to do anything short of robbing themselves to see its prosperity. They worked with the employers to achieve a reduction of the Indian tariffs, in many cases initiating local campaigns prior to the employers' involvement. Later they were involved in the movement to establish the Manchester Ship Canal, working through the union and local Chamber of Commerce to promote the scheme. Free trade for them was an unassailable principle on which their own interests as well as the employers' depended. Unfair competition was morally wrong for it impoverished everybody in the long run, even those unscrupulous foreign manufacturers who temporarily benefited. All they wanted was an equitable opportunity to sell their product, having demonstrated, at least to their own satisfaction, that they could still undersell foreign competitors who used cheap labour for longer hours. When their own employers acted contrary to the interests of the whole trade and the reputation of British goods, they were quick to condemn them. Using so much size in the manufacture of inferior goods, so that cloth had to be dug out of the holds of ships, as some mill owners had done, was seen as particularly damaging to the industry on which the operatives prided themselves. Similarly the greed of speculators, especially those encouraging the over-expansion of the Limited Companies, earned their rebuke. Such action would lead to an overstocked market, while what should be done was the building of railways to open up new territories. Instead of increasing supply until the price fell to unprofitable levels, the employers should have helped them to ensure that the purchasing power of their existing customers was adequate and extend the market to new ones. Wars that dislocated trade were abhorrent to them, and the Lancashire operatives and their unions were generous in Indian famine relief. At the heart of the Spinners' policy, however, was a desire to prevent unfair competition between their own employers. Their opposition to mills running beyond the legal hours, or as they called it 'time-cribbing' reflected that concern. To allow one's employers to get away with making a marginal reduction in costs by this method would mean he obtained the orders of his neighbours, rather than increasing the total amount of trade.[3]

The prevention of the redistribution of trade, rather than the creation of it, also lay at the root of the defence of wages at individual mills. In both cases, wages and time-cribbing by individual mills, the union had the support of the employers, perhaps at times more strongly than from their own members in the mills affected, in the defence of what was essentially the method used by owners to keep wages out of competition between themselves. The union leaders, of course, gave the policing of agreements a different focus, not only did such action protect members from a downward wage spiral in bad trade, but reinforced the Spinners' concept of fairness within the market economy. Given the Amalgamation's incomplete organisation and relative weakness during the worst years of the depression, their success in maintaining wages and hours at individual mills is explained by the employers as a whole supporting their aims. The problem came when the millowners as a group decided to change the agreements or levels of wages. It was not then a case of the union simply ensuring all employers kept to the same standard, but whether the Spinners were willing to accept the new one. The policy of the Amalgamation to the proposal for a general wage reduction was always to question whether it was justified. Occasionally somebody would argue that wages should be a fixed cost, employers having to remunerate the spinners at the old level of pay irrespective of trading profitability, but this was not the dominant view. Spinners' leaders did accept that, provided the cause of the crisis was external to the actions of millowners, wages ought to come down in bad trade as they ought to rise automatically in good. Other variables certainly played a part, such as the supply of labour, but profit and loss were the key determinants. This did not mean the Spinners thought wage cuts ought to be the first resort of the employers when prices fell. If, for example, the problem was due to over-production, then the Spinners' solution was to run short-time at the old wages and clear the market of its excess stock. Tactically this was a good policy for the Spinners, because once wages were reduced it was more difficult to raise them than simply reverting to full time, but the policy also had moral overtones as well. It was the employers who had created the over-production by expanding the industry's capacity too quickly, and it was only right therefore that they should share in the burden. This same moral view, applicable to other causes of the crisis as well, justified the Amalgamation in rejecting at times the call for wages to come down.[4]

The movement to reduce wages began in earnest during 1877, notices being given in March at Mossley and Bolton. Initial resistance was successful, but Bolton masters renewed their demand in July. In readiness for a struggle, the Amalgamation's strategy was to strike the first town where the reduction of 5 per cent was attempted in the hope of stopping the movement spreading. Bolton was therefore chosen to be the centre, and, as notices in Manchester, Mossley and Stockport were posted in August for similar reductions, Bolton was instructed to resist. Although Thomas Ashton later described the Bolton strike of 1877 as 'an encounter with gloves on', it was not perceived so at the time. Authority had been given up by the local association to the central union, and all the resources of the Amalgamation were brought to bear on the dispute, the interests of other districts being postponed until after the Bolton dispute was won. Eighty-three mills closed, 50 within the Borough of Bolton, and in all 10,755 operatives were out, including 1,020 hand-spinners and 875 self-actor minders. Local levies in Bolton on those still working were increased to 5 shillings per week, while all other Districts, even those with disputes of their own, were ordered to pay 1s. 6d. per week. Collections were made all over Lancashire, and the weavers' union was approached for a loan. As the strike continued solid through September, the Amalgamation looked for a way out, offering both short-time and a two-to-three years moratorium on wage movements, if they remained at the present level. Throughout the strike the members continued to receive strike pay with an allowance for each child, piecers also being given an allowance. Eventually, the Amalgamation produced a face-saving formula and recommended in late October that all of Bolton accept the reduction, provided that the Masters agreed to revise the list. After a ballot the men returned at the 5 per cent reduction. Negotiations on the list proved abortive.[5]

The Bolton strike of 1877 had short-term and long-term consequences, not only for the Amalgamation in losing its first major set-piece dispute, but for industrial relations throughout the cotton industry. During the strike more districts posted notices, and at its end one town after another imposed the 5 per cent reduction during November and December. Rather than resist, the Amalgamation was forced to recommend acceptance without a struggle. Strikes did take place in the small districts, but they were often only token stoppages. There was no money to pay those that came out, Bolton being compelled to suspend all payments except those for funerals and out-of-work benefit. In all the strike had cost the Amalgamation over £17,000, four times the sum of its ordinary levy, wiping out the much vaunted reserve. The special levies that had been imposed also generated dissatisfaction and murmurings of secession began to be heard. The image of a strong Amalgamation melted with the defeat of Bolton. When in December the Cotton Spinners' and Manufacturers' Association (C.S.M.A.) demanded their own 5 per cent reduction, the Weavers rejected the move while the Spinners decided on acceptance if trade had not improved by the beginning of January. Receiving an accolade for their reasonable behaviour from some employers, the Spinners' leaders faced criticism from their membership and a questioning of their authority to make such arrangements. Perversely, this failure by the Amalgamation and the loss of its prestige may have prevented the establishment of a county-wide organisation of employers for a number of years. Previous to 1877, there had been little in the way of formal contact between employers' associations over industrial relations as opposed to legislative and trade questions, although undoubtedly such matters were discussed informally. However, two days before the Bolton Spinners were recommended to call off their strike and with no end in sight, the Secretary of the Oldham Employers' Association, Samuel Andrew, wrote to the other employers' groups suggesting they form 'as powerful an Amalgamation as that of the operatives'. When the strike collapsed this was not pursued, although from that time onwards considerably more co-operation between employers in the various towns was manifest.[6]

Perhaps the most important consequence of the Bolton strike was the foundation of a Piecers' Association connected to the Amalgamation. Almost from the beginning of spinning trade unionism, piecers had received strike pay despite making no contribution to the union. In the years from 1873 to 1878 this had cost the Amalgamation some £13,000 in all districts, £6,000 in the Bolton dispute alone. During the latter strike, however, Bolton decided to ask piecers in their local association areas who were still working to make contributions to assist those on strike, irrespective of whether their spinners were union members or not. The success of this venture led the Amalgamation to call on all districts to use their best endeavours to raise voluntary subscriptions from piecers all over the county, specifically for their Bolton contemporaries. Once the strike was over, the value of these efforts was appreciated and the decision was taken in November 1877 to establish a Piecers' Association. In December an outline scheme, whereby each piecer would be asked to pay 1d per week in exchange for receiving full benefits immediately he became a spinner, was floated, and organisation was already under way in Bolton and Oldham before the Amalgamation's full plan had become official policy in April 1878.[7]

Apart from making a small contribution to the cost of paying their dispute pay, the idea of a Piecers' Association was recognised as a means of inculcating the principles of trade unionism in the spinners' assistants. No longer, suggested Thomas Ashton, would there be the difficult job of teaching new spinners about the value of solidarity. Contributions were fixed at 1d per week for full-time piecers and ½d per week for half-timers, little piecers and creelers, entitling them to six shillings and three shillings per week respectively during strikes; those who did not join were to receive nothing in the future. Each District was to have its own local branch run by a Piecers' Association secretary elected from among the spinners. The new organisation grew slowly and variations in rules existed for some time, Bolton refusing to allow piecers of non-unionists to join. Part of the problem was the unrealistically low subscriptions demanded, which hardly provided enough to cover management expenses. Not only was considerable difficulty experienced in finding suitable individuals to be secretary, but dissatisfaction with those who were appointed was a further source of trouble, involving lengthy dismissal proceedings. In time, further rules were introduced in an attempt to impose some uniformity, but diversity continued, resulting in major differences in the level of organisation. Spinners were banned from paying the subscription out of their own pockets, but mere encouragement to join failed. Oldham, which left it to the shop to collect subscriptions, hardly managed to bring in half of their piecers. In contrast, Bolton introduced a system whereby big piecers took turns in being responsible for collections, but when this proved ineffective, the responsibility was put on each spinner. This proved extremely successful, providing almost total piecer unionisation in the District. Subordinate to the Spinners' Association, and with no rights to attend union meetings or take part in decision making, the Piecers' Association did not always reflect the aspirations of the piecers themselves. But attempts made in later years to form independent unions amongst these workers never succeeded.[8]

Unfortunately for the Spinners the wage cuts begun at Bolton did not end after the first round, and by September 1879 three further reductions totalling some 20 per cent off the wage lists had taken place. At the same time most of the operatives experienced short-time working when earnings were greatly depleted. Drastically weakened by the Bolton dispute, the Amalgamation attempted to resist, pursuing its policy of concentrating on one particular area rather than promoting a general strike. Barely viable when the different employers' associations were acting alone, this strategy was entirely unsuitable against an organised imposition of wage cuts by all the employers' associations. The first attack on wages came in north-east Lancashire where the 5 per cent originally demanded in December 1877 had been rejected by the Weavers and not enforced, despite the Spinners' acceptance. In March 1878, the masters returned with a new demand for a 10 per cent reduction, and this time the Spinners offered 5 per cent plus arbitration while the Weavers signalled opposition. Insisting on the full 10 per cent — regretfully in view of the Spinners' 'reasonable behaviour' — the ensuing strike became renowned for its riots and the burning of the employers' leader's house. Essentially a Weavers' dispute, the local Spinners' Association rejected the Amalgamation's instruction to accept the 10 per cent cut and stood shoulder to shoulder with the rest of the cotton operatives, only 20,000 of the 1.27 million spindles in the area continuing to turn during the dispute. Eventually the Amalgamation granted £1,000 by way of financial assistance to alleviate their distress, but the strike was lost, leaving the local Spinners' unions facing bankruptcy. Meanwhile across the county, masters in other districts imposed their own reductions of 5 per cent with the Amalgamation advising acceptance. Not until Oldham employers attempted to impose a further 10 per cent reduction at the end of the year did the Amalgamation propose resistance, the resultant strike being settled by a compromise of half that amount. By then the Amalgamation was in debt, its reserve fund gone and all but accident benefit payments suspended. 'For the purpose of keeping the organisation intact' levies were reduced to a ½d, but even then some Districts could not pay. When therefore a further round of cuts began in August 1879, the Amalgamation was only able to offer token resistance.[9]

At the end of this period of wage cuts the Amalgamation consoled itself by claiming that the position of spinners would have been worse without their influence, despite the general recognition that the organisation had failed. Not all agreed with Thomas Ashton that defending wages in a recession was a mistake, but most of the leadership felt that a policy which had led to the collapse of central and local funds, a deterioration in industrial relations, and the loss of hard-won procedural agreements, required re-evaluation. Particularly worrying was the fall in membership and the secession of District Associations. Membership had risen in the early 1870s to reach 14,257 by 1874, and had continued to rise until June 1877, when a record of 15,544 was achieved in 53 Districts (the latter figure due mostly to splitting existing Districts). Between then and 1879 membership fell by over a third to 9,977, and the number of affiliating Districts dropped to 43. The major secessions were in the north east, where the Amalgamation had refused fully to back the resistance to the 10 per cent reduction in early 1878. As a consequence Blackburn and later Burnley left the Amalgamation, the former owing some £300 in unpaid levies. Other Districts, particularly those in Yorkshire, did not withdraw from the Amalgamation, but merely ceased to exist.[10]

The problem, the leadership concluded, was that:

> instead of being a real Amalgamated Association, we are simply an alliance of various localities, whose systems of government vary, and whose scale of contributions and benefits are often based upon unsound principles as some of our members know to their cost.[11]

The truth was that while some districts could not afford to pay the levies required with so many of their own members on strike or working short-time, other local associations were not enamoured with the way the Amalgamation was being run. Over the summer of 1878 a number of resignations from the Executive took place, not least the departure of the General Secretary, William Heginbotham. Throwing himself on the mercy of the delegates, Heginbotham was not exonerated for the incompetent way he had kept his accounts, having to pay back half of the £132 deficiency found. Fortunately with the appointment of James Mawdsley of Preston as Secretary, and Thomas Ashton as Chairman, the secessions temporarily ceased. By the end of the year, however, the seceding recommenced, with the Ashton Twiners' Association and Ashton Fine Spinners joining the town's Self-Actor Minders outside the Amalgamation, the latter never having been persuaded that the benefits offered by the Amalgamation warranted the subscriptions. The problem for the Amalgamation was compounded by the decline in membership of those who stayed within its ranks. Only the Bolton Minders' Association significantly increased its membership, from 1,000 in 1875 to 1,450 in 1879, the number in the town's hand-mule spinners' society remaining stable despite smaller district affiliations into its ranks.

Over the same period, Manchester Fine Spinners' membership was halved; Stockport, Stalybridge and Accrington fell by about half; and Preston by over a third. Some of the smaller Districts fared even worse: Pendlebury lost over four-fifths of its members, while Rochdale lost three-quarters. Unionisation was at its lowest ebb across the county. Oldham, which had lost 600 members between 1878 and 1879, calculated that whereas 2,000 spinners had been outside its ranks in 1877, by 1880 this had risen to 2,850. As a result, expenditure ran ahead of income by £80 per week, with extra out-of-work benefit being needed. In desperation benefits were suspended and levies increased by most of the local associations; rules were changed in an effort to strengthen local executive authority, as well as to keep tighter control of finances. By late 1879, at best the situation as far as the Amalgamation was concerned could be described as having stabilised, membership had stopped falling and with benefits suspended further debts were avoided. The last revision of rules in November 1877 — when the word Rovers was dropped from the title, such no longer existing amongst the membership — remained in force until 1882. Any immediate improvement, if there was to be any, would have to come from District reorganisation rather than from the Amalgamation itself.[12]

The first District to undergo fundamental reorganisation was Bolton. Here, where divisions over the acceptance of a wage cut had caused the self-actor minders to break away from the older Hand Society in 1861, the relationship between the two associations had seen a chequered history. Attempts to combine on the suggestion of the Minders in 1865 had failed and apart from jointly organising the spinners' annual trip, the two societies kept to themselves. The Amalgamation, which had promoted a scheme in 1876 for a single society for Bolton after the Hand Spinners had affiliated, failed to reduce the mutual ill-feeling. Instead the relationship deteriorated as a result of the introduction of a new Minders' rule whereby any of their members found teaching hand-mule spinners to operate self-actors would be expelled. In turn the Hand Spinners' Society passed its own rule, allowing any such expelled minder full benefit of their own society and refusing any joint-deputation while what they called 'that obnoxious rule' continued. Instead of both sides withdrawing their position to provide a more amicable atmosphere, each side then escalated the dispute. By the end of the round of wage reductions in 1879, the relationship between the two bodies was at its worst, with accusations of poaching and underhand practices. However, at the end of 1879 the resistance to another possible reduction had brought the two societies together. Plans were mooted for amalgamation and despite a few hitches one society for the whole town came into being in March 1880. Part of the explanation for why the formation of the 'Operative Cotton Spinners of Bolton and the Vicinity', as it was first called, had been possible in 1880 was the near-exhaustion of the Hand Society's funds. The old reason for continuing membership of the Hand Spinners' union, once working on self-actors, was the former society's superior benefits; once these were suspended, resistance was easily overcome. Just as important, however, was the success joint-action had achieved, while negotiations for combining the two societies continued, for an increase in wages. Seeing an upturn in trade in late November 1879 the Amalgamation in Manchester had instructed all Districts to apply for a 10 per cent increase, payable on the last making-up day in January of the new year. Decrying the move as inopportune and premature, the initial resistance of the county's employers quickly evaporated. Apart from Mossley, where a ten-day strike took place, most Districts won an immediate 5 per cent without serious industrial action, together with the promise of a further rise by midsummer if trade continued to prosper. The atmosphere within Bolton at the time, therefore, was at its most sanguine having begun to turn the tide of wage reductions which had been their only experience over the previous few years.[13]

The next development, however, came as a result of failure rather than success. The Amalgamation's wage application for an advance in January 1882 met with effective opposition from employers across the county and the decision was taken to extend Bolton's boundaries and form a Province of local associations. Intended to encompass all those Districts in the fine trade and whose wages to some extent were dependent upon changes at Bolton, by 1885 the Province included 3,829 spinners and 7,793 piecers in ten branches covering Chorley, Atherton, Tyldesley, Leigh, Reddish, Farnworth, Hindley and Manchester. Not as well organised as Bolton itself, these smaller societies had been unable to stem the introduction of work practices not sanctioned by the Provincial centre. The new Association was therefore faced with a plethora of district and mill disputes in an attempt to bring uniformity of practices and preserve the traditions of the trade. Most notable was the campaign to stamp out joining which was prevalent in Chorley and Leigh. Deductions from lists, supposedly for local disadvantage, problems with piecers, and different procedural agreements also figured in the disputes to bring uniformity. On some issues, such as common rates of subscriptions and benefits, the Province was immediately successful, and in others partially so, such as the spread of indicators and the payment by length instead of weight. One inherited problem, however, fining, took a considerable time to eradicate. Unlike at Oldham, where the Masters' lawyer had advised that it was not worthwhile trying to fine because it was difficult to prove responsibility and therefore better simply to sack the suspected offender, in the outlying Bolton Districts the practice continued. At Atherton, the Province ordered a strike against fines, but at Tyldesley the local branch was advised to expel any member who paid a fine. Certainly the new Province was not willing to see the reintroduction of a practice which in Bolton had been effectively wiped out.[14]

The last major issue in the search for uniformity within the Province was that of the employment of women spinners. Although this particular question came to a head in the middle of 1886, when Heatons of Lostock Spinning Mills introduced three female minders, the issue had a long history going back to the 1830s. In the recent past, despite the Amalgamation's rule of 1872 prohibiting them from membership, female spinners continued to be employed in outlying districts, especially at Wigan where reputedly half the spinners were women. In small numbers the women operatives could be tolerated; even at Bolton, where in 1878 a group of spinners only complained of their piecers being taken to assist female spinners then being introduced at one mill, rather than protesting at the larger issue. Women were employed throughout the industry as piecers and again Bolton had previously made no objection, having rejected a proposition to prohibit them from piecing on self-actors. When the Lostock Mill dispute commenced, however, attitudes changed, and where once tolerance had been the order of the day, fixed positions were taken. At first the Bolton Province tried to keep the dispute low key, quietly approaching the employer to agree not to sack the women, but replace them with men when a vacancy occurred. This being refused, the resulting strike became public after two weeks, the employer vowing to break the union. Despite evidence that the women were working below rates and another woman having worked there as a spinner for twelve to fourteen years, the union chose to centre its case on the question of morality. Women would have to work without skirts, boots, stockings, some of their petticoats and their shoulders exposed, argued John Fielding, the Provincial Secretary, which with all the swearing in the shed was morally degrading, a point of view somewhat weakened as one-third of the mills in the town employed women piecers. The Masters' Association replied dismissing Fielding's assertions, and the issue became something of a *cause célèbre*. Letters to the *Cotton Factory Times*, the trade paper founded in January 1885, continued to appear until April 1887.[15]

While all this was going on the strike progressed with the Bolton Province passing a resolution to refuse to teach any more girls piecing. This was not done in petty victimisation, claimed Fielding, but in a spirit of self-sacrifice:

> So long as girls shared the work with the opposite sex, the system operated as a check to there becoming a plethora of skilled mule spinners, because the former, on arriving at womanhood, usually married and left the trade entirely, and this regulated to some extent the number of skilled workers.

By stopping girls piecing, he went on, they had ensured keener competition for any future spinner vacancies:

> they have proved themselves capable of sacrificing their interests as workmen for the higher nobler object of protecting the purity of their women and in doing so have acted the part of true citizens.[16]

Eventually, Heatons, who threatened the female relations of strikers with the sack at their other mills, formed a 'company union' for the knobsticks whom they employed to replace their original workforce. At the end of May 1887 the dispute was officially declared over, the shop made 'illegal', and those left out put on victim benefit which the union continued paying until March 1888. Notwithstanding this defeat, the employment of women minders never became general, although female piecers remained an element of both the industry and the Amalgamation's Piecers' Association.[17]

Already possessing a Provincial Association the reorganisation of Oldham was of a different order. Here the first major changes were in the centralising of authority and finances, establishing a uniform subscription of one shilling per week and more especially the launching of a membership campaign. Levels of unionisation are notoriously difficult to assess, particularly where the boundaries of districts overlap. Thomas Ashton, however, estimated that following the wage reductions only half of the Province's spinners were organised, unlike in Bolton, where more than 99 per cent were enrolled. Oldham's problem, thought Thomas Ashton, was grounded in their previous indifference towards recruitment, but the situation was more complicated. Spinners had been unable to pay the high subscription during spells of short-time and the practice of members being struck off the books when benefit ran out meant a continual, if temporary, loss of members. Recruitment was further made difficult by the system of members paying in the district they lived in rather than at work, with the consequence, according to Ashton, that spinners in the same mill did not know who were members. More importantly, the continued expansion of mill building meant that the Province had to recruit more members merely to maintain its existing level of unionisation. Despite these problems Oldham's membership campaign, which included shop meetings, improvement in benefits and visits, had immediate results — numbers increased by 1,000 (30 per cent) by the end of 1880. Although slowing down after that, increases continued, and membership levels of 77 per cent and 86 per cent were being claimed in 1881 and 1882 respectively, until in mid-1885 over 5,000 spinners were enrolled.[18]

The next major change in Oldham came with the failure to secure an advance in January 1882, the same impetus that in Bolton had brought about the formation of its Province. Both were aware that they had become the 'centres of struggle' on which surrounding districts were dependent for adjustment in wages. To some extent this had always been the case, although in the early part of the century the centre had been Manchester. The formality of the system whereby masters and men in other districts agreed to abide by what happened in these two centres without having a strike or lockout in their own, had been spreading. Apart from the Leigh Spinners, who asked their employers to drop the traditional practice of following Bolton in 1879, the system had been reinforced by the experience of the late 1870s, leading to a mushrooming of ad hoc and formal agreements. Once the wage movement started to operate in the contrary direction the masters were less willing to follow Oldham and Bolton, complained the Amalgamation, but follow they often did, not always to the operatives' advantage. During the summer of 1880, Mossley struck for ten days to gain the second instalment of 5 per cent, but returned to work on the understnading that if Oldham did not pay, the rise would be taken off. A similar arrangement was negotiated in Ashton, which was still outside the Amalgamation, and both towns lost their rises when Oldham failed to gain the advance. Again in January 1882, when another rise was applied for across Lancashire, both the employers and the operatives waited to see what happened in Bolton and especially Oldham. When Oldham refused to strike because they were not yet financially strong enough, all the other claims were withdrawn.[19]

A possible outcome of these 'centres of struggle', based on a fine spinning sector around Bolton and a coarse one around Oldham, was the creation of two separate amalgamations. Indeed the danger inherent in the reorganisation of the two major Provinces was their now diminished dependence on the Amalgamation for support. Logically, because the trade of the two sectors fared differently, separate central organisations would have been better able to pursue the particular interest of each. Certainly the existence of two sectors was a prime reason why the employers themselves had not come together in one unified body and why two bargaining centres prevailed. Such an idea, however, was not seriously contemplated by the Spinners, the advantage of having one organisation while the employers were divided outweighed all other considerations. Had the Amalgamation failed to reorganise perhaps a different view would have been taken, but as it was, even a small attempt to develop an enhanced formal bargaining unit around Oldham following the collapse of the 1882 wage campaign proved abortive. Known as 'The United Moveable Committee', because the venue changed for each conference, the committee met only sporadically, its main function being to provide a monthly report of changes in margins. As margins, the difference between the buying and selling prices of raw cotton and yarn, never became so favourable as to warrant an advance, except briefly in December 1883, there was little reason to meet but to elect officials and pass accounts. Its last meeting took place in December 1885, when the growing strength and influence of the Amalgamation had made even the United Moveable Committee's intelligence function redundant.[20]

The Amalgamation had started its own reorganisation soon after it had begun in the principal Districts, with the establishment of a new reserve fund in March 1880. The idea was to forgo 'local disputes and save'. If only we could 'lay our hands on £50,000,' wrote James Mawdsley later, it would be 'a thousand times more influential than the most logical and convincing argument.' In practice the project was more modest, a weekly levy of 3d per member, reduced to 1½d in November 1881 when a cotton corner brought about short-time working. The idea of enforcing justice through a large reserve fund was one that was continually argued by the General Secretary. Without such a fund, he suggested, the Amalgamation would never be able to act as one man, and the policy of leaving it to specific districts to bear the struggle would continue. In the short term, however, Mawdsley's hopes remained unrealised and instead the Amalgamation's energies were concentrated on raising District subscriptions to a uniform one shilling per week, as at Oldham. In November 1880 Mawdsley complained that despite being one of the oldest unions, 'we cannot congratulate ourselves upon having made that progress solidifying our institution and drawing together our various districts, that might be expected. Scarcely two Districts pay the same benefits, some districts have none.' To remedy this situation the Amalgamation prepared a draft scheme for a weekly subscription of one shilling in 1881 and by plugging away at the issue most Districts gradually adopted it, 90 per cent by December 1884, allowing not only superannuation, accident, sickness and breakdown pay, but also the unemployment benefit necessary in an industry suffering from recurring short-time. The Amalgamation itself continued with its own inadequate subscription of 1½d per week, which had to cover management expenses as well as dispute pay and contributions to the reserve. As a result special levies were still needed to meet the expenses of major disputes.[21]

Financially the Amalgamation might have been weak, but in membership and District affiliations the early 1880s was a time of recovery, although not at first by bringing back the eleven local associations which had left. A number of small districts joined for the first time, and parts of Blackburn, the principal District to secede, broke away from their parent organisation and together with Bury rejoined the Amalgamation by 1880. Gradually others who had left returned, but Blackburn remained aloof, with relationships becoming for a time exceedingly strained. Being covered by the same employers' organisation as Preston and the smaller north-east districts, common action with them was difficult to avoid. Joint deputations of the three leaders of Preston, Blackburn and Burnley took place in all the major attempts to raise wages in 1881-2. This, despite Thomas Banks of the Executive taking part, was disliked by the Amalgamation, which permitted the joint action but regarded it as a mistake, suspecting outsiders. Worse, when financial help to

Blackburn was given by neighbouring associations because a weavers' strike had led to local spinners being laid off, the Amalgamation refused to sanction the use of union funds for such purposes, castigating the north-east districts. In the end, however, the Amalgamation gave up trying to isolate Blackburn, and while not forgetting 1878, it declared that 'blood was thicker than water', and allowed Districts to aid the laid-off spinners. As a result of this new-found comradeship Blackburn rejoined in early 1884. By then the Amalgamation had already seen the expansion of its organisation in Yorkshire, where many branches had been wiped out in the late 1870s. In 1883 Sowerby Bridge, Elland, Bradford and Halifax and Huddersfield came together to form a Province so that a full-time Secretary could be employed. Apart from Ashton-under-Lyne, which did not join until 1885, all the major districts were in by the end of 1884, membership had risen from under 10,000 to 16,000 and the estimated level of unionisation across the county had reached 84 per cent.[22]

It was only at this point, 1884, that the cotton spinners of Lancashire achieved that level of organisational strength upon which their reputation for power and influence was ultimately founded. This new-found authority enabled them to resist changes in technology which could have undermined their privileged and elite position. The mid-1880s were a watershed, when together with the District and shop organisation, the Amalgamation maintained the spinners' status, kept up wages, and protected working practices. Their influence in the T.U.C. had also been enhanced by the election of James Mawdsley to its Parliamentary Committee in 1882 and to its Chairmanship in 1886. Pride in the union was expressed by the commissioning of an emblem in 1881, and within a few years its leaders were being appointed Justices of the Peace. Whereas in 1880 the General Secretary was bemoaning its failures, already by 1882 he found it possible to congratulate the members on more than half the trade gaining payment by indicators. With the growth of its authority, the Amalgamation felt able to help promote the Manchester Ship Canal, lobby again for Indian tariff reform, promote legislation to limit the power of the Limiteds to raise loans, and give evidence to the *Royal Commission on the Depression*. There was still room for improvement, and the question of a reserve fund remained a prominent issue, but the Amalgamation felt no need to make any further changes in its organisation or rules. The last revision had occurred in 1882 and apart from expanding the Executive from seven to thirteen, seven to come from the mules, and the dropping of the arbitration clause, the remaining alterations were minor.[23]

If any charge of complacency with their new-found prestige was justified, perhaps it was to be found in their failure to recruit ring spinners. Spinning on rings instead of mules was beginning to become established and the question arose whether to organise this new branch of essentially female operatives. The Amalgamation already allowed mule spinners' overlookers to retain membership on the grounds that they would be sympathetic in disputes, so possibly a start could have been made with those in charge of ring spinners, but many Districts were against it. The question had been first introduced at Amalgamation level in December 1882, but was deferred until March the following year. Then, the

Amalgamation Representative meeting decided that because of what was considered to be the rapid increase in ring spinning and the displacement of mule
spinners, it 'was absolutely necessary that the right hand of fellowship should be
extended to the workers on ring frames, with a view to keep up wages of the persons
employed thereon, seeing that the object of the employers is to produce yarn at a
less cost by employing females and others at a low rate of wages, in order to undersell
the self-actor minders'. Instead of full membership, however, the proposal was to
include them in the Piecers' Association, with a low subscription rate of 3d per week
and low benefits. Many in fact joined in south-east Lancashire, but Bolton voted
against accepting the council's resolution and following the establishment of a
Cardroom Amalgamation in 1886 and the opening of its ranks to ring spinners, they
became the more representative organisation.[24]

The state of trade in the early 1880s, while better than in the years immediately
preceding it, remained in a dull condition. Temporary recoveries were soon
replaced by lulls in trade, and together with cotton corners, the Egyptian revolt and
the imposition of French tariffs, short-time and unemployment remained. The
Amalgamation blamed over-production, especially by the Limiteds, and capacity
in spinning to outstrip the requirements of the cloth manufacturer and the yarn
export market. However, not all sections of the industry suffered at the same time;
margins could be declining for fine spinning whilst improving for coarse products.
The repercussions of a weavers' strike in Blackburn could be devastating for the
Oldham trade, causing thousands of spinners to be laid off, whilst leaving Bolton's
spinners relatively unaffected. With such conditions the pressure for wage movements from either side was not always firm, employers and operatives withdrawing
claims as trade fluctuated. Oldham, in particular, faced a complex and uncertain
market with no clear-cut trend on which to act. Margins were down, but increased
efficiency meant that profit levels were maintained. The Oldham Limiteds seemed
indifferent to the two-thirds of the north-east Lancashire looms which were running
on short time in 1882, and continued to produce yarn at full capacity, relying on
increasing their exports. Fortuitously, during the weavers' strike of 1883-4, they
managed to export some 90 per cent of the yarn they produced, but more often
margins plunged. Firms began to make more money speculating in 'futures' than
they did in producing yarn, enabling them to present high dividends while margins
were falling. Both sides watched the margins in weaving, fearing a crash in that
sector would throw spinning into chaos; neither masters nor men wanted any kind
of strike, despite the deteriorating position. As 1884 ended margins fell again and
the masters began to contemplate a reduction. The second trough in the long period
of indifferent trade was about to bring a further round of wage cuts for those
operatives who had still only succeeded in recovering half of the reduction experienced in the last one.[25]

By the closing months of 1884, Oldham employers were still reluctant to pursue
a reduction if it involved a strike. Testing the feeling of their members in October,
the proposal for cutting wages was abandoned, ostensibly because trade had
improved, but later it was admitted by the Oldham Masters' Secretary that this

was due to a lack of support. The threat however remained, the Amalgamation in January 1885 advising all its members to stay at work when possible and avoid strikes unless there were exceptional circumstances. By February, Thomas Ashton was echoing this view, claiming from private information that the employers were going to try to force the operatives to strike. Whether it was true that because the masters were divided, especially between private firms and the Limiteds, on how to act, that they wanted a strike by the operatives to help heal their divisions, seems doubtful. By March, the leadership of the Oldham Masters' Association thought the time opportune for a wage cut, and under pressure from some of their members they approached the Limiteds' Association for their views. As a result they proposed a 10 per cent reduction, 5 per cent if accepted without a strike, but when the operatives rejected this and suggested short-time, the movement collapsed again with insufficient support to close the mills. Slowly, through the pressure of mounting stocks rather than a continuing decline in the margins, the Masters were able to obtain sufficient promises for closure and they returned again in late June with their demand for a 10 per cent reduction.[26]

To avoid a strike the Amalgamation and its Oldham Province did everything they reasonably could to meet the employers half-way. Already, by June, the strikes at individual firms throughout Lancashire meant more money was going out in Amalgamation dispute pay than was coming in, and despite claiming that they had funds for a fifteen-week strike, they were looking for a settlement. Their overall offer to accept 5 per cent if coupled with short-time and unofficially without any such strings, was rejected out of hand by the Masters' Association, even though some of the Limiteds favoured the inclusion of a simultaneous curtailment of production. The Masters' Association, having struggled to obtain the authority for the lockout, were not now going to allow a compromise, telling their members that despite the negotiations they had received no definite offer from the Spinners.

The mills closed on 24 July. Recognising that a struggle was unavoidable, the Amalgamation swung behind what they later described as a 'stand up fight'. At the time, while admitting 'they might not win', they were intent that the Oldham Masters 'would be taught a lesson they wouldn't forget'. Their objection to the reduction was on 'moral grounds': trade was bad, but it was the masters' greed that had created it through over-production. The dispute would be fought 'not lightly, but firmly' and if all Districts fulfilled their promises they had nothing to fear. Keeping at first 2,844 and later 3,262 spinners in strike pay was no easy matter, but despite other employers' associations adopting short-time, and in the case of Bolton reducing wages by 5 per cent, the Amalgamation's levy of 2s 6d per member per week saw only 100 defaulters out of 16,000, and the funds never failed. In total the dispute cost the Spinners £36,000, two-thirds of which came from the Amalgamation, who were compelled to borrow money from the membership in £5 shares yielding commercial interest. Others were not so fortunate. With the closure of 80 Limiteds and 60 private companies some two-thirds of the Province's spinners were out, but a further 18,000 operatives in the town were locked out also. Without adequate funds of their own, the other unions and non-unionists were plunged into poverty,

1,000 operatives were receiving outdoor relief before the struggle ended. The *Cotton Factory Times* reported that 1,500 watches had been added to one pawnbroker's collection, whilst the Bible Women's Mission organised relief. Before the thirteen weeks of the lockout were over, many of Oldham's population had seen their life savings disappear.[27]

During the Oldham lockout the balance of power switched from side to side, highlighting the major problems both masters and men had in maintaining such a struggle. Before the lockout commenced the Amalgamation already looked with anticipation at the full-time work the other districts would have once Oldham was out of the market, reckoning without the sympathy of other towns' employers. At first, irrespective of such support, the benefit of the lockout was not evident as stocks remained high and margins down, partly explaining why the employers were so willing to continue the struggle. Towards the middle of August the first cracks in the employers' side emerged, some shareholders in the Limiteds wanting the lockout called off. The following week the employers considered meeting the operatives to see what it was possible to arrange, but deferred this until after an Amalgamation meeting. Now that stocks were being depleted, other towns were poaching Oldham's trade. Although not yet a major movement, as some stock still remained, the threat was obvious. One or two mills reopened whilst others attempted to start on the 5 per cent reduction already achieved at Bolton. Whilst the Oldham Masters boasted that their unity 'was unequalled' in the history of the industry, each side waited for the other to make a move.[28]

Had the Amalgamation and Thomas Ashton had their way, the first to yield would have been the operatives. They organised a ballot with the recommendation to return, but the rank and file rejected this by 1,945 to 771 votes. Had they taken the ballot earlier, a more favourable result for the leadership might have occurred, but by the middle of September the operatives had been radicalised by the attempt of the Masters to open the mills and encourage knobsticks. Warned by the unions to keep away from the workplace, the operatives took it upon themselves to gather in considerable numbers outside one working mill, and frustrated by manoeuvres to get some knobsticks away, hurled stones at those they found. Played down by the *Cotton Factory Times*, abjured by the leadership, these disturbances were quickly dealt with by the police; but relationships were soured and the operatives' determination strengthened. When at the start of October three mills opened on the operatives' terms of 5 per cent, panic among employers set in. Instead of the Amalgamation, who were trying to end the rank and file resistance by reducing strike pay, it was the employers who retreated. Finding a face-saving formula, they accepted the 5 per cent reduction offer from the Spinners' Amalgamation still on the table, and added the clause that if trade worsened in three months a further 5 per cent would be taken, arbitrators to decide if there was disagreement. The Spinners returned on this compromise, many unaware of the three-months clause and nobody sure if the operatives had accepted it. The Amalgamation claimed that they had won, the employers suggested it was a victory for common sense.[29]

By ignoring the riots during the 1878 dispute, and the picketing, victimisation and violence at individual firms, it is possible to argue that the big set industrial disputes in the cotton industry were becoming ritualistic. Superficially, the Oldham lockout would tend to support this view, as the press at the time, and both masters and men, publicly acknowledged the good humour and lack of acrimony. Because there was a lack of victimisation following the lockout, an additional legacy of bitterness was absent. Certainly, after the dispute, the Amalgamation could claim that never before had they met the masters on such equal terms following a major struggle, but that was meant in terms of strength, not of fellow feeling. Going behind the congratulatory public statements about the town's calmness and the good relations, a different picture emerges. The highlight of the disturbances had been the stone-throwing incidents and the injury of pickets, which the Employers' Secretary, Samuel Andrew, initially attributed to outsiders at the T.U.C., which was then meeting at Southport, but later he had to withdraw this statement after legal threats. Disturbances were, however, not the only evidence of an out-and-out struggle behind the façade of friendly relations. The Amalgamation knew that it was the employers' plan not simply to reduce wages, suggesting that they intended 'dispensing with three-quarters or more of the men'. Such plans, including the introduction of the joining system, were not overtly expressed, although readjustments in the wage list were, until September, when Samuel Andrew advised that 'we may now quietly urge the members to get to work, throwing the old minders overboard and, if necessary, adopting the redistribution scheme'. Similarly behind the scenes the language of conflict adopted by the employers was not of the normal civility, the Amalgamation complaining of unjustifiable personal attacks on its leaders. Admittedly employers had received poison pen letters, but despite this Mawdsley thought 'we can fight the employers to the bitterest of endings . . . let it be, as men who are fighting with foe worthy of our steel, so that which ever wins we may at its close, be able to shake hands with them, knowing that neither side had forfeited that self-respect which constitutes the highest dignity of mankind'. Unfortunately the masters were not impressed, labelling the Amalgamation's officials as 'instigators of destruction and misery'. Ritual or not, the Amalgamation congratulated its members on their loyalty and the importance of the victory. The dispute had not only proved the Amalgamation's strength and the commitment of the members to pay such a high levy in place of the reserve needed, but just as importantly it had demonstrated that what they considered to be 'perhaps the most powerful Employers' Association in the Kingdom' was vulnerable and in need of reorganisation.[30]

In retrospect, the period following the Cotton Famine can be viewed as a time of considerable achievement for the Spinners' Amalgamation. Having emerged from the Cotton Famine as a partial federation of poorly organised local associations, by the mid-1880s the regenerated union represented some 84 per cent of all spinners in the wider Lancashire area. Reorganisation had been a gradual process, initiatives following the major crisis of 1869 and the late 1870s, when the Amalgamation had demonstrably failed, but by the end of the period both the union and the status of

the membership was enhanced. Whilst the Cardroom Amalgamation had frag-
mented and the Weavers were still trying to form their first permanent central
organisation, the Spinners had maintained their Association and many of the
Districts secured a firmer footing. Meetings at all levels still took place in public
houses, but the larger Districts had acquired premises of their own, partly under
the influence of the temperance movement and the desire for respectability. The
Amalgamation itself, after a number of moves, settled in Ashton New Road,
Manchester, and with the election of James Mawdsley by an examination aimed at
testing candidates' ability to calculate list prices, set a precedent for this method of
appointment which was followed by local associations. It would be some time,
however, before the majority of local secretaries gained their positions by examination; less than a dozen District Associations in the 1880s had full-time officials.
Despite this there was some recognition that the Executive needed to keep in touch
with rank and file attitudes, hence the inclusion in the 1882 constitution of an
additional seven representatives on that body from the mules.[31]

The greatest successes over the period were the Conference of 1870, which
brought in Oldham and later Bolton, the hours reduction and the District
reorganisations of the early 1880s. With the latter, the Spinners' Amalgamation, as
evidenced by the Oldham dispute of 1885, at last reached the strength to withstand
a concerted employer attack upon wages and force a compromise. In some respects,
however, the Amalgamation still had a long way to go. Indeed it could be argued
that their continuing weaknesses resulted from not having totally collapsed.
Because the Amalgamation remained intact, the more fundamental reorganisation
of central finances was not carried through. It had been the declared policy of the
leadership from 1870 to form a central reserve fund capable of financing the major
disputes without imposing levies. During all the major disputes levies as high as 5
shillings per member on top of subscriptions still had to be made, and the
Amalgamation continued to be a vehicle for Districts helping one another rather
than a powerful organisation in its own right. That the members of other Districts
during the Oldham Lockout carried the burden without protest is testimony to
their solidarity as well as perhaps the recognition of the concept of 'centres of
struggle', but without a reconstructed financial centre the Amalgamation had a
permanent weakness. This problem, together with the existence of two major
bargaining centres, Oldham and Bolton, resulted in the Amalgamation having to
pursue a more defensive role than might otherwise have been the case. Initiatives
came mainly from the Districts, through Representative Meetings, with the Executive merely sanctioning the use of funds as per rule or along with the General
Secretary investigating complaints.[32]

In some ways the success of the Amalgamation in maintaining standards prior to
1885 lay in the failure of the employers to challenge the Spinners' cherished customs
and practices. This is not to say that individual employers did not take the initiative
to attack the union and their members' craft status, in fact the records of District
Associations are full of such attempts. By themselves, however, the individual firms
had not the power to carry their plans through; fierce competition between

employers made innovation risky if a stoppage ensued and the union was strong enough to defy single employers. It was rather the threat from the employers as a whole which failed to develop. Part of the explanation of this, in regard to ring spinning for example, which might have been used to break the power of the mule spinners, lay with the inadequacy of the new technology. Ring frames were not the substitute for self-actor mules producing the majority of counts, although perhaps, too, there was some conservatism in regard to rings among Lancashire cotton masters. Where rings and improved technology were applicable, the employers did take on the union and defeat it. It will be remembered that twining, a type of doubling process, was under threat from new technology. In Oldham, where traditionally twiners were paid more than spinners, no list existed and the employers attempted to impose one in 1881 which entailed reductions. The resulting twelve-month strike by twiners led to the operatives' total defeat: wages fell by up to 30 per cent and membership of the Twiners' branch of the Oldham Province dropped by a third. During the strike employers had managed to keep going, with four to six of the improved machines kept running 'with an overlooker to four children', and follow- ing the union's collapse, joining was introduced on a wide scale. Joining, of course, was a general threat to all types of spinners and, as with rings, it could have been used as a weapon to break the union. The system itself, however, was not any more profitable to operate than the 'spinner to two-piecer' method of manning. Dividing the wages of the old spinning team between two grown men could be just as expensive, depending on whether the standard price list was paid. Employers as a whole, and their associations especially, for the most part saw no real advantage in trying to introduce joining, either to smash the union or to get reductions in wages. Not only had they been able to achieve substantial wage reductions without clouding the issue with new work practices, but as the *Textile Manufacturer*, an employers' monthly newspaper, commented, they had come to recognise the value of trade unions and especially the conciliatory role of their leaders. The threat made during the Oldham Lockout to sack strikers and introduce joining was a potential turning point, but in that dispute not only did the millowners find it impossible to get sufficient blacklegs to commence working on any kind of system, but the Amalgamation demonstrated to the employers that they could no longer gain the wage reductions they wanted. The union was now seen in a new light and its power in need of curbing, but by then the Spinners were strong enough to resist. Employers began to see themselves as weak, and in consequence were more wary of attempting any fundamental changes in the mule room. Their challenge, it seems, came too late; what the employers needed was an Amalgamation of their own.[33]

CHAPTER SIX

The Making of Brooklands

The period 1885 to the early 1890s were years that saw the permanent establishment and growth of other Amalgamations in the cotton industry. All types of cotton unions had to varying degrees suffered in the late 1870s depression and were in need of re-organisation. The Weavers' Amalgamation having settled on a new constitution in 1884 doubled their membership from 37,500 in that year to 75,500 by 1894. The cardroom workers following the formation of their new Amalgamation in 1886 grew even faster, from 9,500 to 31,000 in 1892. Overlookers also took a greater interest in trade unionism. From 1878 when the employers showed no distinction between them and other workers, the focus of their local associations switched from providing insurance schemes to industrial relations. In 1885 they formed their own central association, a year before the Factory Acts Reform Association was re-established. Once the hours reduction of 1874 had been gained, meetings had taken place at various times on specific campaigns, but now the new body held regular conferences, developing the political wing of the movement to deal with a wider range of legislative issues concerning the factory. Changing the name in 1889 to the United Textile Factory Workers' Association, (U.T.F.W.A.) to include these wider interests, it was active in campaigns to increase fines for 'time cribbing', tighten the rules on capital raising by Limited Companies and a host of health and safety issues affecting mill workers. As a body that included the bulk of organised Lancashire cotton operatives, the U.T.F.W.A. with its 120,000 members in 1888 was one of the largest associations of unionised workers in the country.[1]

In general, the whole of the cotton industry was better organised than most other industries, even ones dominated by all male craft workers. In 1888 only an estimated 10 per cent of United Kingdom employees were members of trade unions compared with nearer 25 per cent in cotton. Such figures are, however, misleading, averages masking a wide range of experience. Of the 750,000 trade unionists to be found in that year, most were located in metals, engineering and shipbuilding (190,000), mining and quarrying (150,000), building (90,000), and textiles (120,000). Within these industries, with the exception of textiles where the highest proportion of women were organised, it was mainly the more skilled male workers who belonged to a union. Shipbuilding craftsmen, for example, had around 50 per cent of such workers in their union and the best organised coalfield, Northumberland and Durham, a slightly greater proportion. Cotton weaving trade unions in Lancashire, on the other hand, with a 30 per cent union density, outstripped other unions of semi-skilled workers whilst the Spinners, with around 90 per cent, were better organised than almost, if not all, skilled groups. The Spinners therefore were an elite force among trade unionists and not simply in their level of unionisation. Subscriptions and benefits were the highest and most comprehensive in the trade union world, nearly 25 per cent greater than their nearest rivals the Amalgamated Society of Engineers, then regarded as the leading aristocrats of labour.[2]

If through their union the Lancashire spinners were an aristocracy of labour, at work in the mill they were far from that in appearance. In a humid atmosphere, stripped to their waists, barefoot, they walked some twelve miles per day, back and forth with the mule carriage. As the mules became longer the work became even more arduous and with extra speed more breakages occurred needing greater attention. By the time the spinner reached his fifties the strain of over thirty years working in such circumstances had taken its toll. Failing eyesight was a particular problem causing many to seek outside employment. Altogether the environment was an unhealthy one, the air filled with flying cotton particles. Unlike the old hand-mule, the self-actor presented increased dust problems requiring extra cleaning. In Oldham 1½ hours per week was set aside for this purpose, but elsewhere arrangements were made mill by mill and according to the Amalgamation no employers provided sufficient time. Cleaning had to be done during meal times or while the machinery was in motion and when undertaken, as it usually was, by piecers, this was illegal resulting, when the employer could shift the blame, in the spinner being either summoned or sacked. The spinner, then, might be in a privileged position in regard to his own assistants, but if for any reason he lost his job, a new situation was difficult to come by, often necessitating a temporary return to piecing. Whilst a small minority might make their way up the mill to become managers of Limited Companies, the competence spinners showed in looking after their own mules, meant less overlookers were needed, cutting off opportunities for promotion. Once in charge of his own pair of mules therefore, the majority of spinners had reached the limit of their earning capacity with little possibility of advancement. As a labour aristocrat, the spinner occupied a very limited and often impoverished estate.[3]

The Oldham dispute and more particularly the successful defence of wages in 1886, demonstrated the Amalgamation's capability to defend what had already been achieved. What they had, they would hold. The question in the late 1880s and early 1890s revolved around whether wages and conditions could be improved and in part this was dependent upon the industry's prosperity. Fortunately for the Spinners, the period between 1885 and 1891 saw some improvement in the state of trade. After the deepening of the depression beginning in 1885, during the following year trade recovered. Both 1887 and 1888 were fairly good years for the industry and while 1889 saw a brief dip in trade, 1890 witnessed relative boom conditions. It was only in late 1891 that the third of the major troughs in the long depression came to smash prices and wipe out profits. Throughout the period, however, the industry continued to grow. To the *Royal Commission on the Depression* in 1885, the Amalgamation had given the figure of 54,000 persons employed in spinning in its area, made up of 19,000 adult spinners, 9,500 piecers over eighteen, and 27,300 between thirteen and eighteen years old. By 1892 the figure for adult spinners had risen to 20,500 with

41,000 assistants. Spindles in the Lancashire cotton area rose from 41 million in 1885 to 43 million in 1893, a quarter of them in the Oldham district alone. With no major changes in technology, the period saw the wider dissemination of previous improvements and the multiplication of existing machinery rather than any radical shift in the ratio of capital to labour.[4]

Favourable circumstances in industry and trade, while necessary, were not sufficient in themselves to bring about improvements in the spinners' conditions along the lines envisaged by the Amalgamation. If changes were to come by joint regulation rather than by the unilateral control of the Amalgamation imposed by strikes, employers' organisations would have to be extended and improved to facilitate bargaining. James Mawdsley outlined the problem in 1889. Employers' associations were unable to service agreements: 'What they ought to do is to appoint practical men as their agents who should devote the whole of their time to their duties. These could then attend to disputes as they arose without delay and with a joint central committee to deal with cases in which local officials might disagree, there would we believe be few strikes'. John Fielding, Bolton's secretary, a year later, added that he would like to see his own members, 'being compelled, on pain of dismissal from the Society, to refer all disputed matters to arbitration of the two bodies' in his locality.[5]

In 1885 such proposals for this high level of joint regulation had been an impossibility. Either a permanent employers' association representing the majority of millowners in the various towns did not exist or where they did, part-time lay officials, solicitors, directors and proprietors of companies with other commitments, undertook the work of administration. In the spinning area only Oldham Masters had a salaried secretary, who while allowed other business interests, was supposed to devote all the time necessary to undertake the duties implied in full joint regulation. Understandably a wide variety of bargaining levels were practised on issues other than general wage movements with implications for the work of Amalgamation's local secretaries. In Oldham there was a tendency to promote the greater use of the union secretary because the counterpart official existed. In Bolton there was the opposite tendency, the encouragement was towards managers negotiating with their own workpeople until industrial action was imminent and the union official called in. Where no employers' association was formed, as at Stalybridge, this was the final stage of conflict resolution unless the Amalgamation intervened, and while often to the advantage of the operatives, the lack of expertise of the mill manager compared with the local union secretary presented its own problems. Mutual understanding of the boundaries of common practice was absent and agreement in consequence more difficult to attain. The lack of a central employers' association also presented problems, but one from which the Amalgamation took some benefit. Covering the whole of the county, while the employers were divided, the union was fairly happy with the concept of the two main centres of struggle, trading the loss of a comparable negotiating body to the Amalgamation with the gains inherent in a more comprehensive organisation. It was the employers themselves therefore who began to push for a united body of their own, not with the idea of facilitating greater joint regulation, but rather to curb the union's power.[6]

The need to form a single county-wide masters' association had been manifest to the employers' leaders from the 1870s. As already mentioned an attempt to create such a body was initiated in 1878 without success. Not until the Oldham Lockout, or more correctly the inability of that town's masters to gain the second half of the reduction promised in the settlement, was the idea of a central employers' association resuscitated. Having proved to the operatives' leadership that their case for a further reduction was justified, Oldham Masters' Association was faced with the need of another lockout when the rank and file repudiated the agreement and rejected their leaders' advice. Not wishing to maintain their role as the 'centre of struggle', whilst it appeared they would have to close their mills without the assistance of other Districts, Oldham Masters turned to the whole trade and appealed for an Amalgamation of their own. Unable to obtain support from the Cotton Spinners' and Manufacturers' Association (C.S.M.A.) the initiative only succeeded in obtaining an agreement between Ashton, Bolton and Oldham for joint action provided that three-quarters of the spindles in each town signalled their intention to take part in any movement. Immediately calls for an agreement to pursue a wage reduction were made, but a number of the large Bolton firms refused to join in and 1886 ended with the Oldham Masters' Secretary, Samuel Andrew, complaining that the operatives were so united 'that if the employers did not amalgamate in a similar way capital is certain to become for a time at least the servant and not the master of labour'.[7]

The next attempt came two years later with the establishment of a wages committee within an existing organisation rather than with a new body. Formed in 1867, the Cotton Spinners' Association (C.S.A.) dealt with all trade questions other than wages. Its status and influence had not always been high, despite successfully organising short-time in 1880, but with the growing threat from cotton corners in the middle of the decade, the C.S.A., rechristened the United Cotton Spinners' Association (U.C.S.A.), under pressure from Oldham agreed to deal with the Spinners' 5 per cent claim of 1888. Unfortunately for the U.C.S.A. the resistance of the wage claim collapsed and the operatives obtained their rise without a strike. Similarly in the following year Oldham's call for a 10 per cent reduction failed and when a further rise of 5 per cent was conceded in 1890, dissatisfaction with the U.C.S.A. mounted. Oldham, under their Chairman, J. B. Tattersall, sent in a plan for a complete revision of the rules allowing affiliations from District Associations rather than individual firms. Eventually these plans were adopted in December 1891, invitations being issued to all Masters' Associations to affiliate. The inauguration of the Federation of Master Cotton Spinners' Associations (F.M.C.S.A.) in February 1892, however, saw only the Oldham or American sector in membership. The C.S.M.A. stayed aloof, and Bolton, resenting the power of the Limited Companies and the poaching of their fine trade by Oldham firms, tried to form a federation in the Egyptian sector, and it was not until 1905 that their differences with Oldham were settled and one united body created. The new Federation therefore was not as geographically representative as the old U.C.S.A. but what was lost in coverage was gained in commitment and determination to stand up to the Spinners' Amalgamation.[8]

The years when the employers were attempting to improve their own organisations were ones of progress for the Spinners' Amalgamation. Their primary achievement was on the wages front: not only had they resisted further cuts during the depression of 1886, but in 1888 and 1890, wage advances were achieved. Whereas in 1886 the Spinners saw a high 'out of work' expenditure, Districts too poor to pay their levies and cuts at individual mills, by the end of 1890 they had succeeded in restoring list wages to 10 per cent below the original level. Given increased efficiency and speeding up, wages were well above previous amounts earned when lists were at a hundred per cent, (see Table I), and due to falls in the cost of living during the period, real incomes were substantially higher.[9]

Table I — Estimated Average Weekly Earnings of Minders and Piecers in Lancashire and Cheshire 1871-1891

| | 1871 | 1874 | 1880 | 1886 | 1891 |
	s. d.	s. d.	s. d.	s. d.	s. d.
Self-Actor Minders	30 0	33 0	31 0	31 0	36 0
Big Piecers	12 0	14 0	14 0	14 0	15 3
Little Piecers	7 0	8 0	9 0	9 9	10 6

Membership, which had fallen slightly in 1886 to 15,500, steadily rose to over 19,000 by December 1892. Part of this was achieved through the 'spin off' from successful wage advances, resulting in some expansion of the Amalgamation's existing District Association membership, but just as important were new affiliations. Clitheroe rejoined the Amalgamation in 1888, leaving only the extreme north-east of the county and, with the exception of Haslingden, the notoriously difficult to organise Rossendale valley without a federated branch. Later in the same year, after efforts by the leadership, Rawtenstall was brought into the fold, and no existing body of spinners in all the four counties remained unaffiliated. By the beginning of the new decade the Amalgamation had sixty branches, with, beside the two new Provinces, a number of alliances and groups of districts acting together. Rochdale, in particular, was active in attempting to extend its boundaries, establishing branches in neighbouring towns and villages and bringing in other workers such as the warehousemen and packers. Financially the Amalgamation was also making improvements, not least in promoting the reserve fund. Raising the latter levy to 2d per week, and then 3d per week, on the grounds that once the employers united it would no longer be possible to levy those uninvolved, the locally and centrally held reserves combined had reached nearly £100,000 by the end of 1890. At the same time the Amalgamation, still thinking in terms of 'centres of struggle', introduced special strike benefit rules whereby existing rates would be supplemented by a 25 per cent addition on top of the twelve shillings, plus one shilling per child, to those Districts who fought the battle on behalf of the whole. However, the most notable achievement of these years was the establishment of a Bolton List, which incorporated a number of features of the Oldham List, and the closer informal and formal co-operation between masters and union.[10]

Bolton Masters had been trying to negotiate a new list since 1880, but progress was slow. It was not until 1887 that agreement with the union was finally reached and despite the long gestation period the introduction of the list still resulted in the mushrooming of disputes over interpretation. Such disputes served as an important recruiting agency for the Bolton Masters, who had only just re-organised themselves in 1886 with the appointment of a permanent under-secretary as an expert to contradict what they claimed as the local spinners' leaders' misinterpretation of the original 1858 list. However, the new list did fulfil the expectations of its signatories on most of the provisions it contained. Indeed across the whole of Lancashire, the Amalgamation was able to claim that not a single strike had taken place in 1888 due to an 'infringement of any of our lists'.[11]

In one respect, therefore, the period can be characterised as a high point in collaboration between masters and men with both sides attempting to reach a settlement before taking industrial action. No doubt the three-year period of moderately good trade that began with 1888 partly explains why employers sought to compromise, anxious to capitalise on profitable periods before they disappeared. Co-operation was particularly evident in regard to short time, the Amalgamation and Districts encouraging employers to the point of enforcing reduced working on breakaway firms, in a joint venture to break what was now becoming an annual attempt by speculators to form a cotton corner. On this the C.S.M.A. was willing to negotiate and discuss with the Amalgamation its proposal to beat the speculators, as was the newly reorganised U.C.S.A. This latter body extended co-operation to other issues, inviting the Amalgamation to take part in joint deputations to the Home Secretary on a number of questions facing the industry. Further evidence of co-operation came when Albert Simpson, a Preston master, proposed a conciliation scheme which was taken up by the U.C.S.A. Negotiations were opened with the Amalgamation, who along with the proposers recognised that the cost of strikes were a 'waste of strength'. In the end the idea of a Conciliation Board was allowed to drop, the Spinners' Amalgamation regretting 'that the rank and file of our members' have 'not taken the interest in the question that its importance deserves.' At the same time as employers were proposing conciliation, however, the union at all levels was increasingly engaged in 'taking on' the employers, disputes and strikes becoming widespread, challenges being made to what the masters considered their prerogatives. Possibly the employers' willingness to co-operate sprang from this growing threat, but whatever the connection between the two phenomena, the masters' willingness for accommodation was accompanied by growing union militancy.[12]

The causes of this militancy were diverse. Undoubtedly the favourable state of trade and more particularly the growing confidence gained through the collapse of employers' resistance to wage claims played their part. Probably as important was the re-awakening of trade unionism amongst the lesser skilled and the new unionism movement which occurred at the end of the 1880s. With the establishment of organisations among the dockers, gas workers, labourers, seamen and others, trade unionism was growing in strength and influence. Old unions to a greater or lesser degree, eventually became infused with the new spirit of radicalism that characterised the new unions. Some of the old leaders, amongst them Mawdsley, suspected the motives of those new unions which were led by socialists. So anti-socialist was Mawdsley — he pronounced their ideas fit only for the 'scum of London' — that he resigned his seat on the T.U.C. in 1890 over their growing influence within its ranks. The new spirit, however, was affecting the Spinners also, and while socialism itself took some considerable time, if ever, to permeate the Amalgamation, within twelve months Mawdsley was back in the T.U.C. supporting the policy of a statutory eight-hour day.[13]

Among cotton workers too a new zeal was manifest, especially in the cardroom. Following the formation of the Cardroom Amalgamation in 1886, workers in this department had immediately tried to use their new found strength to gain and hold conditions of employment hitherto denied them. Because they lacked a widely accepted list even at District level, and with no clear understanding of the terms by which cardroom workers were engaged, this meant both an attempt to achieve uniformity of conditions by negotiating with the employers' associations and, more importantly, to raise standards at individual firms. Once unleashed, the Cardroom rank and file took up the campaign in their mills enthusiastically, finding new issues on which to demand improvement. Not only did this present problems for employers and their organisations, but it raised issues for the Spinners' Amalgamation. At one level there was the demonstration effect of workers in the same mill winning concessions, but more especially, there was the problem of 'lay-offs' when only one section of the mill was out on strike and how to make such action effective. Previously, when a dispute had occurred involving only a small section of the operatives, only those workers had been withdrawn. Employers in such circumstances found it fairly easy to keep the mill running, engaging blackleg labour to replace those on strike. Now, with the increasing numbers of single firm disputes involving spinners, together with those of the cardroom, an answer had to be found quickly. Within each union the whole of the membership at particular mills could be withdrawn, but what was needed was a joint body of the Spinners and Cardroom to co-ordinate action. 'If a firm has to be struck,' Mawdsley argued, 'let the striking be right from the shoulder' and close the whole mill. With such a plan in view, the two Amalgamations created a federation in 1890 entitled the 'Cotton Workers' Association' (C.W.A.), meetings of which would precede any industrial action. A levy was raised to pay 8 shillings per week dispute pay to all those who were out on the others' behalf, although it was possible for each side to find their own grievance that could be pursued at the same time.[14]

The idea of the C.W.A. was initiated by the Spinners, who had already offered some cardroom workers strike pay from Amalgamation funds if they came out with them, and it was the Spinners who promoted the new organisation, urging its members to influence the cardroom workers to join their respective union. Perhaps there was a little condescension on the part of the Spinners, but it was not particularly resented, Mawdsley suggesting joint shop meetings once a year 'to make each other's acquaintance'. That the C.W.A. was valued by the Spinners is undeniable, and they asserted that its existence was responsible for the favourable outcome of the 1890 wage campaign. After the Brooklands dispute in 1893, the Spinners even approached the Cardroom leaders with the idea of bringing them fully into the Amalgamation 'as the interests of both are identical'. The employers, on the other hand, viewed the formation of the C.W.A. as a menacing development, another goad to improve its own organisation so that in future they could resist the much resented advance as that of 1890 and protect their threatened prerogatives.[15]

Those threats to what the employers regarded as their managerial rights were by 1892 becoming in their sight intolerable. When the Bolton Masters' Association and employers in other towns refused to agree to improved holiday arrangements, the spinners took them unilaterally. Similarly when failure to re-negotiate the long-standing practice of washing mill blinds and windows did not result in a favourable outcome for the union, even Rochdale, not a strong district, refused to do that work. Indeed the whole cleaning issue for a time became in Mawdsley's words, 'the most important question facing the Amalgamation', with individual mill strikes occurring especially when employers attempted to put the onus on the spinner for the prosecutable offence of piecers doing such work during meal hours. More importantly, new attitudes emerged towards the question of supervision; Bury wanted the power to strike several mills to force their owners to employ overlookers in sheds where previously the small number of mules had been thought not to warrant supervisory staff. Other districts struck against the overlookers they had, claiming petty tyranny, described as 'driving', justified in a few cases with some supervisors being prosecuted for assaulting spinners. Mawdsley commented on the increased number of strikes concerning overlookers' behaviour in 1891. 'Although such strikes have at odd times taken place for generations back, they have never, up to the last few months been undertaken in a systematic manner', adding that 'the time has arrived when if the operatives seek to be employed with any degree of comfort to themselves, they must take their share in the internal management of the concerns in which they are employed'. Whereas in 1888 the Amalgamation was saying 'we make no claim to interfere with an employer's business', now they challenged where the line between their business and that of the employers was drawn.[16]

This new attitude was particularly evident on the issue of non-unionism. Whilst in June 1891, Mawdsley had told the *Royal Commission of Labour*, on which he also sat, that there was not the slightest bad feeling between non-unionists and members and that no action was taken against them, a new policy was apparent by the end of that same year. If these people 'will do nothing to navigate the ship', Mawdsley wrote, 'they must metaphorically speaking be thrown overboard or cast ashore. Our resolution therefore, to refuse to work with non-society comrades is a step in the right direction and has already been productive of much good'. This change had been prompted by the fact that the Cardroom had already started striking individual mills against non-unionists, and local spinners had taken up the idea. The Amalgamation was trying to control a movement that was already taking place, giving belated permission for spinners to support such action. Bolton also insisted on bringing in their non-unionists, forcing employers to tell non-unionists to join or leave their situation. Whilst individual employers capitulated, the C.S.M.A. viewed the development 'as a menace to their order'.[17]

To some extent the employers and their local associations were overwhelmed by what was happening, especially in regard to individual mill disputes. Barely able to facilitate negotiations on general wage questions, their organisation and procedures were incapable of dealing with small disputes on this level. Capable of responding to a town lockout, they had no way of dealing with attacks on single firms. The Oldham Masters' Association pushed forward a comprehensive compensation scheme, but the problem of getting a firm to leave disputes to the Association remained. Firms were more interested in fulfilling their own orders than the precedent they might be setting by granting concessions. In consequence the employers' associations were forced to provide generous payments to encourage firms not to open their mills on the operatives' terms. On the other hand, sometimes Masters' Associations officially refused to get involved in settling disputes because of the added authority to any precedent their interference would give. Definitions of what was covered by procedural joint rules became restrictive, employers and union refusing to meet on non-wage issues before strikes or lockouts. In the heightened agitation the relationship between the two sides became strained. Individual mill disputes had always thrown up practices which caused bitterness. During a general wage strike or lockout for the most part it was not worth trying to import knobsticks, but single firm disputes offered a better opportunity for such action. Once knobsticks were employed, picketing, with the possibility of clashes and the involvement of the police, followed. Employers' associations, who had previously frowned on blacklists, now circulated names to surrounding firms to prevent strikers being employed elsewhere and helped in the recruitment of knobsticks. John Fielding, the Bolton Spinners' secretary, commented in 1892, that the employers took alarm at the growing power of trade unions, so that 'every demand of the operatives for the barest justice was described as a further act of dictation on their part. The new found unity of the F.M.C.S.A. was conceived in a hostile spirit and its policy so far has been, at least so it appears to us, largely that of offering battle to the workpeople's unions in an unreasonable desire to reduce the members of these units into such a condition of abject subjection as would leave them little better than serfs'.[18]

The first major clash caused by the employers' new determination to resist the union's growing militancy occurred over a dispute at Stalybridge in 1891. Here a company renowned for its antipathy towards the union, once forcing its operatives to give individual notice for strike action, persistently introduced inferior quality cotton. Always a complex issue and difficult to prove, problems over bad material already accounted for 90 per cent of disputes by 1890 even before the poor crop of that year arrived to make matters worse. In 1889, a town lockout was initiated at

Bolton over a dispute at one firm, but with the wave of individual mill strikes in the early 1890s nobody expected another one at the Stalybridge Spinning Company to cause any real trouble. In 1888, Mawdsley had calculated about two-thirds of employers were willing, following a joint inspection, to reduce speeds and make recompense, and the principle of compensation had spread since then. However, the dispute at Stalybridge proved less tractable, coinciding with growing union militancy, the beginnings of a downturn in trade and the employers' willingness to make a stand. When the dispute began the firm had stood alone but two days before strike notices expired masters in Mossley, Hyde, Ashton and Stalybridge came together to form the Ashton & District Employers' Association and they took over the negotiations offering a joint inspection to determine the genuineness of the operatives' claim. This the local union rejected on the grounds that the union did not need an inspection to prove the material was bad and the strike commenced at the end of September. No further negotiations occurred until the end of December when the union agreed to have an inspection, but the talks broke down on the question of reinstatement and retrospective compensation. From this point on, the Stalybridge dispute escalated, rumours circulating that the employers of south-east Lancashire were 'making an attempt to force a lockout presumably on account of a strike at one mill,' wrote Mawdsley, 'but really because trade was bad'. This was 'good generalship' for them, he conceded, but the Amalgamation was not about to be forced into a fight which was not of their own choosing. In anticipation of the coming struggle the Amalgamation raised levies from 3d to 5d and Mawdsley arranged to drop all conditions other than a joint inspection. This offer was accepted and the operatives resumed work, but three days later the inspectors failed to agree and the strike recommenced, this time with the introduction of blacklegs, picketing, the stoning of a police wagonette and an appeal to the newly formed F.M.C.S.A. for assistance.[19]

Operative leaders were later to claim that the F.M.C.S.A. jumped at the chance 'to test the efficiency of their newly acquired power' but, at first sight, Stalybridge was an unlikely choice. Most employers accepted the idea of compensation for bad material, and it was necessary to blur the issue rather than concentrate on bad spinning directly. Most important was the question of reinstatement, a basic trade union principle which the employers managed to confuse with the non-unionist campaign. Whereas the Amalgamation simply wanted to get the operatives their jobs back, masters deliberately chose to see this as replacing non-union labour with striking trade unionists. Without attempting to negotiate, the F.M.C.S.A. announced its decision to lockout all the operatives in the mills covered by that body, Samuel Andrew claiming 'the question is, who is to govern the trade, employer or employed'. Some 60 per cent of the Amalgamation membership, working 18 million spindles, found themselves locked out from 15 April and with the cardroom workers and others, a total of 54,000 were idle. Negotiations for arbitration fell through and the Bolton Masters pledged support before the Amalgamation sued for peace, dropping reinstatement. In exchange for an agreement for joint inspections the lockout was called off, just three weeks after it had begun.[20]

The F.M.C.S.A. regarded the lockout as a great success, demonstrating a level of unity amongst employers not previously achieved. The utility of their organisation in defeating the operatives had been proved, their confidence was high and immediately its leaders began to contemplate using their power to reduce wages. The Stalybridge settlement was to be merely a truce, a temporary period of peace. Despite only half of the original strikers getting their jobs back the spinners' leaders tried to promote the settlement as an advance. John Fielding claimed that the principle of joint inspection for bad material embodied in the settlement was 'of a character such as we had previously never been able to obtain and which will do much in the future to secure an intelligent treatment of our complaints'. Admittedly a formal agreement now existed with the F.M.C.S.A., and it is possible to see the seeds of future procedural development in the Stalybridge settlement, but Fielding was exaggerating. To begin with the settlement did not apply to Bolton, their employers were outside the F.M.C.S.A. and secondly, as the *Textile Manufacturer* pointed out, what was done was 'merely the registration of a principle which has been in operation in Oldham and Ashton for several years'. Moreover, no rules were laid down as to who should constitute the investigators of complaints, what criteria they should use, what would happen in the event of disagreement and, more importantly, for the issue of bad material, no time limit was specified for such inspections to take place. The rank and file and district officials therefore were not so easily moved to accept their leaders' assessment and protest meetings were held in many areas. As one local official observed, the Amalgamation had 'boasted of being able to lay their hands on £150,000, but yet surrendered after three weeks stoppage, on one of the greatest principles connected with trade unionism. This meant that the whole plan of campaign against non-unionists laid down by the union leaders was a sham'. Eventually what Mawdsley described as 'the foolish and on the whole untruthful gossip' about a 'sell-out' died down, but its legacy did contribute to the important shift in the Executive's thinking which was taking place. With the growth of militancy in the late 1880s the leadership had attempted to put itself at the head of the movement and thereby control it. Now it appeared those same leaders, while wary of being open to attack for moderation and compromise, intended to oppose the extension of demands to new issues and withdraw their sanction of individual mill disputes, especially on non-unionism. During the Stalybridge lockout, Thomas Ashton had been asked if 'there ought to be, or if there ever will be any Board of Conciliation in the cotton trade'. He replied that he did not think so, 'it would not work well in my opinion. Each district must manage their own affairs. We work pretty well together in Oldham. As a rule the masters are too slow for us in the settlement of trade disputes by a joint tribunal'. When the lockout was over such antagonism to the idea of some form of central joint consultative body was not so unattractive to many of the other leaders.[21]

The year 1891 had begun 'with a margin such as would entitle the cotton trade to be looked upon as a veritable El Dorado', but within months trade turned, leaving employers 'growling like bears with sore heads' and talking about a reduction. Stocks mounted when cloth producers reacting to lower prices for their goods reduced purchases of yarn, and the year ended with further deteriorations in spinners' mill margins. It was for this reason that the Amalgamation argued, with some justification, that the Stalybridge dispute was simply a 'peg on which a stoppage was hung'. But three weeks had been insufficient to make a permanent shift in demand and after a temporary respite mill margins continued to fall. By summer 1892 an estimated 1.5 million bales of cotton were left in Liverpool and the difference between the raw material and finished yarn price fell to 2¼d per pound and as 2⅝d per pound was required to make a 5 per cent profit, employers once again returned to the idea of a wage cut. Indeed before the Stalybridge lockout the Oldham Masters' Association had already discussed the possibility of a reduction, preferring to leave it to others to take the lead. When the F.M.C.S.A. had taken up the question in March 1892, only Ashton and Oldham had been keen, but by the summer support was more widespread. One Oldham mill called for short-time plus 10 per cent off list prices and Samuel Andrew, the Oldham Employers' Secretary, passed their letter to his Chairman, J. B. Tattersall, who was also Vice-Chairman of the F.M.C.S.A. Following an informal talk amongst the leadership in July, a meeting of the trade took place, with representatives from Bolton and the C.S.M.A. attending as observers. Hyde District immediately declared against a reduction but supported short-time. J. B. Tattersall countered by proposing a reduction of 10 per cent coupled with short-time and only when this motion was lost, did the meeting proceed with wages as a separate issue, calling for a ballot of firms about a 10 per cent reduction. The result was disappointing for those hoping for action and Oldham was forced to recommend a fresh ballot at the end of the second week of August, this time for a 5 per cent reduction and while this was being done firms outside the F.M.C.S.A. were canvassed for support. On this occasion although just short of the 80 per cent required, the returns were deemed satisfactory. 'But before proceeding to give the requisite month's notice', the F.M.C.S.A.'s leaders decided to, 'arrange a meeting with the Executive of the Operatives' Association with a view to arriving, if possible, at an amicable agreement on the question'.[22]

That the employers were looking earnestly for a settlement is doubtful, certainly nobody on the union side believed this to be the case. 'What they want is a stoppage and as the employers cannot agree upon that amongst themselves, the turbulent spirits amongst them are trying to get a reduction proposed, in order that the operatives will stop the mills'. Believing this to be the case, even when attempts were being made for the 10 per cent reduction, the Amalgamation's leadership reacted in a justifiably angry manner. The first casualty of the campaign was the traditional civility shown by each side to its opponent's negotiators, those employers from the Limited Companies being chosen for special abuse by the Spinners. 'Having a capacity for sticking to money when it gets in their fingers,' wrote Mawdsley, 'and in consequence having raised themselves from the gutter to opulence, they think they are smart and clever.' As to the amount of the F.M.C.S.A.'s claim, the Spinners thought that 5 per cent was so small a figure given the present crisis as to be of no practical use whatsoever, a view echoed by the *Textile Mercury*, the employers' paper. What was wrong with the industry, argued the

Spinners, was the lack of railways in the Far East, the fluctuating price of silver, and the need for a more rigidly enforced Factory Act. If the employers would put their shoulder to the wheel on these questions as they had done on the Corn Laws, wrote Mawdsley, wage cuts would become an anachronism. The F.M.C.S.A. however, did not see the problem in that way, even rejecting the Amalgamation's offer to impose short-time working on employers who were unwilling to join in any movement the Masters' Association cared to organise. Instead the hope that the employers would not 'upset the trade for a paltry five per cent' disappeared when notices were given in October to lock up the mills from 5 November, with the 'parvenus' from the Limiteds, those 'ignorant, self-sufficient slave drivers, with faces of brass', being blamed. The Amalgamation prepared itself by raising levies to 2 shillings per week while notices ran, an extra 4 shillings per week when the lockout started, and calling for loans at 6 per cent per annum. The F.M.C.S.A. for its part wrote asking Bolton to join in, as firms within its own sphere of influence attempted to resign. Various unsuccessful offers came from local Mayors and the Manchester Chamber of Commerce's Board of Conciliation, but neither side thought any kind of meeting was worthwhile and the lockout began. Mills closed and the *Textile Mercury* looked forward to the trade unions being given 'a lesson in a form that should not readily be forgotten'.[23]

Despite the attempted resignations of a few Oldham firms and Mawdsley's belief that the private employers were 'disgusted at the Federation's action', the lockout began with morale low on the Amalgamation's side. Several districts had signalled their possible inability to raise the levy required. Despite such problems, the Amalgamation declared itself to be in a better position than ever before to engage in such a struggle and determined to resist to the best of its ability. The Amalgamation, argued Mawdsley, had no choice but to defend its members from what they saw as the first of a certain series of cuts, suggesting that the F.M.C.S.A. was out to capitalise on the strength they had shown over Stalybridge. In contrast to a short-time campaign when the Spinners would have made every effort to close all mills, a lockout meant that they would be attempting to keep as many mills running as possible in order to maintain levies from working members. In this they were partially successful, by the beginning of November out of its 20,000 members only 7,619 were locked out, 5,500 of whom belonged to the Oldham Province. Two weeks later only 320 firms had closed their doors, 180 in Oldham, 56 in Ashton, 20 in Rochdale and 62 more in Hyde, Stockport, Manchester, Heywood, Darwen and Bury, accounting for some 12 out of the F.M.C.S.A.'s 19 million spindles. Admittedly another few million spindles continued to run, their owners paying the allowable fine for continuing to work, which went to pay compensation to those closing, but still there were not as many locked out as during the Stalybridge dispute. Over the following weeks the F.M.C.S.A. were able to extend its coverage, especially among those firms who were completing contracts but they also had some failures. Bolton Masters, despite F.M.C.S.A. pleading and its own officials' support were unable to get the requisite ballot vote to join in, partly due to better trade in the fine section and partly due to animosity over their trade being poached by Oldham. The

C.S.M.A. for its part was divided, particularly after the unions had agreed with them to follow any settlement arrived at in south-east Lancashire. Two ballots were necessary before the required two-thirds in favour of running short-time was achieved. By January 1893 therefore although 71 per cent of Oldham Spinners were on dispute pay and 56 per cent in the rest of the F.M.C.S.A.'s districts, in the Amalgamation over all only 34 per cent were out. Seemingly, the *Textile Mercury* was correct in suggesting that the Amalgamation's coverage of a total of 40 million spindles left them better organised than the masters.[24]

This is not to say that managing to keep the lockout from spreading meant that the problem facing the Spinners' Amalgamation was small. Although only just over a third of its members were out central levies had to be raised to 5 shillings per week, which necessitated some spinners paying a weekly total of 6s 6d to the union. Bolton was turned to for a loan of £20,000, which with the income from the levies enabled 7,000 spinners and the 16,000 piecers to be paid their full strike allowance, until almost the end of the dispute. Less fortunate was the Cardroom Amalgamation whose own 20,000 members faced real hardship. With the Spinners unable to provide financial support, bankruptcy had occurred in some Cardroom Districts by December and their Amalgamation began to fragment with disaffiliations from some local associations who could no longer pay the levy. Appeals to other trade unions brought in some money to keep going, but by the end of February 1893 this too was running out. Worse off still were the 10,000 operatives who did not belong to any union: these were forced onto charity and parish relief. Despite such hardship there was little in the way of unrest, with no knobsticks to challenge there were no picket lines, and the deprivation was born stoically and quietly. The union's staunchest critic, the *Textile Mercury*, praised the operatives' behaviour, 'They are going about the matter in a very business-like manner, and so far as we gather, there is comparatively little asperity displayed by them against those who side with capital'. Even when some firms attempted to re-start at the 5 per cent reduction, picketing was unnecessary as nobody went in.[25]

Unfortunately what the operatives considered as their patient sacrifice to protect themselves and the trade by removing stocks, did not result in an immediate improvement in margins. While it was true that the stoppage had stimulated fine spinning, thus helping Bolton, the margin for medium counts remained low. Stocks were simply so high that the increased exports in December 1892 over the previous year made little difference to demand, and despite the silent mills the price of raw cotton rose, necessitating a greater selling price to maintain the margin as it was. In such circumstances the employers felt no need for compromise and neither they nor the Amalgamation called for a further meeting during 1892. Behind the scenes, however, suggestions towards a settlement were already being made, J. B. Tattersall putting forward the idea that employers should not ask for another reduction or the operatives ask for an advance 'until some other important centres' such as Bolton had altered wages first. On the operatives' side at the beginning of December a proposal for accepting the 5 per cent cut provided that short-time of forty-two hours was worked, failed to obtain a seconder, but by the beginning of the new year it had become the Executive's policy. From now on there was always the gap between the rhetoric of the public platform and what was being discussed round the table.[26]

Informal negotiations began in the first few days of 1893 and, following the invitation of Rochdale's Mayor, a full joint meeting was held on 12 January. The operatives' leaders had power to offer the 5 per cent reduction providing that only forty hours were worked, the wages to revert to old levels when full time resumed. The employers countered by insisting on the 5 per cent reduction, no further movement for one year, and no recognition being given in their arguments of the now improving margins. This latter point was returned to at a second conference held a fortnight later when again the F.M.C.S.A. 'intimated that however profitable trade may be, they will insist on having the five per cent. On this declaration being made the operatives declined to prolong the discussions'. Official negotiations broke down but events looked as if they were moving in the operatives' favour when on the following day it was noted that the Bolton Masters once again would not be able to support the F.M.C.S.A. Mawdsley reported unofficial negotiations with individual employers who would be seen again on the compromise of 5 per cent and short-time. Four days later, the Executive went on the offensive suggesting that the employers from the Limiteds 'whose friends never accuse them of having brains' were prolonging the dispute with a view to 'inflicting a crushing defeat on the operatives . . . It is not for us to advise fighting tactics, but it is certain that unless the employers are severely punished for this they will again be domineering when any trouble arises'. Both sides now looked even further apart than ever before. In February J. B. Tattersall was cheered at a full meeting of the F.M.C.S.A. for his firmness on the 5 per cent reduction and on the non-unionist question, while at a Special Representative Meeting of the Amalgamation their usually cautious Chairman, Thomas Ashton, announced that he would 'never advise men to accept the employers' terms'. It was a 'war to the knife' he declared and now that the margin had improved it was 'not a question of 5 per cent, but of mastership'. Yet despite this hardening of attitudes unofficial negotiations were continuing which would eventually lead to a settlement.[27]

Exactly what happened may never be known as no transcripts of unofficial talks were kept, minute books are missing and surviving accounts vary. On the masters' side a reading of the autohagiography of Charles Macara, of Bannermans and the Manchester Association, suggests that the illness of both the F.M.C.S.A.'s Chairman, Arthur Reynor, and its Secretary, William Tattersall, allowed him to take a more active part and move the employers towards conciliation, but this exaggerates his role. More important, as Mawdsley asserted, was the fact that when the margin reached 3½d. per pound, 'This was "pie" to producers and had the effect of making the mouths of those who were stopped water with envy'. The F.M.C.S.A. it appeared had reached the limit of its support and with only breakaways likely in the future, even its most hard-headed members realised there would be no outright victory. Firms who had backed the F.M.C.S.A. because of the poor margins rather than any idea of breaking the unions were already becoming discontented, requiring repeated visits to keep them in line. While the Ashton Masters' Association, the

exception, argued for going back to 10 per cent, Oldham firms wrote to their
Secretary with excuses for resuming production and suggested ideas for compromise.
The changing position on the union side is more difficult to discern, not least
because of the missing evidence, but also in the secrecy of the Spinners' unofficial
meetings with the employers. Writing to one firm on 1 February urging their
continued support, Samuel Andrew noted that 'the 2.5 per cent had already been
decided as inadmissable and I do not expect we shall hear more of it'. He was wrong
on the second point, but the letter suggests that already there had been talk of
splitting the difference.[28]

What is known, is that early in the same month the Cardroom Amalgamation
approached their solicitor, Robert Ascroft, who had helped negotiate a list agreement in 1889 and 1890, and asked him to approach the employers on their behalf
with the proposal for a compromise cut in wages. Ascroft accepted the mission,
contacting local Oldham employers including Hilton Greaves, a personal friend,
and it was from this initiative that a critical undermining of the Oldham Masters'
unity emerged. By 18 February, Samuel Andrew had written to Joseph Lees, M.P.,
asking him to use his influence on Bagley who 'in league with Greaves will start on
2.5 per cent. This will be a serious blow to the Federation'. Meanwhile, on the same
day, with some recognition of financial problems, the idea of splitting the difference
had become official policy of the Amalgamation. Reporting that in the previous
week negotiations with 'other parties representing some of the employers' had
revealed that a compromise of 2.5 per cent would settle the dispute, the delegates
at the Spinners' Representative Meeting endorsed two proposals, a straight 2.5 per
cent or that amount now to be given back or doubled after three months dependent
on trade.[29]

The Spinners' proposals were rejected by the F.M.C.S.A. on 21 February, but
two days later a joint meeting took place when J. B. Tattersall, the acting
F.M.C.S.A.'s Chairman, suggested 2.5 per cent now and a further 2.5 per cent in
three months without reference to trade, adding that:

> Providing the operatives' association undertakes in the event of any dispute
> taking place in a mill that the two committees have an opportunity of meeting
> together and settling the matter before any local strike or lockout takes place.[30]

Furthermore, he went on to propose that in exchange for the F.M.C.S.A. not
supporting an employer who sacked an operative for merely being a union member,
the Amalgamation must drop their insistence on the closed shop. If these two
proposals were accepted, the employers would be prepared to recommend that, in
the future, wage movements be limited to 5 per cent. In order that the two sides
might jointly turn their attention to those questions seriously damaging the cotton
trade, Tattersall concluded his proposals by declaring that the F.M.C.S.A. earnestly
desired a settlement. The operatives also earnestly desired a settlement, but
'without giving either side a claim to victory', and therefore while welcoming the
procedural clause, the 5 per cent limit for piece workers and the help with trade

problems, they could not accept a further 2.5 per cent cut in three months without reference to margins; as to the part concerning union membership, that was ignored. Whilst to a small extent it was clear that both sides were interested in saving face, no further compromises could be made and the talks broke down, their importance having been in the ideas suggested by Tattersall, which would be included in a final settlement.[31]

With the breakdown of the negotiations, the following few days saw the movement among individual employers in Oldham recommence with vigour, work beginning at firms employing some 2,000 hands. Bolton Masters again failed to get sufficient support to work short-time to aid the F.M.C.S.A. and public sympathy together with some sections of the press now began to back the operatives against the employers' uncompromising stand. All this did not appear to upset the F.M.C.S.A. too much, not publicly anyway, perhaps because they believed that the operatives' leaders would have accepted the 5 per cent had their mandate allowed them, but also because they managed to get a number of firms to close who previously had only run short-time. As for the union side, despite rank and file criticism of the offer to accept any cut, the Spinners' Executive moved forward with individual employers in the hope of using 2.5 per cent as a basis of settlement. On 2 March, one of these employers wrote to Mawdsley suggesting work commenced at the compromise reduction, with a restoration or further cut after six months, dependent on the margins at selected mills, which if the operatives would accept, he would obtain the Masters' Association's views. Mawdsley replied immediately with a positive answer and by 4 March, the Masters had the terms under consideration.[32]

Meanwhile further attempts by firms to open at 2.5 per cent met with rejection by the Spinners because they feared that mills then working without a reduction might be tempted to adopt the same, but by 8 March that policy was reversed. What had happened was that on the previous day Robert Ascroft, whose intervention in the Cardroom negotiations of 1890 had been resented by J. B. Tattersall, had invited all sides for dinner at his private residence at Prestwich, where over five hours discussion the operatives' leaders offered an unconditional 2.5 per cent reduction and later 3 per cent. That there was a real commitment to come to a settlement was obvious; the F.M.C.S.A. offered 3.75 per cent (9d in the pound) along with the previous procedural clauses which had been amended by Ascroft to include two stages before a strike/lock-out could take place, meetings of local secretaries and then local committees. Had the employers not insisted that the union 'forego their right to refuse to work with non-unionists' a compromise might have been arranged, but as it was negotiations foundered on this condition. Within two days, however, the employers had prepared a draft agreement, leaving blank the specific amount of a reduction and submitting it to the operatives via Ascroft. This refinement of both Tattersall's and Ascroft's procedural claims suggested that the preceding three years' profits rather than current margins be the criterion for future wage movements and while still containing the anti-closed shop provisions added that they regarded the union 'as a most convenient medium for settling disputes', and, therefore, they would 'rather be inclined to encourage than discourage all operatives who voluntarily join some trade union'.[33].

With the existence of a written draft agreement the process of amendment and counter-amendment began, the Spinners putting in 2.5 per cent where the blank was and dropping the clauses referring to past profits and non-unionism, which surprisingly, apart from the amount, the F.M.C.S.A. accepted. Apparently, employers' local associations objected to the clause referring to union membership, because it would stop a settlement being reached. The sticking point of the amount, however, proved more difficult to agree. Ascroft informed the employers that the Spinners were 'tired of being played with' and that further talk was useless until they accepted the operatives' compromise. It was clear that by mid-March the Spinners were in no mood for further concessions, refusing to meet the F.M.C.S.A. unless the 2.5 per cent was agreed upon. An impasse had been reached with neither side being willing to make an adjustment prior to negotiations re-opening. Constant pressure from the press for news and speculation that a breakthrough was imminent, meant that all parties involved needed a break to restore strained nerves. Ascroft invited Mawdsley away for the week-end and although it is not known whether his influence changed Mawdsley's mind, the following week an arrangement was made for a joint meeting with the F.M.C.S.A. without any prior pledges on how much any reduction would be.[34]

The historic meeting that took place on 23 March 1893 at the Brooklands Hotel, seven miles from Manchester, was attended by a large delegation most of whom had no idea where the conference was to be held until they arrived at Oxford Road station in Manchester. The meeting place was being kept secret to avoid the eyes of press and public and as a result its deliberations took on an air of mystery. Of all the various reports of what happened, perhaps the most unelaborated and certainly the most frank was that which first appeared in the *Christian World* by 'One Who Was There'. According to this writer, the two sides met separately in the morning, coming together for the first time at the railway station. Arriving at the hotel just after mid-day the delegates again met separately, before finally opening a joint session around three o'clock, when the 'goody-goody clause number one, setting forth the desirability of settling all disputes in an amicable manner, was ticked off at once in the most prompt and agreeable fashion — equivalent to the performance of shaking hands before entering into the conflict'. The second clause, on the amount, however, took a little more time, both Mawdsley, leading the operatives' side, and Tattersall the employers, retiring with their respective parties before responding to offers. The first major move came from the employers who dropped their demand down to 3 per cent instead of the operatives' offer of 2.5 per cent, but because the unions took a long time discussing this, tea intervened. After grace said by Arthur Reynor, the F.M.C.S.A.'s President recently returned from illness, both sides sat down together. Negotiations after tea began by exchanging notes rather than face-to-face discussions and eventually the employers were prevailed upon to move to 7d in the pound equivalent to 2.9 per cent, which was accepted. Further negotiation on the remaining clauses continued until 5 o'clock the following morning, when the Brooklands Agreement — the industry's so-called 'Magna Carta' — was signed with no mention of previous profits nor of trade union membership.

Instead, apart from an addition to the procedural clause allowing for an appeal to the central bodies representing masters and men, little in the way of new sections were incorporated into the settlement that had not been virtually accepted in previous negotiations (Appendix XI). However, this simple addition was significant, for with it an agreement now existed whereby the final authority to settle disputes was no longer a local one. Tired, the employers left to catch the six o'clock train, while the operatives stayed behind to thank Ascroft for his work, not only for his draftmanship, but also for the proposals he had submitted at his home earlier in the month. The mills reopened on 27 March after twenty weeks, and the unprecedented expenditure by the Spinners' Amalagamation of almost £152,000 of their funds.[35]

The immediate reaction to the news from the conference was that while some spinners' District Associations welcomed the agreement, a minority showed their disapproval by threatening not to return to work. The delegates who assembled on 25 March however gave, in contrast to the Stalybridge settlement, a unanimous vote of thanks to the General Secretary and the whole Executive Committee, ratifying the agreement by a large majority. Mawdsley himself viewed the dispute as having achieved its purpose and the compromise over the wages reduction as a victory. They had 'rectified the markets and brought one of the most powerful combinations of employers in the Kingdom to divide a comparatively small demand of a five per cent reduction'. Fielding was more outspoken declaring that 'we have shown that reducing wages in future to be an undertaking so costly and hazardous that the game will not be worth a candle'. On the employers' side, the leaders claimed an 'honourable settlement', with the hope that its provisions would in the future prove useful. Press reaction from those traditionally supporting the employers however was divided. The *Textile Mercury* claimed they had 'only heard dissatisfaction' with the settlement; the *Textile Manufacturer*, on reflection, saw both good and bad in it, while the *Textile Recorder* welcomed the agreement under which masters and men 'henceforth will meet not as enemies, but as friends in council'.[36]

The reason for these diverse reactions to the settlement was the various and widely differing ideas of what the dispute was about. For those who saw the lockout as an attempt to break the unions it was either a victory or a defeat depending which side one supported. Apart from a wish to bring about an improvement in the market, what the F.M.C.S.A.'s leaders wanted was contained in the procedural clauses. It was J. B. Tattersall for the Oldham employers who had set out in 1889 to bring the procedures up to date. He wanted a joint meeting even when the issue was one on which the employers believed their managerial prerogatives ought normally not to be challenged, but all the same 'undue advantage' might have been taken. In 1890 he at last got a verbal agreement from the Oldham Spinners to make it a condition that neither side take action until the two committees had had an opportunity to discuss the matter within seven days of notices being given. This understanding was later ignored by Thomas Ashton, who refused to set up a joint committee to draft a written rule, but Tattersall continued throughout 1891 to try and implement it. Similarly, it was Tattersall who, once the F.M.C.S.A. existed, began referring disputes to that body, no doubt to delay settlement and bring the maximum pressure to bear, but at the same time informally introducing what was later to be the centralised bargaining Brooklands procedure. With such evidence it is easy to see that the employers were not trying to do away with the unions in the Brooklands dispute, but rather bring them into a system of bargaining which limited the power of the Spinners' rank and file. Indeed, even the *Textile Mercury* saw the unions as useful, arguing that the F.M.C.S.A. 'should counteract — not coerce — the power which the workers possess'.[37]

The employers' original rationale for district wage lists was to control competition between themselves over labour's price; with it had come the bonus of trade union officials acting as interpreters, either jointly with the Masters' Secretary or on their own, of the list clauses. This had limited the union's role in the work place, allowing for the most part the employers to manage as they wished within the traditions and practices of the industry, enforced when necessary by the Spinners' shop. When the Spinners' militancy of the late 1880s and early 1890s came to challenge those customs and practices, attempting to extend their rights and curb the employers' ability to restrict existing ones, or introduce new work patterns, it was the employers who began pressing for procedures like those incorporated in Brooklands in order to keep non-wages disputes out of the mill as well. The extra tier of an appeal to the F.M.C.S.A. level was added to take not only any dispute as far away from the individual mill as possible, but also to allow the influence of less militant spinners' districts and their officials to play a part in the conciliation process. For the employers therefore the success of the Brooklands settlement was not to be found in the immediate wage issue at stake, but in the long- term consequences for joint regulation. At the end of 1893 Oldham Masters were already recording that the joint rules were 'getting nicely into practice and with a little alteration here and there', are 'likely to be generally satisfactory to both sides.'[38]

In accepting the procedures laid down in Brooklands, the Spinners did not agree with the employers as to their purpose. Essentially what they wanted was a more orderly conducted day-to-day relationship with capital and the protection of their funds. As far as the procedures contributed to that end they were welcomed. Indeed the various clauses of Brooklands contained many of the proposals the leadership had been advocating for years and to some extent were merely the extension of Oldham's procedures to neighbouring towns. The wider practice of joint regulation to that half of the cotton spinning industry in Lancashire covered by the F.M.C.S.A. was therefore seen as a good thing. Together with the similar arrangements existing in the C.S.M.A. area and under the Bolton list which provided for dispute procedures, the Brooklands agreement meant all the county had some form of formal negotiating rights and conciliation machinery. Apart from Thomas Ashton, who already had more procedures than anyone else, the appeal to a central body for final conciliation in the F.M.C.S.A. area was also welcomed by the Spinners' leaders. Poor employer organisation and expertise at the local level could be compensated for by the F.M.C.S.A. officials and to some extent the Amalgamation's leaders would gain greater control over the District and their rank and file. Now that non-wage issues were more firmly included in joint regulation such control over the ordinary members meant the policy pursued since the Stalybridge lockout of discouraging what might turn out to be financially disastrous disputes was more easily attained. Challenges to the boundaries of employers' prerogatives would in future have to go through procedures and only after the Amalgamation's leaders had failed to bring about a settlement could action take place. Provided the employers bargained in good faith and implemented the spirit as well as the letter of the agreement the Spinners' leaders saw in the procedures an opportunity to promote the kind of industrial relations they, perhaps more than their members, desired.[39]

The Spinners' leaders' reservations concerning the employers' good faith were well justified. Within weeks the differences in interpretation were becoming evident. Worst affected was the Cardroom Amalgamation whose lack of agreements on job content and wage lists meant more cases to go through procedures; but the Spinners ran into immediate difficulties too. Employers deliberately delayed calling meetings and even when a joint conference took place showed no commitment to conciliation. Often the same employers who had been part of the negotiating team at local level, reappeared when appeals to the F.M.C.S.A. were made and all the same arguments had to be gone through again. Over the same period as the Oldham Masters recorded their satisfaction at the way the procedures worked, Mawdsley noted 'loud complaints are being raised by the operatives that the employers persistently refuse to carry out its provisions in the temper in which they were drafted contenting themselves with saying 'No' to most of the questions submitted for consideration and adjudication'. The Amalgamation was so frustrated at the delaying tactics adopted that they even talked of striking all mills 'if the employers cannot bring themselves to deal' with disputes 'within the agreed fourteen days' promised in the Brooklands Agreement. Thomas Ashton, in putting forward a resolution in April 1897 to withdraw from the agreement, commented that the 'four years' experience we have had in dealing with individual mills . . . convinces us that the formalities cause extraordinary delay . . . give rise to considerable dissatisfaction amongst our members, and place them at a great disadvantage compared to the position which it gives the employers'. What the employers had lost over 'a trifling 5 per cent' it appeared, they had won by regaining control in the mills. In 1893, however, consideration of what the procedures of the Brooklands Agreement meant for the long term was not at the forefront of the Spinners' leaders' minds. Their Amalgamation had withstood one of the major industrial battles of the nineteenth century and justifiably they felt congratulations were in order.[40]

By 1894 with membership level and finances restored, from the Amalgamation's new address at 3 Blossom Street, Great Ancoats, Manchester, the officials looked back over the previous nine years with some sense of achievement. Wages had been improved and even the cleaning question had seen progress with agreements for extra time being signed at Bolton in 1893 and Oldham in 1894. In terms of organisation, too, advances had been made, so that all areas of the county had spinners affiliated to the Amalgamation and in the C.W.A. and the U.T.F.W.A. relationships with other unions in the industry had been strengthened. Over the period the Spinners' Amalgamation had also become less exclusive, Districts opening their ranks to warehousemen, roller coverers, under-engineers, stokers and overlookers. On the other hand not all of the Spinners' leaders' aims for better industrial relations had been fulfilled. In the creation of the F.M.C.S.A. and the procedural clauses of the Brooklands Agreement some advances had been made towards the structure and system necessary to facilitate joint regulation, but not all. Now district employers' associations had been formed and a few more local officials had been appointed to full-time posts, but for a time the employers still had inadequate organisations and staff to administer their required function properly. To get those 'practical men' Mawdsley had asked for, the employers were forced to recruit from amongst the active trade unionists who had the expertise. For the moment, the burden of administrating agreements fell disproportionately on the Amalgamation and its District Association officials. On occasions this led to the Union secretaries appearing to be between the members and the masters, as policemen rather than advocates for the operatives' cause. The image of the cotton spinners' leader had become one of the union bureaucrat.[41]

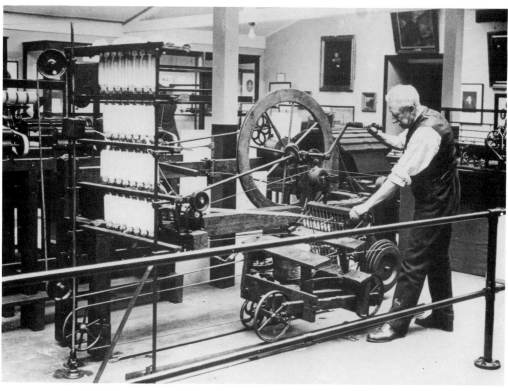

Samuel Crompton's mule being demonstrated in c. 1930. The carriage has been shortened.

*Mule spinning factory c. 1835 showing the spinner by the hand-wheel, a female piecer
and a scavenger cleaning under the machinery.*

Emblem of Associated Cotton Spinners of Manchester c. 1829.

Interior of mule spinning factory c. 1840.

TO THE

OPERATIVE COTTON & SILK SPINNERS

SELF-ACTING MINDERS, TWINERS, & ROVERS,

Of Lancashire, Cheshire, Yorkshire, and Derbyshire.

This Society is based on the following principles, viz:—To afford assistance when any district is turned out for an advance, or against a reduction in prices; and for the redressing of any grievances between employers and employed; but that no turn-out be allowed, under any circumstances, until every legal means have been tried to adjust the same honestly and fairly to both parties.

At a Meeting of Delegates held at Manchester, on Sunday, May 24th, 1846, Delegates were present from the following places, viz:—Manchester No 1, Manchester No 2, Bolton, Oldham, Ashton-under-Lyne No. 1, Ashton-under-Lyne No 2, Waterhead Mill, Lees, Saddleworth, Preston, Duckenfield, Newton Moor, Woodley, Chowbent District, Wheelton, Mossley, Shaw Chapel, Hadfield, Burnley, Blackburn, Padiham, Glasgow, Hebden Bridge, and Central.

NUMBER OF DELEGATES 33, FROM 23 DISTRICTS.

The following Resolutions were agreed to:—

1.—That the minutes of last meeting be confirmed.

2.—That a deputation wait upon Mr. Wilding, of Padiham, and endeavour to prevail upon him to give the advance required; if he will not comply with their request, the deputation be allowed to give notice for the men.

3.—That the secretary go to Staley Bridge, to give instructions to the men on strike at Mr. Thomas Kirk's mill.

4.—That the Piecers at Mr. Lawrence Law's mill, Lees, in case of a strike, be taken on pay by the Central Committee.

5.—That a deputation attend a meeting, to be held at Sowerby Bridge, on June 7th, 1846, to explain the principles of the Association.

6.—That a deputation be appointed by the above meeting, to wait upon the employers of Cragg Vale, and endeavour to prevail upon them to give their men an advance.

7.—That no mill in any district be allowed to give notice for an advance, until the district in which that mill belongs, has sent its list of prices to the Central Committee.

8.—That if a deputation be requested to wait upon the men of Hadfield, their request be complied with by the Central Committee.

9.—That each delegate meeting in future, appoint three persons, who shall that day audit the accounts of the Central Committee.

10.—That the delegates from Scotland be requested to visit those districts that they have not yet visited; and if a general strike takes place, we support them to the utmost extent in our power.

11—That the levy to the Central Committee be twopence per member per week; but if they find it to be inadequate to meet all the disbursements, they advance it to threepence per member.

12.—That the next delegate meeting be held at such time and place as the Central Committee deem most beneficial for the interest of the Association.

PROPOSITION FOR DISCUSSION AT THE NEXT MEETING.

That each delegate (at the time of paying the levy) state the number of spinners &c., in his respective district, also the number of paying members.

MANCHESTER RACES.—Mr. William Fair, of the Woodman's Hut, Gt. Ancoats-street, Manchester, begs leave most respectfully to inform his Friends and the Public in general, that he has again taken No. 17, BRICK BAR, where he intends to have a choice assortment of the best Ale, Porter, & Spirits, and begs that by strict attention to the comfort and convenience of those who may favour him with a call, to merit their patronage and support.

N.B.—The BAR lies between the Starting Chair and the Grand Stand, and will be distinguished by the rim of a Spinning wheel placed on the Stand over the BAR.

WAITERS DURING THE RACES:—Messrs. Arrowsmith, Brindle, and others connected with the Spinners' body, will be in constant attendance.

Signed on behalf of the Central Committee

THOMAS BRINDLE, *Secretary.*

R. WHEWELL, PRINTER AND STATIONER, LITTLE BOLTON.

Handbill of Spinners' Association, 1846.

Three generations of spinners in an Oldham mill c. 1900.

Little piecer cleaning up cotton waste in the mule-gate c. 1900.

A mule spinning team c. 1910.

Spinners and piecers in the mule-gate c. 1910.

Fine spinning team c. 1910 pause during the process of doffing; note the bare feet and the oil stained and torn trousers.

William Leigh, first President of the Amalgamation (1870-76).

*William Heginbotham, General Secretary of the Amalgamation
(1875-78).*

James Mawdsley, General Secretary (1878-1902).

Thomas Ashton, President (1878-1913).

CHAPTER SEVEN

The Spinners and the Rise of Labour

The years between the conclusion of the Brooklands Agreement and the First World War saw a dramatic reshaping of the industrial and political landscape. Throughout industry employers tended to develop trade associations or federations as part of a general strategy of confronting the growth in the power of industrial labour. The trade unions also found themselves embroiled in a variety of legal actions relating to their rights with regard to picketing and immunity from civil action arising out of industrial disputes. At the same time, the trade unions were also faced by the opportunities and challenges presented by the emergence of the Labour Party at the turn of the century.

Alongside these general developments which came to impress themselves on the Spinners' Amalgamation were the multiplicity of issues dealt with by the union arising out of the particular circumstances of the cotton trade. Among the most pressing were the general, often sharp, fluctuations in the prosperity of the industry, the recurring problem of the piecers, and the operation of the Brooklands Agreement itself. In tackling these issues the leadership of the Amalgamation, together with their full-time officials, appeared to display behaviour characteristic of the prevailing labour aristocratic ethos of the 'old' unions. Consequently an emphasis upon negotiations and the avoidance of industrial disruption and the search for agreements and procedures to produce automatic dispute resolution underscored the cautious moderation of the leadership. Such leaders were characterised by respectable appearance, a commitment to self-improvement, and a businesslike approach to industrial questions.

However, as with so much of the discussion of the nature of the 'old' unions, the emphasis upon the style of leadership and the emphasis on collaborative approaches to employers obscures more than it reveals. At all times the Amalgamation was willing, and often very able, to engage in effective militant industrial action. Indeed it constantly prided itself on its preparedness and capacity to undertake sustained industrial action. While leaders and officials held out the Brooklands Agreement as a model form of industrial conciliation, an industrial Magna Carta, they did not do so from a sense of social inferiority or lack of resolution. They did so because they believed it to be in the interests of the industry as well as the union. But while looking for more co-operation with employers, they understood the limits of that self-interest. Thus throughout this period the Spinners' leaders reflected that complex, often contradictory and paradoxical mixture of labourist attitudes; a desire for conciliation, administrative arrangements and collaboration co-existing with a fierce independence, determination and militancy in support of union objectives. Above all else the Spinners displayed a highly developed sense of sectional interest which could be pursued in various ways and in a variety of forums.

With the conclusion of the Brooklands Agreement the structure of the Spinners as an amalagamation was firmly in place. At the end of 1893 the Amalgamation had some 19,326 members and was divided into two Provinces, Oldham and Bolton, with a further division into Districts. While the two Provinces comprised a number of local Districts, some 31 individual, relatively small Districts existed outside those Provinces. This produced a marked diversity in size between the Districts such that the Bolton District of the Bolton Province had 2,260 members in 1893, some 22 other Districts had less than a hundred members each, with Warrington, Little-borough and Ramsbottom the smallest Districts with only 20 members each.

The supreme legislative body of the Amalgamation was the Representative Meeting which was composed of members from the Districts and/or Provinces elected in proportion to paid-up members. In 1895, for example, the Representative Meeting comprised some 115 representatives, of whom 25 came from the Bolton Province and 38 from the Oldham Province. There was some variation in these figures over this period, but the essential balance remained stable, underlining the key role exercised by the Provinces in the Amalgamation as a whole. The Representative Meeting appointed the President, General Secretary and Treasurer of the Amalgamation. In addition it elected 15 members to sit on the Executive Council with the three appointed officers. The Executive Council then elected a sub-council responsible to it, comprising six members of the full Council, normally full-time officials, with the General Secretary and Chairman of Council present ex-officio. The Amalgamation performed two principal functions. Most importantly it was responsible for tackling general industrial disputes, local strikes and lockouts. Secondly, to carry out this function it was required to accumulate a large fund to conduct disputes. The Amalgamation also paid benefit to those left out of work after a strike and administered various benefits payable in the case of death or permanent injury. Later the Amalgamation came to administer the Mawdsley-Ashton Memorial Fund, which provided a pension to the five oldest spinners or former members.[1]

The Provinces and Districts possessed considerable autonomy over the administration of a variety of local friendly society benefits. They dealt with employers on a day-to-day basis over wage questions and conditions of work, and fixed their own friendly society subscription rates and benefit levels. Some of the larger Districts and Provinces paid unemployment and strike pay in addition to the Amalgamation's benefit, as well as normal sickness and funeral benefit. These local units tended to guard their functions jealously and there was always a degree of tension between themselves and the Amalgamation on the relative merits of centralisation versus decentralisation of functions. This often took the form of disputes about whether or not to centralise friendly society benefits, which the Amalgamation favoured but which the local areas successfully resisted after it was mooted in 1903. Such issues were not merely technical questions but rather questions of principle involving the independence of the Provinces and Districts.

However, notwithstanding the existence of local autonomy the real dynamic in the union was the Amalgamation. It was the key to the long-term prospects and effectiveness of the Spinners because in the final analysis the basis of the union's position rested on its ability to undertake general, co-ordinated and protracted strike action. To do this necessitated the possession of sufficient funds together with a firm organisational grip on the productive process, and it was the Amalgamation which provided these for the spinners. The lockout of 1892-3 had cost the union almost £152,000 in strike pay, yet by 1894 funds had been restored to the pre-lockout level. This was achieved because members paid a high union contribution for a low scale of general benefit. In the words of James Mawdsley, the Conservative-inclined General Secretary, this was essential to provide:

> a good margin for fighting purposes as money cannot be spent by the hundred thousand unless it is there to spend. Low contributions and large benefits have ruined half the trade unions . . . and are sapping the usefulness of most of the other half. If there were less sentimental talk about moral force and a little more practical recognition of the power of material wealth the bulk of the workers . . . would not long be grovelling under the heels of unscrupulous exploiters of labour.[2]

In 1894 the Spinners, along with the other cotton unions, were confronted by two important issues; the question of labour political representation and the demand for the eight hour day. The question of labour representation emerged at a time when cotton unions were beginning to doubt the effectiveness of their traditional methods of applying political pressure on those Members of Parliament representing cotton constituencies. The Liberal Government had recently imposed a duty on the importation into India of cotton yarn and cloth despite a promise to the United Textile Factory Workers' Association (U.T.F.W.A.) that nothing would be done without consulting Parliament.

> The wonderful thing about the whole business is that none of the 50 or 60 M.P.s who represent constituencies more or less dependent on cotton . . . could even enter a protest in Parliament . . . until they were driven to it . . . Taken in aggregate they are about as incompetent a set of old women as ever sponged on an industrial community.[3]

One solution appeared to involve the direct representation of cotton operatives in Parliament. The first tentative steps in this direction were taken by the U.T.F.W.A. in 1894 where it was decided to seek the opinion of the members on the question of labour representation. In their report the Legislative Council of the U.T.F.W.A., no doubt prompted by James Mawdsley and David Holmes of the Weavers, suggested that one or two candidates be put forward as Parliamentary candidates. It was pointed out that such an initiative could only succeed if 'members are prepared to sink politics and tolerate differences of opinion on other subjects so long as those who might be elected are sound on labour'. This was an interesting interpretation of labour representation but necessary for unions whose members were divided between Liberal and Conservative Party supporters. At a meeting of the U.T.F.W.A. held in January 1895, the new political departure was carried a stage further with the suggestion that two suitable candidates be put forward. This led to the convening of a further meeting of the U.T.F.W.A. at which it was moved that James Mawdsley and David Holmes be nominated. It was clearly hoped that Holmes standing as a Liberal and Mawdsley as a Conservative would constitute a balanced 'Party' ticket and thus prevent a political split amongst cotton operatives. In the event Mawdsley declined to stand and the issue was dropped.[4]

In fact the Spinners' Executive had decided in March not to participate in any scheme for promoting labour representation believing, in response to 'strong party feeling', that it would damage the internal unity of the union. This decision followed the ballot of the members in late 1894 which showed them to be about equally divided on the issue, with 6,496 favouring labour representation and 6,145 voting against. The same ballot showed 8,053 in favour of the eight hour day, with 5,550 members voting against.[5]

The leadership tended to link the two issues, seeing effective Parliamentary representation as essential in securing the Eight Hour Day, and interpreted the result of the ballot as a support for the existing status quo. It seems clear that Mawdsley was disappointed at the outcome. He felt that without a separate form of Parliamentary representation cotton workers could only secure their legislative objectives by converting the existing Members of Parliament. This possibility seemed remote to Mawdsley, who asserted that:

> only a few MPs were really friendly to the legislative aspirations of the Union . . . So long as the majority of Cotton Operatives are either indifferent to the Eight Hour Day with a large minority even opposed to it, we shall find it difficult to make headway . . . Even if all the operatives were in favour of the proposal it would make no difference so long as they sent M.P.s to Parliament who were of the opposite way of thinking . . . of some sixty to seventy men who in Lancashire and Yorkshire sit in Parliament as representatives of more or less textile districts, there are not more than half a dozen who are pledged to an Eight Hour Day . . . What is wanted is that workers should vote as they talk, or better still stop talking for a time and vote the right way.[6]

While the Conservative Mawdsley seemed willing to countenance a new political departure for the union, others, notably Thomas Ashton, the veteran leader of the Oldham Province and President of the Amalgamation, and John Fielding, Secretary of the Bolton Province, were more sceptical. Fielding, like Ashton, was a Liberal in politics and doubled as the Secretary of the Bolton Trades Council.

The political question for the Spinners throughout this whole period concerned not independent labour representation, but labour representation as such. Was it prudent to intervene directly in party politics? On the one hand there were certainly legislative objectives to pursue, but on the other was the threat to the unity and hence industrial strength of the Amalgamation which might follow in the wake of partisan politics. Parliamentary objectives might have distinctive labour characteristics like workmen's compensation or the eight hour day, but they might just as often be wholly sectional and shared by the employers, as with the issue of Indian Cotton Duties. This variety, coupled with the political spread of spinners, who at least shared in the considerable working-class Toryism of Lancashire, argued for a prudent and above all pragmatic response to party politics.

This dilemma had not so much been 'reconciled' as deflected by the creation of the U.T.F.W.A. to handle political questions, as it were, at one step removed. However, the classic formula for abstention from political involvement was always the notion that industrial strength would itself suffice. The great dispute of 1892-3 had apparently reinforced such feelings amongst spinners, and its resolution had confirmed their exclusive and aristocratic position at the top of the textile industrial structure. Its political implications were consequently more limited than many socialist activists anticipated.[7]

If the Spinners displayed an ambivalent attitude to the question of labour representation, their relationship with socialism was unambiguously hostile. Industrial self-confidence, the ability to help oneself within the confines of a trade, was a most effective antidote to socialism and no trade union had greater justification for this feeling than the Spinners. No union had less reason to replace its trade identity with a class identity. It has even been argued that the Spinners were hostile to the idea of mass trade unionism in the cotton industry. H. A. Turner is responsible for pointing to this negative face presented by the Spinners to the development of mass class-based unionism in cotton, suggesting that

> as the group with an established and prior hold on the industry, it must have
> at least appeared to them that the organisation of other workers was as likely
> to be to the Spinners' own cost as to that of their employers.[8]

In fact, by the time of the arguments about labour representation the Spinners had encouraged the development of the Cardroom and Weavers' Amalgamations who shared their non-socialist political instincts. The Spinners saw the developments as favourable in the sense that they were seen as likely to reduce the number of local disputes and as a contribution to an orderly system of industrial relations in the industry. Socialists, on the other hand, could be identified, in terms of union organisation, as those disruptive elements who made periodic attempts to organise the piecers independently of and implicitly hostile to the Spinners' Amalgamation. J. R. Clynes and Tom Mann had both separately figured prominently as socialists engaged in such an endeavour.

The attitude of the Spinners to socialists was largely reciprocated by many socialists of this period, who were at best equivocal in their attitude to the union, and often simply hostile. British socialism in the 1890s had not yet prostrated itself on the altar of indiscriminate, sectional, industrial strength. There remained a substantial tradition from Chartist times of regarding trade unionism as inherently sectional and intrinsically divisive. In the particular case of craft unionism, this divisive sectionalism was combined with a high level of conservatism and an economic logic which made it as much the enemy of the unorganised poor as of Capital.

Even as unions like the Spinners gravitated towards the idea of labour representation, they did so within the confines of a perspective shaped by the limited objectives and aims of their particular interests. This movement did not require of them a political affirmation or commitment; rather, it represented a kind of political denial. The argument for labour representation was articulated in terms of the need to put aside party political differences in favour of labour interests. It was not a question of labour politics but labour interests which transcended 'normal' party politics.

When the Spinners finally resolved on direct political intervention it should not have surprised the Independent Labour Party (I.L.P.) that the impact was not in accordance with the aspirations of that party. Indeed, at the 1895 T.U.C. the cotton unions gave notice of their anti-socialist instincts when, under the direction of Mawdsley, they combined with the Miners' Federation to block the advance of the socialists. They forced through a series of amendments to the T.U.C.'s rules in three areas. The Socialist-dominated trades councils were disenfranchised, the system of block voting was introduced, thereby strengthening the hand of the cotton and coal unions, and socialist activists were effectively excluded from the Congress. This latter point meant that Keir Hardie could no longer participate at the T.U.C., but Mawdsley's main political target may actually have been Henry Broadhurst, the Liberal-inclined Secretary of the T.U.C.'s Parliamentary Committee.[9]

However, having rejected the idea of labour representation in 1895, the Spinners were thrown back on the established medium of the U.T.F.W.A. to pursue their political objectives. The General Election of 1895 represented a high point in the exercise of such pragmatic pressure politics. In Lancashire the election was dominated by the issue of Indian cotton duties and allowed the cotton unions and employers to mount a joint campaign against the Liberals. The effect was an agitation that the Conservative M.P., R. G. C. Mowbray, recorded as so 'overpowering and unanimous . . . [that] . . . if one does not vote with one's constituents one may as well save oneself the trouble of standing again'. Mowbray was one of two Conservative electoral casualties in Lancashire and saw his defeat as a direct consequence of his support for the Liberal measure.[10]

Elsewhere the election saw a sustained swing to the Conservatives, most pronounced in Oldham where Robert Ascroft and J. F. Oswald were elected. The election of Ascroft, a well-known Oldham solicitor, is particularly revealing about the relationship between cotton trade unionism and politics in a cotton town.

It was not so much that he was thought of as an ardent Conservative as that he was regarded as the man most likely to win the seat under that party colour. It was understood that he . . . desired a 'business member' for Oldham . . . the trade interests of the great cotton spinning town required special Parliamentary attention . . . When the matter was more widely considered it was felt that no one could better give this attention than the man who had done excellent service for the labour interest of the town.[11]

When Ascroft died in 1899 the cotton unions sent warm messages of condolence to his family testifying to his efforts on their behalf. He had been actively involved in the affairs of the Cardroom Amalgamation and was closely involved in the Brooklands Agreement. But Ascroft was one of a vanishing breed and with its passing the cotton unions began to reconsider their political tactics.

However, the immediate problem confronting the Spinners at this time was the depressed state of the trade which lasted until 1897. The Executive clearly anticipated an imminent employers' offensive against wage levels and was anxious to avoid the possibility of any major, general dispute. The membership was urged to show discipline and caution: 'There should be no unwise raising of disputes at individual firms, where it can possibly be avoided, and our members will do well to do their utmost to give satisfaction in their work'. To that end the Executive's advice to its Provinces and Districts on individual disputes throughout 1895 and 1896 was a variation on the theme ' . . . it was not thought advisable to push the case'. By the close of 1896 there was much satisfaction that a major conflict with the employers had been avoided. Such strikes as had occurred had mostly involved firms unconnected with the Federation of Master Cotton Spinners' Associations (F.M.C.S.A.) and even these had been generally settled amicably. The membership was informed that union funds stood at an impressive £198,000 and that a few 'more years such as the last will put the Amalgamation in an impregnable position so far as the general reduction of wages is concerned.'[12]

As trade began to improve, a new potential source of industrial conflict emerged over the operation of the Brooklands Agreement. It was argued by many Districts, most particularly in Oldham, that local firms were using the Brooklands disputes procedure in a way designed to stall the resolution of localised disputes. In virtually all instances these disputes concerned the perennial problem of bad spinning which came to haunt the Brooklands Agreement and threatened its very existence. Bad spinning occurred when inferior cotton being spun broke, which slowed down the whole productive process, with obvious consequences for those paid by the piece. Spinners tended to blame sub-standard cotton for the problem, although it may also have been due to the increase in spinning speeds.

Whatever the cause, it was a constant source of friction for spinners, and led to disputes with employers when trade was good. The Spinners held talks with other union signatories to Brooklands and pressed the F.M.C.S.A. to amend the agreement to ensure that its 'spirit' was reflected in practice. The issue dragged on for over a year before it was apparently, though not finally, resolved by an amendment which entitled the operatives to take action sooner than previously allowed if complaints were not dealt with promptly.[13]

The resolution of the constitutional wrangle over the Brooklands Agreement was followed almost immediately in the autumn of 1897 by the F.M.C.S.A.'s demand for a 5 per cent cut in wage levels. Both sides accepted the principle that the demand be put to arbitration, but in practice neither side could agree on the precise terms around which arbitration could be based. However, before the issue could be put to the test the wage cut demand was withdrawn in the face of improving trade in early 1898.

The lesson which the Spinners' Executive drew from this withdrawal by the employers, which took place almost contemporaneously with the defeat suffered by the Amalgamated Society of Engineers, was typically hardheaded:

> This is that industrial conflicts are not decided by sentimental twaddle about 'rights' . . . Employers are undoubtedly on the war path and . . . we must not make the mistake of assuming that the capitalist lion is, in future, going to lie down with the labouring lamb. What is wanted is not only a good central reserve fund but plenty of money locally.[14]

The revival of the cotton trade which gathered pace throughout 1898 and remained buoyant until 1903 enabled the Spinners to mount a campaign to regain the wages lost in the 1892-3 dispute. Armed with an overwhelming mandate for industrial action from its membership, the Executive successfully pressed the F.M.C.S.A. to restore in full the wage cut which the Spinners had conceded in 1893.[15]

The ability of the Spinners' Amalgamation to maintain their industrial position and even regain lost ground at a time when unions like the Amalgamated Society of Engineers were suffering major defeats needs some comment. At the end of the century, technological advances allowed employers the opportunity of undermining the strength of craft unionism by means of new machinery allied to new sources of labour. The Engineers had been defeated on this issue and on the face of it the Spinners were singularly vulnerable. The emergence of ring spinning marked a technical advance on the traditional mule system which threatened to undermine the spinner. The cotton industry in the world at large, and in the U.S.A. in particular, had been transformed by the new technology. Yet in Britain the self-actor mule remained predominant and the spinner continued to exercise an important role in the spinning process.

A number of historians, notably Lars Sandberg and William Lazonick, have confirmed and documented this phenomenon, although interpretations of its causes differ. In broad terms Sandberg argued that the mule remained more profitable, given British costs, for the finer, higher count yarns, and that consequently the pattern of demand for British cotton goods accounted for the persistence of the mule. Lazonick, however, claimed that the preference for mules was more thorough-going, and is explained by the English patterns of industrial relations and the organisation of the industry, particularly its vertical specialisation.[16]

Most interesting is Lazonick's claim that the unique strength and posture of English cotton trade unionism was an important factor in the rapid development of technological backwardness in the cotton industry of Lancashire. This posture was integrally associated with the spinner-piecer relationship and the exclusion of female operatives from mule spinning. Lazonick details a series of technical developments which had earlier been conditioned by the features of this unique system. Its central position in the mind of the union can be expressed thus:

> . . . by the late nineteenth century the minders recognised full well that their relatively high wages were based, not on special technical skills or mental abilities, but rather on the power of their unions to keep their wages up, which, in the context of the threat of the joining system at least, meant their power to keep the wages of piecers down.[17]

The proscription of female labour not only continued but was extended. The strike in 1886 against the employment, at Lostock Mill near Bolton, of three female minders, resulted directly in the Bolton Province voting 'that members in the future decline to teach or cause to be taught the trade of piecing to any female child'. Thus the exclusion of females from spinning was extended in Bolton to piecing after decades of acceptance. Interestingly the Spinners were involved in a dispute relating to the use of women spinners at the Brown and Nephew Mill in Wigan as late as 1895. Non-union female spinners are known to have persisted in the Wigan and Manchester areas and may actually have been more widespread than has generally been supposed.

In these circumstances employers were unwilling to rationalise the division of labour and refrained from any serious attempt to introduce the female operated ring-frame. However, where the traditional labour structure of mule spinning already existed, they could intensify the work process as the one area where collaboration with the Spinners' union to increase productivity was possible within the accepted framework. Intensification of work was acceptable to spinners, paid by the piece, and its consequences largely suffered by piecers, generally paid on a fixed wage.

> . . . the minders could pass much (but by no means all) of the extra work onto piecers, with no extra remuneration to the latter . . . they were willing to trade-off more work (for the minder-piecer unit as a whole) for more earnings (for themselves).[18]

It is important to recognise that this resistance to the ring-frame technology was not direct or confrontational on the part of the Spinners' union. The Amalgamation was always highly aware of the competitive position of Lancashire cotton and consistently took a long view on matters concerning both technology and competition. Their opposition to the ring frame was based on the contention that it was a technology only applicable to the production of lower or coarser cotton yarn, and not to the higher counts which they associated with their skill. Consequently the industrial relations position dovetailed with a variety of factors in making employers, who after all still derived managerial advantages from the minder-piecer system, disinclined to embark on unknown territory.

The Spinners, consequently, concerned themselves little with the threat of the introduction of ring spinning on a wide scale, although its vague possibility may have had some effect in hastening their co-operation in productivity-boosting measures on the alternative mule technology. In fact the average number of spindles per self-actor mule increased from between 720-960 spindles in 1870 to around 1,080 in 1910. At the same time the average speed rose from 7000/8000 revolutions per minute to 8000/9000 by 1910.[19]

This was not primarily a gain for the cotton masters. According to G. T. Brown: 'The reasonable conclusion seems to be that a large proportion of the economies reaped from technical progress have been offset by the high cost of meeting the demands of workers . . .' Incentives to efficiency in general were further muted, both by the union's and the Factory Acts' obstruction of the introduction of a double-shift system. The persistence of the one-shift system tended to 'limit the market shares of the most efficient mills and, what is the obverse, permit a larger number of less efficient mills to remain in the industry'.[20]

If the Spinners were able successfully to deflect the threat posed by new technology, the potential threat posed by the piecer was always present. The big piecer was capable of carrying out the function of the spinner and might emerge as a strike breaker at any point. To offset this possibility the Spinners sought to organise piecers within their own organisation, and while not allowing them full 'citizenship' generally undertook to give them dispute pay and in certain Districts various benefits. The extent of this type of organisation and benefit provision varied from district to district and was generally more extensive in the larger districts. In the returns to a questionnaire sent out by the Amalgamation in 1898, it appears that in Bolton and Oldham a combined total of more than 19,000 piecers were organised in the union. In Bolton the main piecer paid a weekly subscription of 2d, which entitled him to general and local dispute pay and funeral benefits.[21]

From the perspective of the Spinners it was vital to prevent any independent form of piecer organisation from gaining currency. Attempts at such independent organisation occurred in 1889 and at the turn of the century, when Tom Mann tried to organise piecers in the Workers' Union. Further attempts were made to develop piecers' unions, most notably in 1908 and 1914 when a Bolton union was formed with a claimed membership of 1,000. Nonetheless it seems beyond dispute that the Spinners were able to contain the piecer problem quite effectively before 1914. Perhaps the particular localised nature of the cotton industry and the youth of the piecer allowed the spinners to create a kind of occupational hegemony. The spinner explained his relationship to the piecer in terms of the idea of apprentice-ship. The main piecer was generally between 18 and 24 years of age and was supposed eventually to graduate to the position of spinner. The normal method for filling vacancies was on the basis of seniority, but the whole conception of an apprenticeship required an expanding industry, in which an increasing number of spinning opportunities could be created.[22]

Between 1893-1905 the number of spinners remained stationary and indeed fell at various times. In 1893 there were 19,327 spinners in the union and this figure was not surpassed until 1905 when the membership stood at 19,451. It reached a low point in 1897 when the recorded figure was 17,760, and averaged about 18,000 over the period as a whole. This meant that while the piecer might aspire to the position of spinner, the opportunity was generally lacking. The expansion of the related textile engineering industry represented an important safety valve in these circumstances and it appears that many piecers gravitated to the industry in their middle twenties. Those who were tempted to participate in independent piecers' unions had to recognise the potential cost in terms of their aspiration to spinner status. As the *Cotton Factory Times* observed in 1899, those who joined the Workers' Union would forfeit the interest of the spinner and the right to posts based on seniority would be similarly forfeited. In the event the rapid expansion of the cotton spinning industry in the decade before 1914 relieved much of the pressure by increasing the piecer's chance of his own set of mules. Indeed, between 1905 and 1908 membership of the union went up by 3,386 to 22,837.[23]

However the most pressing issue at the turn of the century was the political sphere, with the textile unions re-entering the political arena in 1899 by reactivating the U.T.F.W.A. This was a significant development, given that the unions had only decided to suspend the direct operations of the U.T.F.W.A. some three years previously. On that occasion suspension had been accepted on the basis that the organisation had achieved better law and administration for textile operatives than any other section of workers and little more in the way of legislative benefit seemed likely in the near future. The decision to reactivate the U.T.F.W.A. was initially a response to the creation of an Employers' Parliamentary Committee on which leading cotton employers occupied prominent positions. However, it was soon involved in a variety of related campaigns on issues close to the interests of its constituents. In particular it urged legislative amendments to the 1875 Employers and Workmen Act, the 1897 Workmen's Compensation Act and the 1895 Factory and Workshop Act. In addition the F.M.C.S.A. advocated the complete abolition of mealtime working and the closure of all mills at midday on Saturdays.

At one level the reactivation of the U.T.F.W.A. might be interpreted as a return by the cotton unions to traditional pressure politics. At another it can be seen as one aspect of a process of development and change in the nature and course of spinner trade unionism. Certainly the period between 1899-1903 witnessed a level of activity on the part of the spinners which had scarcely been equalled before, for its scope and intensity of purpose had not been equalled since 1889-93.

On the wages front the Spinners' Amalgamation were able to take advantage of the favourable trading position of cotton by seeking a further increase on that obtained in 1899. In March 1900, Mawdsley instructed the Districts to give one month's notice of a demand for a 5 per cent increase in wages. This demand was first conceded by employers in the Bolton District and then throughout all the spinning districts which were organised, leaving most members 'on as high a piece rate as . . . for forty years'.[24]

In August 1900 the Spinners' Executive reached an agreement with the F.M.C.S.A. on the issue of mealtime work. The demand for an end to such work, which involved extensive maintenance work on the machinery, was initiated by the Rochdale District at the end of 1899. The agreement which was finally accepted involved the ending of all mealtime working except that of oiling the machinery. Implementation and enforcement of the agreement was held to be the responsibility of the local Districts.

One of the most significant consequences of this arrangement was the boost it gave to shop floor organisation. The existence of organisation within individual mills was well established, but it was often social in character and where it assumed an industrial dimension, in terms of enforcing norms of industrial behaviour, it tended to be secretive to prevent victimisation. Now the local representative or embryonic shop steward was well known to mill managers, as were those on the mill committees. It was increasingly common for internal problems to be resolved in meetings between the mill manager and the mill committee. The overall effect was the emergence of an increasingly powerful layer of lay officials who proved more militant than the F.M.C.S.A. anticipated. Indeed, in Oldham, where the development was most pronounced, the increase in militant industrial activity just before 1914 can be attributed in large measure to the influence of such lay officials. Its full significance was not seen until the end of 1918, when rank and file activism posed a threat to the power of the union leadership itself.[25]

The gains in terms of wages and mealtime working had been achieved relatively easily and with little initial acrimony. However, two further problems confronted the Spinners: the raising of the minimum age at which children could be employed as half-timers, and the demand for the ending of Saturday work at twelve o'clock and not one o'clock. The first problem posed an awkward dilemma for Spinners' leaders, while the second represented an aspiration long held by the membership. At around the turn of the century as many as 100,000 half-timers were employed in the textile industry of Lancashire. Most were involved in weaving, but many were involved in spinning as 'little piecers'. The Education of Children Bill introduced in Parliament in 1899 contained a provision for raising the minimum age at which children could be employed on a half-time basis from eleven to twelve years. This measure was opposed by rank and file cotton operatives, notably weavers, and formally by the U.T.F.W.A. Indeed it has been suggested that one factor in the revival of that body was the need to fight this legislative proposal.

In fact it seems clear that the leaders of the textile unions, while formally opposed to the measure, were basically sympathetic to its objectives. George Harwood, Liberal M.P. for Bolton and Chief Parliamentary Spokesman for the U.T.F.W.A., along with John Kenyon, M.P. for Bury, actively supported the raising of the age. Harwood informed the House of Commons that while the Spinners were concerned, 'they have made no protest at all, either in public or private . . . their opposition, if opposition it can be called, has been of a feeble and half-hearted character'. It is clear that the half-time question was something of an embarrassment to textile leaders, and the enactment of the minimum age to twelve years was accepted with some relief. However, the embarrassment was to recur throughout the next decade as attempts were made in Parliament to eliminate the practice, with general trade union support outside the textile areas.[26]

By contrast, the demand for the midday stoppage on Saturdays was taken up by the textile unions, led by the Spinners, with enthusiasm. There had been no reduction in the 56½-hour week worked by textile operatives since it had been laid down in 1874. However, the demand for half-day Saturdays had been raised first in 1871 and had resurfaced periodically thereafter. At the 1895 General Election it had been an issue in Lancashire and Yorkshire textile constituencies and was again taken up by the Amalgamation in September 1899. The Spinners then took the leading part in the attempt by the U.T.F.W.A. to negotiate the reduction from the employers, which in turn foundered on the argument that it would undermine the international competitiveness of British cotton goods. The issue was resolved in 1901, when George Harwood and John Kenyon forced an amendment to the Factory and Workshop Acts and Bill currently under discussion in Parliament. Technically the amendment on the reduction of Saturday working was to apply to women and children, but the reality was to bring about a general reduction for textile operatives. Opponents argued that the whole issue was artificially created by those interested in attending soccer matches, a 'football stop', and that it had little support among the operatives themselves. In the event, a ballot on the question called by the U.T.F.W.A. showed overwhelming support for the reduction, by 165,447 to 6,191. Among spinners, including piecers, the vote was 43,102 to 521.[27]

George Harwood headed off a final attempt by the employers to defeat his measure by pointing out that throughout Lancashire 'every machine and every engineering shop' closed at twelve o'clock on Saturday and that a reduction in the hours of work to 55½ per week could not seriously threaten the health of the cotton industry. The reduction which came into operation in 1902 represents the only general reduction in working hours achieved by textile workers between 1874 and 1914. According to Mawdsley it brought the hours of spinners into rough approximation with those of comparable groups of organised workers.[28]

While Mawdsley had been actively at the forefront of the various agitations and negotiations initiated in 1899 he also found himself in demand on the political front. Oldham found itself in the unusual position of facing a double-member by-election in 1899 and Mawdsley was approached by the local Conservative Association to run in tandem with Winston Churchill. He decided to stand, having secured permission from the Spinners' Executive and with a concession from the Conservative Association that allowed him a free voice on all labour questions. In the event neither Mawdsley nor Churchill secured election and Mawdsley was criticised by some who suggested that had he stood as an independent trade unionist he might have united the textile vote and thus prevented a Lib-Lab vote being deployed against him.

Whatever the merits of this argument, Mawdsley was clearly a unique phenomenon within the Spinners, and indeed the wider trade union movement. He was the
only example of a leading trade union official who appeared as a Conservative in
politics, and yet he proclaimed a general, even 'unequivocal' commitment to
independent labour representation. What he did not possess was any belief in
socialism, which he saw as irrelevant to the trade unionist. What he did articulate
was a particular conception of labour representation based on a pragmatic appreciation of labour interests rather than labour politics. In essence, for Mawdsley,
labour interests were self-evident and could be separated from political opinions,
which were the personal possession of individuals. Where labour interests were
concerned Mawdsley was relentless in their pursuit, and this gave him a radical
quality. He supported Tom Mann's minority report on the *Royal Commission on
Labour* (1892-5) and endorsed the candidature of the socialist Harry Quelch at the
Dewsbury by-election of 1902. However, Mawdsley's dominating presence in the
Spinners' Amalgamation was brought to an abrupt end with his death in February
1902. Mawdsley was succeeded by William Howarth following the now established
practice of a competitive examination designed to test the candidate's technical
and statistical understanding of the industry's operations. Ironically, Howarth
was subsequently recruited as Secretary of the Employers' Federation in a move
which caused no friction between the two organisations. The Secretaryship of the
Amalgamation then passed to William Marsland in 1904.[29]

While much of the activity of the Spinners at this time was concentrated on their
particular interests, they were involved in the wider changes taking place within
trade unionism. The industrial environment of the 1890s was characterised by an
increase in tension between employers and unions and the growing involvement
of the legal system in trade disputes. The growth of employers' federations was
accompanied by a more aggressive attitude towards trade unions. Within the
T.U.C. moves were afoot to strengthen the industrial position of individual unions
by constructing a new federation which could provide assistance, especially financial
assistance, to unions involved in major disputes. This idea came to fruition in 1899
with the formation of the General Federation of Trade Unions (G.F.T.U.).

The G.F.T.U. attracted affiliations from more than fifty trade unions and saw its
object as promoting industrial harmony by ensuring that members would have a
central reserve fund from which they might be authorised to draw money to sustain
disputes. This fund was to be created out of affiliation fees and could only be drawn
on in amounts related to fees and in certain circumstances. The concept was
attractive to the Spinners and the other cotton amalgamations, particularly since
its philosophy of industrial self-sufficiency through large centrally collected and
administered reserve funds reflected almost exactly their own. In May 1899 the
Spinners obtained a mandate to join the G.F.T.U., with Thomas Ashton and James
Mawdsley appointed to the General Council as their representatives.[30]

The G.F.T.U. appeared to mark an important development in British trade
unionism and certainly attracted enthusiastic support from the Spinners' leaders.
Yet its promise remained largely unrealised and it was rapidly overtaken in

significance by the contemporary movement which brought the Labour Party into being. This movement was a response to the growing insecurity felt by many trade unions and especially to their vulnerability to legal interpretation of their activities by the courts.

At the T.U.C. of 1899 a resolution permitting affiliates to participate in a conference to be held in the new year, with outside bodies, notably the I.L.P., Fabians and Social Democratic Federation, was passed. This was carried because the miners and textile unions decided to abstain on the issue, although Thomas Ashton on behalf of the Spinners claimed that 'if their Society was to interfere in politics it would go down immediately'.[31]

Despite Ashton's strictures the Spinners' Executive decided to send two members, A. H. Gill and James Billington to the foundation conference of the Labour Representation Committee (L.R.C.) in February 1900. At the same time the event attracted little real attention, being seen as just another body seeking to further the political aspirations of trade unions. Even the presence of Gill and Billington should not be overstated for, as the *Cotton Factory Times* observed:

> Although the Amalgamated Cotton Spinners have decided to be represented
> . . . it does not follow that they will fall in with the decision of the Conference
> . . . The Operative Cotton Spinners are very much divided on political
> questions, and there is very little chance of their being brought to a frame of
> mind for acting together on the subject.[32]

However, the case for direct, independent labour representation was given a decisive boost by the legal decision handed down by the Final Court of Appeal on the Taff Vale case. This case centred on a strike organised by the Amalgamated Society of Railway Servants against the Taff Vale Railway Company. The company successfully sued the union for damages arising out of the claim that the union had acted unreasonably. This decision, which threatened the efficacy of the strike weapon, was initially treated by the Spinners' Executive as a rather academic issue somewhat external to the union's affairs. Indeed the Spinners thought that the Taff Vale decision merely clarified the terms of the 1875 Conspiracy and Protection of Property Act which they felt did not allow 'peaceful persuasion' during picketing. The Spinners pointed out that members would '. . . see clearly that all that men, when picketing, are allowed to do is to attend at or near the place where the business is struck . . . for the purpose of giving or obtaining information'. Thus the implication was that the legal decisions were correctly applied against 'very ignorant men' engaged in intimidation.[33]

The contemporaneous case involving the Blackburn Weavers helped to shake the rather complacent attitude of the Spinners' Executive. The Blackburn case, besides being much closer to home, was specifically brought on the question of picketing without any implication of intimidation. In 1902, the Weavers accepted legal advice to settle the issue out of court and this, together with the realisation of the amount of money which Taff Vale had cost the railwaymen, induced the Spinners to draw a political lesson. This lesson was emphasised in the annual report of the U.T.F.W.A. for 1901, which asserted:

> There is one point in the work of 'lobbying' M.P.s that drives home . . . it is this: the want of a member in the House of Commons that understands what is desired from the workers' standpoint; and the sooner textile workers make up their minds to be represented by one of their own class, the better it will be.[34]

The following year the Weavers' Amalgamation decided to enter the political arena directly by nominating their Vice-President, David Shackleton, to stand as an independent Labour candidate at the forthcoming by-election at Clitheroe. At the July 1902 conference of the U.T.F.W.A., Thomas Ashton moved the resolution supporting Shackleton's candidature and the Conference resolved that 'this organisation of textile workers should endeavour to obtain direct representation in the House of Commons'. To that end it was agreed to ballot the memberships of the affiliated amalgamations on support for Labour Representation, and secondly on the payment of a levy to effect such representation.[35]

The result of the ballots was overwhelming support for both propositions. In the case of the Spinners the vote was 9,978 in favour of Labour Representation with 3,057 against and 9,634 for a political levy with 3,407 against. Within the vote there were interesting variations between Bolton and Oldham. In Bolton the vote on Labour Representation was carried by 1,045 to 182, while in the Oldham Province it was carried by 3,535 to 1,735. Oldham accounted for more than 60 per cent of the 'against' votes. This was a significant variation with implications for the subsequent attempts to develop labour politics in the two strongholds of the Spinners' Amalgamation. However, following the ballots it was decided by the U.T.F.W.A. to put up one candidate each in Oldham and Bolton, which were two-member constituencies, whenever an opportunity arose. The candidates chosen were A. H. Gill and Thomas Ashton, the Spinners' leaders in Bolton and Oldham Provinces.[36]

The surface appearance of politics in Oldham and Bolton could not present a greater contrast. The former was fraught with conflict and disappointment for the enthusiasts of independent labour, whilst the latter exhibited a smooth transition from the apolitical postures of the 1890s to a stable and successful pattern of labour representation. Gill was elected to Parliament in 1906 and successfully returned at the two elections of 1910, while no Labour candidate actually fought a Parliamentary election in Oldham before 1911. Yet the politics in both towns were the same — resistance to the I.L.P. and a rejection of political involvement. As a consequence the dominant influence of the Spinners' Amalgamation in Bolton and Oldham made it difficult for the I.L.P. to thrive and this prevented the establishment of any real independent tradition of labour politics.

When the Spinners did enter the political sphere it was with their own brand of moderation, which was imposed with little difficulty, and their domination of the trade union sphere was translated into a similar relationship with the political, wholly without rank and file vitality or any groundswell of change in political attitudes. It is noteworthy that the ballot of 1902 on labour representation asked the same precise question as in 1894, apparently oblivious to the idea that the meaning of 'labour representation' had undergone any transformation since 1900. The location of Spinners' political activity had changed, but the underlying political values remained largely unaffected.

However, it remains the case that the electoral success of Gill in Bolton was in marked contrast to the state of labour politics in Oldham before 1914. In Oldham the Trades and Labour Council called representatives of various societies together in July 1903 to promote the cause of Thomas Ashton as prospective Labour candidate. By early 1904 it was stated that the Oldham L.R.C. had some eighteen separate committees with a total membership of some 440 individuals of whom a quarter were spinners. The Oldham L.R.C. seemed to be developing in a solid fashion, appointing an election agent, until it was reported in October that

> owing to unforeseen circumstances Thomas Ashton . . . has found it necessary to retire from the position of Parliamentary Labour candidate.[37]

This withdrawal, which came abruptly, apparently without prior warning, in late 1905, made it impracticable for labour to put a credible replacement into the fray, and set an unfortunate precedent for the future course of trade union-labour politics in Oldham.[38]

In Bolton, A. H. Gill fought and won a seat in 1906 on a platform which provides a fascinating insight into labour politics mediated through the Union. Bolton, like Oldham, was a two-member constituency, but unlike Oldham had some minor tradition of labour politics. At the 1895 General Election an I.L.P. candidate standing without union support obtained a vote of 2,694, which suggested some potential for a Liberal-Labour ticket with cotton union support. The 1895 election saw a Liberal candidate win one of the Parliamentary seats by splitting the two Conservatives and at the subsequent General Election in 1900 the Liberals and Conservatives divided the seats without an election taking place. With the emergence of the Free Trade versus Protection issue post-1903, Bolton represented a classic opportunity to run a Liberal-Labour ticket along the lines prescribed by the secret MacDonald-Gladstone electoral pact. But in this case the ticket was ideologically as well as tactically apposite, in that the ideological content of Gill's platform was classically Liberal. Gill distinguished himself as a 'Free Trader without limitations', meaning that he did not believe in any retaliation over protective tariffs. He was particularly concerned with the high level of public expenditure and attributed the depression of domestic trade to its relentless rise since the 1880s. His proposals for reform of the electoral system are equally interesting. They anticipated an easier system of registration, the abolition of plural voting and the holding of elections on one day. The extent of reform did not reach manhood suffrage, let alone votes for any category of women.

Gill was very much a Spinners' candidate and reiterated that Bolton's industries needed looking after by men who knew the 'technicalities'. Gill certainly did, and the major controversies of his candidature were inter-labour disputes concerning the piecer. Predictably Gill defended the traditional structure of the industry and claimed that big piecers had a bright future occupying a similar position to engineeering apprentices. He also defended the practice of imposing a fixed wage on piecers, arguing that if the Spinners allowed their members to pay piecers as they saw fit it would be a recipe for dissension. This produced correspondence in the local press, with 'Mill Worker' arguing that a piecer's chances of becoming a spinner were not bright. On the occasion of 'sick minding', the one bright spot in a big piecer's life, he had to pay a 'footing' of 2d. per spinner throughout the mill room. 'An Old Spinner' objected to Gill's defence of the disciplining of any spinner who paid more than the piecer's maximum, saying it smacked of 'employers' language', and advocated the piecer's right to sell his labour to the highest bidder. In the event Harwood (Lib) and Gill (Lab) were elected well ahead of the Conservative, Goschen.[39]

The movement of the Spinners' Amalgamation into the L.R.C. coincided with a period of marked fluctuation in the well-being of the cotton trade. The boom which began in 1898 had completely evaporated by the spring of 1903, ushering in the most widespread and sustained curtailment of production experienced for a generation by all classes of trade. The year 1904 saw an intensification of the slump which was likened to the Cotton Famine of 1861. The main cause of distress was the increase in the price of raw cotton which began after 1896 and reached a peak in 1903-4 due to a combination of poor harvests and the activities of American speculators operating a price ring to raise prices.

At this point important developments took place on both sides of the trade union and employer divide. In May 1904 the Spinners had entered into an agreement with the Cardroom Amalgamation, committing both parties to sympathetic action in the event of trade disputes. Its significance lay in the growing strength and importance of the Cardroom in relation to the Spinners. The key element in the Cardroom was its male section, concentrated in the trade of carding engine mechanics — the strippers and grinders. These men were increasingly well organised and their union, the Cardroom Amalgamation, became increasingly aggressive in its attempts to attain 'the same high wages for their male members as the spinners . . . and . . . institutional prestige and rewards within the labour movement'.[40]

The 1904 agreement was psychologically important for the Cardroom in its search for a position of parity with the Spinners' Amalgamation, but rather than creating an harmonious relationship between the two Amalgamations, it actually produced a context within which their uneasy relationship became embittered. At the end of 1904 there was a fusion on the employers' side between the existing F.M.C.S.A. and the Bolton Cotton Employers' Association. This brought the Oldham and Bolton employers together for the first time, in a move interpreted by the Amalgamation as another indication of the tendency which exists amongst the employing classes to put themselves in the strongest possible position for dealing with their workpeople.[41]

These new forces came into collision in the early summer of 1905 as the general trade in cotton improved, creating a condition described as the 'brightest . . . that has come to the Lancashire cotton trade within a generation . . .' In May 1905 the Cardroom Amalgamation decided to press for a 5 per cent wage increase and this was adopted as a joint objective by the Spinners. At a meeting with the F.M.C.S.A. at the end of the month, it was agreed to adjourn the question for six weeks, which the Federation thereafter wanted extended for a further three months. The unions responded to this demand by giving notice under the terms of Brooklands of their intention to initiate strike action in support of the wages claim. This notice to strike followed ballots in which the overwhelming majority of the spinners, almost 90 per cent of those voting, endorsed the call for a strike. The Bolton employers countered by announcing a proposed 5 per cent cut in the wages of those employed within their jurisdiction.

However, after a conference of all parties chaired by Sir Thomas Swann, Lord Mayor of Manchester, it was agreed that the employers outside Bolton would pay a 5 per cent bonus on wages for twelve weeks after 1 September. Thereafter wages would return to the pre-existing position. In fact the continued revival in trade throughout 1906 allowed the Spinners to consolidate the temporary gain of the previous year into a 5 per cent increase for all those employed by firms in the F.M.C.S.A., excluding Bolton. Bolton fared badly in the outcome because the trade boom was less concentrated in the fine yarns in which it specialised. This increase was also obtained from many Yorkshire employers, where the Spinners' strength had grown from an isolated district around Sowerby Bridge into eight branches with a total membership of some 700 spinners.[42]

The extraordinary boom in the cotton trade at this time produced a number of changes for the industry in general and the operatives in particular. The most immediate consequence was quite a dramatic speculative boom in new mill construction, and a substantial increase in the number of spindles. Between 1900-13 the number of spindles in Oldham increased by 49 per cent and in Bolton by 35 per cent. This created opportunities for piecers to obtain work as spinners, but also resulted in a shortage of little piecers. The employers sought to meet this shortage by encouraging the importation of juvenile labour from non-textile areas. The unions were concerned at the implications of this development for their organisational effectiveness and sought to counter the more extravagant claims of labour shortage while seeking to extend the unionisation of textile operatives.[43]

The Cardroom took the initiative in this matter by seeking an extension of the terms in their agreement for joint action with the Spinners to include '. . . disputes resulting from the members of either Association refusing to work with non-unionists'. This was acceptable to the Spinners' Executive, who had seen their membership rise from 20,928 to 22,506 between the start and close of 1907 and

... felt that the time had come when non-members can no longer be quietly tolerated ... In the present highly organised conditions of the employers, non-unionists on our side are a decided menace to our position.[44]

Clearly the three years of unprecedented growth, 1905-7, had induced a feeling of real self-confidence amongst Spinners' leaders. This allowed them to countenance measures to strengthen union discipline within the spinning process but also to make more general claims for the role of trade unionism in cotton. The Annual Report for 1907 confidently proclaimed:

> The year's facts and figures furnish a striking commentary on the wailings of those pessimistic employers who, not long ago, were telling us that trade unions were ruining the Lancashire cotton industry ... it is evident that trade union progress need be no barrier to industrial success.[45]

To that end the Spinners took advantage of the boom conditions to secure a further 5 per cent increase in wages in June which took wages to their highest point to date. In fact the average weekly wage of a spinner varied, but in Bolton it was 45s 9d against 41s 10d in Oldham. The big piecer was earning about 18s 4d per week and his junior 11s 11d. This wage structure compared with an average wage of 35 shillings per week for skilled workers and 20 to 30 shillings for unskilled and semi-skilled workers. Another local dispute which threatened to spread into a general dispute involved fine spinners in the Oldham Province whose wages were below those paid to comparable spinners in Bolton. In December 1907 Lloyd George, as President of the Board of Trade, intervened to facilitate a solution which gave such spinners an increase of three shillings per week. The actual number of Oldham spinners affected by this change is difficult to estimate, although it was probably a substantial minority.[46]

Yet just as the boom had developed rapidly from a deep depression, so it collapsed virtually overnight. By April 1908 the Spinners' Executive was warning its districts of the pronounced nature of the slump and advising on the need to conserve funds to be better prepared to meet the anticipated attacks from employers. The gloomy prognosis of the Executive was realised by the events of July 1908, by which time short-time working had been introduced on an extensive scale. In that month the F.M.C.S.A. began the process to effect a 5 per cent reduction in wages which set in train a series of events which produced the first general lockout in the industry since 1892-3 and caused a rupture between the leaderships of the Cardroom and Spinners' Amalgamations which had profound industrial and political consequences.

The 1908 dispute proceeded by a tortuous route determined by the operation of the Brooklands Agreement, the internal democratic machinery of the Amalgamation and the 1904 pact with the Cardroom. Having resolved to obtain a 5 per cent wage reduction across the industry, the F.M.C.S.A. was required under Brooklands to give one month's formal notice of their intent. This meant that although the employers first intimated their objective in July, it was not until late August that they formally announced that new wage rates would operate from 21 September. All this meant that both Amalgamations had plenty of warning of what was in the pipeline, and the leaders had ample time to formulate a considered response. In the case of the Spinners' Executive it was clearly felt that resistance to the employers' demands was impracticable in the circumstances of the trade and therefore futile. However, their advice was decisively rejected in a ballot of members, with 16,154 rejecting the proposed cuts and only 1,312 accepting them.

At the same time it was apparent that the Cardroom leaders with the support of their members were intent on resistance. This placed the Spinners' Executive in the difficult position of seeing their industrial allies, the Cardroom, taking a stand against wage cuts, a move supported by the rank and file spinners. Moreover, the implication of the Cardroom's position was industrial action of a kind which the Spinners' leaders thought bound for disaster. The uncertainty engendered by this state of affairs had some effect on the F.M.C.S.A., which sought to defuse the immediate risk of a major dispute while still achieving their principal objective. They offered to defer the actual implementation of a wage cut until January 1909 so long as the unions accepted the principle of the cut immediately. The Spinners' Executive wished to accept this offer, but the Cardroom strongly objected and both sides agreed to let the matter rest for a few days after which a Joint Council of the Amalgamations would make a final decision.

The Spinners' Executive reported back on the negotiations to a Special Representative Meeting of their Amalgamation in September and urged that the amended employer offer be accepted. The meeting rejected this suggestion and instead decided to ballot the membership on the revised terms. This ballot rejected the revised terms by 12,677 to 4,530. However, the Executive noted that only 73 per cent of those voting had rejected the terms and this fell short of the 80 per cent required for industrial action under union rules. They therefore determined to accept the terms offered, despite the vote. But any hope which the Spinners' Executive held that they had been able to sidestep neatly an industrial confrontation was dashed by the policy of the Cardroom. Despite the Spinners' action in accepting new terms the Cardroom reaffirmed its intention to resist, and the F.M.C.S.A. announced that without a general agreement their mills would remain closed to all textile operatives. In these circumstances the Spinners' leaders instructed their members not to return to work until a final settlement had been reached.

The strike-cum-lockout lasted seven weeks, during which time the Spinners' Amalgamation paid out some £141,000 in dispute pay. Arguments between the Executives of the two Amalgamations about the merits of their respective postures permeated the whole dispute, but what embittered relations to the point of a complete rupture was the fate of the Spinners' application for strike benefit from the G.F.T.U.

Both the Spinners and Cardroom Amalgamations were affiliated to the G.F.T.U. and were theoretically entitled to strike benefit in the current dispute. However, the Cardroom objected to the Spinners' claim for benefit on the grounds that the Spinners had accepted the Federation's terms and could not be in dispute and eligible for benefit. This objection cost the Spinners some three weeks' lockout benefit from the G.F.T.U., amounting to more than £10,000. But more galling to the Spinners than the financial loss was the sense that they had been humiliated by their 'junior' partner. Certainly the action of the Cardroom was politically inept and insulting, the more so since their position on the substantial issue at stake, the wage cut, was supported by the vast majority of rank and file spinners. The conduct of the Cardroom Executive is best explained as part of a growing willingness to challenge the predominant position of the Spinners amongst cotton operatives. In the context of the 1908 dispute this challenge appeared to have failed. The dispute was settled in early November on the terms which had been available at the outset. The Cardroom was forced to accept the 5 per cent cut, which was deferred for four months until the first pay day in March 1909.

This result clearly represented a substantial defeat for the operatives in general and the Cardroom in particular. In fact Spinners did not achieve a general increase in wage rates until July 1915. The Spinners' leaders felt that the outcome was a vindication of their position throughout the dispute, and commented grimly:

> During the dispute the officials of the Cardroom Workers' Amalgamation displayed a spirit of bitterness·. . . regrettable and altogether uncalled for . . . From the operatives' point of view the lockout cannot be regarded as having been anything but a huge mistake . . . the cotton employers were better organised than at any previous time . . . trade was in such a wretched condition as to make a stoppage a most desirable eventuality from the employers' point of view . . . If there be any credit in . . . spending £260,000 of trade union money, and finishing up with giving the employers everything they wanted, we are quite prepared to allow the Cardroom Workers' Amalgamation to take it.[47]

However, if the Spinners thought that the dispute had taught the Cardroom an expensive lesson likely to induce more caution, they were mistaken. The Cardroom continued to adopt an aggressive, radical industrial posture which had important implications for relations between the Amalgamations. While formally bound by the alliance of 1904, the relationship was increasingly marked by tense rivalry which sometimes burst into the public arena. In 1908 James Crinion, President of the Cardroom and the man who succeeded Thomas Ashton as prospective Labour candidate in Oldham, withdrew his candidature largely as a result of inter-union ill-feeling. Once again, labour politics in Oldham had been effectively sabotaged by the internal politics of the textile unions.

On the wider industrial stage the two month dispute in 1908 was seen as particu-larly damaging in an industry so vital to the prosperity of Britain and the Lancashire region in particular. Following the conclusion of the dispute the new President of the Board of Trade, Winston Churchill, brought together all the parties to discuss the possibility of creating some machinery which would enable wages to become largely self-regulating along the lines of the sliding-scale system which had operated in the coal industry. Such discussions were not new and periodic attempts had been made to reach such a solution, most notably between 1899-1901. What made the search for a solution so difficult was the complexity of the cotton productive process, which meant neither side could agree on a standard basis of wages and profits from which to evaluate future demands. This again was the principal reason for the failure of the talks in 1908-9, especially since the Spinners viewed any scheme for compulsory arbitration of wages with outright hostility. The Spinners continued to maintain the central importance of collective bargaining backed up by healthy bank balances. Indeed, they advised their members at this time that only by maintaining 'financial reserves large enough to enable them to give a good account of themselves will the operatives be able to secure anything like justice at the hands of the employers'.[48]

Yet it would be a mistake to interpret relations between operatives and employers in the cotton industry as dominated by hostility. Indeed, there was a persistent desire to co-operate on issues of mutual interest and the cotton unions were subject to criticism within the Labour Party because of this tendency to promote legislation jointly with employers. Inside the industry unions and employers sought to act in concert on the issue of short-time working in the post-1908 depression, and both acknowledged that the slump was largely a consequence of over-production caused by the speculative boom in mill construction post-1905.

In times of slump the traditional remedy of the unions was to urge the general application of short-time working. The F.M.C.S.A. felt unable to concede short-time in principle, believing that those producers outside the organisation would use the opportunity to increase their production. However, in practice short-time working was widely in evidence in 1908-9, which encouraged the growth of support within the Spinners' Amalgamation for a statutory reduction in the working week from 55½ hours to 48. In fact the Spinners' support for the Eight Hour Day was largely a product of a desire to avoid the need for short-time working. Thus agitation for the Eight Hour Day reached peaks and troughs of intensity, depending on the state of the trade. In good times it was muted, but in bad times it was vigorously advocated.

The initiative was taken by the Bolton Province on this occasion, who sought to move a resolution in June 1909 calling for a ballot of all cotton operatives on the question. The resolution was subsequently discussed at the July conference of the U.T.F.W.A. where the decision for the ballot was taken. This produced a vote in favour of the 48 hour week by 111,567 votes to 77,355. Amongst Spinners the vote for reduction was carried by 13,204 to 6,420 votes, which the Executive interpreted as indicating support for a policy of a gradual reduction in hours.[49]

The U.T.F.W.A. felt unable to press the demand with more than moral force, given the large vote for the status quo and particularly since the Cardroom Amalgamation was almost equally divided. Conferences with the employers were held in London with interested M.P.s present, but the issue failed to generate sufficient support to enable the unions to take the issue beyond this traditional form of lobbying. In addition, at the General Election of 1910, candidates in textile constituencies were sent a questionnaire by the U.T.F.W.A. which included a question asking whether candidates would support a measure to reduce, gradually, working hours throughout the cotton industry.

While the U.T.F.W.A. and the union-sponsored M.P.s maintained a number of legislative campaigns, the dominant issue within the industry was the depressed state of trade which continued throughout 1909-10. At the start of 1910 the Spinners' leaders were in no doubt that the F.M.C.S.A. would invoke the twelve-months clause in Brooklands and seek a further 5 per cent reduction in wages. On this occasion the Spinners' Executive was determined to resist and not to be outflanked by the Cardroom. Negotiations between the employers and Spinners continued throughout the spring of 1910 resulting in an ambitious agreement in June. The Spinners' Executive described this agreement as '. . . the most important settlement of a wage dispute that has ever taken place in the history of our Amalgamation'. It was agreed that the F.M.C.S.A. would withdraw the proposed 5 per cent wage cut, in return for which the Brooklands Agreement would be amended so that such agreements would now remain unchangeable for two years rather than twelve months. However, the Spinners' leaders also suggested that in the current situation the present wage agreement should be binding on all parties for five years, although the wage lists would still be open to adjustment. This suggestion was accepted by the employers and thus the question of wage rates throughout the industry was settled, with the Spinners having taken the initiative on the operatives' side and with the Cardroom being presented with a virtual *fait accompli*.[50]

This agreement was made without any recourse to rank and file opinion and was based on the need to maintain the principle of collective bargaining while avoiding a confrontation in circumstances which the leaders deemed particularly inauspicious. The agreement was defended as an honourable compromise, which would produce confidence and stability in the trade and without which it was 'practically certain that we should have had to pass through the most disastrous lockout that Lancashire has ever seen'. The decision of the Spinners to offer a five-year wage freeze in 1910 was clearly based on a pessimistic assessment of the immediate prospects of the cotton trade. In fact this assessment was ill-founded in that the years up to the outbreak of the First World War saw a significant recovery in the trade. There was little evidence of unemployment or short-time working among textile operatives, and 1913 saw cotton production reach its historical peak in Britain. Although unable to push for increased wages, cotton spinners sought to increase their earnings by means of adjusting the lists, which was permissible under the 1910 agreement, and this led to considerable unrest at local level.[51]

In fact a lockout did occur in late September 1910 which affected some 14,000 spinners for one week, originating in a dispute at the Fern Mill, Shaw. This dispute, which was organised by the Cardroom in defence of the craft status of strippers and grinders, attracted national attention. It also involved the Spinners, who were required by the 1904 pact to withdraw their members in support at the mills in dispute. The strike began at Fern Mill in June but dramatically escalated in mid-September when the F.M.C.S.A. decided on a general lockout which began on 3 October.

In the event a settlement was reached through the efforts of the government's chief industrial conciliator, George Askwith. The Spinners paid out more than £11,000 in lockout pay and asserted that

> . . . in our opinion the causes alleged by the employers for resorting to a general lockout were altogether too trivial, and such as they would never have dreamed of closing their mills for if trade had been in a prosperous state.

The whole episode was taken as a valuable lesson which needed to be learned by the membership:

> The general lockout is becoming more and more a favourite weapon, and the employers now appear ready to lay their hands on it on any flimsy pretext . . . We need hardly point out that the only method of ensuring ourselves against this liability . . . lies in the direction of improving our financial position.[52]

The period after 1910 also saw the re-emergence of the old perennial grievance of bad spinning and allegations by the operatives of foot-dragging on the part of employers when dealing with such complaints. The issue was especially sensitive in the Oldham area, where bad spinning assumed epidemic proportions. The Oldham spinners had always enjoyed a combative relationship with their employers, and their demand for a positive response on the bad spinning question met with an obstinate refusal by employers. At the Quarterly Representative Meeting of the Spinners in September 1912, the Oldham Province gave notice of their intention to move a resolution at the following meeting in December which would require the Amalgamation to withdraw from Brooklands.

In the meantime discussions between the Amalgamation's leaders and the F.M.C.S.A. failed to produce a solution and the resolution to leave Brooklands duly appeared at the December Representative Meeting. An attempt by the Bolton Province to adjourn the issue was defeated by 104 votes to 33, and the Oldham resolution was deemed to have been carried. Immediately thereafter the Spinners' General Secretary, William Marsland, wrote to the F.M.C.S.A. giving one month's notice that the Amalgamation would cease to be bound by Brooklands after 31 January 1913.[53]

The Spinners now began to prosecute a vigorous strategy of strike action against employers, mainly in Oldham on the bad spinning question. This action brought them into dispute not only with employers but with their former allies the Cardroom Amalgamation in a manner reminiscent of 1908 but in reverse. The Spinners were taking the militant industrial initiative and the Cardroom found itself involved in a dispute not of its choosing and over which it had no control. In February 1913 the Cardroom Executive requested a meeting with their counterpart in the Spinners' Amalgamation because of newspaper reports suggesting that the Spinners were preparing to strike in as many as thirty cotton mills. This required the Cardroom to withdraw their labour under the terms of the 1904 pact and they clearly felt uncomfortable about such large-scale action. They asked the Spinners to delay action until they had met the F.M.C.S.A. to discuss the whole question of the Brooklands Agreement. Thomas Ashton told the Cardroom that the local associations of employers were refusing to discuss bad spinning questions with them and the Spinners were now approaching individual firms to reach agreements. He said that no strikes would be initiated until each employer approached had been given the chance to reach a settlement. However, Ashton emphasized that where firms declined to reach a settlement, strikes would commence.

The Cardroom Executive appeared satisfied by Ashton's explanation, believing that strikes would not be undertaken on a large scale. But soon after, the Cardroom called a further meeting and their secretary, William Mullin, argued that his members were being embroiled in sympathetic strike action on a scale amounting to a general dispute. He explained that while the Cardroom was prepared to withdraw their labour in all cases where requested, any future instances of joint action could not be guaranteed. Thomas Ashton responded that what the Cardroom did was its own affair and of little consequence to the Spinners who would continue with their own strategy.

The industrial alliance between the Amalgamations had reached breaking point. An attempt by the Cardroom to amend the 1904 pact so that joint action could only operate in one mill at a time was rejected by the Spinners and by the end of March 1913 it was apparent that Cardroom workers in Oldham were being instructed not to tender notice of strike action in support of spinners. At a meeting of the Spinners' Executive on 29 March, William Marsland, the General Secretary, was instructed to inform the Provinces and Districts that the pact with the Cardroom was at an end and they were neither to ask nor to give support to the Cardroom in trade disputes. This industrial fragmentation amongst cotton operatives was soon paralleled by a political split in the U.T.F.W.A. involving the Cardroom.[54]

Political questions became increasingly important to the Spinners and other cotton unions, particularly following the election of a radical Liberal Government in 1906. This government initiated a number of interventionist measures of particular importance to trade unions, most notably in the areas of workmen's compensation, national insurance and child labour. On the wider political front, the legal judgement on the Osborne case in 1909, which made the possession of political funds by trade unions illegal, and the 1913 Trade Union Act, which reversed that decision where a ballot of members authorised such a fund, placed the question of political affiliation to the Labour Party at the forefront of the union agenda. In between, the Oldham by-election of 1911 highlighted the somewhat ambiguous relationship of the cotton unions and the local Labour Party, and set in train a series of events which led to a split in the U.T.F.W.A.

The political strategy and tactics of the Spinners, as with the other cotton unions, continued to be mediated through the U.T.F.W.A. notwithstanding their affiliation to the Labour Party. This meant that candidates for Parliamentary elections were sponsored by the U.T.F.W.A., which decided how many candidates would be sponsored and for which constituencies. In reality it was accepted that each of the main affiliated unions, Weavers, Spinners and Cardroom, should be allowed at least one prospective candidate. In addition the major legislative initiatives and campaigns undertaken by the textile unions were mounted under the auspices of the U.T.F.W.A. which became the main immediate focus and forum for the political objectives and aspirations of the affiliated bodies.

It does not appear that affiliation to the Labour Party represented a fundamental change in the nature and objectives of cotton union politics. While the Labour Party was seen as a necessary, even essential, medium for trade union politics, it was not seen as exhaustive. Traditional methods of pressure politics were still resorted to on a widescale basis, and as late as 1912 the U.T.F.W.A. was actively co-operating with the employers in drawing up and promoting amendments to the Limited Liability Act. At the local level the unions adopted an insensitive attitude towards Labour parties in those constituencies over which they claimed a primary jurisdiction. This inability or unwillingness to recognise the political aspirations of local Labour parties was ultimately damaging to the idea of sponsored textile and parliamentary representation.

In essence the development of cotton politics was largely shaped by the sectional industrial interests of the affiliated unions. The three textile sponsored M.P.s elected on the Labour Party platform before 1914 were sent by the U.T.F.W.A. primarily as representatives of the textile operatives. A. H. Gill, David Shackleton and his successor at Clitheroe, Albert Smith, were assiduous guardians of the cotton interest and their main Parliamentary activity was devoted almost entirely to that interest. Certainly the issues which attracted the U.T.F.W.A. were those relating to workmen's compensation and national insurance, as well as those such as 'time cribbing', the reduced working week and the abolition of fines at work, which were of particular interest to the cotton operatives.

The issue of 'time cribbing' was a long-running problem which was particularly sensitive for the Spinners. Time cribbing was a method by which employers were able to gain additional time from their employees by means of running machinery for a short time beyond the normal point of stoppage. It was argued that this could increase the work time for operatives by as much as two hours in a week, and although illegal under factory legislation it was difficult to stamp out in practice. It was a sensitive issue for spinners because unlike day wage labour it was widely believed that they accepted the practice as being financially beneficial. At a meeting held with Herbert Gladstone, Home Secretary, in 1907, William Marsland pointed out that the Spinners were opposed to the practice and did not want it thought they connived in its operation. In fact the issue continued to be a source of irritation to the unions, but following their persistent agitation on the question, fines on employers were increased, as were the number of factory inspectors appointed to enforce the Factory Acts. By the outbreak of the First World War, 'time cribbing' had been brought under stricter control.[55]

Undoubtedly the most embarrassing issue confronting the U.T.F.W.A. and its affiliates was that of half-time workers. Legislation restricting the use of child labour had been introduced in the nineteenth century, yet child labour remained a feature of cotton factory life. Now pressure from educational and medical, as well as trade union opinion, began to mount for effective action to eliminate the practice. At a conference in August 1908, the U.T.F.W.A. voted by 186 to 27 that the age of the half-timer be raised from twelve to thirteen years. This question was then put to the ballot with a firm recommendation for the change, but it was overwhelmingly rejected by 150,723 to 33,968 votes. Amongst spinners the vote in favour of continuing with entry at twelve years was by 15,296 to 3,166.

This was a severe embarrassment to the leaders of the unions, who were in favour of a change, and a further attempt was made to secure a positive vote from the membership at the start of 1912. Once again the leadership urged the members to vote for an increase in the minimum age to thirteen, since it was apparent that Parliament would enforce a reform in the immediate future. However, the membership maintained its support for child labour by 122,893 votes to 31,352 with the spinners voting 15,014 to 4,431 for the current position. Interestingly, A. H. Gill spoke and voted against the Education (School Attendance) Bill, which aimed to end the half-time system, justifying his action in terms of his role as representative of the Lancashire textile workers.

Overshadowing all else on the political front was the Osborne judgement of 1909. This judgement threatened trade union sponsored labour politics by outlawing the union possession of political funds. The Spinners and subsequently virtually all the cotton unions found themselves subject to a local version of Osborne in November 1910 when a Bolton spinner, Henry Catterall, applied for an injunction preventing the Amalgamation from spending funds for the purpose of securing Labour representation. Prior to these legal interventions the U.T.F.W.A. was actively considering increasing its sponsored candidates to three. Following the withdrawal of James Crinion as the prospective candidate for Oldham, it was accepted that the third candidate should be nominated by the Cardroom to replace Crinion. This would have ensured that each of the three large cotton unions could place a candidate before the electorate. With Gill and Smith defending Bolton and Clitheroe respectively, Oldham represented the natural target for a third candidate. But Oldham possessed two Liberal M.P.s and the Cardroom had broken with the local Labour Party over the Crinion affair. This ensured that the Cardroom's nominee, W. H. Carr, would not fight Oldham but instead stood as the sponsored U.T.F.W.A.'s candidate at Preston, where he failed to secure election despite a creditable performance.[56]

At Bolton, Gill followed his success of 1906 with re-election at the two elections of 1910, where again there was a close correspondence between Gill's vote and that of his Liberal running mate, George Harwood. This correspondence owed much to Gill's moderation which ensured that there was no conflict in Bolton between the Liberalism of local cotton dignitaries and the Labour candidacy. This allowed the *Bolton Evening News* to explain the smooth success of the Lib-Lab ticket as largely due to the 'excellent spirit of camaraderie, a freedom from jealousy between Liberals and Labour men in their common attack on the Unionist positions at the time'.

The General Elections of 1910 left textile representation where it had been since 1906, namely Gill of the Spinners and Smith representing Weaving in Parliament, and the Cardroom without an elected member. The following year a political vacancy occurred in Oldham, when one of the Liberal members, Alfred Emmott, accepted a peerage. On the face of it this presented the Cardroom with an opportunity to secure a Parliamentary seat. However, relations between the Oldham Labour Party and the Cardroom were completely fractured and the local party desired a 'political' candidate to fight the seat.

The National Labour Party suggested that W. C. Robinson, a member of the National Executive Committee and a previous Party chairman, be approached to stand. Robinson was a member of the I.L.P. and a relatively advanced advocate of independent labour representation. In addition he was also Vice-Chairman of the U.T.F.W.A. and General Secretary of the Beamers, Twisters and Drawers, and apparently an ideal Labour candidate for a constituency like Oldham. Yet his adoption affronted the Cardroom and divided the cotton unions. Both A. H. Gill and William Marsland appeared on Robinson's election platform along with leaders of the Weavers' Amalgamation, but Cardroom leaders were absent. The election produced a victory for the Conservative candidate, Bartley-Dennis, with 12,255 votes against 10,623 for the Liberal A. L. Stanley and 7,448 for Robinson. Robinson's intervention showed there was widespread support available for a Labour candidate in Oldham. More immediately it cost the Liberals a formerly safe seat and set in train a process which led the Cardroom to withdraw temporarily from the U.T.F.W.A.

The issues surrounding Robinson's candidature in Oldham and the behaviour of leading members of the U.T.F.W.A. in not endorsing that candidature were raised at the Labour Party Annual Conference in 1912 and at the Conference of the U.T.F.W.A. in that year. The main target for criticism was William Mullin, Chairman of the U.T.F.W.A. and leader of the Cardroom, who had refused to sign Robinson's nomination papers. The first indication of serious disharmony emerged when the election of officers of the U.T.F.W.A., which took place at the 1912 Conference, produced a discussion on the procedure for electing a chairman. In response to a question as to why each District was not invited to send in nominations the Secretary, James Cross, pointed out that while no rule applied to the situation, the positions of chairman, secretary, treasurer and vice-chairman had been allocated to the cardroom, weavers, spinners and mixed trades respectively for as long as anyone knew. Mullin was then elected to the chairmanship of the Legislative Council of the U.T.F.W.A.[57]

Having established that there was no rule to prevent rival nominations to the top official positions within the Legislative Council, Robinson was put forward to oppose Mullin for the Chairmanship in 1913. The Cardroom was incensed by this breach of traditional etiquette and refused to participate in the Conference unless Robinson withdrew. Their fear was that although Mullin would win, it would be in the face of a substantial opposition. Feelings against Mullin were still running high, and the position of the Cardroom had been damaged by their industrial dispute with the Spinners over joint action on bad spinning. Moreover, the growing equivocation of the Cardroom on the vigorous prosecution of the campaign for a 48-hour week had also alienated the union-political activists who dominated delegations to the U.T.F.W.A. All this meant that their threat of withdrawal did not produce the expected response and Robinson's candidature remained on the table. The Cardroom, acting on their threat, withdrew from the Conference and the U.T.F.W.A., leaving Robinson to be elected Chairman.[58]

While the Oldham political fiasco dominated much of the U.T.F.W.A.'s political preoccupation, the issue of Osborne and Catterall remained a difficult problem for the cotton unions. In the event the passage of the Trade Union Act of 1913 provided them with the option of amending their rules to create political funds on the affirmative vote of their members. In November 1913 the Spinners' Amalgamation put the question to a ballot of members and secured a vote in favour of creating such a fund by 4,826 votes to 3,376. Perhaps the most striking characteristic of this ballot was the apparent sense of apathy surrounding the issue and the contrasting responses of the Bolton and Oldham Provinces. In fact just over one third of the membership bothered to vote, and only one in four spinners was prepared to register a positive endorsement of the political fund. In the case of Oldham, there was a narrow vote against the fund by 768 to 746 votes, in a Province with more than 8,000 members. By contrast in Bolton, where the conduct of labour politics had been both smoother and more successful, a positive vote was secured by 1,887 to 1,393.

For the Spinners' Amalgamation on the eve of the First World War, prospects reflected both the surface confidence of the wider industry and the deeper fragility of that confidence. Since Brooklands, the Spinners maintained their position at the peak of the industry's industrial hierarchy. The membership had grown to more than 22,000 and it represented more than 90 per cent of all spinners. In terms of financial strength it enjoyed an almost unrivalled position amongst British trade unions. Its organisational structure had changed little over twenty years, except that Blackburn, Preston and Yorkshire had emerged as Provinces of the Amalgamation, though nowhere near as large or as influential as Oldham and Bolton. In essence the real power in the union was still vested in the Amalgamation and its two major Provinces, although there were already signs of the shop steward-based rank and file activism which was to manifest itself dramatically in the near future.

Perhaps the most serious disappointment for the leadership was the Brooklands Agreement, which had been seen as an innovative model agreement between unions and employers. While it may have contributed to the absence of general trade disputes, it proved less adaptable when applied to the resolution of localised conflicts. In particular Brooklands, despite modifications, seemed powerless to solve the endemic issue of bad spinning which was the overwhelming cause of local disputes. The abrogation of the Brooklands Agreement by the Spinners in January 1913 was followed by a one-clause agreement designed to facilitate the resolution of local disputes without immediate recourse to strike action. But the cotton industry at the outbreak of war lacked the kind of industry-wide agreement which had contributed, in large measure, to the general industrial tranquillity of the Brooklands era.

If relations between employers and unions were more strained than for many years, so too were inter-union relationships. The apparent identity of outlook which had allowed the Spinners and Cardroom to forge an alliance in 1904, and which might have led to further collaborative activity, had now broken down in a welter of bitterness and accusation. The source of this breach would seem to have been the desire of the Cardroom to assert its growing demand for prominence within the wider sea of cotton trade unionism, and the unwilllingness of the Spinners to allow their position and authority to be challenged. The form of that struggle was both industrial and political, and in both areas the Cardroom saw its ambitions largely thwarted. The consequence was their brief departure from the U.T.F.W.A. at a time when a united body was clearly vital to the interests of all cotton workers.

Taken as a whole, the prospects for the cotton industry and for Spinners appeared largely benign. In 1913 the industry ranked third behind coal and engineering, employing more than 600,000 people and accounting for about a quarter of total British exports. Although Britain's share of the world consumption of raw cotton had fallen from 37 per cent in the early 1880s to 20 per cent by 1913, it still possessed more spindles than either the U.S.A. or Europe. Indeed, as Joe White has pointed out, there was a 29 per cent increase in spindles for 1906-14 over the decade 1896-1905, a 17 per cent increase in cotton consumption, and an almost 19 per cent increase in cloth exports measured in linear yards or pounds. In addition the earnings of spinners had risen by some 35 per cent between 1886 and 1906, and the absolute number of cotton workers was increasing, especially after 1901. Indeed, as we have seen, the number of spinners rose by around 17 per cent between 1905-8 before stabilising at around 23,000 until the First World War.[59]

All this suggested an essentially healthy industry and the growing number of spinners indicated that the piecer problem was lessening as opportunities for the big piecer to gain a spinning position increased. Despite this overall improvement in the fortunes of the cotton industry, the position was not entirely secure. The ultimate health of the industry largely depended upon the continued access to plentiful supplies of cheap raw cotton and the ability to maintain and expand overseas markets, including Europe. There were already difficulties in terms of cotton supply due to the rapid growth of the U.S.A. cotton industry and problems associated with expanding the production of raw cotton in the southern United States. The problem of markets for cotton goods was also potentially difficult given the impending war, particularly since Europe was emerging as the most favourable market for exports, especially of cotton yarn. The appearance of a buoyant cotton industry on the eve of the First World War could not entirely hide the underlying problems of supply and markets which cast a shadow over the industry and were now to become acute.

CHAPTER EIGHT
War and Labour Unrest

The First World War was a turning point in the history of the Lancashire cotton industry. In 1912 the industry produced over 8 million square yards of cloth, of which 7 million were exported, and employed over 600,000 operatives working 60 million spindles and nearly 800,000 looms. By 1938 the industry produced 3 million square yards of cloth, exported 1.5 million and employed 300,000 operatives working 40 million spindles and 500,000 looms. The industry had been effectively halved. The main cause was simple: the loss of export markets. The Lancashire cotton industry was from its very beginning in the industrial revolution an exporting industry, approximately three-quarters of production was exported during the nineteenth century and those who worked in the industry before 1914 considered that they met the demands of the home market before breakfast. Lancashire provided a quarter of Britain's total exports by value before 1914 and was the largest exporting industry in the country.[1]

In 1914 the main export market was India, taking 2.5 million square yards of Lancashire cloth out of the seven million square yards exported. China was the next largest market with one million square yards of cloth, followed by the British Dominions and Colonies, Middle and Near East, then South America, all three areas importing approximately 0.75 million square yards each. Europe took around 0.5 million square yards. The change by 1937 was dramatic, the Indian market imported 0.3 million yards of cloth and had ceased to be the largest market. The British Dominions and Colonies were the only major market to be relatively unaffected by the collapse of world trade, remaining at 0.75 million square yards; elsewhere the collapse was as dramatic as in India. Losses in the Indian market were associated with the introduction of tariffs against Lancashire cotton cloth, they had reached some 25 per cent in the mid-1930s. The consequence was that Lancashire, which had provided just under half the world's exported cotton cloth in 1913, by 1938 provided only a quarter and had been replaced as the premier exporter by Japan.[2]

The outbreak of the First World War affected the industry in two main ways. Initially, there was high unemployment in the autumn of 1914 as a result of the economic dislocation caused by the onset of the war, but by 1915 there was a growing shortage of male labour in the industry as many spinners and piecers volunteered for the armed forces. In particular there was a shortage of piecers who, because they were younger, volunteered in great numbers. One obvious solution to this problem was the substitution of women and girls as piecers for the male labour that had gone to the Front. Increasingly by 1915 women were being substituted for men throughout the economy. The most significant development was in engineering and munitions where women's labour was substituted for unskilled and semi-skilled male labour. The Spinners' Amalgamation traditionally opposed the employment of women in the spinning room, presenting its opposition to women working in the spinning room as a moral objection. High temperatures in the spinning room meant that operatives wore light and loose clothing which they changed into in the spinning room. It would be immoral, it was claimed, for women to work alongside men in such circumstances. The reality, of course, was that the union feared that the introduction of women would lead to an erosion of wage rates. They were aware that they were the only major section of the industry's labour force that was dominated by men and they were also the best paid section of that labour force. In the spring of 1915 the union discussed the position with David Shackleton, the former Weavers' leader who had become a civil servant and was acting on behalf of the Government. They were unable to reach any general agreement and the question of women was left to the Provinces and individual Districts. The strength of the opposition was reflected in some of the proposed alternatives; these included the recruitment of 'Belgian boys', war refugees from Belgium, and the reduction of the school leaving age. Both Bolton and Oldham did introduce some women as piecers for the duration of the war, but this labour was largely phased out after the end of hostilities.[3]

Whilst the shortage of labour dominated most industries during the war, the major problem faced by the cotton industry was in fact a shortage of raw cotton. This placed the cotton trade unions in a difficult position compared with other trade unions during 1914-18. The period of the war saw a substantial growth in the influence of trade unions both politically and industrially, but the basis of this increased power was the shortage of labour and the Government's need for co-operation from the trade unions. The cotton trade unions lacked the bargaining power of many other trade unions, especially the coal and engineering unions, because the industry was not considered crucial to the war effort. The decline of the power of the cotton unions was set against the background of the decline of the cotton industry. The industry had had a major influence on Government policy in India before 1914, but during the war this influence declined. This was evident in 1917 when the Government allowed India to raise a tariff against Lancashire cotton, ostensibly to raise funds for the war but in reality as a concession to Indian opinion in return for support for the British war effort. Both cotton employers and operatives protested to the Government, but these protests fell on deaf ears. In retrospect the decision to allow India to raise a tariff against Lancashire cotton can be seen to be a turning point in the history of the industry. It was the loss of the Indian market that was a fundamental cause of the depression in the industry during the 1920s and 1930s.[4]

Government intervention had already begun to affect the industry by 1915. The growing wartime inflation had caused unrest amongst the membership by the summer of 1915 and coincided with the end of the five-year agreement to freeze wages. The Spinners agreed to accept a reference of their wage claim for 10 per cent on the wage list to the Government's Committee of Production headed by George Askwith. The alternative, according to the Government, was for the cotton industry to be included in the Munitions Act of 1915, making strike action illegal. However, the Government was concerned about the threat of a lockout in the industry, arising from the fact that the Cardroom Amalgamation was already striking certain mills for a 10 per cent war bonus, to which the Federation of Master Cotton Spinners' Associations (F.M.C.S.A.) had responded by the threat of a lockout of all operatives in spinning. After a two-day hearing the Committee of Production recommended a wartime bonus of 5 per cent on the wage list.[5]

The following year, 1916, the Spinners' Amalgamation sought another wage advance, only for the employers to claim that the previous award by the Committee of Production was granted on the understanding that no further bonus or advance would be given for the duration of the war. The issue was referred to the Committee of Production who ruled in the Spinners' favour and then went on to award a further 5 per cent advance. By 1916 spinners' wages had risen 10 per cent compared with the rise in the cost of living of 46 per cent. Early in 1917 this discrepancy was recognised with the award of a further 10 per cent.[6]

The shortage of raw cotton reached crisis point in the summer of 1917 because of the success of the German U-boat campaign. The German attempt to isolate Britain by the use of submarine attacks on British merchant shipping was largely successful, seriously reducing shipping space. Cotton was given low priority compared to munitions and food, and as the stocks of raw cotton held in Liverpool warehouses declined, the industry panicked. The Government's response was to suspend the Liverpool raw cotton market and establish the Cotton Control Board in June 1917.

The Cotton Control Board consisted of twelve members representing employers, trade unions, merchants and the Government. It was chaired by Sir Herbert Dixon, Chairman of the Fine Spinners' Association, the largest single employer in the industry. Edward Judson, President of the Spinners' Amalgamation and Secretary of the Ashton Spinners, was probably the most influential of the three cotton trade unionists on the Board. The Government's motives in setting up the Board are important in understanding later events. The growth of state intervention was one of the major features of the war, especially after Lloyd George became Prime Minister in 1916. Lloyd George was particularly concerned to avoid social unrest which might undermine Britain's ability to win the war and the Government feared that a shortage of raw cotton would lead to an economic and social crisis in Lancashire comparable to the Cotton Famine of the 1860s.

The Cotton Control Board was left largely to its own devices by Whitehall and the industry took considerable pride in its ability to handle its own affairs. The basis of the Board's authority was an order from the Board of Trade forbidding the purchase of raw cotton except under licence from the Board. The policy was to issue licences to raw cotton merchants when they had less than a fortnight's supply of cotton. Demand for raw cotton was prevented from outstripping supply by restricting the use of spindles and looms. The Board fixed a maximum percentage of machinery which firms could work without licence. To work machinery above this percentage firms required a licence from the Board which was obtainable only on payment of a levy. The levy was collected by the Board and used to provide unemployment pay for those operatives who were made unemployed as a result of the scheme. Unemployment pay was 25 shillings for male operatives but only 15 shillings for female workers. The operatives were employed on a strictly enforced rota system, thereby avoiding permanent unemployment. Employers in spinning were allowed to work 60 per cent of their spindles without a licence. Licences were issued to spinners using American cotton to increase their production to 70 per cent of capacity, but this was to be a maximum. Firms with Egyptian cotton could use all of their machinery because this was in plentiful supply. Shipping space from Egypt was in less demand than that from America because troop ships going to Egypt were coming back with plenty of excess space.[7]

The formation of the Cotton Control Board had a number of advantages for the unions. Even without the Board, unemployment would have existed and the unions would have had to use up part of their assets in trying to mitigate the distress. Under the Board they were able to relieve the distress without undermining their own funds, the unions were responsible for distributing the unemployment relief to unemployed operatives whether they were union members or not, and this enabled them to preach the values of trade unionism to non-unionists. The cotton unions provided a third of the Board's membership, equal to employers' representation. Formally they were able to play an equal part in determining the policy of the Board but according to H. D. Henderson, Secretary to the Board:

> The operatives' leaders fulfilled essentially the role of a friendly opposition, now pleading for concessions, now issuing warnings, but at no time playing an equal part in the determination of policy.[8]

Incorporated into the Cotton Control Board, they were held accountable for the Board's decisions by their membership, the industry and the Government. Yet their influence on decision making was minimal. What was even more damaging was that their role on the Board affected their ability to bargain successfully with the employers.

At the time of the formation of the Cotton Control Board wages in the industry had only advanced by 20 per cent on the wage list since 1914, well below the increase in the cost of living caused by wartime inflation. In the summer of 1917 the Spinners' Amalgamation applied for a rise of 30 per cent but agreed to postpone their demand for three months because of the uncertainty caused by the formation of the Board. When it became clear that the Board had stabilised the industry, the Spinners renewed their wage demand. The Cotton Control Board announced that levies for the payment of unemployment relief would end and only be resumed if a modified wage agreement was reached. The Spinners took the hint, and a wage advance of 15 per cent on the wage list was agreed with the F.M.C.S.A. At the same time the Board promised to continue with levies and unemployment pay, Dixon, the Board's

Chairman, played a leading role in the negotiations acting as both conciliator and arbitrator. Part of the employers' argument was that they could not meet the wage demand in full because of the levies they paid to the Board. They argued that the unemployment pay was effectively a wage payment thus linking the Board directly to wage negotiations despite its protestations to the contrary.[9]

New wage negotiations began in May 1918. These were path-breaking in the industry's history because for the first time the three main Amalgamations — Spinners, Cardroom and Weavers — made a joint claim. The impetus to a joint wage claim was the Cotton Control Board. The two major employers' associations, the F.M.C.S.A. and the Cotton Spinners' and Manufacturers' Association (C.S.M.A.), also combined for the first time. Negotiations took place at a critical point in the war — the German Spring offensive of 1918. Growing war weariness in Russia had led to the Revolution of 1917 and to the Bolsheviks taking Russia out of the war. Germany transferred its troops from the Russian Front to the Western Front in the hope of delivering a knock-out blow, before the arrival of large numbers of American troops tipped the balance in the Allies' favour. The Spring offensive was initially successful for Germany and among its repercussions was a shipping crisis in Britain which meant that even less shipping space for raw cotton was available.[10]

The Executive Councils of the cotton unions met and agreed on a joint application for a 30 per cent advance on the wage list on the condition that unemployment benefits paid by the Cotton Control Board continued. Henry Boothman, the Spinners' new Secretary, stated to the membership that 30 per cent 'was somewhat less than your Executive Committee would probably have asked . . . but it was thought that, at the present juncture, a uniform application for all sections was desirable'. At the joint meeting of the cotton unions and the two employers' associations, Judson argued that the operatives were entitled to a wage increase because of the rising cost of living and the profitable state of trade. The employers announced they were unable to give an answer until they knew the proposals of the Cotton Control Board. At this point Dixon, Chairman of the Cotton Control Board, chose to announce an entirely new policy. Levies were to be paid on all machinery operated; there was to be a sliding scale and the more machinery run the higher the payment; a 40-hour week instead of 55 hours was to be introduced in American spinning, though there would be no unemployment pay for short-time working. At the same time the rota system which many operatives had regarded as fair was to be abolished, which meant that those who were unemployed were now to become permanently unemployed.

There were two major factors behind these changes. Firstly, the growing shortage of shipping space for raw cotton as a result of the military situation. Dixon had visited London alone to see the Shipping Controller who allocated shipping space and was informed that the industry would receive no raw cotton for two months, and further, that there was a question mark over whether supplies could be resumed after that. This raised the frightening possibility that the whole industry would have to close down. The Board's response was to increase from June the levies on employers in order to meet what it believed would be a critical situation. The changes in the levy system and unemployment pay were clearly a panic reaction on the part of the Board. They were concerned about unemployment in the industry rising rapidly and leading to social unrest. They believed the changes were the only way of containing the situation. Secondly, the Board's decision to abolish the rota system stemmed from Government concern that labour was urgently needed in munitions. The Government had been particularly outraged to find that their plan to build an aircraft factory in Oldham was likely to be undermined by the fact that there was no labour available to work in it. The Oldham munitions case appears to have influenced the Government's attitude to the rota system and they consequently brought pressure on the Board to end it.

When the cotton unions met the employers again John Smethurst, the Secretary of the F.M.C.S.A., argued that the change in levies had created a new situation, contending that the new increase was equivalent to a 30 per cent wage advance. The employers offered 20 per cent. The conference remained deadlocked for eight hours and was only broken with the intervention of Sir Herbert Dixon, who threatened the unions that unemployment pay would be ended unless agreement was reached:

> If you leave the unemployment out of it, and come back to us and ask for 100 per cent, ask what you like, and the Masters will consider it again, and probably throw their hats in the air and give you what other working people have got, but you must keep your own people that are out of employment.[11]

Dixon's intervention ended the disagreement; he suggested to the unions that if they accepted 25 per cent he would persuade the employers to agree to that figure. Dixon also signed the final agreement on behalf of the Cotton Control Board. This was an extraordinary act, given the Board's claim to have nothing to do with the wage negotiations. The effect of the wage award combined with short time was to effectively cut the wages of the Oldham spinners from June 1918. The advance of 25 per cent was worth approximately 18 per cent on weekly wages, but hours were being reduced by 25 per cent, leaving Oldham spinners with a wage reduction of approximately 10 per cent. Bolton spinners felt the full benefit of the advance because hours in the Egyptian sector were not being restricted. When the Representative Meeting of the Amalgamation met in June there was considerable opposition to the agreement by the Oldham delegates, but they agreed to accept the wage settlement while at the same time rejecting the new regulations of the Cotton Control Board. They argued the rota system should be retained and there should be compensation for short-time working, but the wage agreement and the new regulations were so closely interlinked that the rejection of one was effectively the rejection of the other. The Weavers soon joined with the Spinners in opposing the abolition of the rota system. The Cotton Control Board attempted to head off the protest by postponing the abolition of the rota system, due to begin in June, for six weeks, but this only encouraged the unions' opposition and they took their case to the President of the Board of Trade, Sir Albert Stanley. When they met Stanley he agreed to suspend ending the rota for a further two weeks while the case was investigated. At the end of the fortnight he upheld the decision of the Board but appealed to Dixon to raise the level of the permanent unemployment pay and in return the Government offered increased shipping space for raw cotton.

The attitude of the President of the Board of Trade, Sir Albert Stanley, is revealing because it indicates that one of the Government's concerns was with the possibility of social unrest in Lancashire. The Government was clearly conscious that Lancashire could become like Clydeside and South Wales, areas which had witnessed major strikes in the engineering and mining industries. The Government looked to the cotton trade unions as an example of moderation. Its aim, therefore, was to hold social unrest in check by unemployment provision. The Board's new concessions included a rise in unemployment pay of 20 per cent, raising weekly unemployment pay to 30 shillings for men and 18 shillings for women. American spinning mills were allowed to run 55 per cent of their spindles for 45½ hours, as opposed to the original regulation of 50 per cent capacity for 40 hours. The Board believed that the effect of this would be to absorb the unemployed operatives.

The United Textile Factory Workers' Association (U.T.F.W.A.), which had conducted the negotiations with the President of the Board of Trade, met in August 1918 to discuss the concessions and voted narrowly by 116 to 114 votes to accept the new proposals. Later on the same day, the Spinners' Executive met and recommended the acceptance of the new agreement, but this was rejected by the Representative Meeting which by a large majority voted to hold a ballot of members on whether to strike for short-time payments and retention of the rota system. The ballot produced a majority of 81 per cent in favour of strike action, just over the union's 80 per cent rule. Voting varied according to Districts, Oldham was solidly for the strike by almost nine votes to one, but in Bolton the vote was only two to one in favour. The strength of feeling in the Oldham area was not surprising given that the Province had already voted to call a strike and it was in Oldham that the brunt of short-time working would be felt. The Executive were summoned to London to meet Sir David Shackleton, by then the Permanent Secretary at the Ministry of Labour, who informed the Spinners' Amalgamation that the decision to strike was in contravention of the Defence of the Realm Act and therefore the union could not legally make strike payments. He justified this by arguing that a considerable portion of the output of cotton mills was required for the production of war materials, a surprising assertion given that the cotton industry had suffered throughout the war because of its lack of military priority.[12]

The threat of the strike was so significant that the Cabinet discussed it, believing that it was caused by the new unofficial shop stewards' movement based on Oldham. They therefore saw no advantage in putting the Spinners' President and Secretary in prison for leading a strike the Executive were opposed to, but rather they decided to make strike payment illegal, in the belief that the strikers' support would rapidly diminish without it.[13]

After hearing Shackleton's statement made to them in London, the Executive postponed the strike for a week and called a Special Representative Meeting. The meeting decided to implement the strike, which began in September. The Government's response was to seek an injunction preventing the Amalgamation from paying strike pay. At the same time Lloyd George, who was in Manchester, where he had received the freedom of the city, wrote to the Amalgamation:

A strike in the cotton trade would seriously interfere with the production of war material, and we are all most anxious that nothing should occur to make more difficult the task of our brave men who are engaged in deadly struggle with the enemy. Consequently, although I am for the moment confined to bed, and forbidden by my doctor to take part in public business, I cannot refrain from making an appeal in the interests of the men who are fighting, to the operative cotton spinners whose notices to cease work have now expired, to return to work, and leave the decision of the matters in dispute to the Government after an enquiry by a tribunal to be at once appointed by the Government.

The patriotism of Lancashire men has been tested in many fields, and has never yet failed.[14]

Such an appeal was difficult to resist for the Executive, who recommended acceptance; but the Representative Meeting referred the matter back to Districts. When the Representative Meeting re-assembled it accepted Lloyd George's recommendations. The strike ended after a week, but with the lifting of the injunction the Executive distributed retrospective strike pay.

The tribunal was held in the Manchester Town Hall in October under the chairmanship of Sir Dudley Stewart Smith K.C., with Sir A. Kaye Butterworth and George Rowe as the other members of the tribunal. Smith was a leading lawyer and Kaye Butterworth and Rowe were employers. The Cotton Control Board was represented by Sir Herbert Dixon and H. D. Henderson. Edward Judson and Henry Boothman represented the Amalgamation. The tribunal discussed three major issues: the advantages and disadvantages of the rota system; whether there was any precedent in the existing policy of the Cotton Control Board for making payments for short-time working; and whether the acceptance of the May wage agreement by the Amalgamation implied the acceptance of the Cotton Control Board's new regulations in June 1918.

Sir Herbert Dixon explained that it was the trade unions who were behind the original idea of the rota system:

These gentlemen will admit that I did not want the rota system from the very beginning, but I am rather soft, and when these gentlemen promised me 'if you only let this rota system go we will see that the people go to work' I gave way and gave it a trial. At the end of six months I was perfectly certain that it had not worked to the nation's aid.[15]

He then specified his reasons for the abolition of the rota.

> I don't deny for a moment that it is an excellent arrangement for the workmen,
> but the view of the Cotton Control Board ... was that it was not in the national
> interest. We had about 40,000 to 50,000 people out on the rota, and we had I
> think at least 10,000 to 15,000 places, jobs that wanted operatives for at least
> three months, and we could not get them under this rota system. The result
> is that labour was being wasted.[16]

The Amalgamation's opposition to the abolition of the rota system was by this time
not very strong, as Judson informed the tribunal:

> I must candidly admit straightaway that it has not been the hardship that we
> expected it would be. There are reasons for that. The first reason is because
> the age limit has been raised by which men can be taken into the army. The
> second reason is because many of the employers, recognising that if they were
> not short-handed they were going to be short-handed, have retained the
> services of those men and paid them wages to hang about the place rather
> than let them go and somebody else get hold of them.[17]

Out of a membership of 15,000, only 181 spinners were unemployed.

The main thrust of the union's argument centred around the question of short-
time pay. It was short time and the consequent reduction in wages which had wiped
out any gains to the Oldham spinners. What was particularly upsetting for the
union was that the economic distress of the operatives had not been shared by the
employers. Profits had been rising since the setting up of the Cotton Control Board
and reached new heights in 1918. The increased levies that the employers had paid
to the Board had not been required because unemployment had been lower than
expected. The crux of the Amalgamation's argument was that the money from
levies was theirs in lieu of wages and therefore they were entitled to decide how it
should be paid. If they wished to have short-time pay they could, as it was their
money. Surprising as this view may seem, it had been deliberately encouraged by
the employers. During the wage negotiations of May 1918, John Smethurst, the
Secretary of the F.M.C.S.A. had stated:

> Whether the money was paid as levies to the Cotton Control Board or
> advances in wages it was money for the operatives.[18]

However, Dixon informed the tribunal that when the increased levies were introduced in June he had told the employers that if any of the increased levies were
unnecessary the money would be returned. Dixon's statement took the union by
surprise:

> Judson: This rather contradicts the statement that Mr Smethurst made. He

said that this was money — he did not care whether it was in wages or levies
— it was money for the operatives.

Dixon: I have nothing to do with Mr Smethurst.

Judson: You will remember he made that statement in the Victoria Hotel,
when you were presiding.

Dixon: I have nothing to do with the statement. There were a heap of
statements made . . .[19]

The effect of this was to remove the underlying assumption behind the Spinners'
case for short-time payments.

Dixon's comments about the Amalgamation and the May wage agreement were
equally revealing. Dixon was annoyed that an agreement negotiated and accepted
by the union's leaders had then been rejected by the membership. He had regarded
the Amalgamation's rule requiring the agreement to be placed before the membership as a mere formality:

We are perfectly certain . . . that this movement has arisen from below. This
agreement was arrived at after eight hours' discussion. It was an agreement
which was intended by all of us to be kept — by the leaders of the men — kept
as they always have kept their agreements with us; and if the feeling gets
through the country that they are not in a position to keep agreements which
they sign, well then, God help the trade.[20]

While Dixon was correct to see the shop stewards' movement based on Oldham as
a growing influence within the Amalgamation, he ignored the extent to which the
influence of the shop stewards was a result of the falling real wages of the Oldham
spinners — a fall which contrasted vividly with the rising profits of the industry.
The tribunal in their recommendations clearly recognised this. Although they
rejected the Amalgamation's case, both on the rota and short time, they accepted
that given the level of profits in the industry the fall in wages was not justifiable.
The tribunal recommended that the Spinners' Amalgamation and the F.M.C.S.A.
meet before the wage agreement ended in December 1918 to seek a modification in
it in order to raise wages. The tribunal had recognised the Spinners' grievance as
legitimate, but condemned their solution to it.[21]

The F.M.C.S.A., not being represented at the tribunal, felt under no obligation
to carry out the recommendations. Negotiations between the Spinners and their
employers did not begin until after the end of the war in November 1918. The
Spinners applied for a wage advance of 40 per cent on current rates, equivalent to
over 68 per cent on the wage list. When they put their case to the F.M.C.S.A. they
placed great emphasis on the tribunal's recommendations, but the employers
claimed that the ending of the war had generated great uncertainty. They finally

offered 40 per cent on the wage list, which the Spinners rejected. The Amalgamation then balloted their members for strike action, voting 10,132 to 424 in favour. The strike began in the first week of December 1918 and was organised jointly with the Cardroom Amalgamation. At the same time the Weavers submitted a claim for a wage advance which was being examined by a Court of Arbitration.[22]

The Prime Minister, Lloyd George, again intervened. A General Election was about to take place and Lloyd George was concerned that a cotton strike would increase the vote for Labour in Lancashire. The Amalgamation refused the offer of arbitration by the Government, but Lloyd George invited the Executive Committee of the Spinners' Amalgamation and the Cardroom Amalgamation together with the F.M.C.S.A. to meet him in London. The Court of Arbitration on the Weavers' claim was rushed through in record time and they were awarded a 50 per cent advance on the wage list. Lloyd George suggested to both Amalgamations and the F.M.C.S.A. that the Court's recommendations should be the basis of an agreement between them. Both sides accepted this suggestion — the Spinners' Amalgamation's opposition to arbitration appears to have been overruled by the presence of Lloyd George and the setting of 10 Downing Street — and the strike was called off after two weeks.[23]

The end of hostilities in 1918 was immediately followed by a post-war boom which lasted till the summer of 1920. This boom was characterised by a very high level of profits on a scale not seen since the industrial revolution, and by massive speculation in the industry. Approximately 40 per cent of the spindles in the industry changed hands between 1918 and 1920. The bulk of this occurred in the Oldham spinning sector where the tradition of limited liability encouraged these developments. The main factor behind the boom and subsequent speculation was that Lancashire, due to a shortage of raw material and transport difficulties caused by the war, had been cut off from many of its main markets, so that the boom was largely a re-stocking boom as former customers bought up Lancashire cotton for the first time since 1914.

Significantly, the boom differed from the pre-war booms in that it had not lead to any expansion in the industry due to the speed and the difficulties of wartime dislocation which held up building work. Speculators, in order to participate in the boom, had to buy up existing capacity so that in 1919 the industry was characterised by a growing demand for existing mill companies to either sell out or to be re-capitalised. The nature of mill finance in Lancashire meant that the boom was financed by large-scale borrowing, especially from the Lancashire banks such as Williams Deacon's and the District Bank. The Amalgamation protested jointly with the Cardroom Amalgamation against the speculation during 1919 to the F.M.C.S.A. They received a complacent reply, being told that as the cost of building new mills had greatly increased since the war, it made sense to increase the value of cotton companies to take this into account.[24]

In 1919 the growing militancy of the Spinners was expressed in the demand for the 48 hour week. There was opposition to starting work before breakfast and increasing recognition that the industry would not attract labour if workers were forced to start work at six o'clock in the morning, especially in an industry which employed so many women and children. The movement was also part of a wider campaign by the trade unions for a reduction in hours — engineers and railwaymen had already won a reduction. Two factors contributed to the general campaign, the belief that a reduction in hours of work was part of the promise of a 'land fit for heroes', and, secondly, the fear of unemployment created by the ending of the war. The boom of 1919 created the classic combination of factors that led to a reduction of hours, an ability for trade unions to win major concessions combined with a growing fear of unemployment. The two earlier votes by cotton operatives for the 48 hour week in 1894 and 1909 had taken place against the background of depression; the 1919 vote took place in much more favourable circumstances. The movement for a reduction of hours was also international and cuts in the working week took place in major competitor nations, thus reducing the effect of the employers' counter-argument that only foreign competition would benefit from a reduction.

Both the Oldham and Bolton Provinces had passed resolutions in favour of a reduction in hours, Oldham for 48 hours and Bolton for 44 hours per week. This movement was also reflected amongst other cotton operatives, especially the Weavers who were passing similar resolutions. The hours issue was a question for the U.T.F.W.A. rather than individual unions, and they applied jointly to the two employers' organisations, the F.M.C.S.A. and the C.S.M.A., for a reduction in hours to 44 hours per week from the existing 55½ hours in February 1919.

The employers' organisations rejected the application, offering a 49½ hour week. The negotiations continued into early May, when the employers made a final offer of a 48 hour week and a 15 per cent wage advance. By then the 48 hour week no longer looked such a substantial concession, since the National Industrial Conference, an attempt by Lloyd George to head off labour unrest, had already voted for a 48 hour week. The general belief was that the Government would have to legalise this and therefore all employers would be forced to grant it. The offer from the cotton employers, therefore, looked even less attractive, especially as the 15 per cent on the wage list only covered half the predicted loss in wages as a result of the reduction in hours. All the cotton unions balloted their members and had majorities for strike action. The Spinners voted 18,531 to 393 in favour of a strike.

After the ballot the unions gave notice of strike action, the first ever general strike by cotton operatives. The Ministry of Labour intervened and Sir Robert Horne, the Minister, summoned both sides to a meeting in London. Horne expressed his concern about the consequences of a strike as 'we always look upon the cotton industry in this Ministry as one of the steadiest elements in the country'. His hopes, however, were dashed by the absence of the F.M.C.S.A. who refused to attend the meeting. Their claim that there had been insufficient notice and the difficulty of getting accommodation was hardly credible. The headline in the *Cotton Factory Times* was 'Couldn't get digs'! Horne reconvened the meeting the next day when it became clear that the F.M.C.S.A. was opposed to any intervention by the Ministry of Labour and the Minister was left to withdraw with a bloody nose.

However, Horne did arrange a meeting between all the employers and unions at Manchester Town Hall on the Friday prior to the start of the strike. The employers made a new offer of 48 hours a week and 25 per cent on the wage list, but this was refused. The U.T.F.W.A. put forward two propositions to the employers. They suggested that the employers grant either a 46½ hour week with a 25 per cent wage advance, or a 48 hour week with a 30 per cent wage advance, but both were rejected.

The strike, which involved 450,000 operatives, started the following Monday, 21 June 1919, but on the very first day of the strike a meeting of the Cotton Control Board took place under Sir Herbert Dixon. The President of the Manchester Chamber of Commerce suggested that the negotiations between the operatives and the employers should resume under Dixon's chairmanship. This was agreed, and after a meeting lasting several hours an agreement was reached for a 48 hour week and a 30 per cent advance on the wage list. The dispute appeared to be over.

The Spinners' Executive, meeting at Southport where they were attending the Labour Party Conference, rejected the new agreement and called a Special Representative Meeting to discuss the matter. When the U.T.F.W.A. met to consider the award it was only accepted narrowly by 166 votes to 138. This did not end the matter though, because two days later the Spinners' Representative Meeting met and rejected the award.

The relationship between the Spinners and the other cotton unions was strained even further when the Secretary of the Oldham Spinners, Fred Birchenough, publicly accused representatives of another Amalgamation of having 'sold' the Spinners. He alleged there had been a secret agreement with the employers to accept 48 hours and 30 per cent on the wage list. His remarks appear to have been aimed at the Cardroom Amalgamation and to have been motivated by the growing criticism that the Spinners' opposition to the agreement was due to the influence of the shop stewards' movement.

There is some evidence to sustain Birchenough's accusation. Writing of the negotiations in the Manchester Town Hall, Peter Bullough, the Bolton Spinners' Secretary, observed: 'Our side went inadvisedly, I thought, to the length of offering to accept a 48 hour week and a 30 per cent increase on standard. This was refused, although some on our side asserted they had the best of reasons for believing it would be accepted'. He also commented after the meeting which negotiated the settlement: 'I am afraid the whole thing is hurried, and in the face of the employers' refusal, only so lately as last Friday, of the same proposals, rather suspicious. I fear trouble will arise.' His prophecy was certainly correct and the strike continued for a further three weeks.

The Spinners were not alone in their opposition to the new agreement. A number of weaving districts continued to oppose it and even in the Cardroom Amalgamation there was growing opposition led by an emerging shop stewards' movement again based in Oldham. In south-east Lancashire there were disturbances in Hyde, Stalybridge and Ashton, when operatives marched from mill to mill calling workers out in a similar manner to the 1840s. Apparently they were led by dissatisfied Cardroom operatives and weavers, whose grievance was as much against their own union as the employers. The Spinners refused to continue negotiations via the

U.T.F.W.A. and insisted instead that combined cotton union executives form the negotiating body. The employers were reluctant to meet the new body arguing that what was now taking place was not a strike against them but an inter-union conflict. Finally persuaded to resume negotiations, they were adamant about not reducing hours below 48 per week. Their main argument against reducing hours was their fear of increasing foreign competition. They did agree, though, that the wages part of the agreement should be re-negotiated at the end of twelve months rather than eighteen months as originally agreed, the Spinners believing correctly that the forthcoming boom would enable them to seek a further wage advance. The strike came to an end after three weeks. In all the strike resulted in over 8 million working days being lost and was the largest strike in 1919.[25]

The 1919 dispute was the first general strike in the industry that involved all sectors and offered the best opportunity for the unions to turn their co-operation into a more permanent organisation. There was growing discussion at the U.T.F.W.A. about the idea of an industrial union. The 1919 dispute was a missed opportunity. The circumstances it ended in were farcical and provide some justification for the comments of contemporaries like the Webbs, who suggested that sectionalism held back cotton operatives. Sectionalism, though, was not the motive of the Spinners in rejecting a settlement. It was clearly an attempt by the leadership to regain its credibility amongst the membership and to head off the growing influence of the shop stewards' movement.[26]

The absence of any detailed records apart from correspondence in the *Cotton Factory Times* makes it difficult to judge the nature of the shop stewards' movement in cotton spinning. In 1919 the movement claimed to represent some 7,000 spinners, but its influence seems to have been confined to the Oldham Province, whose secretary Birchenough was a vigorous critic. There is no evidence that the movement was politically radical as well as industrially militant, which was the feature of the shop stewards' movement in engineering also active in Lancashire. The unofficial engineering strikes of the spring of 1917 started from Rochdale and must have influenced the Spinners. The Amalgamation was unique among the three main cotton unions in having a shop organisation, though even within the Amalgamation the role of the shop differed. The government of the Bolton Province was based on the shop system which sent delegates to the Province. In Oldham it was based on branches. The shop met regularly discussing both shop, district or provincial business and Amalgamation affairs, it elected a chairman and secretary and also had its own funds. The shop was the key element in the organisation of the Amalgamation and the creation of a rival centre of power based on representatives of the shop threatened the full-time officials. Its existence was relatively brief— 1918-20 — but during this period it was perceived by both employers and the Amalgamation's leadership as a threat to the existing pattern of industrial relations. The lack of any political ideology in the shop stewards' movement meant that, unlike engineering, the movement was not a particular advocate of industrial unionism.

Although the shop stewards' movement represented a threat to the Executive of the Spinners' Amalgamation and forced the Spinners into a position of industrial militancy, the shop stewards' movement within spinning represented a conservative rather than a radical force within cotton. The shop stewards' movement within spinning did not want an industrial union that brought all cotton workers together. They wanted to maintain their privileged position and their differentials in wage agreements. They were more industrially militant not simply because they wanted to fight the employers, but because they were anxious to keep their distance from other workers in cotton, both within the workforce and within their own union organisation. For this reason, then, the chance to form an industrial union which could have benefited all cotton operatives was lost.[27]

The Amalgamation decided to take advantage of the continuing boom to seek a further wage advance and even threatened to seek one before the existing wage agreement ended. The F.M.C.S.A. recognised the case, given the level of profits being generated in the industry, and towards the end of 1919 paid special bonuses to their employees. In the spring of 1920 the cotton operatives won their largest ever wage advance, 70 per cent on the wage list, bringing the wage list to 210 per cent above the 1914 list price, with the result that for the first time since 1914 wages in the industry were ahead of prices. Despite the level of profits in the industry, the wage agreement had only been made possible by the intervention of Sir David Shackleton acting on behalf of the Ministry of Labour. The employers had begrudgingly granted the wage increase and as later events were to show, greatly resented this agreement.[28]

Wages were now at their high point for the inter-war period, according to a F.M.C.S.A. survey of 1920, a Bolton spinner earned £5 16s. 11d. and Oldham £5 6s. 5d., compared with the 1906 figure of £2 5s. 9d. and £2 1s. 10d. Big piecers earned in Oldham £2 10s. 7d. compared with £1 15s. 10d. in Bolton, while little piecers earned £1 14s. 2d. and £1 1s. 11d. respectively. Bolton, though a high wage district for spinners, was a low wage area for piecers, whilst Oldham piecers had traditionally earned a higher proportion of the spinners' earnings, 47.5 per cent for the big piecers and 32 per cent for little piecers, compared with Bolton where the respective percentages were 30 per cent and 19 per cent. The proportion had fallen in Bolton between 1906 and 1920. Traditionally this distinction had been explained in terms of the greater demand for labour from engineering in Oldham, which forced spinners to hand over a larger proportion of the total wage of the team to the piecers. However, it is clear that part of the explanation of higher spinners' wages in Bolton was the lower wages of piecers. Despite this, piecer membership of the union was higher in Bolton.[29]

The benefits of the advance were only felt for a short period by the spinners. By the summer of 1920 unemployment was increasing in the industry and by October 1920 short time was introduced in both the American and Egyptian spinning sectors. Large-scale unemployment and short-time working took a heavy toll on the Amalgamation's funds and the Executive began to be apprehensive that there would be a demand from the employers for a wage reduction. This proved to be correct when they demanded 95 per cent off the wage list, equivalent to a 30 per cent reduction of current wage rates.

The F.M.C.S.A. met the Amalgamation, and their secretary, John Smethurst, argued that the previous wage advance had only been given because of the level of profits in the industry and not because of any increase in the cost of living, and this was the reason they were now seeking a wage reduction. He argued that the price of Lancashire cotton was too high and as a result the demand abroad was falling and that it was the wages that were the major cause of declining competitiveness. According to Smethurst wages were over three times higher than before the war, but Henry Boothman pointed out that dividends were eight times higher in 1920 than they were before the war.

The cotton unions met and decided to co-operate in their resistance to general wage reductions. Negotiations began at the end of May 1921 with the operatives offering to accept a 20 per cent reduction off the wage list on the grounds this represented the fall in the cost of living. The employers, who also negotiated jointly, refused to budge. Discussion with the employers revealed the strength of the resentment about the previous 70 per cent wage advance. The weaving employers were adamant that it was not justified and it was clear that they had not enjoyed the prosperity of spinning employers in 1919 and 1920.

The unions were particularly bitter about the employers' failure to make a counter-offer after they had offered to accept a wage reduction. Henry Boothman complained 'we have started from nothing and got up to 25 per cent and they had started at a high figure but had only come down 5 per cent. They had not come down the ordinary route'. The F.M.C.S.A.'s secretary, Smethurst, replied 'Eliminate from your minds the possibility that because you go up we are coming down.' He further added 'so far as this side of the table is concerned we are going to break with the old lines.' Nothing could illustrate more clearly than this exchange the change in atmosphere in industrial relations that had taken place in 1921. Further negotiations eventually led to the cotton unions offering 50 per cent and the employers indicating that they would accept 70 per cent. Negotiations collapsed. According to a report sent to the Ministry of Labour by one of its officials in Manchester, the breakdown was a great shock to the cotton trade union leaders, who remarked to the official that had the employers shown a little more forebearance a stoppage would have been avoided.

The stoppage began on 6 June and according to the *Cotton Factory Times* with over half a million operatives locked out this was the largest ever dispute in the industry. Its size and significance soon brought about the intervention of the Ministry of Labour, which summoned both parties to London in the first week of the strike. The employers were adamant that the trade should solve its own problems and were particularly keen to keep out Sir David Shackleton, who they held personally responsible for the 70 per cent wage advance in 1920. The employers' antipathy towards the Ministry had been so great that during the negotiations prior to the strike the Ministry's officials had been cold-shouldered by them and had to rely on the trade union side for reliable reports on what was happening. The Minister of Labour, Dr McNamara, was concerned about the fact that the cotton strike coincided with the miners' dispute.

McNamara persuaded both sides to resume negotiations at the end of the first week of the strike. The cotton unions had expressed to him a desire for a Ministry official to act as the chairman of the new negotiations. The employers, though, made it clear to the Minister that under no circumstances would they accept his intervention. Smethurst stated that:

> the employers desired that negotiations should be direct with representatives of the unions and without the intervention of any third party. This desire was not animated by any lack of respect for the Minister. It was due to what might be termed prejudice in Lancashire as to intervention. It was felt that both sides understood each other and would probably make better progress once they got together if they were left to themselves.[30]

Negotiations between the two sides continued into the second week of the dispute, with the employers refusing to reduce their demand for wage reductions below 70 per cent. The union negotiating team had been instructed not to move above a 55 per cent reduction without a further move from the employers. It was at this point that John Smethurst attempted to break the deadlock and suggested a settlement whereby the final reduction was 70 per cent, but this was to be reached in two stages.

The unions' negotiators met the employers again and proposed that there should be a 60 per cent reduction for six months, followed by a further 10 per cent reduction. Judson told the employers 'We should be under great difficulties in carrying through a recommendation on these lines greater than any settlement he had been at during the past twenty years.' This suggestion became the basis of the agreement that both sides agreed to recommend to their members. The cotton unions agreed to meet two days later after their respective unions had discussed the question. The meeting of all the cotton unions ended in a similar fiasco to 1919. At their own meetings the Cardroom had agreed to accept the wage agreement despite having considerable doubts about the way the negotiations had taken place. James Crinion, the President of the Cardroom, had objected to the constant face-to-face meeting with the employers, preferring the traditional approach of passing notes between each side! The Weavers had voted to oppose the proposed agreement against the advice of their President and Secretary. The Spinners' Amalgamation met with the Bolton and Oldham Provinces already committed to opposing the agreement. Judson and Boothman persuaded the meeting to postpone a decision until they had balloted the members, suggesting that there had not been enough time for the members to be fully consulted. Whether they would have felt so strongly about the issue of consultation had they not faced defeat is doubtful.

All the cotton unions met on the afternoon of the same day to discuss their joint attitude, and the Weavers' Amalgamation moved the reference back of the agreement much to the embarrassment of the Weavers' leaders. When the Bolton Spinners' President, Albert Law, announced that he wished to move postponement of the resolution for a week, uproar broke out in the meeting. Once again the

Spinners appeared to be the disruptive element. The Chairman ignored this call to postpone the decision and went ahead with the vote, which accepted the agreement by 266 votes to 227. The Spinners abstained. Clearly, had the Spinners' delegates voted, the agreement would not have been accepted and their decision to abstain guaranteed acceptance of the wage agreement.

The following week as the strike continued, the Weavers balloted their members who voted to accept the agreement and return to work by two to one. Similarly, the Spinners held shop meetings throughout each District and reversed the vote which had rejected the agreement, thus ending the lockout which had lasted three weeks. The change in attitude amongst the Spinners is explained partly by the acceptance of the wage agreement by the meeting of all the cotton unions, which helped to demoralise opposition to the agreement throughout Lancashire and that the Spinners' Executive put all its authority behind the wage agreement, recommending it to the members and suggesting that no better deal was possible.[31]

During this period of labour unrest a number of advances were made by the Amalgamation, the most important being the introduction of the 48 hour week which had been a goal of the Amalgamation since the early 1890s. The abolition of starting work before breakfast made work a more civilised experience for the cotton operatives and was the major gain from the wartime period. Another significant change in the industry was the abolition of the half-time system, bringing to an end the system of child labour in the cotton factory, one of the great blots on its progress from the industrial revolution onwards. Though this was not how the operatives viewed the system, their children's contributions to the family wage always having been an important part of their standard of living. Even in 1918 the operatives voted for the continuation of the system by approximately two to one, the result of the Spinners' ballot being 7,230 for the half-time system and 4,655 for its abolition. At the same time, the Amalgamation signed both oiling and cleaning agreements with the F.M.C.S.A. which ended many years of abuse in the factory, as both employers and operatives broke the Factory Act by oiling and cleaning working machines before the start of the working day or during the dinner break. The spinner did not want to stop machinery during working time for oiling and cleaning unless he was compensated for the loss of production; the new agreement did this.[32]

The First World War also led to a change in the Amalgamation's attitude towards the piecer; from 1919 onwards they were to be members of the Amalgamation. Prior to that Provinces and Districts had separate membership for piecers, and payment of strike and lockout pay varied. By making them members of the Amalgamation, strike pay and benefits were made uniform and the likelihood of smaller districts being unable to pay their piecers and therefore jeopardising a strike was avoided. Also, by enrolling them into the organisation, total membership was doubled overnight and this the Executive believed was likely to increase the influence of the Amalgamation. However, piecers were not to be full members of the organisation, they could not attend shop meetings and therefore still relied on others to raise their grievances within the organisation.

By June 1920 the Amalgamation's membership had reached an all-time high of 55,521, of whom 24,537 were spinners and 30,984 piecers. The composition of the Amalgamation at this time was a membership of 19,954 in Oldham and 17,176 in Bolton, though the Bolton figure had a much higher number of piecers reflecting its traditionally higher membership of piecers. This was achieved by insisting that the piecer's subscription should be paid by the spinner, thus ensuring almost complete membership, the piecer having no choice in the matter. The other Provinces were Preston 1,543 members, Yorkshire 1,700 and Blackburn with 1,762 members. The largest Districts were Ashton, 2,675; Hyde, 1,116; Mossley, 1,078; and Rochdale, 2,400. The Amalgamation was largely a south-east Lancashire organisation with its centres of strength in Oldham and Bolton.[33]

The most significant change in the period 1914-21 was the re-awakening of the Spinners' industrial militancy, there were a number of factors that explain this crucial change. The freezing of wage rates between 1910-15 at a time of rising prices was followed by the war which saw rapid price inflation while wage rates rose slowly, only catching up by the end of 1918. This experience was similar to that of many other workers, but the spinners differed in that they also suffered from unemployment and short-time during the war whilst other workers offset a fall in real wages through regularity of work or overtime. The traditionally militant Oldham Spinners were the worst hit due to the shortage of American raw cotton. These developments took place against the background of very high profits in the industry during the latter part of the war. At the same time expectations were rising due to a combination of the growth of the trade union movement and the Labour Party and Lloyd George's promise of a 'land fit for heroes'. In order to ensure that wartime unrest did not spread, the Government's message was that there would be no return to the pre-1914 world. The effect of all this was to give the spinners both a sense of grievance and a sense of the possibility of change, they seized this opportunity to a degree which surprised their leadership. This level of militancy began to threaten the Amalgamation's leadership with the emergence of an unofficial shop stewards' movement, largely based on Oldham. The threatening feature of the shop stewards' movement was that the strength of the union was in its shop organisation. If shops were to set up their own shop stewards' organisation then the very basis of the Amalgamation's authority would be challenged. It was this fact that explains the more militant attitude of the Executive in 1919 during the hours dispute. But this militancy was to be short-lived, it was crushed by the onset of the depression which began in 1921.

CHAPTER NINE

Spinners in the Inter-War Years

The depression of the 1920s in the cotton industry was not a general depression but was based on particular sectors. The most severely hit was the American cotton spinning Province of Oldham. The Bolton Province of the Amalgamation remained relatively prosperous throughout the 1920s and even managed to increase its membership. The cause of the depression was twofold: the recapitalisation of the industry between 1918 and 1920 and the growth of economic nationalism amongst developing countries, especially India. The depression was made more severe by government policy, in particular the decision to return to the Gold Standard in 1925 which had the effect of making it even more difficult to succeed in increasingly competitive export markets.

The recapitalisation of the industry had affected some 40 per cent of the spinning sector's capacity, with the coarse yarns of Oldham most affected. The history of limited liability combined with the shortage of raw cotton during the First World War, and the existence of a large pent-up demand for coarse goods in the immediate aftermath of the war, created a seller's market. The high profits that resulted attracted speculators who, in order to participate in the boom, had to buy up those companies already established in the industry. The boom of 1919 was essentially a price boom, and no major expansion in productive capacity occurred. The consequence was that firms were bought and sold on the assumption that the post-war boom in profits would continue. The reality was that the position of the Lancashire cotton industry in the world market had been transformed by the war. The growth of protection in India and the rise of Japanese competition were the two major developments. Approximately two-thirds of its lost markets were beyond the industry's control because of the economic nationalism of India. The other third was due to Japanese competition in the markets of the Far East, and it could be argued that a more competitive Lancashire could have held on to some of that trade.

The effect of recapitalisation was to place a significant proportion of the industry in the hands of the banks. The banks prolonged the agony by keeping firms in existence longer than was commercially viable, their aim being somehow to rescue their loans. The result was that many firms in the 1920s were competing at prices on which they made a loss, and in doing so they dragged down more viable firms as well.[1]

The experience of the Amalgamation in the 1920s was dominated by wage cuts, short-time and unemployment. The 70 per cent wage reduction of 1921 was followed by a further reduction in 1922 of 50 per cent off the wage list. The effect of these two wage cuts was to remove the two major post-war advances of 1918 and 1920, leaving as the only gain of the immediate post-war period the 48-hour week and the 30 per cent advance achieved in 1919. The latter advance had been granted to compensate operatives for loss of wages due to the reduction in hours. The 1920 wage advance had raised the wage list to the record high of 215 per cent, some 210 per cent above 1914, which represented a wage increase of 160 per cent over 1914, compared with an increase in the cost of living of 150 per cent. By 1922, when the cost of living had declined to 83 per cent above 1914, wages had fallen even faster, representing an advance of only 60 per cent on 1914. The continued fall in the cost of living in the 1920s, combined with wage stability, nearly restored real wages to their 1914 levels by 1929, when a further wage cut occurred.[2]

The 1922 wage cut was again a joint movement by employers, the two employers' organisations, the Federation of Master Cotton Spinners' Associations (F.M.C.S.A.) and the Cotton Spinners' and Manufacturers' Association (C.S.M.A.). This time, unlike in 1921, the cotton unions did not resist, agreeing to accept the principle of a wage reduction. Though the employers negotiated jointly the cotton unions were not united, the Cardroom Amalgamation negotiating separately. In fact it was the Cardroom Amalgamation's decision to accept a 50 per cent reduction of the wage list in two stages, 40 per cent and a further 10 per cent reduction six months later, that made any resistance by the Spinners and Weavers useless. All the Amalgamations feared that a prolonged strike or lockout, coupled with the high cost of unemployment benefits, would destroy the financial basis of their organisations. They also appear to have accepted, to some extent, the employers' argument that in the long run the reduction would work to the operatives' advantage by increasing trade and therefore employment. In 1923, after further negotiations between the two sides, wages were stabilised. The stabilising of wages reflected the growing stability of the industry as it recovered from the slump of 1920-2. By 1924, the industry was producing some 6 million square yards of cloth, exporting 4.5 million and employing 500,000 workers, compared with 8 million square yards produced and over 600,000 operatives employed in 1912.

The effect of the depression had been to reduce the industry's level of production by a quarter, though not its capacity to produce. The membership of the Amalgamation was not immune from such changes and it fell from 55,521 in June 1920 to 47,551 in 1928, the major loss being in the Oldham Province, whilst membership in Bolton actually increased. Though the industry declined in these years, the effect was not general and the Bolton fine trade enjoyed a measure of prosperity between 1922 and 1928. It was therefore still possible for both employers and trade unionists in Lancashire to believe in a return to Edwardian prosperity. Employers were still paying dividends, though under 5 per cent for most of the 1920s, and as low as 2 per cent in some years, compared with the dizzy heights of profits experienced in 1919 and 1920. The industry was even buying new machinery, though the total number of spinning mules fell slightly and most of the new investment was concentrated in ring spindles. Despite the comparative stability of the industry after 1923 unemployment remained high, and estimates suggest that over a quarter of the labour force were unemployed in the early 1920s and that even with the recovery, unemployment remained around 15 per cent for the remainder of the 1920s. The majority of this unemployment and short time in spinning was based on the coarse spinning towns, especially Oldham. The assumption made by economic historians such as Lars Sandberg that short-time working was a policy supported by the cotton trade unions at this time is questionable. In January 1922, Henry Boothman observed:

> We are constantly being told that a reduction in the cost of production must be effected, but it is difficult to see how such a reduction can be brought about when employers find it expedient to run their mills at about half capacity, and in numerous instances to stop them altogether for long periods . . . it is not obvious how production costs can be reduced unless full-time running is resumed.[3]

The Amalgamation continued to be critical of the use of short-time throughout the 1920s, and for many members in the Oldham Province full-time working was a novelty during these years.[4]

The political attitudes of spinners do not seem to have been radicalised by the experience of the 1920s. Two members of the Amalgamation were elected as Labour Members of Parliament between 1918 and 1929: Alfred Davies for the weaving constituency of Clitheroe in 1918, and Albert Law for Bolton in 1923 and 1929. Both were working spinners and it was a noticeable feature of the inter-war period that the leading full-time officials of the Amalgamation were no longer prepared to stand for Parliament. Alfred Davies was President of the Hyde Spinners and a member of the Amalgamation's Executive when he was elected M.P. for Clitheroe. Though the Parliamentary Labour Party had only 60 members in 1918, four of whom were cotton trade unionists, he failed to make an impact in the Party or in the House of Commons. Albert Law was elected M.P. for Bolton in both 1923 and 1929, the years of the minority Labour Governments. While well-known in Lancashire, having been President of the Bolton Spinners' Association, he also failed to make an impact on the Parliamentary Labour Party. Working men were at a disadvantage when elected compared with full-time trade union officials, and when Davies and Law were defeated in 1922 and 1931 they had great difficulty in finding work in the industry, partly due to political prejudice but also to the seniority rule in the spinning room, by which the longest-serving piecer had to be promoted to the first vacancy.[5]

The Lancashire cotton constituencies slowly swung to the left in the 1920s and by 1929 all the main cotton towns returned Labour Members of Parliament. In the Amalgamation the pattern still remained the same, with Bolton rather than Oldham showing the greater interest in political questions — three of the Bolton Presidents in the inter-war years stood as Labour candidates, John Battle, Albert Law and George Illingworth. The difference in political attitudes was starkly revealed when following the General Strike the Trade Disputes Act was introduced in 1927. The General Strike, the most dramatic event in the history of labour in the inter-war years, made little impact on the Amalgamation. Members were to be balloted to find out if they were prepared to answer the T.U.C.'s call for sympathy action in support of the miners, but the strike was called off before the ballot was taken. The Conservative Government's response was the Trade Disputes Act which, as well as outlawing general strikes, included the provision that trade unionists paying the political levy to the Labour Party had to 'contract in', reversing the practice established by the 1913 Trade Union Act. The result was a large loss in trade union support for the Labour Party, with only 21,000 out of 48,000 Amalgamation members paying the political levy in 1928. Nationally, the Labour Party lost one third of its support, but in the Amalgamation support was more than halved, and the loss was greater than that of the other cotton unions. In Bolton approximately 10,000 out of a membership of 18,000 paid the levy, whereas in Oldham only some 4,500 of 15,000 members contracted in, further indication of the different attitudes towards politics, although despite this difference both Bolton and Oldham returned Labour Members of Parliament in 1923 and 1929.[6]

The background to these changes was the general decline of the influence of the cotton unions on the Labour Party in the 1920s. In 1918, when 60 Labour M.P.s were elected, four were cotton trade unionists; in 1923, when the first minority Labour Government was formed, only three of the 191 Labour M.P.s were cotton trade unionists; in 1929, when Labour was for the first time the largest party in the House of Commons, four out of the 287 Labour M.P.s were cotton trade unionists. The decline in influence reflects the unwillingness of the cotton trade unions to raise their political levy in order to sponsor more Labour candidates and to pay constituency Labour parties a greater contribution.

The result was that when Lancashire swung to the left in 1929, and elected for the first time a majority of Labour MPs, the main beneficiaries were the general unions rather than the cotton unions, as would have been the case in 1918. A major factor in the growth of support for Labour in 1929 in Lancashire was the Labour Party's adoption of the cotton unions' demand for a government inquiry into the industry. This demand became part of the Labour Party's new programme, *Labour and the Nation*. The cotton unions believed that such an inquiry would expose the real cause of the industry's problems, the recapitalisation of the post-war boom, and would thus undermine the employers' case for a further wage reduction.[7]

The election of the minority Labour Government in 1929 coincided with an intensification of the depression in the industry. The employers' response was to demand a wage reduction. Many cotton operatives thought the threatened wage reduction had been proposed as an act of revenge for them voting Labour. In the previous year both employers' organisations had approached the unions seeking a wage reduction and an increase in the working week. A series of conferences between the two sides had taken place but had broken down. The Lancashire press had been particularly hostile to the cotton employers' proposals, and when both the F.M.C.S.A. and the C.S.M.A. put their proposals for a lockout to their members neither achieved the required support for action; the Bolton employers even voted against the proposals, a reflection of the continued prosperity in that part of the trade. The cotton unions had successfully beaten off the employers' attempts to reduce their wages and increase their hours, but their success owed a great deal to the employers' own disunity. By 1929 the depression had begun to affect the fine spinning firms of Bolton, and this convinced all the employers of the need for a wage reduction. In fine spinning, the situation was exacerbated by coarse spinning firms moving into the higher counts.[8]

The employers' offensive of June 1929 persuaded all the cotton unions once more to work together to oppose the wage reduction. The Spinners balloted their members and there was overwhelming support for strike action. The employers' vote for a lockout had been similarly decisive and this brought the intervention of the Ministry of Labour in the form of its Permanent Secretary, Sir Horace Wilson. He arranged for the two sides to meet in July but little progress was made, even the employers' suggestion that both sides form a small negotiating committee was rejected by the unions until the employers withdrew the lockout notices. A few days later Wilson again intervened, inviting both sides to meet him. The cotton unions' negotiating team included Henry Boothman, the Amalgamation's Secretary, Fred Birchenough, the Oldham Secretary who had become President of the Amalgamation following Judson's death, and William Wood, Vice-President of the Amalgamation and Bolton Secretary. The initial suggestion of the unions was that wages should remain the same until the new Labour Government's enquiry into the industry reported, but the employers claimed they were unable to meet this demand because of the uncertainty the waiting would create.

The two sides did agree to meet to discuss their respective cases. The cotton unions' argument was that they saw little difference between the employers' present case for wage reductions and those arguments presented in 1921 and 1922. Then the employers had argued that a reduction in wage rates would lead to greater trade and less unemployment. If this was so, the unions wanted to know, why did they now want another wage reduction, and where was the trade? The unions decided after some discussion to make an offer of arbitration to the employers under the Industrial Courts Act of 1919. This suggestion threw the employers' representatives, who had been expecting the unions to accept a wage reduction. They made a counter-offer suggesting that they would reduce their demand from 25 per cent if the unions would agree to a reduction in principle. Henry Boothman made a powerful speech in favour of acceptance, arguing that 'in every dispute that has resulted in a strike, we could have got the result before the stoppage that we got afterwards. I submit that is the case now.' Despite Boothman's speech the unions voted to reject the principle of a wage reduction.

It was at this point, after three days of negotiations, that the cotton unions' unity began to break up. Executives of the Spinners and Cardroom met after the vote and demanded from the other Executives that the decision be reconsidered. This led to a long and heated discussion and it was Boothman who suggested a further approach to the employers to once more seek arbitration. However, the employers remained firm. On the following day, as the employers' notices were set to expire, the combined Executives of the cotton unions met, though the Weavers had already decided they could not accept the principle of a wage reduction. This decision again upset both the Cardroom and Spinners' Executives and effectively ended any chance of a settlement. In fact the Weavers' Executive had no choice in rejecting the principle of a wage reduction, as they had not been given the power to negotiate a reduction by their General Council. The employers were resentful of this as they were keen to avoid a dispute as it was likely to lead to a number of firms being forced out of business. The threatened lockout had been a tactic by the employers to get the unions to agree to the principle of a wage reduction, but the intransigence of the Weavers ensured that their bluff was called. The Weavers' Executive faced the problem that the Spinners' Executive had experienced in 1919, a growing upsurge of militancy amongst their members which restricted their room for manoeuvre in negotiations. The Weavers argued that they were the worst paid workers in the industry, and should be the last to suffer a reduction. This view was resented by both the Spinners and the Cardroom, who also had low-paid operatives amongst their membership, many of the women in the Cardroom and the piecers in the Spinners' Amalgamation having wages comparable to, if not lower than, the Weavers.

The talks collapsed on Saturday, 27 July 1929, with the lockout due to begin the following Monday. The Spinners' Executive led by Boothman then decided to try to negotiate a separate settlement with the employers. They approached the Cardroom Executive, who also agreed to negotiate, even though their Representative Council had rejected the idea that same day. The Cardroom Executive had told the Spinners they did have power to negotiate a separate settlement on the basis of their original ballot of the members in May. Even the Spinners' Executive were taken aback by this and decided not to proceed with the separate negotiations.

When the lockout began the Spinners' Executive called a Special Representative Meeting and asked for powers to negotiate an agreement. The delegates were to go back and consult their Districts about the members' attitude to this. The Special Representative Meeting reconvened a week later and took only a quarter of an hour to refuse to give negotiating powers to the Executive. This was a decisive rejection of Boothman and the Executive's position and indicated that militancy was not dead amongst the Spinners, even after nearly a decade of depression in Oldham.

This decision ended any hope the employers had of a separate agreement with the Spinners and Cardroom. The lockout carried on for another week, with pressure growing on the employers to accept arbitration. The Labour Prime Minister, Ramsay MacDonald, summoned the employers' representatives to meet him at Edinburgh and he succeeded in pressurising them to accept the idea of arbitration. The lockout was called off, having lasted for three weeks. This was the last general dispute of the cotton operatives: involving 388,000 operatives and with 6.5 million working days lost, it was the largest dispute since the General Strike.

The Board of Arbitration was held in August 1929. The Chairman was a High Court judge, Rigby Swift, a former Conservative M.P. for St. Helens, who had been nominated by the employers. The other four members of the Board were two Trade Union nominees, Charles Cramp of the National Union of Railwaymen and A. G.

Walkden of the Railway Clerks, both members of the T.U.C. General Council, and the two employers' nominees, Sir Archibald Ross and Sir Arthur Balfour, both leading employers in the metal industry. Balfour had been Chairman of the Committee on British Industry and Trade set up by the 1924 Labour Government. The Board had been happy for the proceedings to be in public, but protests from the employers resulted in the hearing being held in private. The cotton union gave joint evidence with James Bell, Secretary of the U.T.F.W.A., speaking on their behalf. The verbal evidence of the F.M.C.S.A. was given by William Howarth, Chairman of the Bolton employers, who had been the General Secretary of the Spinners' Amalgamation in 1902-4. He stated that after the cost of raw material had been accounted for, wages formed over 50 per cent of the cost of production. The unions' argument was that any movement in the wages of operatives had little impact on the price of the finished article, and therefore any cut in wages was likely to result in increased profits rather than greater trade. Boothman cross-examined Howarth, and as might have been expected, there was bad feeling between the two men, Boothman occupying the position Howarth had once held. When Howarth claimed that the operative was effectively forced to vote for strike action by the pressure of the shop-man who collected his ballot, a practice which he could recall from the time when he had been a trade unionist, Boothman responded sharply, pointing out that the voting system had changed since those days.

In an attempt to undermine the unions' argument that recapitalisation was the chief cause of the industry's problems, Howarth provided details of costs from firms that had not been recapitalised. This conveniently ignored the impact of the recapitalised firms on those firms which had not been recapitalised. Effectively the Arbitration Board was becoming the enquiry into the cotton trade that the operatives had been demanding. What particularly upset Howarth was that Boothman repeatedly quoted from documents of the newly founded Joint Committee of Cotton Trade Organisations, on which Boothman represented all the cotton unions. They had all been signed by representatives of the F.M.C.S.A. and were critical of the present position being adopted by the employers.

James Bell gave the cotton unions' evidence. Their case concentrated on the consequences of recapitalisation during the post-war boom: high charges to the rest of the industry by the finishing sections, and the failure of Manchester merchants to market cotton goods effectively. Particular emphasis was placed by the unions on the necessity to reorganise the industry both horizontally and vertically in order to get greater co-ordination and efficiency between the various sectors. While Bell was being cross-examined by John Grey, the weaving employers' representative, the Chairman, Rigby Swift, asked Grey, 'Are you leaving them a living wage?' Grey replied, 'I believe it will impose a real hardship on some section of the operatives.' Grey pointed out to Rigby Swift that the effect would depend on the extent of the wage cut and effectively dissociated himself from the demand for 25 per cent. Grey then complained that because the Weavers had refused to negotiate they had not been able to reduce their demand for a wage reduction, at which point Rigby Swift, who had taken no notes during the whole proceedings, asked:

then can you not agree to settle it? Why do you not settle it now? After all, you do not want us five strangers to settle it for you. You settle it for yourselves. Wages have got to come down, but they do not need to come nearly as much as the employers want.[9]

He then went on to recommend them to split the difference. The unions and the employers were rather taken aback by this turn in events, and after negotiating for some hours were unable to come to an agreement. The Weavers' leaders were particularly concerned because they did not feel they could accept a wage reduction, but Rigby Swift told them not to worry as 'nobody need know and they need take no responsibility because the Board would accept the figure and put it into a unanimous award at once.' Finally, when they could not come to an agreement — the employers sticking at a 15 per cent reduction and the unions at 10 per cent — Rigby Swift suggested a wage reduction of 12.5 per cent off the wage list. The cotton unions then told him that they had already made that offer to the employers, and would accept it.

There was great disappointment when the wage reduction was announced. The general view was that the operatives should never go for arbitration again, especially in view of Rigby Swift's cavalier chairmanship. A few days later, when Cramp and Walkden, the union nominees, attended the T.U.C. which was meeting in Belfast, they were denounced by Communist delegates for having agreed to a wage cut. They defended themselves by telling the cotton unions that had they not agreed to 12.5 per cent, they would probably have had an even greater reduction. This story seems most unlikely. Rigby Swift seems to have decided everything, and the two railwaymen's role appears to have been that of onlookers.[10]

The Labour Government set up an enquiry into the economic problems of the cotton industry in 1929 and it was already in existence at the time of the Rigby Swift arbitration court. The Chairman was the Home Secretary, J. R. Clynes, a former piecer, who in the early 1890s had tried to form a piecers' union in Lancashire. The U.T.F.W.A. submitted evidence similar to that which it had given to Rigby Swift. The Committee already had an example of a new development in the industry with the founding of the Lancashire Cotton Corporation in 1929. The scheme was intended to rationalise the cotton industry by the removal of inefficient firms. Capital for the scheme came from the Bank of England and the initial firms that came into the scheme were those already controlled by the banks. The combined effect of borrowing during the post-war boom and losses during the 1920s' depression, had been that a minority of American spinning firms were now in such heavy debt that control had passed to their bankers. During the 1920s banks continued their support of these firms in the belief that when prosperity returned to the industry they would regain their money. The result of this support was to endanger Lancashire banks, in particular Williams Deacon's, as well as the cotton industry, so that the intervention of the Bank of England was motivated by banking considerations as much as by concern for the cotton industry. The Lancashire Cotton Corporation acquired over 9 million spindles in its first year of existence, of which 4.5 million were scrapped by 1939 as the Corporation cut capacity and attempted to centralise decision-making. At the same time a similar but smaller scheme was started in the fine spinning section, the Bolton-based Combined Egyptian Mills, with some three million spindles. The Amalgamation strongly supported these re-developments, believing they were the first steps towards dealing with the consequences of recapitalisation[11]

In July 1930 the Clynes Committee came to the conclusion that 'Lancashire must choose. She can lose her trade, she can reduce her standard of living, or, perhaps, she can keep her trade and wage standard by reducing costs and improving methods.' Survival, it was argued, depended upon greater use of Indian cotton and the introduction of ring spinning, which it was believed would help to reduce costs in the spinning sector because of the cheapness of Indian cotton compared with Egyptian or American cotton. The Committee also called for the introduction of automatic looms, although it recognised that their introduction would require double shifts. Examining the structure of the industry they hoped to see a move towards greater horizontal and vertical integration. The crucial section of the report dealt with finance where it was stated that 'we are assured that, for any comprehensive and satisfactory rationalisation scheme having for its object the reduction of production costs and improved marketing, the necessary finance will be forthcoming.' Employers in both spinning and weaving took this to mean that government finance would be available, possibly from the Bank of England.[12]

The cotton employers had not been happy about the Government's decision to publish the Clynes Report. However, the debate about the Report and the belief that finance was available for the industry kept employers' minds off wage cuts. The Weaving employers were busy trying to persuade the Weavers' Amalgamation to accept 'more looms' and this appears to have stood in the way of a joint employers' initiative and increasingly the employers' organisations in weaving and spinning went their separate ways. The idea of financial support for the industry soon proved to be an embarrassment for the Labour Government, which was concerned at all costs to avoid a financial commitment to the industry. The Clynes Committee, when it made its recommendations, had clearly accepted the vague platitudes of Montagu Norman, Chairman of the Bank of England, and assumed that the Bank would provide the finance as it had already done for the Lancashire Cotton Corporation. But unlike 1929 there was no banking crisis to force the Bank of England to intervene into the cotton industry.

The resignation and subsequent defeat of the Labour Government in August 1931, and the realisation by employers that there was no likelihood of government money, led them to re-examine costs. The problems of the industry had greatly increased during the period of the Labour Government. The combination of world depression, rising Indian tariffs, and the Gandhi boycott of Lancashire cotton goods, combined to produce the greatest crisis in the Lancashire cotton industry. By 1931 over 40 per cent of cotton operatives were unemployed, and Lancashire's loss of the Indian market was almost complete. The enforced decision to leave the Gold Standard in September 1931 gave the industry a sudden boost, helped by the boycott of Japanese goods in China. However, as other countries, especially Japan, abandoned the Gold Standard, the advantage disappeared, employers once again turned to wage cuts as their response to the industry's problems.

The F.M.C.S.A. began discussing with the Spinners' Amalgamation and the Cardroom Amalgamation ways of reducing costs. They gave one month's notice to end the 48 hour week agreement. The F.M.C.S.A. had always been hostile to the 48 hour week, arguing that it was a major factor in rising wage costs and that labour costs were the fundamental cause of the high prices which were losing Lancashire her markets.

A joint conference took place at the end of 1931 between both employers' organisations and the main cotton unions, at which the F.M.C.S.A. justified their action. Fred Mills, the F.M.C.S.A.'s chairman, claimed: 'We are as proud as you are of the standard of living in this country, which has set a very high example to the rest of the world, but I say unhesitatingly that if the standard of living is a false one, and threatens the foundation of the industry, then some lowering of the standard becomes necessary'. Henry Boothman replied:

> Now let us get down to brass tacks. Does anybody think that hours are going to be increased even if the 48 hours are substituted by a higher figure? Does anybody imagine that these hours are going to be worked? You cannot. If there is any virtue in another figure being substituted, why do you not work the 48 hours?[13]

It was clear, with short-time working endemic in Lancashire, that the employers could not provide the majority of operatives with 48 hours' work, never mind the 52 hours they were proposing. Their purpose in arguing for an increased working week was in reality to reduce wages. The conference ended without agreement and the F.M.C.S.A. made no sustained attempt to increase hours.[14]

In the summer of 1932 the F.M.C.S.A. gave notice of a reduction of 25 per cent off the wage list, approximately a 12.5 per cent cut in wages. Negotiations about the wage reduction began in September against the background of a strike in weaving, where employers were also seeking a wage reduction. The F.M.C.S.A. agreed to postpone their demand, hoping that success for the weaving employers would enable them to reduce their own employees' wages without a dispute. The Cardroom and Spinners' Executives both accepted the principle of a wage reduction, but talks were adjourned until after the Weavers' dispute had ended. It did so with a reduction of 15.5 per cent, and negotiations in spinning were resumed in October with the help of the Ministry of Labour. The Assistant Secretary to the Ministry, Frank Leggatt, who had played a key role in the settlement of the weaving dispute, acted as chairman. He was keen to introduce a new conciliation system into spinning similar to the one introduced in weaving, believing that without conciliation machinery the cotton industry would continue in conflict, and he skilfully arranged the agenda to leave the most contentious matter of wages until the end. Agreement was found on the question of extending the industry's collective negotiating machinery and the question of reinstating the 48 hour week. The majority of time was spent discussing wages, but finally the two Amalgamations were persuaded by the F.M.C.S.A. to accept a reduction of 14.5 per cent off the wage list, which was effectively a wage reduction of 7.5 per cent. The employers did agree, though, to consider preferential treatment for certain low-paid workers, including piecers.[15]

The relief expressed in the press about the agreement was short-lived when a Special Representative Meeting of the Spinners rejected the agreement by 84 votes to 38. The two main provinces, Oldham and Bolton, had already voted to reject the agreement by substantial majorities, and they were joined by Rochdale and Bury, although some support for the agreement came from smaller districts who were less financially stable and therefore more threatened by a long lockout. The Special Representative Meeting agreed to a ballot of the members. Boothman defended the agreement on the grounds 'that a reduction of wages has been in the air for a time, certainly for not less than two years, and to have staved it off for so long must be regarded as no mean achievement.' As a consequence of the Special Representative Meeting's decision, the employers locked out the spinners. The lockout had already been on for a week while the ballot was taking place, though the employers were optimistic that the dispute would soon end. The ballot showed a majority to reject the agreement but the 60 per cent vote for strike action fell short of the 80 per cent required under the Amalgamation's rules. The most interesting feature of the ballot was that the greatest resistance to the agreement had been based on Bolton. By 1932 Bolton had replaced Oldham as the militant area in the Amalgamation. This clearly reflects the relative prosperousness of Bolton in the 1920s, the self-confidence of Oldham spinners having been destroyed by a decade of depression. Though the dispute lasted for only a week it was the last major strike in British industry until after the Second World War. The press had accused the delegates of the Representative Council of not being representative in voting to reject the agreement, but the ballot showed that none of those Provinces and Districts which had voted for rejecting the agreement supported it when the ballot was taken, whereas four Districts — Ashton, Hyde, Stalybridge and Stockport — who had voted for the agreement at the Representative Meeting, all showed majorities for strike action.[16]

Subsequent negotiations took place on the question of piecers' wages. The piecer question had been recognised before 1914 as a major social problem, and the impact of the depression worsened their situation. By the boom of 1920 piecers were earning an average of £2 0s 0d a week, reaching £2 10s 0d in Oldham. Piecers had traditionally been paid more in Oldham than Bolton because of the difficulty of attracting juvenile labour into the mill when there was alternative work in engineering and ironworks. By 1932 piecers' wages had been reduced to £1 8s 0d in Bolton and £1 13s 0d in Oldham. Even more significant was the decline in opportunity for the promotion of piecers. Whilst James Mawdsley had estimated that only one in three piecers were finding employment as spinners in the 1890s, Jewkes and Gray in their study estimated for the early 1930s that the figure was one in six. A little piecer began work at the age of fourteen, now that the half-time system had been abolished, and usually became a big piecer at eighteen or nineteen years of age. He was likely to remain a big piecer until his mid-twenties, and an increasing proportion were remaining piecers until their late twenties or early thirties. At this age many were married men, but receiving a wage which was often less than the dole.

The piecer's wage was low because in theory he was rewarded when he became a spinner, but this depended on there being expansion of the industry. As the industry contracted and opportunities declined, many former spinners who had themselves been made redundant were also seeking work. The seniority rule in the mill insisted that vacancies for spinners went to the senior piecer, but many shops encouraged a system where one out of every two vacancies went to an unemployed spinner.

The little piecer was also a question of concern. Weekly wages of £1 14s 0d in Oldham and £1 0s 0d in Bolton in 1920 had fallen by 1932 to £1 3s 0d and 16 shillings respectively. Although these were quite high wages for juvenile labour, it was the dead-end nature of the jobs that began to attract criticism. By the end of the 1930s there was extensive evidence that parents were discouraging their children from entering the spinning room, and a shortage of juvenile labour was beginning to arise.

Piecers formally became members of the union in 1920 and were counted as part of the union membership from that date. They were able to vote on strike questions and receive strike benefit, but otherwise did not have full membership, though, of course, they did not pay the same contributions as the spinners. Most importantly, they could not attend the shop meetings that were a vital part of the union's organisation and had to rely on their grievances being raised by others. Attempts continued throughout these years to form a separate organisation for piecers. A rival piecer union was founded in Oldham in 1920, but failed because of the impact of the depression. In the late 1920s a piecers' reform organisation based on Bolton was denounced within the Amalgamation as a communist organisation, although this appears to have been wishful thinking by those who wished to discredit it. Communist Party influence amongst cotton operatives was largely confined to north Lancashire and the weavers. Bolton traditionally had been more likely to produce an independent piecers' movement because of the low pay of its piecers. In 1920 a big piecer in Oldham earned 47.5 per cent of a spinner's wage, in Bolton the figure was only 30 per cent. Similarly, a little piecer earned 32 per cent of a spinner's wage in Oldham, but only 18 per cent in Bolton. This anomaly caused comment from even the Bolton employers. When the 1932 wage reduction was settled there was general agreement that the low wages of piecers should be protected, and in 1933 the big piecer received an advance of two shillings per week, the amount to be paid by the employer, not the spinner.[17]

The dispute of 1932 was to be the last of the Spinners' Amalgamation. This partly reflects a change in attitudes of employers, who no longer looked to wage cuts as the solution to their difficulties, recognising the industry's decline as permanent. Instead they sought to improve their own profitability and competitiveness by a reduction in the industry's capacity. The F.M.C.S.A. believed that there was surplus capacity in the industry and this encouraged weak selling, which reduced prices and profits.

Encouraged by the success of the weaving industry in persuading the National Government to pass the Cotton Manufacturing Act of 1934, the F.M.C.S.A. approached the Government to introduce a scheme for the spinning industry. The Cotton Spinning Industry Bill of 1935 was the result, despite the fact that only just over 60 per cent of employers had voted in favour of the scheme. Introduced by the National Government on the assumption that it would enjoy wide support in Lancashire amongst both employers and operatives, a section of employers representing the combined firms in the industry led a vigorous campaign against it, much to the Government's dismay. They were also joined in their opposition by the Spinners' Amalgamation. The Bill proposed to destroy redundant spindles, for which the owners were to be compensated from money raised by a levy on the rest of the industry, but there was to be no compensation for the operatives.[18]

The Amalgamation's attempts to persuade both employers and Government to introduce compensation for operatives failed. The President of the Board of Trade, Walter Runciman, stated that he thought the operatives ought to be compensated. This outraged the employers, who were not prepared to alter their scheme, arguing that as it would be only redundant spindles that were destroyed no operatives would be affected. The Amalgamation never accepted this, estimating correctly that some employers would destroy machinery in use, thus throwing operatives out of work, and the Amalgamation asked the Parliamentary Labour Party to oppose the Bill.

The Bill was postponed because of the 1935 General Election, and this gave the U.T.F.W.A. a chance to appeal to the electorate on the issue. Although a number of Lancashire Conservatives appear to have been frightened by the prospect of fighting the General Election against the background of the Spindles Bill, the result showed little swing to Labour in Lancashire or nationally.[19]

In contrast to the employers' scheme, the Spinners' Amalgamation supported the setting up of a Cotton Control Board for the industry. This was to be based on granting licences to spinners and weavers to carry on their business by a Control Board which would overview the industry. The Cotton Control Board scheme was drawn up by the T.U.C. for the cotton unions, on which Henry Boothman was the senior cotton trade unionist. He was a member of the influential Economic Committee of the T.U.C. formed by Ernest Bevin, and it was this committee which was largely responsible for the scheme. The cotton employers opposed the Cotton Control Board scheme, and this encouraged the more radical weaving unions to propose nationalisation of the industry and the U.T.F.W.A. voted in favour of this in rather curious circumstances at their conference in 1934. Many of the delegates appear to have been leaving the room when the vote was taken, and of the rest a large number abstained, feeling they did not have a mandate on the issue. The T.U.C. drew up a further scheme for the nationalisation of the industry which became the Labour Party's policy in the 1935 General Election. The scheme had only lukewarm support amongst the cotton operatives generally, and helped to contribute to the failure of Labour in textile Lancashire in 1935.[20]

The new Parliament passed the Spindles Bill in 1936. The Cotton Spinning Industry Act established a Spindles Board with the power to buy and scrap spinning mills and machinery. The Board had borrowing powers of up to £2 million and was empowered to levy individual employers 1½d per mule (or equivalent in the case of ring spindles). When the Board came into existence in 1936 there were 46 million spindles compared with 63 million in 1930. By 1939 the Board had succeeded in scrapping 6 million spindles.

The Act was passed at a time of recovery in the industry and 1936-7 was the most prosperous period in the 1930s. This encouraged the cotton unions to try to restore the wage cut of 1932. The Weavers were the first to take the offensive and their wage demand had already been referred to their new conciliation machinery, set up under the 1932 Midland Agreement, by the summer of 1936. The Weavers were finally successful in autumn 1936, effectively restoring their wage cut of 1935 associated with the Cotton Manufacturing Act, but not that of 1932.

Similar conciliation machinery had also been introduced in spinning in 1932, but unlike weaving it had been allowed to lapse by the Spinning and Cardroom Amalgamations. The Cardroom Amalgamation had brought a number of cases under the scheme, but had lost them all. The two Amalgamations applied for a wage advance in the summer of 1936, the Spinners' Executive having rejected the idea of an advance when it was first suggested by the Oldham Province in January 1936. Their attitude had changed when the Bolton Province proposed a similar motion in June, the Executive's view in January being that an application for an advance was likely to lead to the F.M.C.S.A. making a counter proposal for a reduction, it being less than six months since the Weavers had suffered a reduction. The Amalgamation's case for an advance in 1936 rested on the restoration of some prosperity to the industry, a rise in the cost of living, and the restoration of 1931-2 wage cuts in public service and other industries. Particularly resented by the Spinners was the accusation that they earned higher wages, largely at the expense of their piecers. Boothman wrote in October 1936:

> One of the major hallucinations or misapprehensions of a number of persons and one which is not unshared by certain scribes of the press is that spinners or minders are in receipt of abnormal or swollen wages due to the small wages that are paid to piecers. We desire to disabuse the minds of these credulous people of this delusion by assuring them that the average wages of a spinner are nothing like the fabulous amounts as are sometimes mentioned. We shall be erring on the generous side if we put the average wage of a spinner over the whole cotton spinning area as being anything more than £3 per week . . . The only way in which the piecers' position can be improved is by some concession from the firms employing them and not by reducing the spinners' moderate earnings.[21]

Serious negotiations with the F.M.C.S.A. did not take place until December 1936, with the Amalgamation having balloted their members as to whether they were prepared to strike in order to achieve the restoration of the 14 per cent wage reduction of 1932. The vote was overwhelmingly in favour and this threat, with the continued improvement in trade, persuaded the employers finally to offer a wage advance of 9.5 per cent on the wage list, the first wage advance since 1920. Big piecers were also to receive an extra 2s. 6d. per week in an attempt to improve the piecer problem.

The cotton unions decided by 1937 to drop their campaign for nationalisation. They were influenced in this decision by the actions of the Joint Committee of Cotton Trade Organisations which represented employers, merchants and unions. In 1937 this organisation produced a pamphlet, *Lancashire's Remedy*, which advocated reorganising the cotton industry. The National Government under the new Prime Minister, Neville Chamberlain, was sympathetic, believing that if it was to hold on to Lancashire at the next election, action to solve the cotton industry's problems was necessary. Henry Boothman was also the leading cotton trade unionist on this committee and took part in the negotiations between the committee and the Government. The National Government made it clear they would only accept a scheme which covered the whole industry and had the support of all sections, including the operatives. The 1939 Cotton Industry Bill caused considerable controversy amongst the unions because under any proposed scheme of redundancy, compensation was still not guaranteed. When the Bill was debated by the U.T.F.W.A. it was accepted by a majority of two to one. The aim of the Act, like the Spindles Bill, had been to reduce capacity and to hold up prices by the establishment of a Cotton Board which bore a strong resemblance to the one proposed by the cotton unions in their 1933 scheme. However, the outbreak of the Second World War meant that the Act was never put into effect, a Cotton Board was set up to meet the wartime emergency, rather than to deal with the long-term problems of decline.[22]

During the inter-war years the Spinners' Amalgamation faced its greatest ever crisis, with cotton exports halved and spindles reduced by a third. The membership of the Amalgamation in June 1920, 55,521, had fallen by 1928 to 47,551, though the main loss was amongst piecers. The decline in membership also hid another development, the growth of Bolton. The 1920s were in general a period of prosperity for Bolton, reflecting the continued strength of fine spinning, and as a consequence Bolton membership showed a marginal increase from 17,637 in 1920 to 18,366 in 1928. It was the Oldham Province and the other coarse spinning areas, Rochdale, Blackburn and Yorkshire, whose membership was falling. Membership in Oldham declined from 19,575 in 1920 to 15,059 in 1928, for the first time making Bolton the largest Province. However, this numerical shift in the balance of the Amalgamation was not as significant as it would appear, for in terms of spinners Oldham still outnumbered Bolton by 8,372 to 6,122, and it was the higher piecer membership in Bolton that gave that Province the larger membership.[23]

But by 1932 the crisis in the industry had become general and affected Bolton as well as Oldham. Compared to 1920, the membership of the Amalgamation had fallen almost one quarter to 41,541, though even in 1932 the Bolton membership was approximately the same as 1920, at 17,617. It was Oldham that had the more severe crisis, its membership figure of 12,617 in 1932 representing a fall of 35 per cent on

1920. At the beginning of the 1920s Oldham had provided 36 per cent of the Amalgamation's members; in 1932 it had fallen to 30 per cent. The economic recovery after 1932 did little to slow down the rate of decline in membership. By 1938 the union had lost almost 25,000 compared to 1920, some 45 per cent of its membership. Slightly over one half of its 29,052 members in 1939 came from Bolton, where membership decline was less pronounced than in the other Provinces. Oldham's decline had continued, and by 1938 its membership, 7,456, was almost half the size of Bolton's, and since 1935 spinner membership in Oldham has been exceeded by Bolton.[24]

The basis of the Amalgamation's strength before 1914 was the large central fund designed to enable it to withstand a long dispute with the employers. This, combined with the friendly benefits paid by the Provinces and Districts, were two of the main characteristics of the union. The high cost of disputes and unemployment between 1918 and 1932 undermined the financial stability of the Amalgamation. The cost of disputes was high for the Amalgamation: the 1919 strike cost £141,000, the 1921 lockout cost £126,000 and the 1929 lockout cost £116,000. Out of work pay cost the union £217,459 in 1921 and continued to be high throughout the 1920s, peaking again in 1930 at £215,487. By 1932 unemployment pay had ceased or had been considerably reduced and was, by that year, no longer of any value to a member on the dole. The tightening of the means test by the National Government of 1931 for those seeking unemployment relief resulted in the deduction of trade union benefit from state payments. Between 1919 and 1921 the union paid out in benefit £0.75 million, and in 1929 and 1930 the figure was £0.5 million, while the amount members could afford to pay in contributions declined. Twice the Amalgamation had to suspend levies by Provinces and Districts. The consequence was that the union's fighting fund, which in 1918 had stood at the massive sum of £530,967, had fallen by 1933 to £158,881.[25]

For most of its members, the inter-war years had been a saga of uncertainty, the main features being wage cuts, unemployment and short time. Unemployment never fell below the national average and peaked at over 40 per cent in 1931. Even in the relatively prosperous mid-1920s unemployment had been 15 per cent, and it reached 30 per cent in 1930 and did not fall below 20 per cent until 1936. Wages, according to an employers' survey, averaged over £5 a week in 1920 compared with the pre-war average of £2; Bolton spinners earned an average wage of £5 16s 11d compared with £5 6s 5d for Oldham and an average for all spinners of £5 3s 4d. By 1932, according to a similar survey done by employers, average weekly wages were £3 15s 8d, with the figures for Bolton and Oldham £4 5s 3d and £3 15s 9d respectively. This was only a little above the average industrial weekly wage of £3, though a marked contrast with the wages received by big piecers, which stood at £1 17s 3d in Bolton and £1 10s 7d in Oldham.

These figures were calculated by the employers on the assumption of operatives working a 48 hour week. Such an assumption had no impact on the result of the 1920 survey, but for 1932, averages calculated on such an assumption were unrealistic in an industry where short-time working was endemic and unemployment epidemic. The figures the employers produced for 1929 were strongly challenged by the unions, the Amalgamation claiming an average wage of just over £3 0s 0d compared with the £4 0s 0d of the employers. In the same year Freda Utley, relying on trade union sources, calculated spinners' wages as £3 15s 0d in Oldham and £3 9s 0d in Bolton, well below employers' figures of £4 2s 0d and £4 10s 0d. After the 1932 reduction wages reached their lowest point in the inter-war period, 68 per cent above the wage list and 37 per cent above the wage level of 1914, whilst the cost of living stood 44 per cent above 1914, which suggests that the real wages of operatives were below the 1914 level throughout the inter-war years taking into consideration short time and unemployment. The effects of the economic crisis in the cotton industry during the inter-war years was to undermine the aristocratic position of the spinner and his union.[26]

The financial strength of the union was reduced by the combined impact of unemployment and labour disputes. The cost of these two items seriously reduced the financial reserves of the Amalgamation. The aim of the Amalgamation had been to have high reserves in order to be able to outlast the employers in any dispute, and this, combined with greater geographical coverage than the employers, had been the basis of the success of the Amalgamation in the late nineteenth century. In order to use the reserve fund effectively the officials of the Amalgamation were chosen for their knowledge of wage calculations and their ability to judge when the market conditions were favourable to achieve wage advances or stopping employers reducing wages. The strike rule requiring an 80 per cent majority for a strike was designed to stop the membership overruling the Executive; such occasions were going to be rare, as 1908 showed. This was why the wartime strike of 1918 was such a shock to the Amalgamation's leaders when they had been prepared to accept the ruling of the Cotton Control Board, and helps to explain the Executive's own militancy in 1919. The problem of the disputes during the depression in 1921, 1929 and 1932, was that they were fought under market conditions unfavourable to success, which helps to account for the attitude of Henry Boothman and the Executive who were unwilling to make a stand until the very end of each dispute. The Spinners led the wave of labour unrest in the industry in 1918-21, when they resumed their traditional role as the 'vanguard' of cotton operatives. In contrast, the second wave of labour unrest in the industry during the inter-war years was led by the Weavers' Amalgamation. It was the Weavers' opposition to wage cuts in 1929 that led to the lockout and they fought alone in 1931 and 1932, the spinning dispute taking place after the Weavers had already been defeated. The Weavers' resistance is explained not just by the fact that they were lower-paid than the spinners; so were the piecers and members of the Cardroom Amalgamation. The cause of the Weavers' 'More Looms' disputes of 1931 and 1932 was the alteration in traditional work practices, with weavers being asked to work six or eight looms rather than the traditional four.[27]

No comparable attempt was made to alter work practices in spinning. There are a number of possible explanations for this difference. Mule spinning was less labour intensive than weaving on the Lancashire loom, and potential savings to employers in spinning from cuts in labour costs were considerably less than those in weaving. In spinning there was an alternative form of technology, ring spinning, which was already being introduced and represented approximately a fifth of the industry's capacity by 1914. Ring spindles were worked by cheap female labour organised by the Cardroom and not the Spinners. Ring spinning had advantages for the production of coarse yarn, at the cheaper end of the market, and it therefore made sense to introduce ring spindles rather than alter work practices for the mule spinners. However, an examination of the pattern of investment in the inter-war period shows that while there was a rise in ring spindles as a percentage of total spindles, from 20 per cent in 1914 to 35 per cent by 1939, there was no major substitution of ring spindles for mule spindles. In fact ring spindles were scrapped in the inter-war years, probably because those firms that had introduced new machinery were the very same firms where speculation had taken place in the 1919 boom. They were therefore heavily burdened by debt and needed to rationalise urgently. A further explanation of the failure by employers to change work practices is that in the fine spinning sector, where Lancashire still remained strong, the mule still had considerable advantages over ring spinning and it was quality rather than price that gave Lancashire its predominant position in these markets. A change in work practice might well undermine the skill of the operative that was the basis of success in the fine trade. It is possible that the strength of the Spinners' Amalgamation discouraged employers from altering work practices. The Amalgamation was always a stronger union than the Weavers and it is possible that confronted with the 'craft' practices of such a well-organised and crucial sector of the labour force, spinning employers were reluctant to take on an issue with no guarantee of success. Savings from the introduction of new technology in the industry would have been greatest if both ring spinning and automatic looms were introduced together, but such rationalisation would have required the whole industry working together, which was impossible given the horizontal divisions of the industry.[28]

A further factor in the employers' failure to attempt to change work practices in spinning was their decision to use cheap and inferior raw cotton. Employers in both spinning and weaving used 'bad' material as a strategy for saving money. This was not a new device, and there had been regular complaints from the operatives about bad materials before 1914, but these complaints increased during the depression of the 1920s. W. Lazonick has argued that for the period before 1914 this was a substitute for technical change: if employers were able to use poor quality raw materials yet keep up previous levels of productivity, they were effectively raising productivity without any increase in the rate of pay, and this rationale still continued in the inter-war years.[29]

Industrial militancy in the union was reduced during the depression as a combination of three major defeats, unemployment, short time and employer belligerence. The F.M.C.S.A. was much more prone to threaten an industry-wide lockout over an incident in an individual mill than before the First World War. A further factor in the decline of militancy was the fall in membership in Oldham. The Oldham Province was from 1880-1914 the centre of industrial militancy, and the growing militancy of the years immediately after the war was based on Oldham rather than Bolton, but it was the Oldham Province that was the worst hit during the depression. The result was that by 1932 resistance to wage cuts was greater in Bolton, which had been relatively prosperous in the 1920s.

The Amalgamation also suffered from the general decline in prominence of cotton trade unionism that occurred in the inter-war years. This reflected the fall in membership of the cotton unions, whose membership was halved, plus the lack of impact of cotton trade union leaders. The Spinners had in Henry Boothman the most prominent of the inter-war cotton leaders, and he was a member of the T.U.C. General Council from 1919-36, but he refused the position of Chairman of the T.U.C. and appears to have played a minor role at the T.U.C. except where cotton affairs were involved. The depression forced cotton trade union leaders to concentrate on their own problems, rather than take a wider view of the role of trade unionism and though the Spinners retained a seat on the General Council until 1939, they had ceased to be a force to be reckoned with.

One obvious response to the depression would have been to reform their own organisation, especially with the sharp reduction in membership. The feature of the Amalgamation was that power was decentralised, but despite the closure of several branches and Districts and one Province, Blackburn, there was no agreement on centralisation. The suggestion made by the Weavers' Amalgamation that the cotton unions should form one industrial union was never entertained by the membership. Reorganisation of those Districts or Provinces most affected did not take place, and Districts continued with full-time officials where it was no longer justified because change would threaten the all-important local autonomy. A structure of organisation that worked well for the Amalgamation when the industry was prosperous proved inappropriate for the economic decline of the inter-war years. This conservative attitude towards organisation was also reflected in the political attitudes of the members during the 1930s, when no member of the Amalgamation was elected to Parliament.[30]

The depression depleted both the Amalgamation's central fund for disputes and the financial strength of Districts and Provinces to pay friendly benefits, and in so doing it undermined the rationale of the union. The Amalgamation, despite its reduced membership, did manage to preserve traditional work practices, but against the background of dramatic decline in the industry this was not a great consolation. Finally, with ring spinning now representing over a third of the spindles in the industry, the threat was that any return to prosperity would see a replacement of mules by ring spindles. The spinner in 1939 was no longer the aristocrat he had been in 1914.

CHAPTER TEN
Mule Spinners' Cancer

Skin cancer was one of the first occupational diseases to be positively identified. In 1775, Percival Pott published his pioneer observations on scrotal cancer amongst chimney sweeps, arguing that it was due to the irritant effects of soot. By the late Victorian period there was an increasing awareness that certain occupations were liable to skin diseases and that workers employed in the shale oil industry and in the distillation of coal tar suffered from skin cancer (epithelioma). The Workmen's Compensation Act of 1906 introduced the principle of an employer paying compensation for certain diseases which were 'due to the nature of the employment' and, in the following year, skin cancer amongst chimney sweeps and tar workers was added to the list of compensatable trade diseases. Knowledge of the causes of occupational cancers continued to advance and, in 1919 'epitheliomatous ulceration due to tar, pitch, bitumen, mineral oil, or any compound, product or residue of these substances contracted in a factory or workshop' was made a notifiable industrial disease which doctors and employers were required to report to the Factory Department.[1]

In the late Victorian spinning industry the regular oiling of the longer and faster working self-acting mule was essential to ensure its efficient operation, and the lightly clothed and barefoot operatives came into daily contact with oil. However, the routine oiling of the mule had its critics.

> It can scarcely be denied that the application of oil to the many thousands of spindles in the mill is done in a very rough, careless and hurried manner by very indifferent workers . . . In the muleroom spindle oil gets lashed about everywhere, and many mules are a disgrace as a consequence of it.[2]

Such casual oiling practices not only led to dirty yarn, but the oil contaminated the clothing and feet of the operatives. The oil which soaked into the floors made them slippery, and this became a cause of minor and serious accidents as operatives slipped when walking up and down the mule gate. However, although oil was acknowledged as a cause of accidents, no specific steps were taken to deal with the problem, and there was no suggestion during the late Victorian and Edwardian years that spindle oil was also the cause of a lethal disease. When William Marsland, the secretary of the Spinners' Amalgamation, suggested to the *Departmental Committee on Accidents . . .* in 1909 that the oil used in the spinning room might have been responsible for an increase in the number of cases of blood poisoning amongst mule spinners, there was no medical evidence to support the view. Oil acne, a minor skin disease, had been recognised amongst those employed in cotton spinning by the time of the First World War, but there was no public suggestion that epithelioma was a life-threatening disease amongst mule spinners.[3]

This situation altered in November 1922, when the *British Medical Journal* published the research findings of A. H. Southam and S. R. Wilson, both surgeons at Manchester Royal Infirmary, into scrotal cancer. Having identified 141 cases of scrotal cancer at the Infirmary between 1902 and 1922, Southam and Wilson discovered that some 53 per cent were amongst cotton mule spinners. In attempting to explain this astonishingly high proportion they combined a study of the mule spinning process with knowledge about the carcinogenic properties of mineral oils to reach the conclusion that the oil which was used to lubricate the spindles, and which sub-sequently contaminated the spinners' clothing, especially around the area of the groin, was partly responsible for the cancer. As the majority of the lesions had been on the left side of the scrotum, they further argued that the friction caused on this part of the body by the faller bar at the front of the mule carriage was a contributory cause. Piecing was almost exclusively done with the left hand, and as the spinner bent over to piece up the broken thread this part of his body was regularly brought into contact with the faller bar. It was a brilliant piece of medical investigation and the only circumstance which marred Southam and Wilson's 'discovery' was the fact that it had not been made public before 1922. As their research demonstrated, scrotal cancer had existed amongst cotton spinners for some time, and it was never satisfactorily explained why an essay on the disease, written by Wilson in 1910, had remained unpublished although its contents were said to have been well known amongst sections of the medical community in Manchester.[4]

Southam and Wilson's research findings reverberated rapidly throughout the spinning industry. A joint committee representing the Spinners' Amalgamation, employers and the Factory Inspectorate was established to investigate the problem, and in October 1923 they issued a leaflet on the disease, epitheliomatous ulceration, to those working in the spinning room. This emphasized the importance of prompt diagnosis and treatment of the cancer, as the medical evidence indicated that a cure was possible if the disease was treated in its early stages. The cost of neglecting the disease was a long and painful illness culminating in death. Although not specifically mentioning the oil, workers were urged to keep their skin clean by regular washing with soap and water. The emerging awareness of this occupational cancer was soon reflected in the cases notified to the Factory Department. Whereas no cases had been notified in 1922, 15 cases (one death) were reported in 1923. In the following year the number had increased to 79 cases (17 deaths), whilst in 1925 there were 78 cases (35 deaths). Thus within a few years of its 'discovery', epitheliomatous ulceration amongst cotton mule spinners had become one of the most lethal of occupational cancers. Scrotal cancer, which had long been colloquially called chimney sweeps' cancer, now began to be referred to as mule spinners' cancer.[5]

Although the Amalgamation acknowledged the necessity of further research into methods of preventing the cancer, there was the immediate problem of ensuring that its members who had contracted the cancer, and who were receiving sickness

payments from the union, obtained compensation from the employer. The Workmen's Compensation Act of 1906 had introduced the principle of an employer paying
compensation for diseases arising out of the nature of the employment, and correspondence with Thomas Legge, the Medical Inspector of Factories, indicated the
strong likelihood of obtaining compensation as mineral oil was already recognised
as an agent in epitheliomatous ulceration. However, an approach to the Federation
of Master Cotton Spinners' Associations (F.M.C.S.A.) made it clear that a test-case
would be required to determine liability. The case opened in January 1924 at
Stalybridge County Court when Harry Whiteley, a Dukinfield spinner, sued his
employers, the Atlas Mill Company of Ashton, for loss of earnings due to the scrotal
cancer he had developed whilst employed by them. The Amalgamation's evidence
that the cancer was primarily due to the action of the lubricating oil used in the
spinning room was presented by their President, Edward Judson, and supported by
various medical witnesses including Arthur Southam. The F.M.C.S.A. marshalled
their own experts, who naturally highlighted the obscurities surrounding the
disease, arguing that the relationship between mule spinning and the cancer was
coincidental, not causal. Extended by technical objections, it was not until July that
Judge Mossop — who had visited a spinning mill during the case — concluded that
Whiteley was eligible for compensation from his employers. The Amalgamation
welcomed the decision establishing the employers' legal responsibility, although its
experience in obtaining compensation for accident cases made it clear that it was
not a guarantee that other claims would be settled smoothly. As Peter Bartrip has
argued, the road to compensation under the Workmen's Compensation legislation
was full of procedural potholes and litigious lay-bys, and, in the following years, the
Amalgamation grew experienced in the county courts of the cotton towns, as well
as in the higher courts, fighting the F.M.C.S.A.'s Accidents Department, individual
employers and their insurance companies in order to obtain compensation for
spinners who had contracted scrotal cancer. The failure, for example, by an
individual to acquire a medical certificate at the appropriate time was only one of
the circumstances which could jeopardise compensation. The Amalgamation
battled hard for adequate compensation for individual members and exerted
pressure through the U.T.F.W.A. and T.U.C. to remove anomalies and injustices in
the Workmen's Compensation legislation. When it became clear that compensation
was not being awarded for the wages lost by spinners who had undergone operations
for the early but pre-malignant stage of the cancer, Amalgamation pressure led, in
1930, to the establishment of a *Departmental Committee on Compensation for Industrial
Diseases* and the eventual recognition of the condition as a compensatable one.
Predictably, this extension of the Workmen's Compensation legislation became the
subject of further litigation. As the Amalgamation observed, such legal proceedings
were costly and, no doubt with an eye on its membership figures, only available to
those spinners who belonged to the Amalgamation.[6]

    Alarmed by the growing number of cases of mule spinners' cancer, the Amal-
gamation did not rely solely on obtaining compensation but was prominent in
calling for further investigation into methods of controlling the disease. A leading

article in the *British Medical Journal* in November 1924 was reflecting such demands when it called for a commission, composed of representatives from the industry, cancer researchers and technical experts to investigate the disease and identify preventive measures. This was established in 1925 with Edward Judson representing the Amalgamation on the Home Office committee. Published in April 1926, the *Report of the Departmental Committee appointed to consider Evidence as to the Occurrence of Epitheliomatous Ulceration among Mule Spinners* not only advanced medical understanding about the disease but identified a number of strategies which, if implemented, could have done much to reduce its incidence. However, the Committee's recommendations for action steered away from compulsory measures, and in making the industry chiefly responsible for their implementation, an important opportunity to attack the cancer effectively was missed.[7]

As a result of the painstaking research into death certificates and hospital records by Dr Sidney Henry, a Medical Inspector of Factories who served as the Committee's secretary, considerable detail was added to the epidemiological silhouette provided by Southam and Wilson. Henry succeeded in identifying 539 cases of epitheliomatous ulceration among mule spinners to the end of 1925, the earliest case being in 1876. He confirmed that its incidence was well above that found in the general population; the mortality from the cancer among cotton spinners between the ages of 55 and 75 years was 100 times greater than that found among the general population between the same ages. Examining the age at which the cancer appeared it became clear that it was rarely found among the younger section of the workers in the spinning room and, whilst the length of exposure required to contract the disease could not be definitedly established, it was unusual for the disease to appear in those who had been employed in the spinning room for less than twenty years. Forty years was the average duration of employment amongst the identified cases. Such an apparently long incubation period was a problem from the point of view of controlling the disease as it became clear that spinners who had left or retired from the industry were still liable to develop the cancer. The Committee was also able to demonstrate that whilst the scrotum was the main site of the cancer, in one in six cases it affected other parts of the body. Paradoxically, in clarifying the epidemiological picture it also highlighted the uncertainties surrounding the disease, especially for those who subscribed to the view that its chief cause was the lubricating oil used in the spinning industry. Why was the cancer apparently not found among waste-cotton spinners or mule-spinners in the worsted industry? If the spindle lubricating oil was the vector, why did the cancer not appear on the feet or penis? Why did it only affect a minority of the mule spinners?[8]

The Committee made a careful review of various hypotheses which could account for the cancer, but concentrated on Southam and Wilson's explanation that it was the mineral oil used to lubricate the spindles which was the cause. Conducting experiments into the twice-daily oiling of the spindles, the Committee demonstrated that a not insignificant quantity of oil was thrown off either directly onto the spinner's clothing or onto the front of the mule carriage, and was then transferred onto his clothes. Breaking new ground, its inquiries into the different types of lubricating oil used revealed that during the third quarter of the nineteenth century mineral oils had gradually displaced animal and vegetable oils (sperm oil, neatsfoot oil) for the lubrication of spindles. Along with the practical knowledge of occupational cancers in other industries and the scientific evidence that mineral oils had been shown to be carcinogenic in animals, the Committee concluded that long exposure to the mineral oils used in the spinning room was the most convincing explanation. It stated confidently that:

> The broad fact is beyond reasonable dispute, namely, that in the absence of exposure to such mineral oils there would be no more mule spinners' cancer.[9]

Given the clarity of this conclusion, and the experience which was being acquired in devising effective methods to control other occupational diseases, the Committee's recommendations veered towards imprudence. Instead of calling for enforceable legislation to eradicate what was generally agreed to be a preventable disease, the Committee was persuaded to allow the industry to develop the main methods of control. The Committee identified four lines of attack against mule spinners' cancer. First, the need for research to discover a safe, non-carcinogenic spindle oil. Second, the fitting of splash guards to existing mules in order to prevent oil soiling the operatives' clothing. Third, the establishment of a system of regular medical examinations in the industry to identify the cancer in its earliest stage. And last, the encouragement of education about the disease amongst the workforce so that they would be in a better position to prevent it.[10]

The Committee's main recommendation was for research to be undertaken in order to develop an innocuous lubricating oil. However, although acknowledging that such research would be 'exceedingly difficult', it did not suggest a return to the animal and vegetable based oils, which had been shown to be entirely safe, at least until a non-carcinogenic mineral oil was discovered. It was the recently established Manchester Committee on Cancer which became the chief research centre in the search for a safe spindle oil. Composed of representatives from Manchester Corporation, the University of Manchester and local hospitals, it relied on charitable donations to finance its researches; among these were ones from the Amalgamation, the F.M.C.S.A. and the large oil companies. Directed by Dr C. C. Twort, its laboratory work soon provided additional incriminating evidence of the tumour-producing properties of the existing spindle oils and, most importantly for the prevention of the disease, Twort and his colleagues were able eventually to devise practical tests based on the specific gravity and refractivity of oil which enabled the carcinogenic properties of an oil to be identified. By 1934, the Manchester Committee on Cancer felt itself able to prescribe with some confidence mineral oils with a low carcinogenicity for use as spindle lubricants. Significantly, the research had also shown that only animal and vegetable-based oils and certain highly refined white oils were entirely non-carcinogenic. Complementing the main research programme, Twort also demonstrated that a degree of protection could be obtained against the cancer by applying a cream, composed of lanolin and olive oil, to those parts of the body liable to oil contamination. In a nutshell, by the mid-1930s the Manchester Committee on Cancer, whilst not having found an entirely safe mineral oil, had extensive laboratory evidence to underwrite its optimism that mule spinners' cancer could became part of medical history if a number of relatively straightforward preventive measures were consistently and thoroughly adopted throughout the spinning industry. Twort and his colleagues had gone a considerable way to solve the problems raised in the first recommendation of the 1926 Departmental Committee.[11]

Meetings between the Amalgamation and the F.M.C.S.A. eventually led to the recommendation that the 'Twort oils', as they became known, would be used throughout the industry. Cost was not considered to be an obstacle, and indeed the F.M.C.S.A. advised its members that 'in fact many oils complying with the specification cost less than many others which do not'. But although the F.M.C.S.A. publicised the Twort formulas to its members, and a system of issuing certificates from oil suppliers was devised, their use was not mandatory. The safer oils appear to have been adopted slowly in the spinning sector. A survey conducted by Twort of the spindle oils being used in 1937 revealed a disturbing picture of usage, concluding that although the most dangerous shale and petroleum oils were less evident, 'a large percentage' of the mineral oils in use were 'still active cancer-producers' and that the really safe Twort oils were 'met with rarely'. In the absence of a detailed and legally enforceable system of supervision, there was a strong propensity towards laxness among firms inside as well as outside the F.M.C.S.A. Indeed, given its crucial contribution to the efficient operation of the mule, mill managers were said to give scant consideration to the selection of the most appropriate oil(s) for lubricating the various parts of the mule. Certainly William Scott-Taggart was not alone in his view that 'probably the majority of mills show the greatest indifference in the purchasing of lubricating oils than in any other department of mill management'. Even though oil costs were a minor proportion of total production costs, the use of cheaper, less efficient lubricants was a false economy as it resulted in increased power and machine maintenance costs. Yet even when the human and financial costs associated with mule spinners' cancer were added to these considerations, traditional procedures in purchasing and mixing oils were apparently slow to change.[12]

The weakness of the voluntary system was highlighted in 1943 when the Spinners' Amalgamation 'accidentally discovered' that the oil being issued to the industry no longer met the Twort specification. With the F.M.C.S.A., the Amalgamation approached the Petroleum Board, which tried to quell the union's alarm by showing that there had been a misunderstanding and that the appropriate oil was available for issue. Whatever the precise circumstances of the case it underlined the fact that best practice was, knowingly or otherwise, easily jeopardised, and the scare prodded the Amalgamation into calls for legislation to make the use of the Twort oil compulsory and errant employers liable to prosecution. Interest also began to be shown in the possibility of using animal and vegetable oils, especially as it became clear that the Twort oils, even when properly formulated and used, were not entirely non-carcinogenic. This concern was strongly reflected in the *Interim Report of the Joint Advisory Committee of the Cotton Industry on Mule Spinners' Cancer* in 1945, when it called for renewed research into the non-mineral lubricating oils with a view to adoption in the industry. In the meantime the Twort oils were to be scrupulously used, a procedure which was to be scrutinised in individual mills by representatives from the Amalgamation and the management. The research into the animal and vegetable oils, which had been shown to be innocuous by the 1926 Departmental Committee and the Manchester Committee on Cancer, did not proceed far, for in the same year a new white oil appeared which its manufacturers claimed was entirely non-carcinogenic. Given the earlier conclusions of the Manchester Committee on Cancer, Twort's deepening bewilderment with these immediate post-war developments was understandable. The Amalgamation encouraged the use of the new white oil, but the employers demanded further research into its properties. The research and trials proved a lengthy operation and it was not until 1951 that it was possible to issue a safe specification for the technical white oil. By this time the Amalgamation's impatience was manifesting itself in calls for a statutory order to enforce the use of these entirely non-carcinogenic oils. However, discussions involving the Amalgamation, the employers, the oil industry, the Factory Inspectorate and technical experts dragged on and it was not until October 1953 that the Mule Spinning (Health) Special Regulations were passed. They were to come into operation from July 1954. Proclaimed as the beginning of a new era of safety in the industry, the regulation specifying the types of oil which could be used to lubricate spindles must have left some people in the industry wondering why it should have taken almost thirty years to reach the conclusion that:

> No oil other than the following should be used for oiling spindles of self-acting mules, that is to say, *white oil or oil entirely of animal or vegetable origin or entirely of mixed animal and vegetable origin*.[13]

It was a directive which some spinners never lived to read.[14]

Conscious that the discovery of a safe mineral oil would take time, the 1926 Departmental Committee concluded that oil contamination would be considerably reduced by the fitting of anti-splash guards to existing mules and redesigning the spindle-bolster mechanism on new mules. However, it left the pursuit of these engineering solutions to be 'decided by a series of tests to be mutually agreed upon and arranged by the Masters' Federation and the Operative Spinners'. The confidence that the two parties would be able to work together and encourage the adoption of suitable safety devices was misplaced. In a period dominated by contracting markets and mill closures, employers were reluctant, at least voluntarily, to meet the costs of altering ageing machinery which might shortly be scrapped. Such investment was not a priority in an industry where between 1929 and 1939 the number of spindles fell by one-third from 59.134 million to 36.949 million. Some research was undertaken and patents were taken out for anti-splash devices, but their fitting seems to have been the exception rather than the rule. Even claims that such anti-splash devices would help reduce the problem of oil-stained cops — a long-standing problem in the industry — appears to have failed to encourage their adoption. It was significant that when the Joint Advisory Committee of the Cotton Industry reported in 1945 it had no precise data on the number of anti-splash devices installed. In the following year the Amalgamation's Secretary, Charles Schofield, informed the U.T.F.W.A. that only 3 per cent of the industry's mule spindles had been fitted with suitable anti-splash devices.[15]

The Amalgamation's verbal pressure to speed up the fitting was politely ignored by most employers who, not for the first time in the history of the cotton industry, showed a stubborn reluctance to invest in measures which would improve the safety and health of their employees. Throughout the history of the cotton spinning industry the health of the mule spinner had been a peripheral concern to the majority of employers, and in a declining industry it appears to have remained an area of low priority for most managements. In this context it was revealing to see how eagerly some employers embraced the novel theory put forward in 1926-7 that mule spinners' cancer was entirely unconnected with mineral oil but caused instead by the friction upon the scrotum of the tightly braced overalls worn by spinners. Such an explanation conveniently shifted liability from the employer to the spinner, and for some employers, at least, requiring a spinner to wear a belt instead of braces was a far more palatable response than introducing and adapting existing machinery or searching for a benign oil. The disdain that such employer attitudes generated amongst the Amalgamation's leaders was epitomised by Fred Birchenough, secretary of the Oldham Province.

> To think that lives have been lost and hundreds of workpeople have suffered and are suffering from the disease, and then be told if our men would wear belts instead of braces, the disease would be avoided. It would be interesting to know whether this wearing of belts instead of braces would have prevented the cases on many other parts of the body. From practical experience of spinning room life I think we can place the reasoning and views referred to in the same category as the suggestion made 'that long legged operatives should be employed in the spinning rooms'.[16]

Whatever preventive measures might be taken, there already existed a reservoir of spinners who had been put at risk by their long exposure to the dangerous oils, and it was for this group that the 1926 Departmental Committee considered establishing a system of regular medical examinations. This was considered necessary because *all* the medical evidence agreed that effective treatment depended upon prompt diagnosis. Disagreement, however, surrounded the precise form of the scheme and in the end it was the Amalgamation's case for a voluntary system which was reflected in the Departmental Committee's recommendation. A system of voluntary medical inspection for all spinners over thirty years old, conducted by approved medical personnel once every four months, was to run for a one-year trial period. If this proved unsuccessful then a compulsory system was to be introduced.

The trial failed and, in the absence of a statutory obligation, efforts to develop a compulsory scheme floundered amongst the arguments of the employers and the Amalgamation about the organisation and financing of an industry-wide scheme. Whilst the Amalgamation condemned the employers for their reluctance to finance the scheme they were not, initially, enthusiastic supporters of a compulsory medical examination. Given the experience of such schemes in other industries, such as shale oil refining, the Factory Inspectorate's indecisiveness further exacerbated the situation when action was required. In the 1930s some mills did operate a system of voluntary examinations, but even in these mills not all operatives made use of the service. In many mills spinners were left to the unsatisfactory procedure of self-examination. Inevitably, opportunities for the early identification and treatment of the cancer were missed as men, through a combination of fear, embarrassment and ignorance, sought medical advice only when the cancer had become well-developed. In addition, there was the problem of monitoring those spinners who had left the industry. The Amalgamation showed more commitment and urgency in demanding compulsory medical examination in the 1940s. However, the recommendation made by the Joint Advisory Committee of the Cotton Industry of a six-monthly medical examination for mule spinners was not acted upon immediately. By 1951 the Amalgamation's impatience was leading to demands for a statutory order to introduce a system of regular medical examinations. Belatedly, it had to wait until July 1954 before a system of compulsory medical examinations every six months was brought into operation. The system appears to have met the operatives' anxieties over privacy and confidentiality and it appears to have worked well, although for some it came too late. The Annual Report of the Chief Inspector of Factories for 1955 recorded the following case:

> A man employed in a mule spinning department as a minder's assistant for five years had never availed himself of the voluntary periodical medical examinations provided by his firm; he retired at the age of 65, one month before the statutory examinations were instituted. Shortly after retirement he noticed a 'pimple' on the scrotum but it was eleven months before he consulted his doctor; a large fungating growth considered to be beyond treatment was found. In some organisations, retired workers who have been at risk are examined periodically and this practice is highly commendable.[17]

Tragically, such brief, sad case histories were not unique to 1955; they could be found in every year during the previous thirty years. The failure of the industry to devise and operate an effective system of compulsory medical examination from the 1920s onwards undoubtedly contributed to the deaths of spinners. Procrastination was the thief of health and life.[18]

The final recommendation of the 1926 Departmental Committee focused on increasing the operatives' knowledge of the disease. Cancer education was a particularly sensitive area of health education, and the following years saw the Amalgamation produce a number of leaflets about the cancer for its members, emphasising the necessity of regular washing and the crucial importance of seeking early medical advice. Aided by bodies like the Manchester Committee on Cancer, lectures about the disease were also arranged. Of course, such information could substantially increase anxieties about the disease, and this may have been one of the reasons why in booklets about mule spinners' cancer distributed to the men photographs of the condition were not included. But such concerns could only partly explain other instances of reticence such as the reluctance of the Factory Inspectorate to provide a cautionary wall poster about the cancer in an effort to remind spinners of the health risks they faced. General advice was better than none, but more specific advice might also have been provided. The exhortation to wash the carcinogenic oil off one's body was sound, but it could have been strengthened by reminding spinners to wash their hands before going to the lavatory.[19]

However, health education was not simply a question of general exhortations, it was also a matter of ensuring that workers had adequate facilities to act upon them. Thus whilst the Amalgamation distributed leaflets urging personal cleanliness, the washing facilities available in most mills were frequently inadequate. Some 'progressive' employers did recognise the benefits of installing adequate sanitary and washing facilities, but in many mills conditions were slow to improve. Indeed, if the criticisms of the U.T.F.W.A. made during the 1940s are substantially correct, conditions in some mills may have deteriorated since the 1920s. But as a preventive measure against mule spinners' cancer a sink with a bar of soap was not an adequate facility. Hot showers, foot-baths and a laundry service to clean oil-impregnated clothes efficiently were required. Barrier creams and lotions should also have been made more widely available. Working through the T.U.C., in 1948, the Amalgamation's success in obtaining additional rations of soap because of the health risks faced by its members was no doubt welcomed by spinners and their wives, but it was essentially a mis-allocation of Amalgamation energy. Of course, the Amalgamation was not chiefly responsible for the lack of adequate washing facilities. It was only after the Second World War that such facilities began to match those provided in other major industries. Inevitably facilities varied between firms, but for the final generation of mule spinners there was an increasing opportunity to remove some of the sweat, dust and oil which was part of the physical legacy of a day in the mule-gate before going home.[20]

Between its 'discovery' in 1922 and the implementation of the Mule Spinning (Health) Special Regulations in 1954 there were some 1,500 recorded cases of epitheliomatous ulceration amongst cotton spinners, of whom over 400 died. For the ever-decreasing numbers of mule spinners the years after 1954 should have been regarded as a period of safety as a result of the obligatory use of non-carcinogenic oils and regular medical examinations in the industry. The Amalgamation's feeling that a long struggle had come to a successful end was further sweetened by the inclusion of mule spinners' cancer in the Industrial Diseases Benefits Scheme in 1954. This removed the anomaly whereby only those spinners who had been employed in the industry within 12 months of contracting the cancer were eligible for compensation. Given its long incubation period, it was not unusual for spinners to have left the industry for a number of years before the disease appeared, and the Amalgamation had conducted a long campaign to remove this injustice. However, the problem of mule spinners' cancer was not yet over. The 1953 Regulations only required that the safe oils should be used for lubricating spindles, and it soon became clear that other parts of the mule were still being lubricated with potentially harmful mineral oils. Initiated by the Amalgamation in 1955, the campaign to ensure that only non-cancerous oils were used on the complete mule was a pathetic coda to the longer movement which had resulted in the 1953 Regulations. Discussions and investigations involving the Amalgamation, employers, scientific bodies, oil companies and the Factory Inspectorate were prolonged, and it was not until 1961 that the employers finally agreed to 'recommend strongly' to their members that the safe technical white oils be used for lubricating all parts of the mule. Almost forty years after Southam and Wilson had argued that the oils used in the spinning room were chiefly responsible for mule spinners' cancer, the industry's mules were at last entirely lubricated by a safe, non-carcinogenic oil. However, even then the Amalgamation's interest in the subject did not cease, and in its final years of operation it made sure that its members leaving the industry were issued with cards reminding them of the risks they had been exposed to and of the necessity of immediately seeking medical treatment should suspicious symptoms appear.[21]

The Spinners' Amalgamation played an important part in the struggle to combat mule spinners' cancer. It worked relentlessly to obtain compensation, fighting in the courts and lobbying government in an effort to remove the hurdles which stood between its members and the speedy payment of adequate compensation. Although there were suggestions that the Amalgamation had hesitated to make public the true incidence of the disease, in general it did much to make its members conscious of the risks which resulted from a free-flowing oil can, and the preventive measures which ought to be observed. Detailed evidence on oiling practices is unavailable, but it does appear that oil was applied more sparingly after the 1920s than had been the practice before. However, the Amalgamation did show a remarkable patience with the delays which surrounded the introduction of anti-splash devices and the comprehensive adoption of the Twort oils from the mid-1930s onwards. It was only during the Second World War that dissatisfaction with voluntary agreements began to be replaced by calls for statutory orders. It is possible that if the Amalgamation had taken a more determined line against the employers, a reduction in the health risks would have occurred earlier. But, as the record of the Cardroom Amalgamation's campaign to get byssinosis recognised as an industrial disease indicates, it is easy to underrate the achievements of the Spinners' Amalgamation in helping protect the health of its members.

In attempting to reduce the incidence of mule spinners' cancer the Amalgamation was closely involved with the Factory Inspectorate. During the inter-war years the under-resourced Inspectorate pursued a policy of obtaining voluntary agreements, such as the 1928 Cotton Spinning Agreement — which dealt with the guarding and cleaning of mules — to improve health and safety practices in the industry. But it was only possible to persuade some of the firms some of the time, and the limitation of the voluntary approach was evident in the slow adoption of a system of regular medical examinations and the slow take-up of the Twort oils. (Indeed, the Factory Inspectorate had raised doubts about the findings of the Manchester Committee on Cancer and its specifications of safe oils which resulted in a further investigation by the Medical Research Council.) Had the Factory Inspectorate been more forceful in supporting moves for statutory orders, then it seems likely that some reduction would have occurred. Even given its inability to enforce effectively a regulation which, for instance, prohibited the use of specific oils, a legislative order would have underlined to employers and management the importance of using the correct type of oil, whilst the occasional prosecution would have served as a reminder to firms that the neglect of statutory orders did have a cost. As Charles Schofield informed the U.T.F.W.A.'s conference in 1946, 'there were still many backwoodsmen among the employers, and whilst many employers would act on the recommendations, there were many who would require some pushing and shooing even to having a Court order made against them'. Yet, the Factory Inspectorate was not alone in its failure to pursue policies which would have more speedily and effectively reduced the risks of cancer in cotton spinning. Given the clarity of the 1926 Departmental Committee's findings on vegetable and animal oils, it is surprising that little research was done by scientific and engineering bodies to demonstrate their qualities as lubricants compared to mineral oils. Similarly, in the pioneering work undertaken by the Manchester Committee on Cancer, it was unfortunate that additional research was not pursued or even suggested into the practical application as spindle oils of those hydrocarbon and animal and vegetable oils which they had positively identified as innocuous. These were missed opportunities which might have decreased the risks which the mule spinner was exposed to.[22]

However, in the final analysis it was the employers who were responsible for the welfare of the workers. Clearly it would be misleading to characterise the attitude of all cotton employers towards mule spinners' cancer as one of indifference, or of coldly calculating the risks of having to pay compensation. As in earlier periods of its history, the industry did have employers who, for a variety of reasons, were willing to invest in improving the factory environment and who were genuinely concerned about their employees' health. It may also be argued that in a contracting industry the problems facing the economically marginal firm were considerable; with profitable domestic competitors and fierce foreign competition, for some firms the means of implementing the necessary health-increasing measures may have been unavailable even if there was a willingness to do something. But this may be a charitable view of employers' behaviour. If economic considerations might partly explain the sluggish adoption of anti-splash guards by some firms, it cannot entirely account for the patchy response to using the Twort oils from the mid-1930s onwards, let alone the employers' propensity to delay the introduction of technical white oils as a spindle lubricant and, later, its use for oiling all the moving parts of the mule. For many employers the health of their employees was a peripheral issue, and they preferred to pay higher dividends than voluntarily to spend money on reducing the health-risks of mule spinners. Initiatives to improve the health and safety of their workers rarely came from employers. Like the cotton masters who were responsible for the development of factory-based cotton spinning during the Industrial Revolution, those who served the industry during its long decline showed comparatively little concern for the conditions in which their employees worked and the risks they ran. Had they demonstrated a greater concern it seems probable that some of the risk-reducing measures proposed by the 1926 Departmental Committee would have been more rapidly and more extensively introduced. This did not occur, and it was the fate of those employed in the spinning room to have added to the other economic and social costs of working in a contracting industry the tragic human costs of mule spinners' cancer.

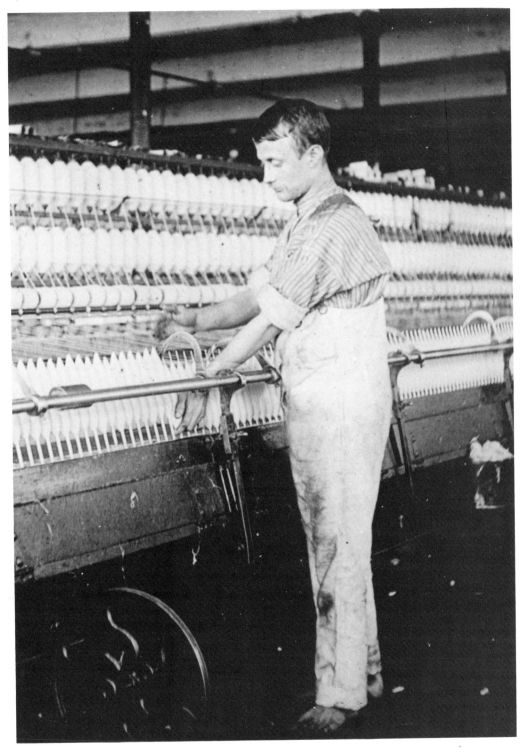

Big piecer at work, c. 1920.

Little piecer at work, c. 1920.

Legislative Council of the United Textile Factory Workers' Association at Blackpool Conference, 1927. Henry Bootham, General Secretary of the Spinners (1917-43) is seated second from right.

Charles Schofield, General Secretary (1944-60).

Fred Birchenough, President (1926-36).

Spinner and his assistant in a clean mule-gate, c. 1955.

Spinner piecing on fine spinning mule, c. 1955.

Charles Schofield (left), Sir Walter Monckton (centre) and Archibald Robertson, President of UTFWA (right), 1953.

Executive of Spinners Amalagamation, 1970. Standing: Arthur Wardley, Jack Hunter, John Dollan.
J. Green, J. Alderson, William Disley, Bill Timlin. Seated: J. Smalley, Clifford Wynn,
Fred Mayall, Joseph Richardson, Tom Bulger, Bill Nally.

CHAPTER ELEVEN
Decline of the Amalgamation

The decline of the cotton industry which had begun in the inter-war period was halted by the impact of the Second World War, which temporarily removed Britain's major competitor in export markets, Japan, and gave the industry a short period in which to reform itself. This period, 1945-51, coincided with the new Labour Government and was a time of reform and modernisation in the industry. It was clearly unsuccessful as the 1950s and 1960s, with the re-emergence of world competition saw a continued decline and the effective disappearance of the Lancashire cotton industry by 1970. The industry's problems in the 1950s and 1960s were different from those of the 1920s and 1930s in that unlike the inter-war years it was not the loss of export markets but the invasion of the home market by Third World producers which was the major cause of decline. By 1959 Lancashire was importing more cloth than it exported, and as a result the Conservative Government introduced new legislation aimed at both contracting the industry and modernising it. The legislation was unsuccessful and the industry's decline continued in the 1960s, but the 1959 Cotton Industry Act effectively brought to an end mule spinning in Lancashire. The Amalgamation's membership, which stood at 22,866 in 1951, fell to 14,571 by 1958, 7,100 by 1961, and had dwindled to 1,758 by 1970, with the Amalgamation formally closing in 1976.

The Second World War continued the contraction of the industry that had been taking place in the inter-war years. The wartime contraction, however, was at least organised by the Cotton Board and operatives were moved either into the armed forces, if eligible, or munitions work. Initially the war stimulated demand for the industry's products either in the form of war-related products such as uniforms and blackout material or for exports in order to raise foreign currency to fight the war. By 1941, with the introduction of 'lend lease', followed by America's entry into the war, exports were no longer so important and the industry was further reduced. After 1941 the main determinants of the industry's size were shipping space, the need to save space for food and war material, the need to release labour for the munitions industry, and the industry's ability to meet certain essential war needs. The result was that although by 1942 the industry had been concentrated to half its spindles, it was also designated an essential industry and a reserved occupation. These changes were reflected in a major contraction of the Amalgamation's membership, which was halved from 30,052 in 1938 to 16,672 in 1944, 3,000 of whom were in the armed forces. At the same time, there was a constant shortage of labour, especially juvenile labour. Partly in order to meet this shortage women were employed as piecers, whilst there was a growing tendency for a pair of mules to be worked by two operatives rather than three. Young male workers were difficult to obtain, partly because of conscription, though it was a problem that had already emerged before the war and reflected the raising of the school leaving age in 1918 and the general unattractiveness of the industry in the inter-war years.

For those who remained in the industry the war years saw regular wage rises. A joint claim for a 20 per cent increase on behalf of all the cotton unions had already been made in the summer of 1939. The two employers' organisations, the Federation of Master Spinners' Associations (F.M.C.S.A.) and the Cotton Spinners' and Manufacturers' Association (C.S.M.A.), refused to negotiate jointly and a rise of 12.5 per cent was given separately in the autumn of 1939. The Spinners' settlement included an extra payment of 4 shillings a week to big piecers and 2s 6d to little piecers. The Amalgamation also agreed to a cost of living wage agreement for the duration of the war, whereby wages changed with movements in the Ministry of Labour's cost of living index. This guaranteed regular wage advances between 1940 and 1943, and combined with the ending of unemployment after 1940 it helped to restore the economic position of spinners; indeed, overtime and double shifts were introduced where necessary, also raising incomes. A further application was made for a wage advance in 1942, above those granted for increases in the cost of living, the Amalgamation arguing that wartime profits in the industry plus low wages compared with other industries meant that operatives deserved and employers could pay higher wages. When the claim was refused it was taken to the wartime National Arbitration Tribunal, as strikes were illegal during the war, but rejected. A further claim was made in 1943 which was more successful, resulting in a war bonus with a further wage advance at the end of the year.

In 1941 cotton operatives experienced, after three years of bargaining, their first ever paid holidays due to the successful negotiations conducted by the United Textile Factory Workers' Association (U.T.F.W.A.). Government legislation had overriden employer resistance to paid holidays, a long-standing aim of cotton operatives; at last Wakes Week could be enjoyed with less worry about the cost to the family budget. The absence of paid holidays had been the reason why some operatives, especially big piecers, had spent their holidays at home, in some cases working in nearby towns whose own Wakes Week came at a different time.

Towards the end of the war, the Amalgamation began negotiations with the F.M.C.S.A. about the position of piecers. The growing interest in the piecer question reflected earlier concerns expressed in the 1930s, plus an awareness that the shortage of juvenile labour during the war was likely to continue in the post-war world, especially as the school leaving age was due to be raised to fifteen. A graduated scale of payment for piecers was agreed for fifteen to twenty-three year olds. The big piecer was to become the spinner's assistant, the assumption being that two rather than three would form the normal team to operate the mules. This proposal represented a major change for the spinning room. Female piecers were finally accepted by the Amalgamation as a permanent means of meeting the shortage of labour, though their recruitment was not to interfere with male promotion and they would not themselves be entitled to become spinners.[1]

It was during the war that the U.T.F.W.A. again discussed the industry's future. Their conference in 1942 responded by setting up a committee to consider 'ways and means of improving the economic stability of the cotton textile industry.' The report, published in 1943, was a contribution to the war and post-war discussion about the future of the industry. It called for the nationalisation of the industry, although this was a demand which received little sympathy from the Spinners' Amalgamation, despite the fact that the new President of the Amalgamation, Albert Knowles, had been a member of the committee. The report was an impressive document but Hugh Dalton, President of the Board of Trade in 1944 and a leading member of the Labour Party, was already committed to a private enterprise solution to the industry's problems. Also influential was the Platt Report of 1944, the report of a delegation led by Sir Frank Platt, wartime cotton controller, and consisting of leading cotton employers and trade unionists who visited the U.S.A., comparing American production methods in cotton mills. This Report was especially critical of the differences in productivity between the two countries, and emphasised the contribution of ring spinning to this difference. Ring spinning had been dominant in the U.S.A. cotton industry before 1914 but still only accounted for a minority of the spindles — some 35 per cent in 1945 — in Lancashire. Unlike the Cardroom and Weavers' Amalgamations, the Spinners were not represented on the delegation, and they were critical of the Report's conclusions.[2]

Labour won a sweeping victory at the 1945 General Election. Its success in Lancashire was only spoilt for the cotton unions by the small number of cotton trade unionists who were candidates; of the four who stood, three were elected, one less than in 1918. The absence of any spinners among these cotton Members of Parliament tended to confirm the union's lack of interest in parliamentary representation.

In 1945 the Labour Government rapidly set about implementing its policies which were to alter the relationship between social classes in twentieth century Britain. It had two main tasks on the home front, to restore and modernise the economy after the war and depression, and to introduce major social reforms which were to create the modern Welfare State. Trade unions were to have a leading role in the determination of policy for industry. These aims dominated the Labour Government in its first years of office, although the crisis of 1947 forced it to concentrate on exporting at all costs, and discussion of long-term modernisation of industry, including textiles, declined. The first period coincided with Stafford Cripps' period as President of the Board of Trade, one of the most dynamic ministers in the Labour Government. The Government's aim was to restore some of the cotton industry's former prosperity by reorganising and modernising it. They were helped by the fact that the period 1945-51 was essentially a seller's market for the cotton industry.

Between 1946 and 1951 the industry experienced the most sustained boom it had known since 1919-20. Production, compared with 1945, increased by over 50 per cent and the labour force increased by the same amount. Profits were high, but though exports showed some recovery they declined as a percentage of world trade in cotton from the pre-1939 figure of 27 per cent to 15 per cent by 1951, and the home market continued to have a far greater importance to the industry. Despite the boom the number of mule spindles fell, and the only new machinery being introduced in the spinning sector was ring spindles.

The new Labour Government soon involved itself in the industry's post-war plans. Sir Stafford Cripps presented a programme for the reconstruction of the industry to the Cabinet in August 1945. Cripps, like Dalton earlier, assumed that the industry would not be nationalised, arguing that the Government should assist the industry in its reorganisation. The Cabinet was split on the question between those favouring a clear and unequivocal statement that cotton would not be nationalised and those who wanted to keep the option of further intervention open. Particular concern was expressed within the Cabinet about the spinning industry because of fears that it would not reform itself.[3]

Cripps agreed that spinning was the main problem, an analysis based largely on the Platt Report of 1944, though his immediate concern was with the shortage of labour. He believed, correctly, that the shortage was due to poor working conditions and wages, and for this reason he wished to set up a joint commission of employers and trade unions to work out a better wage structure for the industry. Cripps visited Lancashire in mid-August 1945 and explained his plans to both employers and unions. The main features of this policy were to be, firstly, a reform of distribution to secure long runs of production, and secondly, the re-equipment of mills with modern machinery, to be combined with the amalgamation of firms in the spinning section. Lastly, and most significantly for the unions, there was to be an extension of double shift working where there was modern machinery. The proposals were regarded as a complete package, so that rejection of one implied the rejection of all. This was particularly important, for the cotton unions traditionally opposed double shifts. According to Cripps when he spoke at Bolton, 'There was abundant raw material but not the labour to turn it into yarn', and he appealed to the operatives to return to the industry. 'I am asking you to trust me and the Labour Government,' he stated. His visit also secured agreement for a commission to review wage arrangements in cotton spinning. The Chairman was to be Justice Evershed, and both the Amalgamation and the F.M.C.S.A. were to be represented.[4]

Completed in October 1945, the *Report on the Cotton Spinning Industry* and its implementation was a landmark in the social history of the industry. The starting point of the Evershed Report was to make the industry more attractive to labour and therefore encourage the return of former cotton operatives to the industry. It called for the abolition of the little piecer and big piecer and the substitution of a spinner's assistant instead. It also recommended changing the system of wage-payment. The big piecer, or spinner's assistant, was to be paid by the employer and not the spinner, thus ending a long source of tension in the industry. The Commission also proposed a uniform wage list and the abolition of District lists. Finally, the report was particularly critical of bad spinning, arguing that a continuation of the practice would destroy all the positive achievements in the Report.

The employers and unions were unable to agree on the uniform list recommended by the Evershed Report. The problem was that the F.M.C.S.A. did not want to raise their costs, but the Amalgamation would only agree to a uniform list if it was based on the higher-paying Bolton list. This would have the effect of raising wages in the Oldham coarse spinning sector. The failure to agree over wages led Evershed himself to make a supplementary report. The question of the uniform list was complicated by 'absentee wages'. The wartime shortage of labour and difficulty in obtaining little piecers had led to the working of mules by a big piecer and spinner, with the little piecer's wage being shared between them. The Evershed Commission's wage census revealed that in 1945 average wages for spinners in Bolton were approximately £6.0s 0d and in Oldham £5 10s 0d. When the 'absentee' wages were added, wages rose by a further 10 shillings for the spinner. A further complication was the difference in length of mules. Bolton mules were shorter, meaning that the wage difference between the two lists was nearer £1 0s 0d than 10 shillings. Taking into account a recent wage advance, Evershed recommended a standard weekly wage for spinners of £7 0s 0d which would vary according to the length of mules between £6 9s 0d and £7 16 0d. The figure included 16 shillings as compensation for the loss of 'absentee wages'. The effect of these recommendations was to raise Oldham wages and bring them to a level equivalent to those in Bolton. Evershed argued that though this might disadvantage the Oldham coarse spinning section in the long run by raising their costs, in the short run a seller's market for cotton guaranteed that Oldham would not be adversely affected. The long run effect might be the complete substitution of rings for mules in coarse spinning but Evershed thought this was desirable. Evershed's underlying strategy was to concentrate mules on Bolton. Evershed made his recommendations in March 1946, but negotiations between the Amalgamation and the F.M.C.S.A. dragged on from 1946 to 1948 before they were finally completed. Welcomed by Oldham, the delay was due partly to the opposition of the Bolton Province to the new list, which would have led to wage reductions for some Bolton operatives. Amendments were made to the original proposals and the Bolton membership voted narrowly for the acceptance of the new list which began operating in 1949. The new list was known as the Evershed list after the chairman of the commission.[5]

Cripps set up a Board of Trade Working Party into the cotton industry in October 1945. This move had only a lukewarm reception from employers, who resented a further investigation of the industry and thought it should be left alone, with a minimum of government intervention. The Working Party had representatives both of employers and trade unions, and the Spinners were represented by their President, Albert Knowles. The final report in April 1946 showed a clear split between the trade unions and employers. The majority recommendation of the Chairman and trade unionists was for continued government intervention. The report recommended increased horizontal amalgamation in both spinning and weaving, as well as vertical amalgamation between the two sections of the industry. A re-equipment levy on the industry was proposed to finance new machinery in spinning, but these recommendations were strongly opposed by the employers on the Working Party, who argued that the industry's structure and its technology should be decided by the market. The recommendations that most affected the unions arose from the introduction of new technology. The Working Party argued that by the introduction of new technology — ring spinning and the automatic loom — costs could be reduced by 10 per cent, while wages could be raised by 20 per cent. Underpinning these calculations was the assumption that double shifts would be worked, a proposal that was directly opposed to the traditional view held by cotton trade unionists. The recommendation placed the cotton unions in a difficult position. Trade union opposition to the Working Party Report would be disastrous in the context of the already existing employer opposition. Cripps came to address the U.T.F.W.A. in early 1947 on the question of the introduction of double shifts, and after his speech they voted by a large majority to accept the double shift. The Working Party Report concluded that 'the time has come when all concerned must make up their minds that they must move towards a major transformation unless they are willing to see the industry shrink to the size of a minor British industry'. Despite the accuracy of this conclusion, the report was largely ignored.

The main result of the report was to make the Cotton Board into a permanent body under a new title, the Cotton Council. The other main consequence was the passing of the Cotton Spinning Act of 1948, which aimed to concentrate the spinning sector into larger units and modernise it. It gave a 25 per cent subsidy for re-equipment on condition that employers closed down certain mills whilst modernising others.[6]

The Amalgamation became increasingly concerned about the Labour Government's proposals for modernising the industry, especially as it was assumed that ring spinning should replace mule spinning. The Amalgamation always believed in the superior quality of yarn spun by mules, which in their view outweighed any cost disadvantage, and sent a deputation in September 1948 to meet Harold Wilson, the new President of the Board of Trade, to discuss the question. They pointed out to him the illogicality of substituting rings for mules when labour was not available for ring spinning. Ring spinning had always been women's work and mule spinning men's. While suggestions had been made by Evershed that men should be encouraged to become ring spinners, mule spinners remained resistant to the idea. Though the industry suffered from a shortage of labour in the post-war period, this shortage was not particularly acute amongst mule spinners, largely due to the age structure in mule spinning. The older workers in mule spinning were less mobile and less likely to seek work in other industries.[7]

The Amalgamation's view was well expressed by its Secretary, Charles Schofield, when he spoke to the U.T.F.W.A.'s conference in 1948:

Some people have got it in their minds that the whole of the textile machinery, because some of it was installed before 1900 or 1918, was completely out of date. That was nonsense. Firms were making profits with machinery that was forty years old or more, and he wanted to say there and then, without fear of contradiction, that a vast amount of machinery in the spinning section, and the mule spinning section, would bear examination by anybody at any time. He knew of one firm with mule spinning machinery dated 1878, and he would challenge anybody to deny it was turning out quality goods in quantity better than any machinery introduced today. Those were Platt mules. Because machinery bore a date of 1878, 1900 or 1910 it did not follow it was obsolescent.[8]

The worst fears of the Amalgamation about the replacement of mules were not immediately realised. Membership of the Amalgamation continued to increase until 1951 when it reached a post-war peak, but it was a growth based on the backwardness of the cotton employers and their unwillingness to reinvest the profits of the post-war boom.

The Amalgamation in 1951 had 22,756 members, of whom 10,675 were spinners. Bolton had 7,862 members and Oldham 8,501, reflecting the recovery of Oldham since 1940, once more the major Province, though its recovery was based on recruiting a larger number of piecers. Amalgamation membership was approximately half the 1930 figure and 40 per cent of the high point of 1920. The Amalgamation, since 1940, no longer had a seat on the T.U.C. General Council or the Labour Party Executive. The Cardroom Amalgamation under Sir Alfred Roberts' leadership had replaced them as the major union in spinning. Despite these obvious signs of decline, the Spinners remained the highest-paid group of workers in the industry. Wages had continued to rise after 1945; there were wage advances in 1946, 1948, 1949, 1950 and 1951, reached by mutual agreement or through arbitration. The strike weapon was rarely used or threatened after 1945.

The major social change was the abolition of Saturday working, with the reduction in hours from 48 to 45 in 1946, the first time cotton operatives had a full weekend of leisure. There were constant appeals for overtime work because of the national economic crisis, especially after 1947, but the response by members was patchy, reflecting their unwillingness to give up the leisure just achieved.[9]

The major rule change during the 1940s arose from the Labour Government's 1945 Trade Disputes Act which repealed the 1927 Trade Disputes Act. Contracting-out rather than contracting-in to the political levy was re-introduced. The result was that by 1950, 19,280 members out of 21,270 paid the levy, compared with 6,772 out of 16,075 in 1946. The other change was the ending of the Amalgamation's own insurance society, which had been formed in 1911 to provide health insurance as a result of the National Insurance Act of that year. The coming of the welfare state abolished this form of organisation and the functions became part of the new social insurance scheme modelled on the Beveridge Report; valuable though the role of the trade union insurance society had been, its replacement reflected the growth of collectivist values amongst trade unionists.[10]

The period of the Labour Government represented a major advance for the Amalgamation and cotton trade unionism in general. The level of consultation about the problems of the industry was far greater than at any period in the Amalgamation's history, and they were much more genuinely partners in the industry. The industry itself appeared to have a future for the first time since 1920, and the Labour Government emphasised the significance of Lancashire cotton to both the export performance and the general prosperity of the economy. But problems did exist for the Amalgamation, most notably the continued emphasis on replacement of mule spindles in all the discussions about the industry's future.

The period of the post-war Labour Government, despite the hopes of contemporaries, did not lead to permanent prosperity and recovery of the industry. The decline of the industry began again in 1952 and continued to the industry's eventual demise. The post-war decline of the cotton industry differed in two important respects from the inter-war crisis. The problems of the industry in the inter-war years had been caused by the loss of Lancashire's export markets, while in the post-war period it was the invasion of the home market especially from 1955 onwards by Commonwealth producers that destroyed the Lancashire cotton industry. The decline took place, unlike the inter-war years, against a background of full employment, which allowed some diversification of the Lancashire economy to take place. The post-war decline was characterised by considerable co-operation between employers and labour; this was because there was agreement that imports were the chief cause of the industry's problems.

Between 1951, the height of the cotton industry's prosperity in the post-war period, and the passing of the Cotton Industry Act in 1959, there were three main years of depression, 1952, 1955 and 1958. The depression of 1952 was due to the collapse of the home market which coincided with the revival of foreign competition. The immediate post-war years had been favourable to the Lancashire cotton industry, as Japanese competition had been effectively eliminated for five years, while the restrictions during the war had created a large post-war market. This position began to come to an end in 1949, but the impact of the Korean war hid the true position for some years. During the period of the Labour Government the main concern was to recruit enough labour for the industry and there was a small rise in productivity, but not large enough to transform the industry's competitiveness.

The 1952 slump shattered the confidence of both employers and operatives, and employment fell temporarily by nearly a half in spinning. The main reason for the recession was the collapse of the home market, brought about by the rise in the relative price of textiles, which led consumers to postpone buying textiles in favour of the new consumer goods of the 1950s. A partial recovery in 1953-4 was followed by a further slump in 1955 when a new phenomenon emerged, the import of cotton textiles into Britain. Though imports were only small in 1955, they helped to push Lancashire into depression. The exports of India and Hong Kong were able to enter the British home market without paying any tariffs due to the imperial preference agreements of the 1930s. The Conservative Government was reluctant to alter the position because it believed that the continued import of cotton cloth from Commonwealth underdeveloped countries, chiefly India, Pakistan and Hong Kong, would help to raise their standard of living and thus enable them to buy the products of other British industries. Where the Government was mistaken was in believing these developments could take place without a major impact on the Lancashire cotton industry. They were in effect sacrificing the Lancashire cotton industry in the interest of other British industries. The Government was able to mask this policy by claiming that the cotton industry's problems arose from a lack of competitiveness, but while this was a contributory factor, it was not the main cause. Various appeals by the Cotton Council to the Government, supported by both the cotton unions and employers, to restrict imports were rejected.[11]

The U.T.F.W.A.'s response to the decline of the industry was to produce in 1957 a new policy for the industry to replace their 1943 programme for nationalisation. The *Plan for Cotton* was written by Harold Wilson, a former President of the Board of Trade and future Prime Minister, and like earlier Labour proposals it believed that modernisation was essential and could be attained by state intervention. A commission to reorganise the cotton industry was to be established, while a government imports commission would review imports, and in the event of a failure to agree voluntarily an acceptable level of imports, the commission would enforce them.[12]

The Amalgamation's attitude towards the *Plan for Cotton* was mixed. Pressure from the Amalgamation had led to amendments to the plan. Harold Wilson's original draft had emphasised the replacement of traditional machinery but this was changed to 'modernisation of machinery of the traditional type', a deliberate reference to mule spinning. The Amalgamation's view was that mule spinning should be retained and improvements should be made to existing technology, rather than replacing it.[13]

The campaign of the cotton unions in 1957-8 spurred the Conservative Government into action. The decline in support for the Conservative Party in Lancashire as a result of their attitude towards the cotton industry was reflected in their poor performance at the Rochdale by-election in 1958, when the Conservative candidate was forced into third place. In the autumn of 1958 the Prime Minister, Harold Macmillan, spoke to the Cotton Board and indicated his willingness to implement proposals to modernise the industry if common agreement could be reached within the industry. At the same time it was made clear that no legal restriction on imports would be made by the Government, and it was up to the industry to make voluntary agreements with the main importers.[14]

By the beginning of 1958 the Amalgamation's membership numbered 14,571 compared with the post-war high of 22,886 in 1951, a fall of one-third. Mule spindles running in 1951 stood at 17.7 million compared with 10.6 million ring spindles; by 1958 mule spindles had fallen to 12.1 million while ring spindles had remained almost unchanged at 10.3 million. Company profits had also fallen by a half, though the fall was not as severe as that experienced in the inter-war years. The continued ability of employers to make a profit was due to the minimum price agreement operated by the Yarn Association since the late 1940s. This in turn enabled the Spinners' Amalgamation jointly with other unions to win wage advances in 1953, 1954, 1956 and 1957, though the awards themselves were not as great as those won by other workers, and cotton operatives again began to slip down the wages league table.[15]

The year 1958 was the third year of depression and the deteriorating condition of the industry led the cotton unions to approach jointly the two employers' organisations seeking redundancy payments for those operatives made unemployed due to mill closures. There was a growing concern that unlike in the recession of 1952 operatives would be unable to find work elsewhere. The Amalgamation pointed out that in a large number of closures directors had received compensation for their services, but none was made to the operatives. The cotton unions wanted a central fund to be established based on a levy of employers equal to 0.25 per cent of the wage bill. The fund would be administered jointly and compensate redundant operatives who had worked over five years in the industry with an extra thirteen weeks' wages, and an additional week's wages for every year's service over six years. The employers opposed this plan, arguing that 'the protection of workers against the effects of unemployment is a matter for the state; it is not a responsibility of an individual industry'.[16]

The sense of crisis in the industry was increased by the fact that 1958 was the first year since the Industrial Revolution that imports of cotton cloth exceeded exports. Lancashire's traditional role had been reversed. In 1951, at the height of the industry's post-war prosperity, exports of cotton cloth had stood at 864 million square yards, but by 1958 this figure had been more than halved to 383 million square yards. Imports of cloth had risen from 99 million square yards in 1953 to 387 million square yards in 1958. Yarn exports showed a similar pattern, with exports falling from 65,481 (thousand lbs) in 1951 to 26,771 (thousand lbs) in 1958, while imports increased from 3,360 (thousand lbs) in 1953 to 14,635 (thousand lbs) in 1958. Attempts to halt imports by voluntary agreement with the major importers were largely ineffective. Agreements which were reached with Hong Kong, India and Pakistan in the late 1950s settled on quotas which were higher than the actual level of imports, offering considerable scope for expansion. The cotton industry had begun to protest about this development as early as 1955 but had been informed by the Conservative Government that they were being alarmist. By 1958 this was clearly no longer true, but the Government was still not prepared to intervene encouraging the industry to make voluntary agreements with the major importers. If these negotiations had taken place against a background of a potential threat of exclusion from the British market, it might have been possible for the industry to have gained a more favourable agreement. The Amalgamation particularly resented the agreement reached with Hong Kong in 1959 taking the view that the textile industrialists of that area had dictated terms to Lancashire and been encouraged to do so because of the British Government's fear of internal disorder in Hong Kong.[17]

The problems of the Amalgamation were compounded in early 1959 by the decision of the Restrictive Practices Court to declare the Yarn Association scheme illegal. According to the Amalgamation the agreement had benefited both the employers and themselves in allowing the industry to set aside reserves for re-equipment and modernisation, and had been an important factor in 'providing better working conditions for our members in so far as there had been very few bad spinning complaints which is something that cannot be said of pre-war days when yarn customers mercilessly beat down the price of yarn, and, to meet the lower prices, the spinning firms purchased lower and lower qualities of raw cotton.' The Court's decision referred to the need for reduction in the size of the industry: 'We are satisfied that the industry can, and ought to, be made smaller', to which the Amalgamation's Secretary, Charles Schofield, responded that 'once again these sentiments have been uttered, and once again the human consequences have been ignored . . . No thought has been given to the men who, in most cases, have spent the whole of their working lives at one mill, representing up to fifty or more years' service.'[18]

In the spring of 1959 the Conservative Government's intentions for the industry became clearer. The speech by the Prime Minister, Harold Macmillan, to the Cotton Board in the autumn of 1958 had suggested the Government was prepared to take a positive view of the industry's problems for the first time since it came into office in 1951. The Cotton Board responded by creating a Development Committee to draw up a scheme for the industry that might be acceptable to both the industry and the Government. When the Cotton Board had successfully made the agreement with Hong Kong for restricting imports, the President of the Board of Trade, Sir David Eccles, wrote to Lord Rochdale, Chairman of the Cotton Board, suggesting setting up a committee of enquiry to review the industry's problems. The Cotton Board quickly replied with a strong preference for immediate Government action rather than an enquiry. Sectional committees of the Cotton Board had already drawn up schemes and gathered information on surplus capacity, and these became the basis for the Government's proposals with further negotiations taking place between employers' associations and itself. Surprisingly, none of these negotiations involved the cotton unions, who only received the vaguest of reports via their membership of the Development Committee.

When Sir David Eccles announced his proposals to assist the industry in April 1959, they were the first intimation the unions had of the changes that were to be crucial to their future. The Government proposed a grant of £30 million to help firms scrap new machinery and re-equip with new plant. The condition for Government support was that the industry would have to compensate operatives made redundant by the contraction. But there was to be no Government financial help for compensating the unemployed operatives; this would have to be provided by employers. The Government's financial aid was only meant to provide two-thirds of the finance for the process of reconstruction and modernisation. There was not a great deal more detail in the Government's statement on the industry's future and this placed the cotton unions, who were negotiating jointly, in a difficult position. Eccles estimated that the industry's over capacity was approximately one-third and suggested that both Government and employers were thinking in terms of at least 30 per cent of the operatives being made redundant.

The Government had made the passing of the Act conditional on the employers successfully negotiating an agreement with the cotton unions about redundancy, but by setting a short timetable and failing to involve the unions in the negotiations they severely handicapped them. Electoral considerations were not unimportant in determining the proposed timetable, but in doing this the unions did not possess the information necessary for successful negotiations, even assuming that the employers had the money to compensate the anticipated redundancies.[19]

Before the negotiations could take place the U.T.F.W.A.'s annual conference was held in May 1959, and proved a rather explosive affair. Growing concern by the Amalgamation about the threat to mule spinning had already led to joint meetings between the Bolton and Oldham Provinces, at which dissatisfaction with the central leadership of the cotton unions had been expressed. The result was a joint resolution from the two Provinces to the Amalgamation's Executive expressing concern at the contraction of the industry, both present and forthcoming, and called on the U.T.F.W.A. 'to actively oppose any policy which would result in additional unemployment amongst our present members'. Although asked to put it forward as an emergency resolution, it was not put before the U.T.F.W.A.'s conference, being replaced by one which merely 'noted' the Government scheme and instructed its officers to 'press for adequate compensation'. Sir Alf Roberts, Secretary of the Cardroom Amalgamation, introduced the new resolution and found himself facing a considerable barrage of hostility from delegates. Ted Mellor of the Oldham Spinners, a well-known figure in the Amalgamation, launched a vigorous attack on the resolution: 'Just imagine "Conference notes", and here we are on our death beds.' He pointed out that most mule spinners would not only be unemployed but unemployable, the average age of mule spinners in Oldham, he claimed, was 53, and there were as many over 65 as under 35; as a result most mule spinners were too old to handle heavy jobs. He did not know what the effect of this proposed scheme would be, 'but he knew what had happened in the past: £10,000 had been paid out to four directors when a mill closed down but up to now all the operatives had got was their cards.' Ted Mellor's attack on the resolution was supported by other delegates and even the normally moderate President of the Amalgamation, James Whitworth, was critical:

> this Amalgamation considers that since 1951 the industry had been treated with the greatest dishonesty . . . mule spinners had been compelled to take jobs as labourers, cleaners, bus conductors . . . because no other jobs were available. Furthermore . . . thousands of people compelled to leave their employment had not even received a letter of thanks from firms to which they had given a lifetime of service.[20]

It was only a personal plea from the Amalgamation's General Secretary, Charles Schofield, to the Spinners' delegates not to oppose the resolution that contained the situation and as a result their opposition was withdrawn.[21]

When negotiations with employers on the redundancy scheme began the cotton unions were placed in an impossible position. The Government's timetable meant that they had to agree a system of compensation for redundant operatives by July 1959, otherwise legislation would be postponed. The consequence of postponement would be that operatives made redundant would receive no compensation. At the same time the unions were negotiating while knowing very little about the proposed scheme for contracting the industry. Their exclusion from negotiations with the Board of Trade meant they were even ignorant of the level of compensation employers were receiving from the State.

The employers presented a scheme for compensation based on the length of service and age of the redundant worker. The level of redundancy pay rose from one week's wage for a 21-year-old to 30 weeks for a 55-year old operative. Compensation was not to be paid if an operative immediately found similar work and only proportionate compensation would be paid if different work was quickly found. Part of the agreement was that employers and trade unions would co-operate in seeking work for redundant operatives. Unlike the trade union scheme, payments were to be made weekly rather than in a lump sum. Most important of all, the scheme only applied to those operatives made unemployed as a result of the scheme.

There were a number of points of conflict between the cotton unions and employers; principally, though, the unions wanted a general redundancy scheme rather than one which just applied to the proposed scheme, and for compensation to be provided in a lump sum rather than by weekly payment. Initially the unions accepted the employers' proposals, but when a union deputation to the Board of Trade learned the details of the proposed compensation levels to employers, they rejected the redundancy scheme and sought a further meeting with employers. They were concerned that redundancy payments should not be eaten away by Government regulations, which would not allow National Insurance payments to be made to those in receipt of weekly redundancy payments. They were also worried that the redundancy payments would be subject to income tax.

Time was by then running out for the negotiations because of the Government's wish to see the Cotton Industry Bill become law before the summer recess. No doubt this desire was influenced by electoral considerations; the Government clearly wished to fight a General Election after rather than before the legislation was passed. Agreement was finally reached in early July on a scheme of compensation that gave operatives a redundancy payment, half of which was paid by lump sum and half by weekly payments. The weekly payments were to be adjusted in order to comply with National Insurance regulations, so as not to affect unemployment pay.

This agreement was discussed by a Special Representative Meeting of the Amalgamation, where a number of complaints were voiced about the failure of the Executive to call a meeting before the agreement had been formally agreed. There was a general feeling 'that the agreement did not come up to expectation' but in the end the delegates accepted that in the absence of any compensation for unemployment since the decline of the industry began in 1920 they would have to accept the proposed scheme. There is probably some truth in the accusation that the cotton unions were 'stampeded into arriving at an agreement' because of the short amount of time that was allowed for negotiation.[22]

The 1959 Cotton Industry Act had a number of new features compared with earlier legislation. Its aim was to contract and reorganise the industry by subsidising employers to scrap existing machinery, especially mules. At the same time the surplus capacity of the industry would be removed, leaving the industry smaller but with a much higher productivity. This the Government believed would enable the industry to become more competitive. Behind the legislation was an implicit belief by the Government that imports were not the primary cause of the industry's problems, a view in conflict with the analysis offered by both employers and trade unions.

The Act enabled firms in the industry to receive compensation for scrapping machinery, whether the machinery was working or not. The rate of compensation was 8 shillings per mule in spinning. This figure was increased by 25 per cent if the firm left the industry, but employers had only from July to September 1959 to decide. The Government paid two-thirds of the compensation to employers while the industry itself paid one-third, which was raised by a levy on those remaining in the industry. The time period covering grants for re-equipment was longer, with firms placing applications for aid before the summer of 1964.[23]

The Amalgamation's chief concern was with the procedure for the scrapping of machinery, because it was clear that there would be no new investment in mules, as the main effect of the Act was to phase out the spinning mule. The Act scrapped over 12 million spindles, the vast majority of which were mules. The largest number of mills closed was in Oldham, 32 in all, with a similar number, 27, being closed in Bolton. Total compensation paid to cotton employers was just short of £10 million. Operatives in spinning received over £500,000 in compensation, the majority going to mule spinners. In the same period the Amalgamation's membership was halved, falling from 14,571 in January 1958 to 7,100 in December 1960.[24]

The Cotton Industry Act effectively marked the end of the Spinners' Amalgamation as a major trade union. Though the Act destroyed over 12 million spindles, many were in fact unused at the time and probably would never have been used. Employers were compensated retrospectively as far back as 1956, in marked contrast with the treatment of the operatives. The Act reduced working spindles from 5.5 million to under 3 million, making 4,500 members redundant as a direct result of the Act itself, but taken together with the depression prior to the Act nearly 7,000 spinners, half of the Amalgamation's membership, lost their jobs permanently. Unlike the Cardroom and Weavers' Amalgamations the Act held out no future for the Spinners. It was clear that as the industry was modernised, remaining mules would be eliminated. As the Amalgamation's Annual Report had remarked at the time, 'the year 1959 must surely go down in industrial history as the most eventful, and for the mule section the most tragic for many years.'[25]

The tragedy of the Act was that though it may have helped the Conservative Government's re-election in 1959, it failed to solve the problems of the industry. The first year of the Act saw a dramatic rise in the prosperity of Lancashire as order books were overflowing to such an extent that higher imports were dragged into the home market. The following year imports rose even more dramatically, creating a sense of crisis once more in the industry, while exports fell from 383,818 (square yards) in 1958 to 286,660 (square yards) in 1961. By 1961 imports were running at a level of 70 per cent of home production, with a sudden growth in imports from Spain and Portugal destroying much of the industry's new confidence. When the 1959 Act was reviewed in Parliament in 1962, it was clear to all concerned that it had failed.

Meanwhile the Amalgamation had begun to discuss organisational change as a result of the decline in membership. A third of the Districts of the Amalgamation closed as a result of the Act, and only Bolton and Oldham remained viable in the sense of being able to pay a full-time secretary. Members and officials were still keen to keep the Amalgamation in existence, and therefore ideas of closer co-operation and organisational unity with the other cotton unions were rejected. Instead, Provinces and Districts in adjacent areas were encouraged to meet, with the hope that they would see the logic of merging. The Amalgamation's Secretary, Charles Schofield, retired in 1960, having served as secretary since 1943, and he was replaced by the Amalgamation's President, James Whitworth, the Ashton Secretary. The Amalgamation also hoped that mule spinners who had transferred to ring spinning could keep their membership, but the Cardroom Amalgamation discouraged this development. The traditional policy of opposition to double shifts on mule spindles was even dropped, both in the hope of finding members more work and of keeping the Amalgamation alive.[26]

There could be little hope after 1960 that the union could continue, and between 1960 and 1970 membership continued to decline, falling from 7,116 to 1,758, with Yorkshire and Haslingden now the largest areas, rather than Bolton and Oldham. James Whitworth retired in 1964 and was replaced as Secretary by Walter Lee, who unfortunately died shortly afterwards. It was left to Joe Richardson to see the union through its last few years of existence. The Spinners' Amalgamation finally closed down in 1976.[27]

During these years there were a number of major problems, of which the decline of the industry continued to be the main one. The 1959 Act having failed, Governments encouraged Courtaulds and I.C.I. to move in and buy up large sections of the cotton industry, transforming it from a horizontally organised industry to a vertical one. This development came too late to rescue the industry, which was changing anyway with the increasing use of artificial fibres, a change that was recognised with the renaming of the Cotton Board in 1967 as the Textile Council. Probably the most disappointing development in the 1960s to the union was the election of the Labour Government of 1964. The decline of the industry since 1952 had taken place under successive Conservative Governments who had shown themselves particularly unsympathetic to the problems of imports. The Labour Government of 1945 was remembered with great affection for having introduced the one period of stability in the long decline since 1920. Furthermore, the new Prime Minister was Harold Wilson, the very politician who had drafted the cotton unions' *Plan for Cotton* in 1957. George Brown, his deputy, had visited Manchester in 1963 and had clearly indicated a willingness to control imports, promising that a future Labour Government would through G.A.T.T. persuade other advanced industrial countries to take underdeveloped countries' textiles so that the burden was not unduly borne by Lancashire. A new body, a Cotton Commission, was to be set up for controlling imports. When in power, though, the Labour Government failed to implement these schemes, and imports continued to take an increasing proportion of the home market.[28]

One major change the Labour Government did make, introduced by the cotton unions' sponsored Member of Parliament, Ernest Thornton, was compulsory redundancy pay. The ending of the 1959 Act had left a great anomaly, as those made redundant after the Act received no compensation. The 1965 Redundancy Payment Act gave those made redundant the legal right to compensation and though its provisions applied throughout industry they were particularly pertinent to cotton. If only its provision had applied throughout the decline of the industry, operatives would have received some compensation for economic changes which were largely beyond their control.

The Amalgamation finally ceased to exist in 1976, over one hundred years after its original foundation though, as we have seen, its real origins go back much earlier to the beginning of the Industrial Revolution. As one of the earliest permanently established trade union organisations in the cotton industry they had played a leading role in laying the basis for the unionisation of the rest of the industry. They had also guided the cotton operatives in many of their industrial struggles and conflicts with Government over issues concerning the industry as a whole. The collective action of the spinners' unions through their Amalgamation, enabled them to do battle with the employers and achieve for themselves a position in the cotton spinning and manufacturing industries that was second to none. They could, with some justice, lay claim to be true aristocrats of labour especially in the late nineteenth and early twentieth centuries. The spinners' pride in craft and success in establishing a permanent organisation, however, could not save the industry from decline and the Amalgamation died not through apathy or lack of interest but because of changes in the international system of production, distribution and consumption of cotton yarn and cloth that were entirely beyond their control.

NOTES

CHAPTER ONE (Cotton Spinning in the Industrial Revolution)

1. D. S. Landes, *The Unbound Prometheus: Technological Change and Industrial Development in Western Europe from 1750 to the Present*, (1969) pp. 41-42; See D. A. Farnie, *The English Cotton Industry and the World Market 1815-1896*, (1979) pp. 330-84 for a select bibliography of the cotton industry. A. P. Wadsworth and J. De Lacy Mann, *The Cotton Trade and Industrial Lancashire 1600-1780*, (1931) still provides the best introduction to the industry's early years.

2. For a survey of technical developments in the early cotton industry see R. L. Hills, *Power in the Industrial Revolution* (1969).

3. H. Catling, *The Spinning Mule* (1970) pp. 31-40; M. E. Rose, 'Samuel Crompton (1753-1827), Inventor of the Spinning Mule: A Reconsideration', *Transactions of Lancashire and Cheshire Antiquarian Society*, 75-6 (1968) pp. 11-32; G. J. French, *The Life and Times of Samuel Crompton* (1860) new edition with an introduction by S. D. Chapman, (1970) pp. 19-22, p. 52; D. A. Farnie, (1979) p. 152, footnote 1; G. W. Daniels, 'Samuel Crompton's Census of the Cotton Industry in 1811', *Economic Journal*, (Economic History Supplement), II (1930) pp. 107-10.

4. E. J. Hobsbawn, *Industry and Empire*, (1968) p. 40; B. R. Mitchell and P. Deane, *Abstract of British Historial Statistics*, (1962) pp. 178-9, 187; D. A. Farnie, (1979) ch. 3.

5. S. D. Chapman and S. Chassagne, *European Textile Printers in the Eighteenth Century*, (1981) p. 41; See H. Catling, (1970) chs. 2 and 3 for the best guide to the mule; W. Lazonick, 'Industrial Relations and Technical Change: the case of the self-acting mule' *Cambridge Journal of Economics*, 3 (1979) is also a good starting point.

6. H. Catling, (1970) ch. 3.

7. H. Catling, (1970) chs. 4-7; G. N. Von Tunzelmann; *Steam Power and British Industrialisation to 1860*, (1978) p. 192; W. Lazonick, (1979) p. 237.

8. H. Catling, (1970) ch. 3; See the notes to Appendix I; P.P. 1842 (31) XXII, *Reports of the Inspectors of Factories*, p. 83; PP. 1833 (450) XX, *Factory Inquiry Commission*; First Report, D1, p. 46.

9. D. A. Farnie, (1979) ch. 2; J. Jewkes 'The Localisation of the Cotton Industry' *Economic Journal* (Economic History Supplement), II (1930) pp. 91-106; A. J. Taylor, 'Concentration and Specialisation in the Lancashire Cotton Industry, 1825-1850' *Economic History Review*, 2nd ser., I (1949) pp. 114-22; A. J. Robertson, 'The Decline of the Scottish Cotton Industry 1860-1914' *Business History*, XII (1970) pp. 116-28.

10. See D. A. Farnie, (1979) for the economic development of the different towns.

11. R. Glen, *Urban Workers in the Early Industrial Revolution*, (1984) and N. Kirk, *The Growth of Working Class Reformism in Mid-Victorian England*, (1985) are the most recent volumes dealing with the cotton districts and are a guide to the debates.

12. V. A. C. Gatrell, 'Labour, Power, and the Size of Firms in Lancashire Cotton in the Second Quarter of the Nineteenth Century' *Economic History Review*, XXX (1977) pp. 95-138; A. Ure, *The Cotton Manufacture of Great Britain*, (1836, reprint 1970), Vol. I, pp. 297-312; D. A. Farnie, (1979) pp. 214-5.

13. H. Catling, (1970) ch. 9; PP. 1834 (167) XIX *Factory Inquiry Commission, Supplementary Report*, p. 136.

14. See W. Lazonick, (1979) for an analysis of the mule and self-actor manning systems and also I. Cohen, 'Workers Control in the Cotton Industry', *Labor History*, 26 (1985); for details of the manning pattern see PP. 1842 (31) XXII, L. Horner, pp. 85-91.

15. G. Stedman Jones, 'Class Struggle and the Industrial Revolution', *New Left Review*, 90 (March-April 1975), p. 51.

16. G. H. Wood, *The History of Wages in the Cotton Trade during the Past One Hundred Years*, (1910); for conditions in the early mills, particularly those at Manchester, see P.P. 1818 *S.C.H.L. Rep.*, (H.L. 90) XCVI and P.P 1819 *S.C.H.L. Rep.*, (H.L. 24) CX.

17. A. Ure, (1836) p. 199; E. F. Tufnell, *Character, Object and Effects of Trade Unions*, (1834) pp. 108-9; G. S. Jones, (1975) pp. 51-4.

18. P.P. 1842 (31) XXII, p. 85.

19. See Appendix I for the methods used to determine the figures cited in this paragraph.

20. On wage trends in different districts see G. H. Wood (1910).

CHAPTER TWO (Mule Spinner Societies and the Early Federations)

1.   This chapter is largely based on recent secondary sources. For a general study of trade unionism in the cotton industry see H. A. Turner, *Trade Union Growth Structure and Policy: A Comparative Study of the Cotton Unions*, (1962). R. G. Kirby and A. E. Musson's detailed and accurately referenced *The Voice of the People: John Doherty 1798-1854*, (1975) is the best account of early cotton spinner trade unionism. I am grateful to Professor R. F. Dyson for kindly making available his work and references on the early history of the spinners.

2.   H. A. Turner, (1962) pp. 79-80; R. Glen, *Urban Workers in the Early Industrial Revolution*, (1984) pp. 83-4; G. Unwin, *Samuel Oldknow and the Arkwrights*, (1924) p. 33; R. Glen, (1984) p. 68; N. J. Smelser, *Social Change in the Industrial Revolution: An Application of Theory to the Lancashire Cotton Industry 1780-1840* (1959) p. 315, 318-9; E. P. Thompson, *The Making of the English Working Class*, (1963, Pelican Reprint 1980), p. 550, 547; N. J. Smelser (1959) pp. 355-6; *Webbs Collection*, Vol XXXVI f. 74-89; G. W. Daniels, 'The Cotton Trade during the Revolutionary and Napoleonic Wars', *Transactions of Manchester Statistical Society*, (1915-16) p. 59.

3.   There is little information on the early shop clubs; information gleaned from parliamentary inquiries, evidence made available as a result of attempts to break them, and rule books are the principal sources. See *Webbs Collection*, vol. XXXVI f. 78; P.P. 1824 (51), V, 5th and 6th Reports, especially pp. 479-80, 556-9, 614-6; R. Boyson, *The Ashworth Cotton Enterprise. The Rise and Fall of a Family Firm 1818-1880*, (1970) p. 149; and pp. 18-20 below. For the district

societies see the rulebook of the Oldham society, and P. P. 1837-8 (488) VIII, *Select Committee on Combinations of Workmen*, pp. 299-305 for rulebooks of the Glasgow and Manchester societies; R. G. Kirby and A. E. Musson, (1975) p. 19.

4. *Webbs Collection*, Vol. XXXVI for the Oldham rulebook; N. J. Smelser, (1959) pp. 318-20 for a discussion of the Manchester rule book; R. Boyson, (1970) p. 149; G. Unwin et al., (1924) p. 33; C. H. Lee, *A Cotton Enterprise 1795-1840: A History of M'Connel and Kennedy Fine Cotton Spinners*, (1972) p. 18.

5. See for example the Oldham (1795), Manchester (1837) and Glasgow (1837) rules; also N. J. Smelser's discussion of the Manchester rule books; J. Doherty, *A Report of the Proceedings of a Delegate Meeting of the Operative Cotton Spinners of England, Ireland and Scotland*, (1829) p. 40; For the financing of disputes see, for example, P.P. 1824 (51), 6th Report, evidence of James Frost, pp. 604-10; A. Aspinall, *The Early English Trade Unions: Documents from the Home Office Papers on the Public Record Office*, (1949) docs. 241, 249, 251.

6. G. W. Daniels, *The Early English Cotton Industry*, (1920), p. 145; G. W. Daniels 'The Cotton Trade during the Revolutionary and Napoleonic Wars' *Trans. Man. Statistical Soc.*, (1915-16) pp. 63, 65; E. P. Thompson, (1980), pp. 219, 576; R. G. Kirby and A. E. Musson, (1975), p. 13; P.P. 1833 (450) XX, *Factory Inquiry Commission, 1st Report*, evidence of A. Lees, D2. pp. 90-1; P.P. 1824 (51) V, 5th Report, evidence of Thomas Worsley, p. 410, and 6th Report, evidence of Peter McDougal, p. 611-13.

7. E. C. Tufnell, (1834) p. 16.

8. E. C. Tufnell, (1834), pp. 13-17, P.P. 1824 (51) V, 6th Report, evidence of James Frost, pp. 573-9, 604-10; See Appendix for estimates of mulespinner numbers; P.P. 1833 (450) XX, evidence of A. Lees, p. 91.

9. H. A. Turner, (1962), p. 67; E. C. Tufnell, (1834) p. 17; G. W. Daniels, 'The Cotton Trade at the close of the Napoleonic War' *Trans. Manchester Statistical Society*, (1917-18), p. 13; R. G. Kirby and A. E. Musson, (1975) p. 15; P.P. 1824 (51) V, 5th Report, evidence of Mr. W. Bolling, master cotton spinner of Bolton, p. 557; R. Glen, (1984) p. 70; A. Aspinall, (1949) pp. 222-3; J. L. & B. Hammond, *The Skilled Labourer* (1978 edition), p. 79; P.P. 1824 (51) V, 5th Report, evidence of Thomas Worsley, p. 411.

10. For descriptions of working conditions in the early Manchester mulespinning mills see the evidence presented to the House of Lords 1818 and 1819 *Select Committee Inquiries into the Employment of Children in Cotton Mills*: P.P. 1818 *S.C.H.L. Rep.*, (H.L. 90) XCVI and P.P. 1819 *S.C.H.L. Rep.*, (H.L. 24) CX; J. L. and B. Hammond, *The Town Labourer*, (1978) pp. 79-80, 110-16 and R. G. Kirby and A. E. Musson, (1975) pp. 346-9 provide the general background to this early phase of the short-time movement.

11. For the Manchester strike see P.P. 1824 (51) V, 5th Report, evidence of James Frost, pp. 575-9; J. L. and B. Hammond, *The Skilled Labourer*, (1978) pp. 78-87; A. Aspinall, (1949), and R. G. Kirby and A. E. Musson, (1975) pp. 18-28; J. Doherty, (1829) p. 33; For quotations in the text see the Second Address of the Journeymen Cotton Spinners of Manchester cited in J. L. and B. Hammond, *The Skilled Labourer*, (1978) p. 79; A. Aspinall, (1949), docs. 253, 260, 298, 280, 294, 319.

12. P.P. 1824 (51) V, 5th Report, p. 414.

13. For the background to the Stockport dispute see J. L. and B. Hammond, *The Skilled Labourer*, (1978) pp. 77-8; P. Giles, *The Economic and Social Development of Stockport*, M.A., Manchester, 1950, pp. 188-91; R. Glen, (1984) pp. 72-5; Information obtained by John Lloyd in the dispute involving Temple is contained in A. Aspinall, (1949), doc. 237; for Temple's account see P.P. 1824 (51) V, 5th Report, pp. 413-5.

14. P.P. 1824 (51) V, 5th Report, evidence of Thomas Worsley, pp. 412-3.

15. J. L. and B. Hammond, *The Skilled Labourer*, (1978) p. 81; A. Aspinall, (1949), especially docs. 234, 280 and 286; P. Giles, (1950) pp. 204-5; R. Glen, (1984), pp. 220-1; For the intrusion of radicalism into the 1818 Manchester Strike see *The Mulespinners' Address to the Public* (July, 1818) reprinted in J. L. and B. Hammond *The Town Labourer*, (1978) pp. 205-6 and a similarly titled address published in September 1818 and reprinted in E. P. Thompson, (1980) pp. 218-21.

16. A. Aspinall, (1949) doc. 366; P.P. 1824 (51) V, 5th Report, evidence of William Scott, pp. 415-6; R. G. Kirby and A. E. Musson, (1975) pp. 28-9; See P.P. 1824 (51) V, 5th Report, pp. 555-61 for accounts of this dispute given by two Bolton masters; A. Aspinall, (1949) docs. 391 and 393.

17. For the Glasgow dispute see A. Aspinall, (1949) docs. 392, 414; P.P. 1824 (51) V, 5th Report, evidence of masters and men, pp. 378-85, 470-84, 611-20; R. G. Kirby and A. E. Musson, (1975) pp. 29-30, 100; E. C. Tufnell, (1834) p. 21; extracts from the *Glasgow Chronicle* reprinted in the *Manchester Gazette*, 11 and 25 December 1824, 15 and 29 January; 5 February, 1825; H. A. Turner, (1962) pp. 72-3; P.P. 1833 (450) XX, evidence of A. Lees.

18. For evidence of actions under the Combinations Acts see P.P. 1824 (51) V, the evidence of employers and cotton spinners. A. Aspinall, (1949), documents relating to the 1818 Manchester strike; R. G. Kirby and A. E. Musson, (1975) p. 33; R. Glen, (1984) p. 75; But see J. Foster, *Class Struggle in the Industrial Revolution: Early Industrial Capitalism in Three English Towns*, (1974) pp. 49-50; N. J. Smelser, (1959) pp. 324-5 and especially p. 324 for an extract from 5 Geo. IV, C.95; R. G. Kirby and A. E. Musson, (1975) pp. 350-2, E. P. Thompson (1980) pp. 546-65.

19. R. G. Kirby and A. E. Musson, (1975) pp. 29-32 for an account of the 1824-5 Federation and the strikes at this time. *Manchester Gazette*, 25 December 1824 for an extract for the *Glasgow Chronicle* giving an account of the Manchester men's visit to Glasgow.

20. N. J. Smelser, (1959) pp. 324-5; R. G. Kirby and A. E. Musson, (1975) pp. 37-9; E. P. Thompson, (1980) p. 564; P.P. 1824 (51) V, 4th Report, evidence of Thomas Ashton, pp. 307-8; S. J. Chapman, (1904) p. 211.

21. R. G. Kirby and A. E. Musson, (1975) in particular Ch. IV relating to John Doherty's first year as secretary of the Manchester cotton spinners.

22. For a contemporary account of the Manchester dispute see P.P. 1837-8 (488) VIII, *Select Committee on Combinations of Workmen*, pp. 241-82 for the evidence of three of the Manchester spinners' leaders (John Doherty, David McWilliams and William Arrowsmith) and the town's magistrate; P. Giles, (1950) pp. 361-71 gives an account of the Stockport dispute; R. G. Kirby and A. E. Musson (1975) pp. 52-78 provide a detailed account of the Manchester strike; *Manchester Gazette*, 28 March 1829.

23. John Doherty's account of the Isle of Man conference which was published as *A Report of the Proceedings of the Meeting of Cotton Spinners at Ramsey* (1829); S. and B. Webb, (1920) pp. 117-20; R. G. Kirby and A. E. Musson, (1975) pp. 76-7, 85-99; S. J. Chapman, (1904) p. 202. The attendance of a Belfast representative at the 1829 Ramsey conference may have been nominal. The district society was defeated in its 1825-6 dispute and was subsequently considered to be of little influence in the industry, see R. G. Kirby and A. E. Musson, (1975) p. 31; P.P. 1837-8 (488) VIII, pp. 62, 229-35, 259.

24. For an account of the Bolton strike see R. Boyson, (1970) pp. 141-9. See R. G. Kirby and A. E. Musson, (1975) pp. 100-13 for an account of the G.G.U.'s early activities and pp. 119-38 for details of the Ashton strike. Also W. A. Jevons 'An Account of the Spinners' Strike at Ashton-under-Lyne in 1830', Social Science Association, *Report on Trades' Societies and Strikes* (1860).

25. For the spinners' account of the 1830-1 dispute see P.P. 1837-8 (488) VIII, p. 270; R. G. Kirby and A. E. Musson, (1975) pp. 142-3; N. J. Smelser, (1959) pp. 231-6.

26. J. T. Ward, *The Factory Movement*, (1962); R. G. Kirby and A. E. Musson, (1975) especially pp. 355-403; J. T. Ward 'The Factory Movement in Lancashire, 1830-55' *Transactions of Lancashire and Cheshire Antiquarian Society*, vols. 75 and 76 (1966) pp. 186-210; See P.P. 1833 (450) First Report D2, p. 116 and P.P. 1833 (519) XXI, D2, pp. 57, 59, and P.P. 1837-8 (488) VIII, pp. 260-2, 265, 270-3, 281-2 for evidence of spinner support of the short-time movement; Also J. Foster, (1974) p. 108.

27. For the controversy surrounding the Oldham dispute see J. Foster, (1974) pp. 110-4; R. G. Kirby and A. E. Musson, (1975) pp. 291-4 and p. 316, fn 82; A. E. Musson 'Class Struggle and the Labour Aristocracy 1833-60' *Social History* I (1976) pp. 339-40; R. A. Sykes, 'Some Aspects of Working-Class Consciousness in Oldham, 1830-1842' *Historical Journal*, 23 (1980) 167-79; R. Sykes, 'General Unionism, Class and Politics: the Cotton District, 1829-34' *Society for the Study of Labour History*, 49 (1984) 20-1.

28. *The Quinquarticular System of Organisation: To the Operative Spinners of Manchester and Salford* (1834). John Doherty gave an account of the Quinquarticular System to the 1837 *Select Committee on the Combinations of Workmen*, see P.P. 1837-8 (488) VIII, p. 251 and pp. 303-5 for the Manchester rules based on an amended version of this system; N. Kirk, (1985) p. 198.

29. R. G. Kirby and A. E. Musson, (1975) p. 308; *Manchester and Salford Advertiser,* 15 October 1836; H. Ashworth, *An Inquiry into the Origins, Progress, and Results of the Strike of the Operative Cotton Spinners of Preston* (1838); T. Banks, *A Short Sketch of the Cotton Trade of Preston for the last 67 Years* (1894) pp. 3-4; C. R. Tabor, 'The Preston Cotton Unions: An Account of their Organisation and Activities 1830-1850' (B.A. Dissertation, Manchester, (1972), pp. 16-24; A. E. Musson, (1976) p. 341; A. Howe *The Cotton Masters*, (1984) pp. 164-5; *Manchester Guardian*, 22 October 1836 and 2 November 1836.

30. P.P. 1837-8 (488) VIII, evidence of employers, operative spinners and authorities, pp. 1-228, 283-303; *Webbs Collection*, vol. XXXIV, f. 380-430; N. J. Smelser, (1959) pp. 234-5, 326-7; H. A. Turner, (1962) p. 75; E. C. Tufnell, (1834) p. 22; R. Sykes 'Early Chartism and Trade Unionism in South East Lancashire' in J. Epstein and Dorothy Thompson (eds.), *The Chartist Experience: Studies in Working-Class Radicalism and Culture, 1830-60* (1982) pp. 156-8.

31. P.P. 1837-8 (488) VIII, evidence of J. Doherty, p. 263; J. Doherty (1829) p. 34.

CHAPTER THREE (Spinners and Minders)

1. See S. and B. Webb, (1920) ch. 4; A. E. Musson, *British Trade Unions 1800-1875*, (1972); for a recent account of industrial relations in the north-west of England see N. Kirk (1984); H. Ashworth, (1838) pp. 9-10; P.P. 1837-8 (488) VIII.

2. *Manchester Times*, 24 January 1829; The wage lists collected by G. H. Wood (1910) indicate the geographical distribution of self-actors in the 1830s; P.P. 1833 (519) XXI, 2nd Report, D2. p. 137, evidence of Peter Ewart; but see S. Andrew *50 Years' Cotton Trade*, (1887) p. 2; *Webbs Collection*, Vol. XXXV; *Bolton Society, Sketch of History* (1892) f.3 although Fielding (vol. XXXV, p. 146) informed the Webbs that there were no self-actors in Bolton prior to 1858; it is possible that they have confused the date of foundation (1837) with the title of a later minute book (see fn. 5); P.P. 1833 (519), XXI, 2nd Report, D2. p. 57, evidence of J. Kenworthy.

3. P.P. 1837-8 (488) VIII, p. 250, evidence of John Doherty; R. Sykes (1892), pp. 166, 168, 156-160; R. G. Kirby and A. E. Musson (1974) pp. 309-12; R. Sykes (1982) pp. 162-3 and 'Physical Force Chartism: the Cotton Districts and the Chartist Crisis of 1839' *International Review of Social History*, Vol. XXX (1985) pp. 207-36; G. S. Jones (1975) p. 60; for the Manchester and Bolton spinners' demands see M. Jenkins *The General Strike of 1842* (1980) p. 146 and R. Sykes (1982), pp. 170-1; for an individual ex-spinner's connections with Chartism see T. D. W. and Naomi Reid 'Abraham Docker' pp. 119-22, in Joyce M. Bellamy and John Saville (eds.), *Dictionary of Labour Biography*, Vol. 2, (1974); R. G. Kirby and A. E. Musson (1974) p. 398.

4. For an account of the 1842 General Strike see M. Jenkins (1980); A. G. Rose 'The Plug Plot Riots of 1842 in Lancashire and Cheshire' *Trans. Lancs. Ches. Antiqn. Soc.*, LXVII (1957); J. Foster (1974), pp. 116-17; T. D. and Naomi Reid 'The 1842 "Plug Plot" in Stockport' *International Review of Social History*, XXIV (1979) pp. 71, 77-8.

5. Webbs Collection, Vol. XXXIV, f. 146; S. and B. Webb, (1920), p. 181; *Webbs Collection*, Vol. XXXVI, f. 4 'History of the Oldham Cotton Spinners'; *Webbs Collection*, Vol. XXXV, Transcript (partial) of the Bolton Spinners' Minute Books (henceforth *Bolton Minutes*); *Manchester Guardian*, 13 Nov. 1844; *Minute Sheets of the Associated Operative Cotton Spinners, Twiners and Self-Acting Minders of the United Kingdom (henceforth Association)*, 19 January 1845; For Arrowsmith see R. G. Kirby and A. E. Musson (1974) P.P. 1837-8 (488) VIII, pp. 278-82; the Association's first chairman seems to have been Samuel Haworth of Bolton, an active short-time campaigner (see the entries under Howard, Samuel, in the index to J. T. Ward (1962)); its secretary, also from Bolton, was Thomas Brindle.

6. *Manchester Guardian*, 5, 9, 16, 19, 23, 26, 30 October, 9, 13, 16, 20 November 1844.

7. Associated Operative Cotton Spinners, Twiners and Self-Acting Minders of the United Kingdom, minute sheet, 15 January 1845. Though a delegate from Glasgow attended meetings of the Association in July 1845 and May 1846, its activities were to be limited to the cotton districts of the northern counties. Twiners (also known as doublers) operated mule-type machines to 'double' already spun mule yarns for a speciality market. The Association's title changed in December 1845 to include Silk Spinners and Rovers; nothing further is known of the former beyond this reference but the latter, societies known as stretchers, who

prepared rovings for the spinner as a mule-type frame and were themselves being replaced by women working on an Arkwright-type roving machine, had long been associated with the mulespinner societies. *Association Minutes* 6 July 1845, record 'That no district or part of a district be allowed to advance, without the consent of the Central Committee or Delegate Meeting. Whether Brindle was also Bolton's secretary and receiving payment in that post, or a working spinner is not known. *Association Minutes*, 3 August 1845, 25 January 1846.

8.   *Association Minutes*, 16 March 1845; on 14 December delegates embarked on plans to organise the Hyde and surrounding districts. *Webbs Collection*, Vol. XXXIV, f. 180, comments by J. Mawdsley; See the *Bolton Minutes*, for details of the disenchantment with the Association.

9.   *Association Minutes*, 20 July 1845; the minutes of 31 August 1845 record 19 districts as being 'wholly or partially advanced'; S. J. Chapman, (1904), p. 264, on 20 July 1845 delegates were urged 'to forward to the Central Secretary, a list of prices paid for all numbers spun in their districts'. For references to lists and prices see the Association minutes. The minutes also detail the deputations to employers; usually this was left to the central committee or delegates but in May 1846, perhaps recognizing the status of the Oldham Province, that organisation's committee was given the conduct of a dispute at Mossley. *Association Minutes*, 31 August 1845; For the disputes of 1845-6 see the *Association Minutes*. *Webbs Collection*, Vol. XXXIV, f. 286, citing letter of D. Holt to *Bolton Daily Chronicle*, 10 October 1877.

10. J. T. Ward, (1962) for a detailed account of the 1840s factory movement; J. Doherty *A Letter to the Factory Operatives of Lancashire on the Necessity of Petitioning Parliament in Favour of the Ten Hours' Bill* (1845); *Association Minutes*, particularly 2 March 1845; *Report and Balance Sheet for October 1844 to October 1845 of the Central Short Time Committee;* The April 1844 meeting of the short-time delegates was attended by a representative from the 'Central Cotton Spinners' Committee', see J. T. Ward, (1962), pp. 292, 295.

11. J. T. Ward (1962) especially p. 322; P. Grant, *The History of Factory Legislation*, (1866) p. 22.

12. *Bolton Minutes*, 1844; *Association Minutes*, 16 March 1845 for delegate support of the Dukenfield Colliers. *Association Minutes*, 30 March, 6 July, 20 July, 3 August; *Webbs Collection*, Vol. XXXVI, f. 237-40, for the annual report, year ending 24 December 1845; *Association Minutes*, 30 November, 14 December 1845, 22 February 1846; On emigration see the *Bolton Minutes* for 1847-8.

13. *Bolton Minutes*, 9 October 1846; *Manchester Guardian*, 18 December 1847; see S. Andrew (1887) p. 4, for references to 'Spinners' gardens' and 'Fergus O'Connor's freeholds'; *Bolton Minutes*, 16 August 1847, 22 February 1848. *Manchester Guardian*, 1 September 1847. See the *Bolton Minutes* for the spinners' support of short-time and the problem of unemployed spinners; *Webbs' Collection*, XXXVI, 66.

14. *Manchester Guardian*, 22, 23 September, 2, 6, 13, 20, 27 October, 3, 24 November; H. J. Dutton and J. E. King, *Ten Per Cent and No Surrender: The Preston Strike 1853-4*, (1981) pp. 23-4; *Manchester Guardian*, 22, 29 December 1847; H. Ashworth (1854) pp. 8-9; *Bolton Minutes*, 14, 16, 20, 23 December 1847.

15. *Manchester Guardian*, 6, 13, 20 October 1847 for lists of societies sending delegates to the Association meetings; *Webbs Collection*, Vol. XXXIV, f. 150. See *Bolton Minutes*, particularly 27 July, 3 August, 10 November, 1848, 9, 12 February 1849, 7 August 1850.

16. Bolton Minutes, 9 February 1849; H. I. Dutton and J. E. King (1981) p. 26; *Ashton Chronicle,*
    12 April 1849; *Manchester Guardian,* 21 March 1849, 21 April 1849; J. T. Ward (1962) p. 366,
    Ashton Chronicle, 15, 22, 29 September, *Manchester Guardian,* 5, 12, 15 September 1849. *Ashton
    Chronicle,* 20 October 1849; J. T. Ward (1962) p. 367, and especially ch. 15 details the decline
    of the Lancashire Central Short-Time Committees, and see pp. 364 and 389; *Ashton Chronicle,*
    22 September 1849, *Bolton Minutes,* 7 August 1850.

17. J. T. Ward (1962) p. 389. For approximate dates of divisions between mule spinners and self-
    actor minders in the local societies see the *Association Minutes. An appeal on behalf of William Fair*
    (c. 1876) stated that the Manchester split occurred in 1843 following 'a severe struggle';
    however Arrowsmith was still secretary to the joint body in the Autumn of 1844. *Webbs
    Collection,* Vol. XXXIV f. 180. Important societies in coarse and low medium areas,
    particularly Preston, Blackburn, Oldham, Mossley and Stockport remained open to both
    spinners and minders. And see *Webbs Collection,* Vol. XXXV for returns of the district
    societies. For an indication of benefits in one of the higher wage districts, see the *Bolton
    Minutes.* On the demises of Glasgow minders and spinners, see *Webbs Collection,* Vol. XXXIV
    f. 413.

18. S. and B. Webb, (1920) pp. 220-3; *Webbs Collection,* Vol. XXXV, extracts from the minutes of
    the Ashton self-actor minders' minute books (henceforth *Ashton Minutes),* 1 July 1858; *Bolton
    Minutes,* 6 February 1853; In 1851 the Bolton society established a co-operative society for its
    members. H. A. Turner (1962) p. 169; and Vol. XXXIV, f. 286, letter of D. Holt.

19. J. T. Ward, (1962) p. 392; *Appeal on Behalf of William Fair* (c. 1876); *Webbs Collection,* Vol.
    XXXV replies of the district societies; J. T. Ward (1962), p. 389.

20. Alderman Baynes, *The Cotton Trade: Two Lectures* (1857) pp. 50-1; Eccles Sharrocks, *Letter to the
    Workpeople of North and North-East Lancashire: History of the Formation of the Blackburn Association
    in 1852, with the Rise and Fall in the Rates of Wages for Twenty-Eight Years,* (1880) p. 3; *Hyde and
    District Operative Cotton Spinners' Association, Historical Sketch: 50 years' Record, Biography, etc. etc.,*
    (Reprinted for the *North Cheshire Herald,* 20, 27 January 1906), pp. 4-5; *Bolton Minutes,* 29
    February, 4 March, 13 April 1852.

21. H. I. Dutton and J. E. King (1981) p. 29; *Manchester Guardian,* 29 January, 6 February 1853;
    Bolton Minutes 31 January 1853. Dutton and King provide a detailed study of the Preston
    strike; J. Lowe, 'Account of the Strike and Lock-Out in the Cotton Trade at Preston in 1853'
    in *National Association for the Promotion of Social Science* (1860) p. 214.

22. Hyde and District Operative Cotton Spinners' Association (1906) pp. 5, 7; *Rules and Regulations
    [of the] Equitable and Friendly Association of Hand-Mule Spinners, Self-Actor Minders, Twiners, and
    Rovers, of Lancashire, Cheshire, Yorkshire* (1860) henceforth *Rules,* 1860) p. 3; *Bolton Minutes,*
    9 June, 31 October 1853 and 19 January 1854; T. Banks (1894) pp. 6-8; *Report and Minutes of
    the Association of Hand Mule Spinners, Self-Acting Minders, Twiners and Rovers of Lancashire,
    Cheshire, Yorkshire and Derbyshire,* 15 January 1854; see H. I. Dutton and J. E. King (1981)
    pp. 23 and 51-3 for connections with the short-time movement and pp. 39, 186-7 and 190 for
    the influence of the Association.

23. H. I. Dutton and J. E. King (1981) p. 195; N. Kirk (1984) p. 251; J. Lowe (1860) pp. 214, 245.
    H. I. Dutton and J. E. King (1981) p. 185 who indicate that the suggestion to the Preston
    spinners to surrender the 10 per cent may have been made by the Blackburn spinners alone.

Association Report, 15 January 1854; *Manchester Guardian*, 9 November 1853; H. I. Dutton and J. E. King (1981) p. 60.

24. See A. Howe (1984) especially ch. V for an examination of employers and their organisations; *H. Ashworth, The Preston Strike: An Enquiry into its Causes and Consequences* (1854) p. 16.

25. *Rules*, 1860; for developments amongst the weavers see H. A. Turner (1962) pp. 126-35; *Bolton Minutes* 30 April 1857. The evidence on Association membership in the mid-1850s is not reliable; Oldham, Manchester Fine and Ashton were certainly out but the societies mentioned in the text either claimed continuity or provided officials for the Association — and Blackburn was almost certainly another important member (see *Webbs Collection*, Vol. XXXV, returns of the district societies.

26. W. Lazonick (1979), p. 237; *Webbs Collection*, Vol. XXXVI, f. 4; H. A. Turner (1962) p. 128; S. J. Chapman (1904) pp. 213-5; *Ashton Chronicle*, 28 April, 1849; N. Kirk (1984) pp. 253-4 — this seems to have been the last major dispute fought by the Manchester coarse spinners; *Bolton Minutes* 22 February 1859; *Bolton Chronicle*, 8 August 1857 (I am grateful to Peter Taylor for this reference).

27. *Rules*, (1860)

28. *Manchester Guardian*, 6 June 1856.

29. D. A. Farnie (1979) p. 138; *Ashton Minutes*, 8 September 1859; N. Kirk (1984) p. 273; T. Banks (1894) p. 8 and British Association for the Advancement of Science, *On the Regulation of Wages by Means of Lists in the Cotton Industry* (1887) p. 11 (and see also pp. 104-7 for the 1844 Bolton spinning list); *Bolton Minutes*, 10 August, 18 September 1859, 15 March 1860. For the Clitheroe dispute see N. Kirk (1984) pp. 254-5.

30. Lancashire Central Short-Time Committee Cash Book, 14 February 1858 — 4 June 1863; the Webbs state (*Webbs Collection*, Vol. XXXV. f. 160) that the Ashton self-actor minders adapted the Blackburn list until receiving their own list in 1860 and the references to the list of the associated minders of Lancashire may be a further indicator of the strong linkage between that body and the Blackburn district. Ashton at this time was outside the Association. Oldham was separately trying to organise the Huddersfield district, *Manchester Guardian*, 24 November, 2 October 1860; *Webbs Collection*, XXXV, f. 16. and see T. Hughes, 'Account of the Lock-Out of Engineers in 1851-2' in *National Association for the Promotion of Social Science* (1860) pp. 203-5.

31. N. Kirk (1984) pp. 256-7 and p. 284; *Bolton Minutes*, 20, 25 March, 20, 28 April, 8 May, 6, 11 June, 2, 16 July; and see the *Manchester Guardian* for this period, particularly 27 April 1861.

32. D. A. Farnie (1979), ch. 4; W. T. M. Torrens, *Lancashire's Lesson or the Need of a Settled Policy in Times of Exceptional Distress* (1864) pp. 102-3; N. Kirk (1984) pp. 258-65; *Bolton Minutes*, 27 October, 1 December 1864; *Webbs Collection*, Vol. XXXV, f. 291.

33. J. Watts, *The Facts of the Cotton Famine* (1866) p. 215.

34. W. T. M. Torrens, (1964) p. 103; *Webbs Collection*, Vol. XXXV, f. 16; J. Watts, (1866) pp. 215-6.

CHAPTER FOUR (The Founding of the Amalgamation)

1. D. A. Farnie, *The English Cotton Industry and the World Market 1815-1896*, (1979) pp. 199, 215, 303, 317; B. R. Mitchell and P. Deane, *Abstract of British Historical Statistics*, (1971) pp. 185, 186, 188; R. Smith, *A History of the Lancashire Cotton Industry between the years 1873-96*, PhD, Univ. of Birmingham, 1954, pp. 16, 56, 59.

2. I. Cohen, 'Workers Control in the Cotton Industry' *Labor History*, 26 (1985); B. Drake, *Women in Trade Unions* (Reprinted 1984) p. 29; R. Marsden, *Cotton Spinning*, (1899) pp. 291-318.

3. *Oldham Chronicle*, 20 September 1919; Oldham Spinners, *Quarterly Report*, March 1868; *Report of the Conference of Trades Delegates of the United Kingdom*, 1866, Sheffield, Appendix 1.

4. *Blackburn Standard*, 22 March, 28 June 1865; Farnie, (1979) p. 165; S. and B. Webb, Trade Union Collection Vols XXXV-XXXVI; A. Williamson, *Historical Sketch of the Hyde and District Operative Cotton Spinners Association*, (1928) pp. 3-4.

5. *Blackburn Standard*, 5 December 1866; *Cotton Factory Times* 30 January 1885, 8 December 1893; CS and MA Minutes, 1866; Oldham Master Cotton Spinners Minutes 1866; Rochdale Spinners Minutes 25 October 1867; *Stockport Advertiser*, 22 February — 29 March 1867.

6. Spinners' Association, *Rule Book* 1868.

7. T. Banks, *A Short Sketch of the Cotton Trade of Preston for the last Sixty-Seven years*, (1888) p. 10; *Blackburn Standard*, 24 March 1869; Farnie, (1979) pp. 165-7; *Final Report (11th) of the Royal Commission on the Organisation and Rules of Trades Unions and Other Associations*, Appendix Vol. 2 1868; Preston Spinners Circular, March, 1869; Rochdale Spinners Minutes 30 July 1868, 22 April 1869.

8. Spinners Association, *Circular*, November 1869.

9. Rochdale Spinners Minutes 5 Dec. 1870; A.A.O.C.S., *Rules*, 1870; G. H. Wood *The History of Wages in the Cotton Trade during the past hundred years* (1910) p. 55.

10. Oldham Spinners, *Quarterly Report* March 1868, *Annual Report* 1871; Oldham Masters Cotton Spinners' Association, Minutes 1869.

11. Saturday Half-Holiday Movement and Factory Act Reform Association Circulars and Minutes 1870-74; Farnie (1979) p. 164, 172; Oldham Spinners, *Monthly Report*, March 1873.

12. Hyde Spinners, *Circular*, February 1872; Oldham Spinners, *Circulars* July 1873; *Oldham Chronicle*, 12 July 1873; *Oldham Express*, 7 July 1873; *Oldham Examiner*, 9 August 1873; A.A.O.C.S., Executive Minutes July 1870 and Rules 1872; Webbs Trade Union Collection, Vol. XXXIV.

13. Preston Spinners, *Circular*, March 1870; *Quarterly Review* 146 (1878) pp. 486-7.

14. F.A.R.A. Account Book 1858-1886 and Minutes 12 May 1872; S. and B. Webb *The History of Trade Unionism* (1920 Edition) p. 309.

15. F.A.R.A. Miscellaneous Manuscripts 1872-74; S. J. Chapman, *The Lancashire Cotton Industry — A Study in Economic Development*, (1904), p. 104.

16. Saturday Half-Holiday Movement Misc. Mss. 1871; Oldham Spinners, *Monthly Reports* September — December 1871 and *Annual Report* 1871-2; Oldham Master Cotton Spinners' Association Minutes and Letter Book 6 December 1870 — 20 March 1871.

17. Saturday Half-Holiday Movement Misc. Mss. 1871; Oldham Spinners, *Annual Report* 1871; Oldham Master Cotton Spinners' Association Minute Book 4-29 April 1871; A.A.O.C.S., Executive Minutes April — May 1871.

18. Saturday Half-Holiday Movement Misc. Mss. 1871; *Oldham Chronicle*, 13 January, 3 February 1872.

19. Bolton Hand Spinners, *Memorial*, 18 May 1871; *Cotton Factory Times*, 8 December 1893; F.A.R.A. Circular 20 September 1872; Oldham Master Cotton Spinners' Association, Minute Book, 10 May, 11 September 1871.

20. F.A.R.A. Circular, 7, 8, 20 January 1872; Minutes 18, 20 February 1872, 4 September 1873; P. Grant, *The History of Factory Legislation*, (1866) p. 160. Oldham Spinners, *Monthly Report*, June 1872; Oldham Master Cotton Spinners' Association Minutes 26 January 1872; T.U.C. Circular May 1873.

21. Extract from the Report cited in F.A.R.A. Circular 5 June 1872, p. 3.

22. *Manchester Guardian*, 11 August 1874. Oldham Spinners, *Annual Report* 1874; S. and B. Webb, (1920) p. 312.

23. Ashton Spinners Minutes, 1 October 1874; Bolton Hand Spinners Minutes 25, 27 October 1874; Oldham Spinners, *Annual Report* 1874-75; Oldham Master Cotton Spinners' Association Letter Book 12 September, 6 October, 9 December 1874.

24. Leigh Spinners Minutes 26 December 1877; Oldham Master Cotton Spinners' Association Letter Book, 18 November 1873, 12 January 1874, 18 November 1875.
Bolton Hand Spinners Minutes 1873-74:
Ages on Becoming members of the Society:

1873	Average 23.7	Mode 20	Median 22
1874	Average 24.1	Mode 21	Median 22

25. Bolton Province Minutes 26 July 1881; *Cotton Factory Times*, 25 December 1885; Rochdale Spinners Minutes, 21 April 1868. Bolton Hand Spinners, Rules 1875; Bolton Province, *Annual Report* 1886; Oldham Spinners, *Annual Report* 1873-74 and *Monthly Report*, October 1872; Rochdale Spinners Minutes 7 May 1872.

26. *Oldham Express*, 3 August 1875; Oldham Masters Letter Book, 14 February 1873, 19 February 1874, Minutes, 11 January 1875; Oldham Spinners, *Annual Report* 1873-75, *Monthly Report* October 1872; Rochdale Spinners Minutes, 27 February 1872.

27. Bolton Hand Spinners Minutes 26 June 1874; *Oldham Chronicle*, 27 February 1875; *Oldham Express* 24 February 1875; Oldham Masters Letter Book, 23 June 1875, Minutes 1870-75.

28. *Blackburn Standard,* 14 August 1875; *Manchester Courier,* 26, 28 July 1875; Oldham Masters Letter Book, 23 June, 9, 11 August 1875; Oldham Spinners *Annual Reports* 1875-8.

CHAPTER FIVE (A Modern Spinners' Union)

1. D. A. Farnie, (1979) pp. 171-4; A.A.O.C.S., Executive Minutes, 16 March, 1 April, 21 June 1874.

2. D. A. Farnie, (1979) p. 305; Oldham Spinners, *Annual Report* 1876 and *Monthly Report,* April, 1878; A.A.O.C.S., Minutes, 22 December 1877, 19 August 1878.

3. Ashton Spinners Minutes, 17 December 1875, 10 February 1876; Bolton Hand Spinners Minutes, 17 November, 30 November 1875; North-East Lancashire Power-Loom Weavers' Association, *Annual Report* 1877-8; Oldham Spinners, *Monthly Reports* March — June 1884; A.A.O.C.S., Minutes 8 June 1875, 1 February 1876, 27 March 1877 and *Annual Reports* 1880, 1885.

4. Oldham Spinners, *Annual Reports* 1876-8; A.A.O.C.S., *Annual Reports* 1880-5; *Textile Manufacturer,* January 1880.

5. Bolton Hand Spinners Minutes 24, 28 July, 8, 22, 27, 31 August, 8, 18, 23 October 1877; Oldham Spinners, *Annual Report* 1878 and Monthly Report February 1879; *Textile Manufacturer,* September 1877.

6. Ashton Spinners Minutes, 11 November 1877; Bolton Hand Spinners Minutes 8 November 1877; Oldham Masters Letter Book, 8, 20, 22 September, 17 October 1877; Oldham Spinners, *Annual Reports* 1878-80.

7. Bolton Hand Spinners Minutes, 3, 18 September, 20 December 1877; Oldham Spinners *Annual Reports* 1878 and *Monthly Report* March 1878; A.A.O.C.S., Minutes, 9 September, 14 October, 27 November, 3 December 1877.

8. Bolton Hand Spinners, Minute Book, 5, 9 January, 16 April 1878; A.A.O.C.S. Minute Book, 31 March, 15 April, 30 November 1878 and Rules 1882; J. White, *The Limits of Trade Union Militancy — the Lancashire Textile Workers 1910-1914,* (1978) pp. 98-102.

9. T. Ashton, *Wages and other Movements etc. in the Oldham Province 1868-1905,* (1906); A. J. Bullen, *The Lancashire Weavers Union — A Commemorative History,* (1984) pp. 9-12; C.S.M.A. Minute Book, December 1877 — March 1878; A.A.O.C.S., Circular 2 February 1879.

10. A.A.O.C.S., *Circular* February, November 1879 and *Annual Reports* 1879, 1880.

11. A.A.O.C.S., *Circular* November 1882.

12. Oldham Spinners, *Annual Reports* 1879, 1880; A.A.O.C.S. *Annual Reports* 1879, 1880; Executive Committee Minutes March — April 1878.

13. Ashton Spinners Minutes, 4, 30 January 1880; Bolton Hand Spinners Minutes, 22 January, 16 July 1865, 16, 17 May 1875, 21 January, 31 October, 1876, 6 August 1878, 12 November, 27 December 1879, 6, 14 January 1880; Bolton Minders Circulars 10, 14, January, 7, 19 February 1880; Oldham Masters Minutes 9, 13, 23 January 1880 and Letter Book 23 January 1880; A.A.O.C.S., *Quarterly Report* December 1879 and *Council Report* April 1880.

14. Bolton Province Minutes, 7 March 1882, 25 January, 14 February, 6 October 1883; *Chorley Standard*, 8 July 1882; Leigh Spinners Minutes 26 January, 21 February 1882, 19 January 1883, 10 March 1884. *Oldham Express*, 22 April 1883; Oldham Masters Letter Book, 5 June 1885 and Minutes 10-24 January 1882; *Manchester Guardian*, 7 July 1882; A.A.O.C.S., Balance Sheet December 1885 and Minutes 25 June 1882.

15. Bolton Hand Spinners Minutes 29 January, 19 February 1878; A.A.O.C.S., Minutes 13 February 1878, 9 January 1892. Although not directly funded by the unions, the weekly published *Cotton Factory Times* (1885-1937), reflected the views and aspirations of the cotton workers' associations and their members, spinners' leaders writing regular columns and articles. *Cotton Factory Times*, 19 November, 3, 31 December 1886, 7, 14, 21, 28 January, 18, 25 February, 11, 18, 25 March, 1, 8, 15, 22, 29 April 1887.

16. Bolton Province, *Annual Report* 1885.

17. Bolton Province Minutes 29 January, 19 February 1878, 17 August, 5 October, 8 December, 14 December 1886, 1, 15 February, 1 March, 31 May 1887; B. Drake, (1984) p. 29.

18. Oldham Spinners, *Monthly Reports* March — August 1880, September, December 1881, March — July 1882, May — November 1883, February — October 1884, January 1885, May, August 1886.

19. Ashton Spinners Minutes, 2 June 1881; *Cotton Factory Times*, 22 December 1885; Leigh Spinners Minutes, 19 February 1879; Oldham Spinners, *Monthly Reports, February — March 1882; A.A.O.C.S., Circular* August 1880, February 1881.

20. *Cotton Factory Times*, 25 December 1885; United Moveable Committee Misl. Manuscripts 8, 13 May, 17 June, 11 July 1882, 24 February, 15 May, 19 June, 18 December 1883, 10 April, 3 July 1884; See also H. A. Turner, *Trade Union Growth Structure and Policy — A Comparative Study of the Cotton Unions* (1962) p. 137, for the idea that the U.M.C. was a possible rival to the Amalgamation.

21. A.A.O.C.S., *Annual Reports* 1884, 1885, 1886; *Council Reports* March, August, November 1880, February, May, November 1881, January, April, July, October, November 1882, March, June, October 1883, January 1884, April, October 1885; Minutes 1 March, 18, 29 September 1882; *Quarterly Reports* December 1879, June, December 1880, January 1881, March 1882.

22. *Cotton Factory Times*, 9 October, 29 November 1885; Cotton Spinners' and Manufacturers' Association Minutes, 28 March 1881, 18 February 1882; Oldham Spinners, *Monthly Report* July 1882; A.A.O.C.S., *Annual Report* 1885; *Council Report* January 1884. Minutes, 18, 29 September 1881; United Moveable Committee Minutes 19 June 1883.

23. Oldham Masters Minutes, 26 May 1881; A.A.O.C.S., *Annual Report* 1881-6; *Council Report*, November 1880; *Quarterly Report*, December 1882; Rules 1882.

24. Bolton Province Minutes 8 November 1882; Leigh Spinners Minutes 14 August 1883; A.A.O.C.S., *Quarterly Report* 17 December 1882, 18 March 1883.

25. Oldham Masters Minutes, 24 May 1881, 18 January, 10 February, 15 August 1884, 22 April 1885; Oldham Spinners, *Monthly Reports*, March, September 1887; A.A.O.C.S., *Annual Report* 1885; *Council Reports*, May 1880, February, November 1881, July 1882, August 1884, October 1885.

26. Oldham Masters Minutes, 7, 21 October, 5 November 1884, 24 March, 10, 17 April, 12 June 1885, and Letter Book 25 March, 1 April 1885; Oldham Spinners Monthly Report February 1885; A.A.O.C.S., *Council Report* January, April 1885.

27. Bolton Province Minutes 7, 22 April 1885; *Cotton Factory Times*, 10, 24 April, 1 May, 1 September 1885; Oldham Spinners, *Monthly Reports*, February, July, September, November 1885; A.A.O.C.S., *Annual Report* 1885; *Circular* 14 July 1885; *Council Report*, January, April, July 1885.

28. Oldham Masters Letter Book, 27 August 1885; Minutes 9 September 1885.

29. Bolton Province Minutes 9 September 1885; *Cotton Factory Times*, 25 September, 16 October 1885; *Manchester Examiner*, 17 September 1885; Oldham Spinners Monthly Report July, September, November 1885; Oldham Masters Minutes, 24 July, 7, 14, 21 August, 1, 9, 11, 15, 22, 25, 30 September, 6, 13, 16, 17 October and Letter Book 4 September 1885; A.A.O.C.S., *Annual Report* 1885; *Circular* 14 July, 5 October 1885; Minutes 29 July 1885.

30. Manchester Examiner, 17 September 1885; Oldham Masters Annual Report 1886, Letter Book 19 September 1885; Minutes, 7 August, 19 September 1885; Oldham Spinners, *Monthly Reports*, November 1885; A.A.O.C.S., *Annual Report* 1885; Council Reports July, October 1885.

31. A.A.O.C.S., *Examination Result Circular* 1878, *Rules* 1882.

32. A.A.O.C.S., *Annual Reports* 1880-5.

33. Oldham Masters Minutes, 1 February 1881; Oldham Spinners Monthly Reports 1881; *Cotton Factory Times*, 9 October 1885; *Textile Manufacturer*, 15 April 1884.

CHAPTER SIX (The Making of Brooklands)

1. A. J. Bullen, (1984) pp. 15-17; A. J. Bullen and A. Fowler, *The Cardroom Workers Union* (1986); Cardroom Amalgamation, *Annual Report* 1887, 1893; General Union of Associations of Overlookers, *Jubilee History* (1935); Northern Counties Factory Acts Reform Association and the United Textile Factory Workers' Conference Reports 1886-93.

2. H. A. Clegg, A. Fox and A. F. Thompson, *A History of British Trade Unionism since 1889* (1964) p. 27, 468.

3. Bolton Province Minutes, 1 November 1881; I. Cohen (1985) p. 75; A.A.O.C.S., *Council Report* January 1890.

4. Bolton Province Diary 1885-93 contained in Annual Reports; *Royal Commission on Labour* Group C. Digest of Evidence, Vol., Textiles, p. 8; A.A.O.C.S., *Annual Report* 1885.

5. Bolton Province *Annual Report* 1890; A.A.O.C.S., *Annual Report* 1889.

6. *Cotton Factory Times*, 20 March 1885; Oldham Masters Letter Book, 26 February 1886, 22 June 1891.

7. Bolton Masters Minutes 10 April — 12 June 1888; C.S.M.A. Minutes 19 June 1888; Old-
    ham Masters, *Annual Reports* 1885-8; Minute 25 February 1886 and Letter Book 7 August —
    6 September 1886.

8. Bolton Masters Minutes, 1 September 1891, 29 January 1892; Cotton Spinners' Association
    Report of the Committee 1886-7, p. 11, 34; Federation of Master Cotton Spinners' Associations,
    Minutes 31 December 1891 — 16 February 1892; Oldham Masters, *Annual Reports* 1886-92;
    United Cotton Spinners' Association, *Report of the Committee* 1887-8, p. 5, 17-18; Minutes, 7
    August — 1 December 1891.

9. G. H. Wood (1910) p. 131.

10. Rochdale Spinners' Minutes, 28 October 1890; 3 February 1892; A.A.O.C.S., *Annual Report*
    1887-91.

11. Bolton Masters Minutes, 3 October 1884, 8 July 1886; A.A.O.C.S., *Annual Report* 1888.

12. Bolton Masters Minutes, 23 May 1890; A.A.O.C.S., *Council Report* July 1890.

13. *Cotton Factory Times,* 16 January 1885; A.A.O.C.S., *Annual Reports* 1885, 1890-1.

14. Cardroom Amalgamation, *Quarterly Reports* 27 December 1890, 28 March 1891; A.A.O.C.S.,
    Council Report November 1889.

15. A.A.O.C.S., *Annual Report* 1892; *Council Report* April 1891; Oldham Cardroom Minutes, 21
    May 1893.

16. A.A.O.C.S., *Annual Reports* 1888, 1891; *Council Report* September 1891.

17. Bolton Province, *Annual Report* 1890-1; A.A.O.C.S., *Annual Report* 1891.

18. Bolton Province, *Annual Report* 1892; Oldham Masters Letter Book 9 August 1890 and
    Minutes 6 June 1889 — 31 October 1890.

19. *Cotton Factory Times,* 4 March 1892; F.M.C.S.A. 31 December 1891 — 16 February 1892;
    A.A.O.C.S., *Annual Report* 1892.

20. Bolton Province, *Annual Report* 1892; Oldham Masters Letter Book, 13, 28 April 1892;
    A.A.O.C.S., Minutes, 5 April — 14 May 1892.

21. Atherton Spinners Minutes, 23 May 1892; *Cotton Factory Times,* 29 April, 14 May 1892;
    A.A.O.C.S., *Council Report* April 1892; Minutes 14 May 1892; *Textile Manufacturer,* 15 May 1892.

22. F.M.C.S.A. Minutes, 13 September 1892; A.A.O.C.S., *Annual Report* 1891; *Council Report*
    July 1892.

23. A.A.O.C.S., *Circular* 15 October 1892; *Council Report,* July, October 1892; *Quarterly Report,*
    January 1893; *Textile Mercury,* 24 September 1892.

24. A.A.O.C.S., *Annual Report* 1892; *Council Report* October 1892; *Textile Mercury.* 12 November 1892.

25. A.A.O.C.S., Minutes, 11 February 1893; A. Bullen and A. Fowler (1986) pp. 58-62; *Textile Mercury*, 12 November 1892.

26. Oldham Masters Letter Book 29 December 1892; A.A.O.C.S., Minutes 5 December 1892 — 11 January 1893.

27. Bolton Province Diary 26 January 1893; A.A.O.C.S., Minutes 11 February and *Quarterly Report*, January 1893.

28. Oldham Masters Letter Book 1 February 1893; A.A.O.C.S., *Annual Report, 1893*.

29. *R. F. Dyson, The Development of Collective Bargaining in the Cotton Spinning Industry 1893-1914*, PhD, University of Leeds, (1971) pp. 305-7; Oldham Masters Letter Book, 18 February 1893; A.A.O.C.S., Minutes 27 January, 18 February 1893.

30. Bolton Province Diary, 23 February 1893.

31. Bolton Province Diary, 23 February 1893.

32. A.A.O.C.S., Letter Book, 2 March 1893.

33. Bolton Province Diary, 7, 13 March 1893.

34. R. F. Dyson, (1971) p. 306; A.A.O.C.S., Letter Book 15 March 1893, and Minutes 16 March 1893.

35. *Christian World*, 6 April 1893, reprinted in *Textile Mercury*, 18 April 1893, p. 258; A.A.O.C.S., *Annual Report* 1894.

36. Bolton Province, *Annual Report* 1893; *Manchester Guardian*, 25 March 1893; *Textile Mercury*, 25 March 1893; *Textile Manufacturer*, 15 April 1893; *Textile Recorder*, 15 April 1893.

37. Oldham Masters Minutes, 22 November 1889, 31 October 1890, 3 November 1891; *Textile Mercury*, 12 November 1892.

38. Oldham Masters, *Annual Report*, 1893-4.

39. C.S.M.A. Minutes 4 February 1890; Bolton and District Net List of Prices, 1 June 1887, p. 10, 'In the event of a dispute arising . . . the matter shall be referred to the two secretaries, who shall take action within seven days . . . should, however, they fail to arrive at a settlement the same shall be referred to the joint committees for their decision.'

40. Bolton Province, *Annual Report* 1893; A.A.O.C.S., *Annual Report* 1893 and Misl. Mss. (Manchester Central Ref. M 133/2).

41. Bolton Province, *Annual Report* 1893; Oldham Masters, *Annual Report* 1894; A.A.O.C.S., *Annual Report* 1894 and Rules 1894.

CHAPTER SEVEN (The Spinners and the Rise of Labour)

1. This account is derived from J. Jewkes and E. M. Gray, *Wages and Labour in the Lancashire Cotton Spinning Industry*, (1935) especially pp. 155-6.

2. A.A.O.C.S., *Annual Report* 1894, pp. 9-10.

3. A.A.O.C.S., *Quarterly Report* ending 1 January 1895, pp. 3-4.

4. U.T.F.W.A., *Annual Report* June 1894, p. 16.

5. For a picture of the development of this attempt at a new political strategy see Resolutions of the Special Representative Meetings of the U.T.F.W.A. 19 January 1895, 28 February 1895; A.A.O.C.S., *Quarterly Report* 23 March 1895; U.T.F.W.A., *Annual Report* (1895) pp. 8-9.

6. U.T.F.W.A., *Annual Report*, (1896) pp. 5-6.

7. See D. Howell, *British Workers and the I.L.P. 1888-1906* (1983) pp. 52-68.

8. H. A. Turner, *Trade Union Growth, Structure and Policy* (1962) p. 149.

9. *Labour Leader*, 29 December 1894, quoted by H. Pelling, *Origins of the Labour Party*, (1965) p. 193.

10. P. Harnetty, 'The Indian Cotton Duties Controversy 1894 and 1896' *English Historical Review* 77 (1962) pp. 690-1.

11. *Cotton Factory Times*, 23 June 1899.

12. A.A.O.C.S., *Quarterly Report* ending 31 January 1896 pp. 4-5; A.A.O.C.S., *Annual Report* ending 31 December 1896, p. 7.

13. See A.A.O.C.S., *Quarterly Report* ending 31 August 1897, p. 2.

14. A.A.O.C.S., *Quarterly Report* ending 31 August 1898, pp. 3-4.

15. A.A.O.C.S., *Quarterly Report* ending 31 September 1899, p. 3.

16. See L. Sandberg, 'American Rings and English Mules' *Quarterly Journal of Economics*, 83 (1969), pp. 25-43; W. Lazonick, 'Industrial Relations and Technical Change' *Cambridge Journal of Economics*, 3 (1979), pp. 231-262.

17. W. Lazonick, (1979) p. 249.

18. *Cotton Factory Times*, 2 March 1894.

19. See R. E. Tyson in D. H. Aldcroft (ed.) *The Development of British Industry and Foreign Competition 1875-1914* (1968) p. 123.

20. Cited by R. Tyson (1968) p. 123; W. Lazonick (1979) p. 252.

21. This is based on an undated questionnaire attached to the A.A.O.C.S., *Annual Report* 1898.

22. J. L. White, *The Limits of Trade Union Militancy* (1978) p. 101.

23. This is based on the annual membership returns contained in the Annual Reports of the Spinners' Amalgamation for the years 1893-1905; *Cotton Factory Times*, 7 April and 19 May 1899.

24. A.A.O.C.S., *Annual Report* 1899, pp. 12-13.

25. This is based on R. F. Dyson, *The Development of Collective Bargaining in the Cotton Spinning Industry 1893-1914*, PhD, University of Leeds, (1971) pp. 400 onwards.

26. *House of Commons Debates*, 4th Series, Vol. 72, cols. 1122-3; P. F. Clarke (1971) pp. 87-8.

27. U.T.F.W.A., *Annual Report* ending 17 July 1901, p. 5.

28. *H. C. Debs.* (4th Series) Vol. 99, col. 516 and cols. 519, 520; *Report of the Conference of Cotton Employers' Parliamentary Association, the U.T.F.W.A. and M.P.s for Textile and other Districts (Held 20 February 1901)*, pp. 5-6.

29. *Manchester Evening News*, 4 February 1902.

30. See A.A.O.C.S., *Quarterly Report* ending 30 April, p. 2, and 31 July 1899, pp. 2-3.

31. T.U.C., *Annual Report*, (1899), p. 64.

32. *Cotton Factory Times*, 21 January 1900.

33. A.A.O.C.S., *Quarterly Report* 31 October 1901, pp. 2-3.

34. U.T.F.W.A., *Annual Report* 27 July 1901; for an account of the Blackburn case see H. Clegg, A. Fox and A. F. Thompson, *A History of British Trade Unions*, Vol I (1964), pp. 323-4.

35. U.T.F.W.A., *Annual Report* 26 July 1902.

36. See A.A.O.C.S., *Quarterly Report* 30 January 1903, p. 4 and 30 April 1903, p. 5.

37. See A.A.O.C.S., *Quarterly Report* 31 October 1905, p. 4

38. See Oldham Labour Representation Committee Minutes 12 January 1904 for a detailed breakdown of rank-and-file trade union affiliations.

39. *Bolton Chronicle*, January 1906 for accounts of the campaign.

40. See the A.A.O.C.S., *Quarterly Report* for 31 January, p. 3, 30 April, p. 4, 1904. For the detailed terms see the A.A.O.C.S., *Annual Report* 1904; J. L. White, (1978) pp. 76-78.

41. A.A.O.C.S., *Annual Report* 1904, p. 8.

42. See the A.A.O.C.S., *Quarterly Report* for 30 July 1905, pp. 3-5; see also the *Quarterly Report* 31 October 1905, pp. 3-8.

43. See J. Jewkes and E. M. Gray, (1935) p. 173.

44. A.A.O.C.S., *Annual Report* 1907, p. 5.

45. A.A.O.C.S., *Annual Report* 1907, p. 3.

46. These figures are derived from J. Jewkes and E. M. Gray, (1935) p. 18 onwards and H. Clegg et al, *A History of British Trade Unions since 1889*, Vol. 1, pp. 457-9 and p. 482; see A.A.O.C.S., *Annual Report* 1907, pp. 6-11.

47. A.A.O.C.S., *Annual Report* 1908, p. 16 and for a more detailed account refer to the A.A.O.C.S., Quarterly Reports of the Proceedings of the Executive Council for those ending 31 October 1908 and 31 January 1909.

48. See *Conciliation in the Cotton Trade — Report of the Negotiations 1899-1900* (1901); A.A.O.C.S., *Quarterly Report* 31 October 1909, p. 4.

49. A.A.O.C.S., *Annual Report* 1909, p. 5.

50. A.A.O.C.S., *Quarterly Report* 31 July 1910, p. 5.

51. A.A.O.C.S., *Annual Report* 31 July 1910, p. 3-5.

52. A.A.O.C.S., *Quarterly Report* 31 October 1910, pp. 3-5.

53. A.A.O.C.S., *Quarterly Report* 31 July 1912, pp. 4-5; 31 December 1913, pp. 3-4; and A.A.O.C.S., *Annual Report* 31 December 1912, pp. 9-12.

54. See the A.A.O.C.S., *Quarterly Reports* 30 April 1913, pp. 10-15.

55. U.T.F.W.A., *Report* (1907).

56. See the A.A.O.C.S., *Quarterly Reports* 31 January 1911 pp. 3-4 for an outline of the Catterall Case.

57. See the U.T.F.W.A., *Annual Report* 29, 30 July 1912, pp. 9, 39-42 and 47-52 for an account of this issue.

58. See the U.T.F.W.A., *Annual Report* 28, 29 July 1913, pp. 3-18.

59. J. L. White (1978) ch. 2.

CHAPTER EIGHT (War and Labour Unrest)

1. Board of Trade, *Working Party Report, Cotton*, (1946) pp. 4-6, Tables 1 and 2.

2. J. H. Porter, 'Cotton and Wool Textiles' in N. K. Buxton and D. H. Aldcroft (eds.), *British Industry Between the Wars*, (1979) p. 29.

3. Amalgamated Association of Operative Cotton Spinners and Twiners (A.A.O.C.S.), *Quarterly Reports* 30 April 1915, 31 July 1915; A.A.O.C.S., *Annual Report* 1915; *Cotton Factory Times*, 29 October 1915; B. Drake, *Women in Trade Unions* (1984) pp. 84-5.

4.   U.T.F.W.A., *Annual Report* 1917.

5.   A.A.O.C.S., *Quarterly Report* 31 July 1915; A.A.O.C.S., *Annual Report* 1915.

6.   A.A.O.C.S., *Annual Reports* 1916, 1917.

7.   H. D. Henderson, *Cotton Control Board* (1922).

8.   H. D. Henderson (1922) p. 11.

9.   A.A.O.C.S., *Quarterly Reports* 31 October 1917, 31 January 1918.

10. See H. D. Henderson (1922) chs. 6-8; A.A.O.C.S., *Quarterly Report* 31 October 1918; A.A.O.C.S., *Cotton Inquiry Tribunal; Report of Proceedings 9-10 October 1918.*

11. A.A.O.C.S., *Cotton Inquiry Tribunal* p. 83.

12. A.A.O.C.S., *Quarterly Report* 30 April 1918, 31 July 1918, 31 October 1918.

13. *War Cabinet Minutes* 10 September 1918, (P.R.O., WC 471/104-5).

14. A.A.O.C.S., *Cotton Inquiry Tribunal* pp. 88-9.

15. A.A.O.C.S., *Cotton Inquiry Tribunal* p. 38.

16. A.A.O.C.S., *Cotton Inquiry Tribunal* p. 38.

17. A.A.O.C.S., *Cotton Inquiry Tribunal* pp. 8-9.

18. A.A.O.C.S., *Cotton Inquiry Tribunal* p. 5.

19. A.A.O.C.S., *Cotton Inquiry Tribunal* p. 70.

20. A.A.O.C.S., *Cotton Inquiry Tribunal* pp. 47-8.

21. A.A.O.C.S., *Cotton Inquiry Tribunal* pp. 95-8.

22. A.A.O.C.S., *Quarterly Report* 31 January 1919.

23. A.A.O.C.S., *Annual Report* 1918.

24. A.A.O.C.S., *Quarterly Report* 31 January 1920; G. W. Daniels and J. Jewkes, 'The Post-War Depression the Lancashire Cotton Industry', *Journal of Royal Statistical Society*, 91 (1928).

25. The account of 1919 is drawn from the U.T.F.W.A., *Minutes of Legislative Council January — July 1919;* U.T.F.W.A., *Annual Report* 1919; *Cotton Factory Times*, 23, 30 June, 4 July 1919; Bolton Spinners', *Annual Report* 1919.

26. See U.T.F.W.A., *Annual Reports* 1919-23 for the debate on Cotton Workers' Federation.

27. *Cotton Factory Times,* 30 August, 15 November 1918 for shop stewards' movement.

28. A.A.O.C.S., *Quarterly Reports,* 30 April and 31 July 1920; *Cotton Factory Times,* May 1920.

29. See J. Jewkes and E. M. Gray, *Wages and Labour in the Lancashire Cotton Spinning Industry* (1935) pp. 15-35, 195-204.

30. Minister of Labour meets deputation of employers in Cotton Industry, 8 June 1921 (P.R.O., LAB 2/1256/11).

31. *Records of Amalgamated Weavers' Association,* (Lancashire Record Office DDX 1123/6/124); *Wage Negotiations,* 1921.

32. U.T.F.W.A., *Annual Report* 1918; A.A.O.C.S., *Quarterly Report,* 30 April 1918.

33. A.A.O.C.S., *Quarterly Report* 2 July 1920.

CHAPTER NINE (Spinners in the Inter-War Years)

1. The main contemporary accounts of the industry in the 1920s are G. W. Daniels and J. Jewkes, 'The Post-War Depression in the Lancashire Cotton Industry', *Journal of the Royal Statistical Society,* 91 (1928); H. Clay, *Report on the Position of the English Cotton Industry* (1931); Board of Trade, *Working Party Report, Cotton* (1946).

2. United Textile Factory Workers' Association (U.T.F.W.A.), *Report on the Ways and Means of Improving the Economic Stability of the Cotton Textile Industry,* (1943) ch. 10, and Table 53.

3. Amalgamated Association of Operative Cotton Spinners, (A.A.O.C.S.), *Quarterly Report* 31 January 1922.

4. Amalgamated Weavers' Association, (Lancashire Record Office Preston DDX 1123/6/125 and DDX 1123/6/126) for Wage Negotiations in 1922 and 1923.

5. U.T.F.W.A., *Annual Reports* 1919, 1923, 1924, 1930, 1932.

6. H. A. Clegg, *A History of British Trade Unionism since 1889* (1985), Vol. II; A.A.O.C.S., *Quarterly Report* January 1928.

7. U.T.F.W.A., *Annual Report* (1929).

8. Amalgamated Weavers' Association (Lancashire Record Office, Preston DDX 1123/6/266 for 1928 'State of Trade' conferences).

9. Proceedings of Board of Arbitration re. Cotton Trade Wages, 21-22 August 1929. Amalgamated Weavers' Association (Lancashire Record Office, Preston DDX 1123/6/303).

10. Amalgamated Weavers' Association (Lancashire Record Office, Preston DDX 1123/6/303) for 1929 Wage Negotiations and Arbitration; Press coverage of the dispute drawn from Bolton Spinners' Press Cuttings Book in possession of Joe Richardson.

11. See J. H. Porter, 'The Commercial Banks and the Financial Problems of the English Cotton Industry 1919-39', *International Review of Banking History*, 9 (1976).

12. Economic Advisory Council, *Report of the Committee on the Present Condition and Prospects of the Cotton Industry* (London, 1930).

13. *Proceedings of Conference between the F.M.C.S.A. and U.T.F.W.A., 15 December 1931* in U.T.F.W.A. Collection, Oldham Local Interest Centre.

14. *Proceedings of Conference between the F.M.C.S.A. and U.T.F.W.A., 15 December 1931;* A.A.O.C.S., *Quarterly Reports* 31 October 1931, 31 January 1932.

15. A.A.O.C.S., *Quarterly Report* 31 July 1932.

16. A.A.O.C.S., *Quarterly Reports* 31 July, 30 October 1932, 31 January 1933; for 1932 dispute also Bolton Spinners' Press Cuttings Book.

17. J. Jewkes and E. M. Gray, *Wages and Labour in the Lancashire Cotton Spinning Industry*, (1935), Ch. 12; A.A.O.C.S., *Quarterly Report* 30 April 1933.

18. J. H. Porter, 'Cotton and Wool Textiles' in N. K. Buxton and D. H. Aldcroft (eds.), *British Industry between the Wars*, (1979) pp. 42-3.

19. A.A.O.C.S., *Annual Reports*, 1936, 1937.

20. U.T.F.W.A., *Annual Report* 1934; *Annual Conference* 1935; *Cotton, T.U.C. Plan of Socialisation*, (1935).

21. A.A.O.C.S., *Quarterly Report* 31 October 1936.

22. U.T.F.W.A., *Annual Conference Reports*, 1938, 1939.

23. A.A.O.C.S., *Annual Report*, 1928.

24. A.A.O.C.S., *Annual Report*, 1938.

25. J. Jewkes and E. M. Gray (1935) Ch. II; A.A.O.C.S., *Annual Reports*, 1918, 1933.

26. J. Jewkes and E. M. Gray (1935); F. Utley, *Lancashire and the Far East* (1931); *Proceedings of the Board of Arbitration Cotton Trade Wages* (1929); U.T.F.W.A., *Report on Ways and Means of Improving the Economic Stability of the Cotton Textile Industry* (1943).

27. A. and L. Fowler, *A History of the Nelson Weavers' Association* (1984).

28. W. Lazonick, 'The Cotton Industry', in B. Elbaum and W. Lazonick (eds.), *The Decline of the British Economy* (1986); L. Sandberg, *Lancashire in Decline* (1974) p. 123.

29. W. Lazonick and W. Mass, 'The Performance of the British Cotton Industry 1870-1913', *Research in Economic History*, 9 (1984).

30. *The Effects of the Depression on Organisation and Structure of the Spinners' Amalgamation* (Copy with the author, kindly lent by Prof. R. F. Dyson); J. Jewkes and E. M. Gray, (1935) Ch. XI.

CHAPTER TEN (Mule Spinners' Cancer)

I am grateful for the helpful comments of Mike Rayner, Steve Jones and Dr Robert Murray on an earlier draft of this chapter.

1. H. A. Waldron, 'A Brief History of Scrotal Cancer', *British Journal of Industrial Medicine*, 40 (1983) 390-401; D. Hunter, *The Diseases of Occupations*, 6th ed, (1978) pp. 797-806; W. R. Lee, 'Emergence of Occupational Medicine in Victorian Times', *British Journal of Industrial Medicine*, 30 (1973) 118-24; R. Murray, 'Mule Spinners' Cancer' in R. Raven, (ed.), *Cancer* Vol. 3 (1956) pp. 319-22.

2. W. S. Taggart, 'The Lubrication of Spindles', *Textile Recorder* 15 June 1926 p. 47.

3. *Report upon the Prevention of Accidents from Machinery in the Manufacture of Cotton* P.P. 1899 (9456) XII pp. 14-16; *Departmental Committee on Accidents in Places under the Factory and Workshop Acts, Minutes of Evidence*, P.P. 1911 (5540) XXIII, Evidence of William Marsland Qs. 3738-41; R. P. White, *Occupational Affections of the Skin* (1915), p. 83; J. Wheatley, 'Manufacture of Cotton' in T. Oliver (ed), *Dangerous Trades* (1902) pp. 702-23.

4. *British Medical Journal*, 18 November 1922, pp. 971-3; *British Medical Journal*, 26 November 1927, pp. 993-4.

5. A.A.O.C.S., *Quarterly Report* ending 31 July 1923, p. 5 and 13; A.A.O.C.S., *Annual Report* (1923) p. 6; *Annual Report of Chief Inspector of Factories and Workshops for 1923*, pp. 69-70.

6. *Manchester Guardian*, 17 January 1924; *British Medical Journal*, 16 February 1924, p. 289, 12 April 1924, p. 679; *Cotton Factory Times*, 18 January 1924, 11, 18 April 1924, 27 June 1924, 1 August 1924; A. Wilson and H. Levy, *Workmen's Compensation*, 2 Vols, (1939); P. Bartrip, 'The Rise and Decline of Workmen's Compensation' in P. Weindling (ed), *The Social History of Occupational Health*, (1985) pp. 163-73; *The Lancet*, 28 November 1925, p. 1137-8; *Bolton Evening News*, 4 February 1928; U.T.F.W.A., *Report of Proceedings, at the Annual Conference*, 1927 pp. 88-92; 1928, pp. 89-91; 1929, p. 61; 1937, pp. 41-4; 1946, pp. 47-8, p. 56; 1953, pp. 64-7; 1955, pp. 13-14; A.A.O.C.S., *Annual Report* 1931 p. 8, 1935 p. 12; *Home Office Departmental Committee on Compensation for Industrial Diseases* (1932) pp. 7-10.

7. *British Medical Journal*, 22 November 1924 pp. 959-60; Home Office, *Report of the Departmental Committee appointed to consider Evidence as to the occurrence of Epitheliomatous Ulceration among Mule Spinners* (1926).

8. S. A. Henry's interest in scrotal cancer culminated in the publication of *Cancer of the Scrotum in Relation to Occupation* (1946).

9. *Departmental Committee* (1926) p. 14.

10. *Departmental Committee* (1926) pp. 20-7; *British Medical Journal*, 24 April 1926, pp. 751-2; *The Lancet*, 24 April 1926, pp. 874-5.

11. This section draws on the *Reports of the Manchester Committee on Cancer*, (1925-44) and the records of the Committee held at the John Rylands University of Manchester Library (L₂F); *The Lancet*, 10 February 1934 pp. 286-7; *Manchester Guardian*, 7 December 1934; A.A.O.C.S.,

Quarterly Report, ending 31 January 1935 p. 6; C. C. Twort and J. M. Twort, 'The Utility of Lanolin as a preventive measure against Mineral Oil and Tar Dermatitis and Cancer', *Journal of Hygiene*, 35 (1935).

12. A.A.O.C.S., *Quarterly Report* ending 31 July 1937, pp. 4-5; *Manchester Guardian*, 9 September 1937, p. 5; W. S. Taggart, 'The Lubrication of Spindles', *Textile Recorder*, 15 June 1926, p. 47; G. H. Hurst, *Lubricating Oils, Fats and Greases*, 4th edition revised by H. B. Stocks (1925) p. 111, 166, 282-5; 'The Mule: Upkeep and Repairs', *Textile Recorder*, 15 December 1929, p. 39.

13. *Mule Spinning (Health) Special Regulations* 1953, (Statutory Instrument No. 1545) p. 2, (my italics).

14. A.A.O.C.S., *Mule Spinners' Cancer File*, Letter to Sir A. W. Garrett, 16 November 1944; Manchester Committee on Cancer, *Records* (L_2F) Letter to E M. Brockbank from C. Schofield, 25 October 1944; A.A.O.C.S., *Quarterly Report* ending 31 January 1944, pp. 7-8; *Quarterly Report* ending 30 April 1944, pp. 10-12; Ministry of Labour and National Service, *Interim Report of the Joint Advisory Committee of the Cotton Industry on Mule Spinners' Cancer and Automatic Wiping-Down Motions* (1945); Manchester Oil Refinery Ltd., *Mule Spinners' Cancer* (1946) (Brochure on Puremor Spindle Oil); C. C. Twort and J. M. Twort, *Textile Weekly* (37) 1946, p. 376; A.A.O.C.S., *Quarterly Report* ending 30 April 1951, pp. 5-6; S. J. M. Auld, 'Environmental Cancer and Petroleum', *Journal of Institute of Petroleum* 36 (1950) 235-53 and correspondence from C. Schofield 36 (1950) pp. 604-5.

15. *Departmental Committee* (1926) p. 27; U.T.F.W.A., *Report of the Legislative Council on the Ways and Means of Improving the Economic Stability of the Cotton Textile Industry* (1943) p. 113; on the anti-splash devices see *Textile Weekly*, 26 October 1945 p. 782, 30 May 1947 p. 872, 1 October 1948 p. 752; *Textile Manufacturer*, October 1948 p. 489.

16. *Oldham Operative Cotton Spinners' Provincial Association Monthly Report*, November 1927 pp. 491-2. On the views advanced by James Robertson on spinners' clothing see *British Medical Journal*, 18 December 1926 pp. 1181-2; *The Lancet* 10 December 1927, pp. 1273-4.

17. *Annual Report of the Chief Inspector of Factories for 1955*, p. 198.

18. A.A.O.C.S., *Annual Report* (1927) p. 8, *Quarterly Report* ending 31 July 1927 p. 16; *Bolton Evening News*, 13 December 1933; E. M. Brockbank, *Mule Spinners' Cancer. Epithelioma of the Skin in Cotton Spinners* (1941) pp. 25-6; A.A.O.C.S., *Quarterly Report* ending 30 April 1951, p. 7; J. L. Williams, *Accidents and Ill Health at Work* (1960) pp. 221-5.

19. Manchester Committee on Cancer Report for 1928 p. 5; *Bolton Evening News*, 11, 19 October 1927; E. M. Brockbank, *Mule Spinners' Cancer* (n.d.).

20. W. F. Dearden, 'Health Hazards in the Cotton Industry', *British Medical Journal*, 12 March 1927 p. 455; U.T.F.W.A., *Report of the Proceedings at the Annual Conference*, 1932 pp. 53-63, 1937 pp. 72-7; U.T.F.W.A., *Report of the Legislative Council on the Ways and Means of Improving the Economic Stability of the Cotton Textile Industry* (1943) pp. 81-3; A.A.O.C.S., *Mule Spinners' Cancer File, Statement to Rationing and Prices Committee of T.U.C.* 11 March 1948; A.A.O.C.S., *Quarterly Report* ending 31 July 1948 pp. 10-11.

21. A.A.O.C.S., *Annual Report* (1956) p. 7; A.A.O.C.S., *Annual Report* ending 31 January 1959 pp. 8-9; A.A.O.C.S., *Annual Report* (1961) pp. 10-11; A.A.O.C.S., *Quarterly Report* ending 31 January 1962, pp. 3-5.

22. U.T.F.W.A., *Report of the Proceedings at the Annual Conference*, 1946; H. Jones, 'Health and Safety at Work in Inter-War Britain' in P. Weindling (1985).

CHAPTER ELEVEN (Decline of the Amalgamation)

1. See A.A.O.C.S., *Annual Reports* 1940-5; U.T.F.W.A., *Annual Reports* 1940-5.

2. See U.T.F.W.A., *Annual Conference Reports and Annual Report*, 1942-5; U.T.F.W.A., *Report of the Legislative Council on Ways and Means of Improving the Economic Stability of the Cotton Textile Industry* (1943).

3. Cabinet Discussion, 3 August 1945, (P.R.O. CAB 66/67 68081).

4. See Bolton Spinners' *Annual Report*, 1945; A.A.O.C.S., *Quarterly Report* 31 October 1945.

5. Ministry of Labour and National Service, *The Cotton Spinning Industry* (1945); *The Cotton Spinning Industry Supplement Mule Spinners' Wages*, Ministry of Labour and National Service 1946; 'Evershed' Mule Spinning List in A.A.O.C.S., *Quarterly Report* 31 October 1948; Bolton Spinners', *Annual Report* 1948.

6. Board of Trade, *Working Party Reports, Cotton* (1946); Bolton Spinners', *Annual Report* 1947; U.T.F.W.A., *Special Conference*, 1947; C. Miles, *Lancashire Textiles: A Case Study of Industrial Change* (1968) pp. 30-40; A.A.O.C.S., *Annual Report* 1947.

7. A.A.O.C.S., *Quarterly Report* 31 October 1948.

8. U.T.F.W.A., *Annual Conference Report* 1948.

9. A.A.O.C.S., *Annual Report* 1951; U.T.F.W.A., *Annual Report* 1946; Bolton Spinners' *Annual Report* 1948.

10. No records have survived of the Amalgamated Association of Operative Cotton Spinners' Insurance Section.

11. See C. Miles (1968) pp. 40-1; A.A.O.C.S., *Annual Reports* 1952-8; H. A. Turner, *Trade Union, Growth, Structure and Policy* (1962) pp. 331-47.

12. U.T.F.W.A., *Plan for Cotton*, (1957); U.T.F.W.A., *Annual Report* 1957.

13. A.A.O.C.S., *Quarterly Report* 31 July 1957.

14. For the background to the Act see C. Miles (1968) pp. 46-9.

15. See A.A.O.C.S., *Annual Report*, 1952-8.

16. A.A.O.C.S., *Quarterly Report* 31 July 1958.

17. U.T.F.W.A., *Annual Report* 1958; A.A.O.C.S., *Quarterly Report* 31 January 1959; U.T.F.W.A., *Annual Conference Report* 1959.

18. A.A.O.C.S., *Quarterly Report* 31 January 1959.

19. U.T.F.W.A., *Annual Report* 1959.

20. U.T.F.W.A., *Annual Conference Report*, 1959.

21. A.A.O.C.S., *Quarterly Report* 30 April 1959; U.T.F.W.A., *Annual Conference Report*, 1959.

22. A.A.O.C.S., *Quarterly Report* 31 July 1959; U.T.F.W.A., *Annual Report*, 1959.

23. See C. Miles (1968) Ch. 4.

24. U.T.F.W.A., *Annual Report* 1959.

25. A.A.O.C.S., *Annual Report* 1959.

26. A.A.O.C.S., *Quarterly Report* 31 October 1959.

27. A.A.O.C.S., *Annual Report*, 1970, 1975.

28. A.A.O.C.S., *Annual Reports* 1962-7.

Appendix I
OFFICERS OF THE SPINNERS' AMALGAMATION

PRESIDENTS

Officer	Former District	Period of Office
William Leigh	Hyde	(1858) – 1876
William Radcliffe	Mossley	1876 – 1878
Thomas Ashton	Oldham	1878 – 1913
Edward Judson	Ashton-under-Lyne	1913 – 1926
Fred Birchenough	Oldham	1926 – 1936
William Wood	Bolton	1936 – 1940
Albert Knowles	Oldham	1940 – 1953
James Whitworth	Ashton-under-Lyne	1953 – 1960
Walter Lee	Oldham	1960 – 1965
Joseph Richardson	Bolton	1966 – 1967
Frederick Mayall	Oldham	1967 – 1976

GENERAL SECRETARIES

Thomas Mawdsley	Manchester	(1848) – 1874
William Heginbotham	Hyde	1875 – 1878
James Mawdsley	Preston	1878 – 1902
William Howarth	Bolton	1902 – 1904
William Marsland	Ashton-under-Lyne	1904 – 1917
Henry Boothman	Oldham	1917 – 1943
Charles Schofield	Bolton	1944 – 1960
James Whitworth	Ashton-under-Lyne	1960 – 1965
Walter Lee	Oldham	1965 – 1967
Joseph Richardson	Bolton	1967 – 1976

TREASURERS

William Fair	Manchester	(1849) – 1876
William Leigh	Hyde	1876 – 1878
William Radcliffe	Mossley	1878 – 1883
Samuel Jones	Manchester	1883 – 1893
James Robinson	Bolton	1893 – 1896
Thomas Dawson	Oldham	1896 – 1932

MEMBERS OF THE TUC PARLIAMENTARY COMMITTEE AND GENERAL COUNCIL

James Mawdsley	1882; 1884 – 1889; 1891 – 1896
Alfred Gill	1903 – 1914
Edward Judson	1917 – 1918
Henry Boothman	1919 – 1936
William Wood	1936 – 1938
Robert Handley	1938 – 1940

MEMBERS OF PARLIAMENT

Alfred Gill (Bolton): 1906 – 1914, died in office.
Alfred Davies (Clitheroe): 1918 – 1922.
Albert Law (Bolton): 1923 – 1924; 1929 – 1931.

Appendix II
ESTIMATES OF THE NUMBER AND DISTRIBUTION OF MULE SPINNERS IN 1811

Lancashire

Manchester	1772
Bolton	556
Ashton-under-Lyne	521
Preston	496
Oldham	327
Bury & Ramsbottom	127
Rochdale	77
Chorley	66
Wigan	38
Heywood	20

Cheshire

Stockport	587
Macclesfield	235
Warrington	83

Derbyshire

Glossop	245
New Mills	140

Yorkshire

Halifax	204
Todmorden	113

Scotland   1333

Source: These estimates were obtained by dividing the mule spindleage for specific areas as identified by Crompton and listed in G. W. Daniels (1930) by 600, the assumed number of spindles per pair of mules. This latter figure has been chosen because it falls mid-way between the 360 spindle mule (720 per pair) common in the Manchester and Preston districts and the 240 spindle mules (480 per pair) common elsewhere. The estimate probably overstates the number of mule spinners in the two former areas and underestimates in the remainder.

Appendix III
ESTIMATES OF THE NUMBER AND DISTRIBUTION OF MULE SPINNERS AND SELF-ACTOR MINDERS IN 1841

AREA	Counts more than 60	Counts less than 60	Mixed counts	Total
Lancashire Parishes:				
Manchester	828	1357	92	2295
Ashton	208	1186	136	1530
Bolton	303	459	274	898
Oldham	79	976	16	1071
Rochdale		719		719
Bury		843		843
Whalley		721		721
Preston (& Leyland)	155	472		627
Blackburn		588		588
Blackburn & part of Preston	24	125		149
Prestwich (& 14 others[1])	55	986	9	1050
Yorkshire:				
12 parishes[2]		180		180
Cheshire & Derbyshire:				
Stockport Borough		427		427
Others (principally north-east Cheshire & north-west Derbyshire)		975		975
Cumberland:				
Carlisle & Dalston		144		144
Totals:	1652	10176	518	12346

Notes

1. Prestwich, Radcliffe, Middleton, Eccles, Leigh, Winwick, Dean, Chorley, Leyland, Chipping, Ribchester, Garstang, Lancaster, Cartmel, Ulverstone.
2. Saddleworth, Thornton, Skipton, Liston, Burnsall, Hampsthwaite, Gisburn, Settle, Gargreave, Giggleswick, Ingleton, Sedbergh.

Source: The estimates are based on data obtained from Horner (1841) except for the Cheshire and Derbyshire figures which were obtained from P.P. 1837-8 (119) XXVIII p. 30 and P.P. 1842 (410) XXII p. 13. The distinction between coarse (<60) and fine (>60) is that used by Horner. Mule spinner numbers for the Horner districts were calculated by multiplying (1) the total spinning labour force (*either* as stated in single process firms *or* as calculated by the spinning:weaving proportions of 0.7 [V.A.C. Gatrell (1977)]) by (2) the proportion of mule spinners in the labour force (the figure of 12.5% was selected as lying within the range 10.7% to 14.8% for mule spinner to spinner labour forces in six identified mills [Horner (1841); Mick Jenkins (1981), p. 53; D. Chadwick (1860) p. 5]). Howell did not divide the Cheshire and Derbyshire districts between fine and coarse spinning, however the area was overwhelmingly coarse with a large number of mixed spinning and weaving firms; here the spinner labour force was calculated assuming a spinner:weaver proportion of 1, thus to offset the assumption of combined enterprises by reference to single firms.

Appendix IV
MEMBERSHIP OF SPINNERS' AMALGAMATION AND THE OLDHAM AND BOLTON PROVINCIAL ASSOCIATIONS 1870 – 1975

Year	Spinners' Amalgamation	Oldham Province	Bolton Province	
			Hand	*Minders*
1870	10000	2231	1104	400
1871	10500	2500		
1872	11500	2276		
1873	12130	2414		
1874	14257	2742	1301	
1875	14619	3278	1180	1000
1876	15115	3417	1088	
1877	15544	3565	1093	1100
1878	11968	3572	1020	1220
1879	9977	3074	1100	1450
1880	11834	3551	2485	
1881	11779	3755	2480	
1882	12437	4078	2674	
1883	14326	4273	3344	
1884	15970	4615	3828	
1885	16579	5057	3820	
1886	15527	4873	3968	
1887	15416	4924	3956	
1888	16910	5309	4066	
1889	17224	5649	4062	
1890	18145	5623	4101	
1891	19662	6157	4233	
1892	19247	6482	4209	
1893	19327	6497	4134	
1894	18615	6341	4150	
1895	18234	6193	4415	
1896	18009	6010	4469	
1897	17760	6056	4459	
1898	17813	6023	4489	
1899	18151	6166	4619	
1900	18384	6319	4779	
1901	18474	6280	4764	
1902	18391	6397	4559	
1903	18315	6363	4545	
1904	18534	6537	4659	
1905	19451	7030	4693	
1906	20928	7611	4865	
1907	22506	8083	5301	
1908	22837	8228	5483	
1909	23124	8325	5584	
1910	22992	8339	5608	

Year	Spinners' Amalgamation		Oldham Province		Bolton Province	
1911	23248		8628		5625	
1912	23500		8769		5630	
1913	23713		8963		5708	
1914	23645		8980		5766	
1915	23885		9472		5874	
1916	23803		10035		5556	
1917	24431		10289		5972	
1918	24806		10256		5904	
1919	25309		10533		5790	

	Spinners	Piecers	Spinners	Piecers	Spinners	Piecers
1920	24064	30822	9538	10037	5892	11784
1921	23628	30752	8841	9014	5901	11802
1922	23291	28690	8792	8586	5916	11832
1923	22965	26840	8676	7675	5899	11798
1924	22953	25672	8672	6676	5914	11828
1925	22988	25430	8723	6767	5981	11960
1926	22820	25209	8672	6581	6071	12142
1927	22499	25357	8516	6645	6167	12334
1928	22248	25303	8372	6687	6122	12244
1929	21613	26673	8090	6916	6177	12232
1930	20724	25990	7747	6987	6081	12160
1931	19826	24342	7535	6602	5967	11932
1932	18625	22916	6869	5802	5873	11744
1933	16545	21405	6207	5132	5737	12183
1934	15533	20443	5895	4808	5675	12075
1935	14654	19702	5525	4520	5590	12087
1936	14059	18173	5281	3823	5321	11466
1937	13629	18103	5131	3884	5270	11071
1938	13161	16891	5030	3426	5094	10668
1939	12479	12392	4861	3212	4919	6300
1940	12389	12774	4662	3209	4719	5661
1941	9950	9088	4265	2918	4527	3633
1942	9582	8849	4072	2742	3803	2182
1943	8615	8331	2974	2200	2978	1946
1944	8604	8068	2911	2110	2957	1751
1945	8708	8321	2922	2309	3407	1793
1946	9763	8836	3152	3318	4055	2775
1947	9963	8604	3255	3553	4199	2554
1948	10295	10176	3383	4127	4385	2825
1949	10440	10983	3505	4562	4370	3025
1950	10592	11434	3629	4739	4373	3118
1951	10675	12181	3642	4859	4572	3290
1952	10146	9856	3601	4701	4297	2158
1953	9557	1078	3371	4555	4021	2287
1954	9254	9856	3175	4278	3945	2402

Year	Amalgamation		Oldham		Bolton	
	Spinners	Piecers	Spinners	Piecers	Spinners	Piecers
1955	8461	8114	2973	3808	3591	1652
1956	7983	7178	2705	3311	3384	1457
1957	7426	7145	2507	3158	3221	1436
1958	6602	6249	2231	2731	2883	1200
1959	5422	4957	1901	2189	2407	924
1960	3486	3614	1090	1436	1462	534
1961	3149	3184	908	1155	1351	452
1962	2626	2348	752	845	1113	300
1963	1950	1970	491	659	756	218
1964	1752	1954	374	491	581	179
1965	1550	1712	366	365	436	130
1966	1180	1441	310	280	280	106
1967	919	1073	220	185	224	86
1968	773	1103	145	125	161	67
1969	680	1078	120	100	129	53
1970	619	743	73	53	129	58
1971	501	673	67	50	107	57
1972	384	496	62	5433	23	
1973	295	374	36	12		
1974	233	339	12			
1975	214	294				

Source: A.A.O.C.S. Annual and Quarterly Reports.

Appendix V

WAGES OF SPINNERS, OTHER TEXTILE WORKERS, CRAFTS, LABOURERS ETC, IN COTTON TOWNS: SELECTED YEARS 1810 – 1859 (WEEKLY WAGES)

Year	1810	1819	1839	1849	1859
Hours of work	up to 80	72	69	60	60
Mulespinners					
40s	20s – 28s over period		23s 0d	21s 0d	23s 0d
60s–100s	{ 42s 6d	32s 0d	25s 0d	21s 0d	23–25s 0d
120s–220s			40–45s 0d	36–40s 0d	40–50s 0d
Big piecer	—	9s 2d	8s 0d	8s 6d	9s 0d
Small piecer		5s8d–7s2d	5s 6d	5s 6d	6s 0d
Self-Actor Minders					
Overlookers			20s 0d	22s 0d	26s 0d
4s to 24s			16s 0d	18s 0d	20s 0d
25s to 40s			18s 0d	18s 6d	22s 0d
Piecers			8s 0d	9s 0d	10s 0d
Throstle frame overlookers			18s 0d	20s 0d	24s 0d
Mill stokers			16s 0d	17s 0d	18s 0d
Nightwatchman			16s 0d	16s 0d	18s 0d
Handloom weavers	21s 0d	10s 3d	16s 0d	15s 0d	16s 0d
Bleacher/Finisher	18s 6d	18s 6d	21s 0d	18s 0d	18s 0d
Calico printers (block)	26s 0d	26s 0d	40s 0d	28s 0d	28s 0d
Block cutter	22s – 30s over period		35s 0d	25s 0d	25s 0d
Other crafts (metal)					
highest	{ 31s 3d	31s 6d	58s 0d	50s 0d	50s 0d
lowest			15s 0d	15s 0d	15s 6d
average			28s 0d	28s 3d	28s 6d
Coalminers			25s 0d	20s 0d	25s 0d
Agricultural labourer			15s 0d	15s 0d	15s 0d
Police Constable			19s 0d	19s 0d	20s 0d
Street labourer	15s 0d	15s 0d	16s 6d	16s 6d	16s 6d
Weekly expenditure for husband, wife & 3 children: Food	21s 0d	16s 8d	20s 8d	21s 6d	24s 7d
Rent, clothing, sundries			9s 6d	9s 6d	9s 6d
Total:			30s 2d	31s 0d	34s 1d

Source: Manchester Mercury, 18 January 1820 for 1810 and 1819; D. Chadwick, *Quarterly Journal of the Statistical Society,* 23 (1860) pp. 23-9; J. L. and B. Hammond (1975) p. 106. For the trends of wages received by spinners and minders in the different cotton towns see G. H. Wood (1910).

Appendix VI
MOVEMENTS IN SPINNERS' WAGES LISTS 1845 – 1914 (% OF ORIGINAL LIST)

Year	Bolton %	Bolton (Self-Actor) %	Oldham %	Ashton %	Preston %	Hours of Working Week
1845	100					60 (1848)
1847	90					
1853	95					
	100					
	95					
1854	90					
1858	90					
1859	93½				107½	
1860	95	105		100		
1861	90	100		90	100	
1865				100		
1866	95	105		110	107½*	
1867	90	100		100	102½	
1869	85	95		95	92½	
1870				100	97½	
1871	90	100		105	102½	59 (1871)
1872	95	105	100*			
1874	90	100				
1875	95	105	100*			56½ (1875)
1877	90	100	95	100		
1878			85	95	92½	
1879	80	90	80	85	87½	
1880	85	95	85	90	92½	
1881			90	95		
1885	80	90	85	90		
1888	85	95	90	95	97½	
1890	90	100	95	100	102½	
1893		97	92	97	99½	
1899	100	95	100	102½		
1900	105	100	105	107½		55½ (1902)
1905	105+5% bonus	105+5% bonus	105			
1906		105	105	110	112½	
1907		110	110	115	117½	
1908		110	110	115	117½	
1909		105	105	110	112½	
1910		105	105	110	112½	
1911		105	105	110	112½	
1912		105	105	110	112½	
1913		105	105	110	112½	
1914		105	105	110	112½	

* New list

Note: By 1914 the majority of the operatives in Lancashire were paid according to a wage list. The wage list varied from district to district but essentially laid down the day rates and piece rates to be paid to operatives for various tasks dependent on the type of yarn being prepared or spun. All wage advances or reductions were additions to or subtractions from the standard list. Because of this the history of movements in the wage rates of cotton operatives can be very confusing. Throughout the history of wage negotiations the base standard for the wage list did not change and all calculations were made to this base standard. Therefore a percentage increase on the base standard was not equivalent to the same percentage increase on the wage received by the operative. This becomes particularly important when considering wages in the period 1914-20 when increases reached some 70 per cent on the list but did not represent anything like this percentage increase on the wage. Wage computations in the cotton industry were so complex that many trade union officials spent much of their time checking on employers' calculations to ensure that their members received the correct payment. These appendices chart the movement in percentage on the base standard and readers should beware of misinterpreting these figures as percentage changes in the wages the operatives received.

Appendix VII
MOVEMENTS IN SPINNERS' WAGES LISTS 1915 – 1948

Year	Bolton %	Oldham %	Hours of Working Week
1915	110	110	
1916	115	115	
1917	140	140	
1918	215	215	
1919	245	245	48 (1919)
1920	315	315	
1921	245	245	
1922	195	195	
1923	195	195	
1924	195	195	
1925	195	195	
1926	195	195	
1927	195	195	
1928	195	195	
1929	182½	182½	
1930	182½	182½	
1931	182½	182½	
1932	168½	168½	
1933	168½	168½	
1934	168½	168½	
1935	168½	168½	
1936	178	178	
1937	178	178	
1938	178	178	
1939	200½	200½	
1940	223	223	
1941	236	236	
1942	241	241	
1943	241	241	
1944	241	241	
1945	241 + 16s 0d	241 + 16s 0d	
1946	257 + £1.0.0.	257 + £1.0.0.	45 (1946)
1947	257 + £1.0.0.	257 + £1.0.0.	
1948	257 + £1.0.0.	257 + £1.0.0.	

Source: A.A.O.C.S., *Annual Reports.*

Appendix VIII
ESTIMATE OF SPINDLE NUMBERS, SPINDLES PER MULE PAIR, AND NUMBER OF MULESPINNERS 1788 – 1870

Year	Total number of spindles (millions)	Estimate of mule spindles (millions)	Spindles per mule pair (hundreds)	Number of mule spinners (I) p	Number of mule spinners (II) q	Proportion of self-actor (r)
1788	1.94 (a)	.049 (e) or .155 (f)	90 (e) 100 (f)	550 (e) 1553 (f)		
1811	4.67 (b)	4.20 (b)	600 (j)	7016		
1817	6.65 (a)	5.9 (g)	600 (j)	9833		
1832 or 1834	9.0 (c) or 12.0 (d)	8.1 (g) 10.8 (g)	700 (k) 700 (k)	11571 or 15428		c. 3%
1841	15.7 (h)	14.1 (g)	750 (l)	18800		
1845 (and 1844-6)	17.5 (c)	15.7 (g)	750 (l)	20933	21375	
1850 (and 1849-51)	20.4 (a)	18.4 (g)	1000 (m)	18400	21487	c. 40%
1861 (and 1859-61)	30.3 (c)	27.2 (g)	1200 (n)	22666	26650	
1870	37.7 (s)					c. 80%

Sources:
(a) Von Tunzelmann (1978) p. 182
(b) Daniels (1930) pp. 107-10
(c) Farnie (1979) p. 180
(d) Blaug (1961) p. 380
(e) Daniels (1920) p. 121
(f) Chapman and Chassagne (1981) p. 41
(g) Estimates of mule spindleage (except for 1788 and 1811) were obtained by making a 10 per cent allowance for throttle spindleage
(h) Spindle numbers for 1841 are calculated from an average of cotton consumption for 1840-2 divided by 30lbs cotton/spindle on estimate between the 26.8m lbs 1834 and 30.0m lbs 1845 (Von Tunzelmann [1978] p. 182)
(j) See footnote to Appendix II
(k) Based on an estimate of 350 spindles per mule — see G. H. Wood (1910) p. 141 for other figures
(l) An estimate based on Horner (1842) p. 88 and Chadwick (1860) p. 5
(m) Gatrell (1977) p. 112 citing Fairbairn for the 1850s
(n) An estimate based on (m) and the 750-900 spindleage common in 1875

(p) Obtained (1788 apart) by dividing spindleage by an estimate of spindles per pair
(q) Based upon estimates of the proportion of mulespinners (see Appendix III) in the total cotton spinning labour force
(r) 1834 figure based upon Ure (1850) assumes ½ coarse counts spun on self-actors; late 1860s assumes all coarse and lower medium counts spun on self-actor; and note that the heavy investment of the 1850s would have considerably increased the proportion of self-actor minders
(s) B. R. Mitchell and P. Deane (1962) p. 185.

Appendix IX
ESTIMATE OF NUMBERS OF COTTON SPINDLES
1882 – 1963

Year	Millions	Year	Millions	Year	Millions	Year	Millions
1882	38.4	1905	46.0	1925	59.9	1946	36.7
1884	40.5	1906	48.3	1926	60.3	1947	36.2
1885	41.3	1907	52.6	1927	60.5	1948	35.5
1886-7	41.0	1908	55.2	1928	60.0	1949	34.9
1887-8	40.9	1909	57.0	1929	59.1	1950	34.4
1889	41.3	1910	57.7	1930	57.7	1951	33.9
1890	41.4	1911	58.0	1931	57.6	1952	33.3
1891	42.4	1912	58.1	1932	55.4	1953	31.8
1892	43.1	1913	58.5	1933	53.6	1954	30.3
1893-4	43.0	1914	59.3	1934	49.2	1955	29.2
1894-5	43.2	1915	59.9	1935	47.1	1956	27.8
1896	42.7	1916	59.8	1936	44.6	1957	26.2
1897	42.1	1917	61.0	1937	43.1	1958	25.5
1898	41.8	1918	59.5	1938	40.9	1959	22.9
1899	42.2	1919	59.2	1939	39.1	1960	12.0
1900	42.6	1920	60.1	1940	38.1	1961	11.6
1901	43.2	1921	60.1	1941	38.3	1962	10.9
1902	44.6	1922	59.8	1942	37.0	1963	9.1
1903	44.6	1923	59.8	1943-4	36.7		
1904	45.2	1924	59.5	1945	36.9		

Source: J. Worrall, *The Lancashire Textile Industry* (1960).

Appendix X
SPINNERS' AMALGAMATION BENEFITS EXPENDITURE 1880 – 1940

Year	Out of Work £	Dispute £	Lockouts £
1880	4220	2554	70
1881	6360	6100	347
1882	6398	7340	514
1883	7106	1392	281
1884	10892	4418	425
1885	15325	30247	570
1886	14377	14721	955
1887	16296	2226	696
1888	14974	1720	77
1889	15891	1905	367
1890	15519	2451	587
1891	13893	7120	120
1892	16819	7917	77955
1893	9282	1790	104081
1894	16393	7993	159
1895	17534	3625	840
1896	14130	5304	428
1897	14774	9819	1672
1898	13737	2603	1185
1899	12034	327	1092
1900	24729	2316	4142
1901	15362	2652	
1902	35373	3078	
1903	56671	4702	
1904	38388	3200	
1905	10391	3400	
1906	12390	2500	
1907	12992	1790	
1908	71601	132782	
1909	71676	22056	
1910	93319	18311	
1911	37981	5269	
1912	27684	10020	

252

Year	Out of Work £	Dispute/Lockouts £
1913	17718	28302
1914	107623	16051
1915	31511	7621
1916	6278	1514
1917	54576	3215
1918	117140	58269
1919	89345	141725
1920	120699	4032
1921	217459	126644
1922	74031	1872
1923	94398	7273
1924	58082	462
1925	49430	1750
1926	145670	1066
1927	67714	2181
1928	70699	4573
1929	90081	116343
1930	215487	5995
1931	104407	22401
1932	54793	69196
1933	26656	24515
1934	49529	4423
1935	36989	3014
1936	19159	5150
1937	12268	7807
1938	60653	399
1939	20311	49
1940	15567	66

Source: A.A.O.C.S., *Annual Reports*

Appendix XI
THE BROOKLANDS AGREEMENT

1. The representatives of the employers and the representatives of the employed in the pending dispute hereby admit that disputes and differences between them are inimical in the interests of both parties, and that it is expedient and desirable that some means should be adopted for the future whereby such disputes and differences may be expeditiously and amicably settled, and strikes and lockouts avoided.

2. That the pending dispute be settled by a reduction of sevenpence in the pound in the present wages of the operative cotton spinners, card and blowing room hands, reelers, winders, and others, such reduction to take effect forthwith, and the mills to resume work on Monday next, the 27th inst.

3. That when the employers and employed next agree upon an increase in the standard wages of the operative cotton spinners, card-room hands, and others who participated in the last advance of wages, such increase shall not exceed the reduction now agreed upon, unless in the meantime there shall have been a further reduction of such wages, in which case, should an advance be agreed to, the employed shall be entitled to an advance equal in amount to the last preceding reduction, plus the reduction of sevenpence in the pound now agreed upon, provided always that no application for an increase of reduction of such wages as now agreed upon be made for a period of six calendar months from the date hereof.

4. That subject to the last preceding clause, and with the view of preventing the cotton-spinning trade from being in an unsettled state too frequently from causes such as the present dispute, to the disadvantage of all parties concerned, no advance or reduction of such wages as aforesaid shall in future be sought for by the employers or the employed until after the expiration of at least one year from the date of the previous advance or reduction, as the case may be, nor shall any such advance or reduction when agreed upon be more or less than five per cent, upon the then current standard wages being paid. Notwithstanding anything hereinbefore contained in this clause, whenever a general demand for an advance or decrease of wages shall be made, the wages of the male card and blowing-room operatives may be increased or decreased to such an extent as may be mutually agreed upon.

5. That the secretary of the local Employers' Association and the secretary of the local Trades' Union shall give to the other of them, as the case may be, one calendar month's notice, in writing, of any and every general demand for a reduction or advance of the wages then being paid.

6. That in future no local Employers' Association, nor the Federated Association of Employers, on the one hand, nor any Trades Union, or federation of Trades Unions, on the other hand, shall countenance, encourage, or support any lock-out or strike which may arise from, or be caused by any question, difference, or dispute, contention, grievance, or complaint with respect to work, wages, or any other matter, unless and until the same has been submitted in writing by the secretary of the local Trades Union, or by the secretary of the local Trades Union to the secretary of the local Employers' Association, as the case may be: nor unless such secretaries or a committee consisting of three representatives of the local Trades Union, with their secretary, and three representatives of the local Employers' Association, with their secretary, shall have failed, after full enquiry, to settle and arrange such question, difference or dispute, contention, complaint or grievance within the space of seven days from the receipt of the communication, in writing aforesaid: nor unless and until, failing such last-mentioned settlement and arrangement, if either of the said secretaries of the local trades union and the local Employers' Association shall so deem advisable, a committee consisting of four representatives of the Federated Association of Employers, with their secretary, and four representatives of the local Amalgamated Association of the Operatives' Trade Union, with their secretary, shall have failed to settle or arrange, as foresaid, within the further space of seven days from the time when such matter was referred to them, provided always that the secretaries or the committee, hereinbefore mentioned, as the case may be, shall have power to extend or enlarge the said period of seven days whenever they may deem it expedient or desirable to do so.

7. Every local employers' association, or the federated association of employers, on the one hand, and every local trades union or the federation of trades unions, on the other hand, shall, with as little delay as possible, furnish to the other of them in writing full and precise particulars with reference to any and every question, difference, or dispute, contention or grievance that may arise with a view to the same being settled and arranged at the earliest possible date in the manner hereinbefore mentioned.

8. It is agreed that in respect to the opening of new markets abroad, the alteration of restrictive foreign tariffs, and other similar matters which may benefit or injure the cotton trade, the same shall be dealt with by a committee of three or more from each federation, all the associations undertaking to bring the whole of their influence to bear in furthering the general interests of the cotton industry in this country.

9. The above committee shall meet whenever the secretary of either federation shall be of the opinion that questions affecting the general interest of the cotton trade should be discussed.

10. The representatives of the employers and the representatives of the employed in the pending dispute do mutually undertake that they will use their best endeavours to see that the engagements hereinbefore respectively entered into by them are faithfully carried out in every respect.

Signed on behalf of the Association of Master Cotton Spinners' Associations,
A. E. REYNER, President
SAMUEL ANDREW, Sec., pro. tem.

Signed on behalf of the Amalgamated Association of Operative Cotton Spinners,
THOMAS ASHTON, President
JAMES MAWDSLEY, Secretary

Signed on behalf of the Amalgamated Association of Card and Blowing-room Operatives,
ENOCH JONES, President
WM. MULLIN, Secretary

Signed on behalf of the Amalgamated Northern Counties' Association of Warpers, Reelers and Winders,
DAVID HOLMES, President
W. H. WILKINSON, Secretary.

HESKETH BOOTH, Solicitor for the Masters' Association
ROBERT ASCROFT, Solicitor for the operatives.

BIBLIOGRAPHY

The main collection of records of the Amalgamated Association of Operative Cotton Spinners is held at the John Rylands Library, University of Manchester. At present they are unlisted but they contain a good run of the printed reports and minutes of the Spinners' Amalgamation. The extant manuscript material includes some general correspondence and subject files but this relates chiefly to the years after 1950. The majority of the pre-1950 manuscript material has been lost. The John Rylands Library also possesses the main archive of the Operative Cotton Spinners and Twiners of Bolton and surrounding Districts. This is a rich collection of printed and manuscript material and it includes the records of local branches from the 1870s onwards. It is in the process of being catalogued. The records of the Oldham Province are located in the Oldham Local Interest Centre and they have been listed. The records of the Preston Province are deposited in the Harris Library, Preston and include the minute books post-1889. The uncatalogued records of the Yorkshire Province are held at the Calderdale Library, Halifax. There is no comprehensive listing of cotton trade union records but an indispensable starting point for research is the bibliography produced by Manchester Studies, *Cotton Union Records* (1980). There is no comparable research aid which covers the records of the main cotton employers' organisations. For these the best introduction is Arthur McIvor, *Employers' Organisations and Industrial Relations in Lancashire 1890-1939*, PhD, University of Manchester, 1983.

1. Manuscript Sources

Bolton and District Textile Employers' Association, Bolton
Bolton Masters' Association Minutes and Reports

Greater Manchester Record Office
Cotton Spinners' and Manufacturers' Associations Collection; Minutes and Reports.

John Rylands University Library, Manchester
Amalgamated Association of Operative Cotton Spinners Collection; Quarterly and Annual Reports, Circulars, Correspondence, Files, Minutes.
Bolton and District Operative Cotton Spinners and Twiners Provincial Association Collection; Reports, Minutes, Circulars, Rules.
Oldham Masters Cotton Spinners' Association Collection; Reports and Letter Books.
Manchester Committee on Cancer Collection; Reports and Correspondence.

Lancashire Record Office, Preston
Haslingden Operatives Spinners' Association Collection.
Amalgamated Weavers' Association Collection.

London School of Economics
Webb Trade Union Collection.

Manchester Central Library
Amalgamated Association of Operative Cotton Spinners Collection.

Oldham and Rochdale Textile Employers' Association, Oldham
Oldham Masters' Cotton Spinners' Association Minutes

Oldham Local Interest Centre
Provincial Association of Operative Cotton Spinners of Oldham and District
    Collection; Minute Books, Reports, Rules and Correspondence.
Factory Acts Reform Association Collection.
United Moveable Committee Collection.
Oldham Labour Representation Committee Collection.
United Textile Factory Workers' Association Collection.

Public Record Office, Kew
War Cabinet Records 1918.
Ministry of Labour Records 1918-50.
Cabinet Minutes 1945.

Rochdale Local Studies Library
Rochdale Operative Cotton Spinners' Association Collection; Minutes and Cash
    Books.

2. Official Publications

Select Committee into the Employment of Children in Cotton Mills, 1818 (H.L. 90) XCVI.
Select Committee into the Employment of Children in Cotton Mills, 1819 (H.L. 24) CX.
Select Committee on Artisans, Machinery and Combination Laws, 1824 (51) V.
Factory Inquiry, Royal Commission 1st Report, 1833 (450) XX; *2nd Report*, 1833 (519) XXI;
Supplementary Report, 1834 (167) XIX.
Select Committee on Combinations of Workmen, 1837-8 (488) VIII.
Reports of Inspectors of Factories, 1842 (31) XXII.
Royal Commission on the Organisation and Rules of Trade Unions and other Associations,
    1867-8 (3980-I) XXXIX.
Royal Commission on Labour: First Report, 1892 (6708 — III) XXXIV.
Report upon the Prevention of Accidents from Machinery in the Manufacture of Cotton, 1899
    (9456) XII.

Departmental Committee on Accidents in Places under the Factory and Workshops Act, 1911 (5540) XXIII.

Annual Report of Chief Inspector of Factories 1919-75.

Home Office Report of the Departmental Committee appointed to consider evidence as to the occurrence of Epitheliomatous Ulceration among Mule Spinners (HMSO, London, 1926).

Committee on Industry and Trade, *Survey of Textile Industries* (HMSO, London, 1928), (Balfour Committee).

Economic Advisory Council, Report of the Committee on the Present Conditions and Prospects of the Cotton Industry (Cmd. 3615) (London, 1930), (Clynes' Report).

Report of the Cotton Textile Mission to the United States of America, (HMSO, London, 1944), (Platt Report).

Ministry of Labour and National Service, *The Cotton Spinning Industry: Report of a Commission set up to review the Wages Arrangements and Methods of Organisation of Work,* (HMSO, London, 1945) (Evershed Report); Supplement. *Mule Spinners' Wages,* (HMSO, London, 1946).

Ministry of Labour and National Service, Interim Report of the Joint Advisory Committee of the Cotton Industry, *Mule Spinners' Cancer and Automatic Wiping-Down Motions,* (HMSO, London, 1945).

Board of Trade, *Working Party Reports, Cotton,* (HMSO, London, 1946).

Ministry of Labour and National Service, Second Interim Report of the Joint Advisory Committee of the Cotton Industry, *Mule Spinners' Cancer,* (HMSO, London, 1952).

3. Theses

Dyson, R. F., 'The Development of Collective Bargaining in the Cotton Spinning Industry 1893-1914.' PhD, University of Leeds, 1971.

Farnie, D. A., 'The English Cotton Industry, 1850-1896.' MA, University of Manchester, 1953.

Giles, P. M., 'The Economic and Social Development of Stockport, 1815-1836.' MA, Manchester, 1950.

Ions, M., 'Industrial Relations in the Cotton Industry in Bolton, 1870-1914.' MA, University of Manchester, 1977.

Jones, F., 'The Cotton Spinning Industry in the Oldham District from 1896 to 1914.' MA, University of Manchester, 1959.

McIvor, A. J., 'Employers' Organisations and Industrial Relations in Lancashire 1890-1939.' PhD, University of Manchester, 1983.

Smith, R., 'A History of the Lancashire Cotton Industry between the Years 1873 and 1896.' PhD, University of Birmingham, 1954.

Tabor, C. R., 'The Preston Cotton Unions: An Account of their Organisation and Activities, 1830-1850.' BA Dissertation, University of Manchester, 1972.

Thorpe, E., 'Industrial Relations and Social Structure: a case study of the Bolton cotton-mule spinners 1884-1910.' MSc, University of Salford, 1969.

Turner, H. A., 'The Development of Labour Organisation in the Cotton Trades of Great Britain: A Comparative Study of Trade Union Growth and Evolution.' PhD, University of Manchester, 1959.

4. Newspapers and Periodicals

Ashton Chronicle

Blackburn Standard

Bolton Chronicle

Bolton Evening News

British Medical Journal

Chorley Standard

Cotton Factory Times

Daily Dispatch

Daily Herald

Fortnightly Review

Lancet, The

Manchester Courier

Manchester Evening Press

Manchester Examiner

Manchester Gazette

Manchester Guardian

Manchester and Salford Advertiser

North Cheshire Herald

Oldham Chronicle

Oldham Examiner

Oldham Express

Quarterly Review

Stockport Advertiser

Textile Manufacturer

Textile Mercury

Textile Recorder

5. Books and Articles

Allen, G. C., *British Industries and Their Organisation*, 4th ed, (London 1959).

Andrew, S., *Fifty Years' Cotton Trade*, (Oldham, 1887).

Ashton, T., *Wages and other Movements etc. in the Oldham Province 1868-1905*, (Oldham, 1906).

Ashworth, H., *An Inquiry into the Origins, Progress and Results of the Strike of the Operative Cotton Spinners in Preston*, (1838).

Ashworth, H., *The Preston Strike: An Inquiry into its Causes and Consequences*, (Manchester, 1854).

Ashworth, H., *Cotton: Its Cultivation, Manufacture and Uses*, (Manchester, 1858).

Askwith, G. R., *Industrial Problems and Disputes*, (London, 1920).

Aspinall, A., *The Early English Trade Unions: Documents from the Home Office Papers in the Public Record Office*, (London, 1949).

Auld, S. J. M., 'Environmental Cancer and Petroleum', *Journal of the Institute of Petroleum*, 36 (1950).

Baines, E., *History of the Cotton Manufacture in Great Britain, (1835)*, 2nd ed., (London, 1966).

Banks, T., *A Short Sketch of the Cotton Trade of Preston for the Last Sixty-Seven Years*, (Preston, 1888).

Baynes, J., *The Cotton Trade: Two Lectures*, (Blackburn, 1857).

Bowker, B., *Lancashire under the Hammer*, (London, 1928).

Boyson, R., *The Ashworth Cotton Enterprise: The Rise and Fall of a Family Firm 1818-1880*, (Oxford, 1970).

British Association for the Advancement of Science, *On the Regulation of Wages by Means of Lists in the Cotton Industry*, (1887).

Brockbank, E. M., *Mule Spinners' Cancer*, (London, 1941).

Bullen, A. J., *The Lancashire Weavers' Union: A Commemorative History*, (Rochdale, 1984).

Bullen, A. and Fowler, A., *The Cardroom Workers Union: A Centenary History of the Amalgamated Association of Card and Blowing Room Operatives*, (Rochdale, 1986).

Catling, H., *The Spinning Mule*, (Newton Abbot, 1970).

Chapman, S. D., *The Cotton Industry in the Industrial Revolution*, (London, 1972).

Chapman, S. D. and Chassagne, S., *European Textile Printers in the Eighteenth Century*, (London, 1981).

Chapman, S. J., *The Lancashire Cotton Industry: A Study in Economic Development*, (Manchester, 1904).

Chapman, S. J., 'Some Policies of the Cotton Spinners' Trade Unions', *Economic Journal*, 10 (1900).

Chapman, S. J., 'An Historical Sketch of Masters' Associations in the Cotton Industry', *Transactions of Manchester Statistical Society*, (1901).

Clarke, A., *The Effects of the Factory System*, (1899, Littleborough, 1985).

Clarke, P. F., *Lancashire and the New Liberalism*, (Cambridge, 1971).

Clay, H., *Report on the Position of the English Cotton Industry*, (1931).

Clegg, H., Fox, A., and Thompson, A., *A History of British Trade Unions since 1889*, Vol I, (Oxford, 1964).

Clegg, H. A., *A History of British Trade Unionism since 1889*, Vol 2, (Oxford, 1985).

Clynes, J. R., *Memoirs*, 2 vols (London, 1937).

Cohen, I., 'Workers' Control in the Cotton Industry. A comparative study of British and American Mule Spinning', *Labor History*, 26 (1985).

Conciliation in the Cotton Trade — Report of the Negotiations 1899-1900, (Manchester, 1901).

Cotton Board, *Report of the Cotton Board Committee to Enquire into Post-War Problems*, Manchester, 1944).

Daniels, G. W., *The Early English Cotton Industry*, (Manchester, 1920).

Daniels, G. W., 'The Cotton Trade during the Revolutionary and Napoleonic Wars', *Transactions of Manchester Statistical Society*, (1915-16).

Daniels, G. W., 'The Cotton Trade at the close of the Napoleonic Wars', *Transactions of Manchester Statistical Society*, (1917-18).

Daniels, G. W., 'Samuel Crompton's Census of the Cotton Industry in 1811', *Economic Journal (Economic History Supplement)* 2 (1930).

Daniels, G. W. and Jewkes, J., 'The Post-War Depression in the Cotton Industry', *Journal of Royal Statistical Society*, 91 (1928).

Doherty, J., *A Report of the Proceedings of a Delegate Meeting of the Operative Cotton Spinners of England, Ireland, and Scotland*, (1829).

Doherty, J., *A Letter to the Factory Operatives of Lancashire in Favour of the Ten Hours' Bill*, (1845).

Drake, B., *Women in Trade Unions*, (London, 1920, reprinted 1984).

Dutton, H. I, and King, J. E., *Ten Per Cent and No Surrender: The Preston Strike 1853-54*, (Cambridge, 1981).

Edwards, M. M., *The Growth of the British Cotton Trade 1780-1815*, (Manchester, 1967).

Ellison, T., *The Cotton Trade of Great Britain* (1886, Reprinted 1968).

Epstein, J. and Thompson, D. (eds.), *The Chartist Experience: Studies in Working-Class Radicalism and Culture, 1830-60* (London, 1982).

Farnie, D. A., *The English Cotton Industry and the World Market 1815-1896*, (Oxford, 1979).

Federation of Master Cotton Spinners' Associations, *Yearbook*, (Manchester, 1930).

Foster, J., *Class Struggle and the Industrial Revolution: Early Industrial Capitalism in Three English Towns*, (London, 1974).

Fowler, A. and Fowler, L., *The History of the Nelson Weavers' Association*, (Nelson, 1984).

Fraser, W. H., 'The Glasgow Cotton Spinners, 1837', in J. Butt and J. T. Ward (eds.) *Scottish Themes: Essays in Honour of Professor S. G. E. Lythe*, (Edinburgh, 1976).

French, G. J. *Life and Times of Samuel Crompton*, (London, 1859).

Gaskell, P., *The Manufacturing Population of England* (London. 1833).

Gatrell, V. A. C., 'Labour, Power and the Size of Firms in Lancashire Cotton in the Second Quarter of the Nineteenth Century', *Economic History Review*, 30 (1977).

General Union of Associations of Overlookers, *Jubilee History*, (1935).

Glen, R., *Urban Workers in the Early Industrial Revolution*, (London, 1984).

Grant, P., *The History of Factory Legislation*, (London, 1866).

Hammond, J. L. and B., *The Skilled Labourer 1760-1832*, (1978 edition).

Hammond, J. L. and B., *The Town Labourer 1760-1832*, (1978 edition).

Harnetty, P., 'The Indian Cotton Duties Controversy, 1894-1896', *English Historical Review*, 77 (1962).

Henderson, H. D., *Cotton Control Board*, (Oxford, 1922).

Henderson, W. O., *The Lancashire Cotton Famine, 1861-1865*, (London, 1934).

Henry, S. A., *Cancer of the Scrotum in Relation to Occupation*, (London, 1946).

Hills, R. L., *Power in the Industrial Revolution*, (Manchester, 1970).

Hobsbawm, E. J., *Industry and Empire*, (London, 1968).

Hopwood, E., *A History of the Lancashire Cotton Industry and the Amalgamated Weavers' Association*, (Manchester, 1969).

Howe, A., *The Cotton Masters, 1830-1860*, (Oxford, 1984).

Howell, D., *British Workers and the Independent Labour Party 1888-1906*, (Manchester, 1983).

Hunter, D., *The Diseases of Occupations*, 6th ed, (London, 1978).

Hurst, G. G., *Lubricating Oils, Fats and Greases*, 4th ed, (London, 1925).

Hyde and District Operative Cotton Spinners' Association, *Historical Sketch: Fifty Years Record*, (Hyde, 1906).

Jenkins, M., *The General Strike of 1842*, (London, 1980).

Jevons, W. A., 'An Account of the Spinners' Strike at Ashton-under-Lyne in 1830', Social Science Association, *Report on Trades Societies and Strikes*, (London, 1860).

Jewkes, J., 'The Localisation of the Cotton Industry', *Economic Journal, (Economic History Supplement)* 2 (1930).

Jewkes, J. and Gray, E. M. *Wages and Labour in the Lancashire Cotton Spinning Industry*, (Manchester, 1935).

Joint Committee of Cotton Trade Organisations, *Lancashire and the Future*, (Manchester, 1937).

Jones, G. S., 'Class Struggle and the Industrial Revolution', *New Left Review*, 90 (1975).

Joyce, P., *Work, Society and Politics: The Culture of the Factory in later Victorian England*, (Brighton, 1980).

Kirby, M. W., 'The Lancashire Cotton Industry in the Inter-War Years: A Study in Organisational Change', *Business History*, 26 (1974).

Kirby, R. G. and Musson, A. E., *The Voice of the People: John Doherty, 1798-1854. Trade Unionist, Radical and Factory Reformer.* (Manchester, 1975).

Kirk, N. *The Growth of Working Class Reformism in Mid-Victorian England*, (London, 1985).

Landes, D. S., *The Unbound Prometheus: Technological Change and Industrial Development in Western Europe from 1750 to the present*, (Cambridge, 1969).

Lazonick, W., 'Industrial Relations and Technical Change: The Case of the Self-Acting Mule', *Cambridge Journal of Economics*, 3 (1979).

Lazonick, W., 'Factor Costs and the Diffusion of Ring Spinning in Britain prior to World War I', *Quarterly Journal of Economics*, 96 (1981).

Lazonick, W., 'Production Relations, Labour Productivity, and Choice of Technique: British and US Cotton Spinning', *Journal of Economic History*, 41 (1981).

Lazonick, W., 'Industrial Organisation and Technological Change: The Decline of the British Cotton Industry', *Business History Review*, 57 (1983).

Lazonick, W. and Mass, W., 'The Performance of the British Cotton Industry, 1870-1913', *Research in Economic History*, 9 (1984).

Lazonick, W., 'The Cotton Industry', in B. Elbaum and W. Lazonick, (eds.), *The Decline of the British Economy*, (Oxford, 1986).

Lee, C. H. *A Cotton Enterprise: A History of M'Connel and Kennedy, Fine Cotton Spinners*, (Manchester, 1972).

Lee, C. H., 'The Cotton Textile Industry', in R. Church (ed.), *The Dynamics of Victorian Business*, (London, 1980).

Lee, W. R. 'Emergence of Occupational Medicine in Victorian Times', *British Journal of Industrial Medicine*, 30 (1973).

Longworth, J. E., *Oldham Master Cotton Spinners' Association Limited Centenary 1866-1966*, (Oldham, 1966).

Lovell, J., *British Trade Unions 1875-1933*, (London, 1977).

Macara, C. W., *Recollections*, (London, 1921).

Manchester Studies, *Cotton Union Records*, (Manchester, 1980).

Marsden, R., *Cotton Spinning*, (London, 1899).

Miles, C., *Lancashire Textiles: A Case Study of Industrial Change*, (Cambridge, 1968).

Mills, W. H., *Sir Charles W. Macara; Bart: A Study of Modern Lancashire*, (Manchester, 1917).

Mitchell, B. R. and Deane, P. *Abstract of British Historical Statistics*, (Cambridge, 1962).

Mosley Industrial Commission to the U.S.A. October — December 1902, *Reports of the Delegates* (1903).

Musson, A. E., *British Trade Unions 1800-1875*, (London, 1972).

Musson, A. E., 'Class Struggle and the Labour Aristocracy, 1833-60', *Social History*, I (1976).

National Association for the Promotion of Social Science, *Report of the Committee on Trades Societies and Strikes*, (London, 1860).

Oliver, T., (ed.), *Dangerous Trades*, (London, 1902).

P.E.P., *Report on the British Cotton Industry*, (London, 1934).

Pelling, H., *Origins of the Labour Party 1880-1900*, 2nd ed., (London, 1965).

Penn, R., 'Trade Union Organisation and Skill in the Cotton and Engineering Industries in Britain 1850-1960', *Social History*, 8 (1983).

Porter, J., 'Industrial Peace in the Cotton Trade, 1875-1913', *Yorkshire Bulletin of Economic and Social Research*, 19 (1967).

Porter, J. H., 'The Commercial Banks and the Financial Problems of the English Cotton Industry, 1919-39', *International Review of Banking History*, 9 (1976)

Porter, J. H., 'Cotton and Wool Textiles', in N. K. Buxton and D. H. Aldcroft, (eds.), *British Industry between the Wars*, (London, 1979).

Proceedings of Board of Arbitration re. Cotton Trade Wages, 21-22 August 1929, (1929).

Reid, T. D. W. and Reid, C. A. N., 'The 1842 "Plug Plot" in Stockport', *International Review of Social History*, 24 (1979).

Report of the Conference of Trades Delegates of the United Kingdom, (Sheffield, 1866).

Robertson, A. J., 'The Decline of the Scottish Cotton Industry, 1860-1914', *Business History*, 12 (1970).

Robson, R., *The Cotton Industry in Britain*, (London, 1957).

Rose, A. G. 'The Plug Riots of 1842 in Lancashire and Cheshire', *Transactions of Lancashire and Cheshire Antiquarian Society*, 67 (1957).

Rose, M. E. 'Samuel Crompton (1753-1827), Inventor of the Spinning Mule: A Reconsideration', *Transactions of Lancashire and Cheshire Antiquarian Society*, 75-6 (1966).

Sandberg, L., *Lancashire in Decline: A Study on Entrepreneurship, Technology and International Trade*, (Columbus, Ohio, 1974).

Sandberg, L., 'American Rings and English Mules', *Quarterly Journal of Economics*, 83 (1969).

Saxonhouse, G. R. and Wright, G., 'New Evidence on the Stubborn English Mule and the English Cotton Industry 1878-1920', *Economic History Review*, 37 (1984).

Shorrocks, E., *Letter to the Workpeople of the North and North-East Lancashire: History of the Formation of the Blackburn Association in 1852, with the Rise and Fall of Wages for Twenty-Eight Years*, (1880).

Singleton, J., 'Lancashire's Last Stand: Declining Employment in the British Cotton Industry, 1950-70', *Economic History Review*, 39 (1986).

Smelser, N. J. *Social Change in the Industrial, Revolution: An application of theory to the Lancashire Cotton Industry 1770-1840*, (London, 1959).

Smith, R., 'An Oldham Limited Liability Company 1875-1896', *Business History*, 4 (1961).

Streat, R., 'The Cotton Industry in Contraction: Problem and Policies in the Inter-war Years', *District Bank Review*, 127 (1958).

Sykes, R., 'Some Aspects of Working-Class Consciousness in Oldham, 1830-1842', *Historical Journal*, 23 (1980).

Sykes, R., 'General Unionism, Class and Politics: The Cotton Districts, 1829-34', *Bulletin of Society for the Study of Labour History*, 49 (1984).

Sykes, R., 'Physical Force Chartism: the Cotton Districts and the Chartist Crisis of 1839', *International Review of Social History*, 30 (1985).

Taylor, A. J., 'Concentration and Specialisation in the Lancashire Cotton Industry 1825-1850', *Economic History Review*, 1 (1949).

Thomas, M. W., *The Early Factory Legislation*, (London, 1948).

Thompson, E. P., *The Making of the English Working Class*, (Harmondsworth, 1968).

Tippett, L. H. C., *A Portrait of the Lancashire Textile Industry*, (London, 1969).

Torrens, W. T. M., *Lancashire's Lesson: or the Need of Settled Policy in Times of Exceptional Distress*, (London, 1864).

Trades Union Congress, *Cotton: The TUC Plan of Socialisation*, (1935).

Tufnell, E. C., *Character, Object and Effects of Trades Unions*, (London, 1834).

Turner, H. A., *Trade Union Growth, Structure and Policy: A Comparative Study of the Cotton Unions*, (London, 1962).

Turner, H. A. and Smith, R., 'The Slump in the Cotton Industry, 1952', *Bulletin of Oxford Institute of Statistics*, April, 1954.

Tyson, R. E., 'The Cotton Industry', in D. H. Aldcroft (ed.), *The Development of British Industry and Foreign Competition, 1875-1914*, (London, 1968).

United Textile Factory Workers' Association, *Annual Reports and Balance Sheets*, (1886-1974).

United Textile Factory Workers' Association, *Inquiry into the Cotton Industry*, (Blackburn, 1923).

United Textile Factory Workers' Association, *Memorandum on the Cotton Industry*, (Labour Research Department, 1928).

United Textile Factory Workers' Association, *Plan for Cotton*, (Ashton, 1957).

United Textile Factory Workers' Association, *Report of the Legislative Council on Ways and Means of Improving the Economic Stability of the Cotton Textile Industry*, (Rochdale, 1943).

United Textile Factory Workers' Association, *Report of the Proceedings at the Annual Conference*, (1907-1974).

Unwin, G., *Samuel Oldknow and the Arkwrights*, (Manchester, 1924).

Ure, A., *The Philosophy of Manufactures*, (London, 1835).

Utley, F., *Lancashire and the Far East*, (London, 1931).

Von Tunzelmann, G. N., *Steam Power and British Industrialisation to 1860*, (Oxford, 1978).

Wadsworth, A. P. and Mann, J. de L., *The Cotton Trade and Industrial Lancashire 1600-1780*, (Manchester, 1931).

Waldron, H. A., 'A Brief History of Scrotal Cancer', *British Journal of Industrial Medicine*, 40 (1983).

Ward, J. T., *The Factory Movement, 1830-1855*, (London, 1962).

Ward, J. T., 'The Factory Movement in Lancashire, 1830-1855', *Transactions of Lancashire and Cheshire Antiquarian Society*, 75-6 (1966).

Watts, J., *The Facts of the Cotton Famine*, (London, 1866).

Webb, S. and B., *Industrial Democracy*, (London, 1897).

Webb, S. and B., *The History of Trade Unionism, 1666-1920*, (London, 1920).

Weindling, P. (ed.), *The Social History of Occupational Health*, (London, 1985).

White, J. L., *The Limits of Trade Union Militancy: The Lancashire Textile Workers, 1910-1914*, (Westport, Conn., 1978).

White, J. L., 'Lancashire Cotton Textiles' in C. Wrigley (ed.) *A History of British Industrial Relations 1875-1914*, (Brighton, 1982).

White, R. P., *Occupational Affections of the Skin*, (London, 1915).

Wiggins, M., 'The Cotton Industry', in F. Gannett and B. Catherwood, (eds.), *Industrial and Labour Relations in Great Britain*, (London, 1939).

Williams, J. L., *Accidents and Ill Health at Work*, (London, 1960).

Williamson, A., *Historical Sketch of the Hyde and District Operative Cotton Spinners' Association*, (Hyde, 1928).

Wilson, Sir A., and Levy, H., *Workmen's Compensation*, 2 vols, (London, 1939).

Wood, G. H., *The History of Wages in the Cotton Trade During the Past Hundred Years*, (Manchester, 1910).

INDEX